THE FATHERS OF THE CHURCH

A NEW TRANSLATION

VOLUME 124

THE FATHERS OF THE CHURCH

A NEW TRANSLATION

ST. CYRIL OF ALEXANDRIA

COMMENTARY ON THE TWELVE PROPHETS VOLUME 3

Translated by

†ROBERT C. HILL

THE CATHOLIC UNIVERSITY OF AMERICA PRESS
Washington, D.C.

The paper used in this publication meets the minimum requirements of the American National Standards for Information Science—Permanence of Paper for Printed Library Materials, ANSI Z39.48-1984.

LIBRARY OF CONGRESS CATALOGING-IN-PUBLICATION DATA
Cyril, Saint, Patriarch of Alexandria, ca. 370-444.
Commentary on the Twelve Prophets / Cyril of Alexandria ; translated with an introduction by Robert C. Hill.
p. cm. — (The Fathers of the church ; v. 124)
Includes bibliographical references and indexes.
ISBN 978-0-8132-0115-3 (cloth : alk. paper) 1. Bible. O.T. Prophets–Commentaries. I. Hill, Robert C. (Robert Charles), 1931– II. Title. III. Series.
BS1505.53.C9713 2007
224'.907–dc22
2007016972
Vol. 3: ISBN 978-0-8132-0124-5

CONTENTS

INDICES

ABBREVIATIONS

AnBib	Analecta Biblica, Pontificio Istituto Biblico, Rome.
Aug	*Augustinianum.*
BAC	Bible in Ancient Christianity, Leiden and Boston: Brill, 2004–.
Bib	*Biblica.*
CCG	Corpus Christianorum series Graeca, Turnhout: Brepols.
CCL	Corpus Christianorum series Latina, Turnhout: Brepols.
DBS	*Dictionnaire de la Bible. Supplément,* IV, Paris: Librairie Letouzey et Ané, 1949.
FOTC	The Fathers of the Church, Washington, DC: The Catholic University of America Press.
GO	Göttinger Orientforschungen, Wiesbaden: Otto Harrassowitz.
HeyJ	The Heythrop Journal.
JECS	*Journal of Early Christian Studies.*
LXX	Septuagint.
NJBC	*New Jerome Biblical Commentary,* ed. Raymond E. Brown, Joseph A. Fitzmyer, Roland E. Murphy, Upper Saddle River, NJ: Prentice-Hall, 1989.
NS	New Series.
OTL	Old Testament Library.
PG	Patrologia Graeca, ed. J.-P. Migne, Paris, 1857–66.
Rahlfs ed.	Septuaginta, ed. Alfred Rahlfs, 7th ed., Stuttgart: Württembergische Bibelanstalt, 1935; repr., 1962.
SC	Sources Chrétiennes, Paris: Du Cerf.
StudP	*Studia Patristica.*
TRE	*Theologische Realenzyclopädie,* Berlin: Walter de Gruyter, 1976–.

SELECT BIBLIOGRAPHY

Boulnois, M.-O. "The mystery of the Trinity according to Cyril of Alexandria: The Deployment of the Triad and its Recapitulation into the Unity of Divinity." In T. G. Weinandy and D. A. Keating, eds. *The Theology of St Cyril of Alexandria. A Critical Appreciation.* London and New York: T&T Clark, 2003. Pp. 75–111.

Brown, Raymond E. *The Gospel According to John I–XII.* Anchor Bible Series 29. Garden City, NY: Doubleday, 1966.

Daley, B. E. "Apocalypticism in Early Christian Theology." In B. McGinn, ed. *The Encyclopedia of Apocalypticism* 2. New York and London: Continuum, 2002. Pp. 3–47.

Doutreleau, L., ed. *Didyme L'Aveugle. Sur Zacharie.* SC 83, 84, 85. Paris: Du Cerf, 1962.

Fernández Marcos, N. *The Septuagint in Context: Introduction to the Greek Versions of the Bible.* Translated by Wilfred G. E. Watson. Boston and Leiden: Brill, 2001.

Harvey, E. R. "Cyrillus von Alexandria." *TRE* 8:254–60.

Hill, R. C. "The Mystery of Christ: Clue to Paul's Thinking on Wisdom." *HeyJ* 25 (1984): 475–83.

———. "Psalm 45: A *locus classicus* for Patristic Thinking on Biblical Inspiration." *StudP* 25 (1993): 95–100.

———. *Theodoret of Cyrus. Commentary on the Psalms.* FOTC 101, 102. Washington, DC: The Catholic University of America Press, 2000.

———. "Jonah in Antioch." *Pacifica* 14 (2001): 245–61.

———. "Theodore of Mopsuestia, Interpreter of the Prophets." *Sacris Erudiri* 40 (2001): 107–29.

———. *Theodore of Mopsuestia. Commentary on the Twelve Prophets.* FOTC 108. Washington, DC: The Catholic University of America Press, 2004.

———. *Reading the Old Testament in Antioch.* BAC 5. Leiden and Boston: Brill, 2005.

———. *Didymus the Blind. Commentary on Zechariah.* FOTC 111. Washington, DC: The Catholic University of America Press, 2005.

———. *Theodoret of Cyrus. Commentary on the Twelve Prophets.* Commentaries on the Prophets 3. Brookline, MA: Holy Cross Orthodox Press, 2005.

———. "Zechariah in Alexandria and Antioch." *Aug* 46 (2006).

Jouassard, Georges. "L'activité littéraire de saint Cyrille d'Alexandrie jusqu'à 428: Essai de chronologie et de synthèse." In *Mélanges E. Po-*

dechard: Études de sciences religieuses offertes pour son émeritat. Lyon: Facultés Catholiques, 1954. Pp. 159–74.

Kelly, J. N. D. *Jerome. His Life, Writings and Controversies.* London: Duckworth, 1975

Kerrigan, A. *St. Cyril of Alexandria, Interpreter of the Old Testament.* AnBib 2. Rome: Pontificio Istituto Biblico, 1952.

Olivier, J.-M., ed. *Diodori Tarsensis commentarii in Psalmos.* I. *Commentarii in Psalmos I-L.* CCG 6. Turnhout: Brepols, 1980.

Petersen, D. L. *Zechariah 9–14 & Malachi.* OTL. London: SCM, 1995.

Pusey, P. E., ed. *Sancti patris nostri Cyrilli archiepiscopi Alexandrini in XII prophetas.* Oxford: Clarendon Press, 1868.

Redditt, P. L. *Haggai, Zechariah, Malachi.* New Century Bible Commentary. Grand Rapids: Eerdmans, 1995.

Russell, N. *Cyril of Alexandria.* The Early Christian Fathers. London and New York: Routledge, 2000.

Schäublin, C. *Untersuchungen zu Methode und Herkunft der antiochenischen Exegese.* Theophaneia: Beiträge zur Religions- und Kirchengeschichte des Altertums 23. Cologne and Bonn: Peter Hanstein, 1974.

Smith, R. L. *Micah–Malachi.* Word Biblical Commentary 32. Waco, TX: Word Books, 1984.

Sprenger, H. N., ed. *Theodori Mopsuesteni commentarius in XII prophetas.* GO. Biblica et Patristica 1. Wiesbaden: Otto Harrassowitz, 1977.

Wilken, R. L. "Cyril of Alexandria as Interpreter of the Old Testament." In T. G. Weinandy and D. A. Keating, eds. *The Theology of St Cyril of Alexandria. A Critical Appreciation.* London and New York: T&T Clark, 2003. Pp. 1–21.

———. "Cyril of Alexandria." In C. Kannengiesser. *Handbook of Patristic Exegesis* 2. BAC 1. Leiden and Boston: Brill, 2005. Pp. 840–69.

Zeigler, J. *Duodecim Prophetae.* Septuaginta 13. Göttingen: Vandenhoeck & Ruprecht, 1943.

COMMENTARY ON THE *TWELVE PROPHETS*

COMMENTARY ON THE *PROPHET ZEPHANIAH*

COMMENTARY ON ZEPHANIAH, CHAPTER ONE

Word of the Lord which came to Zephaniah son of Cushi son of Gedaliah son of Amariah son of Hezekiah in the days of King Josiah of Judah, son of Amon (v.1).

BLESSED ZEPHANIAH prophesied in Jerusalem; he was from a distinguished lineage, and did not belong to those given to false prophecy and to concocting the divine words for the listeners, of whom the divinely inspired Ezekiel said, "Woe to those who prophesy from their heart and see nothing at all," and as well the God of all himself said in Jeremiah, "I did not (168)[1] send the prophets, yet they ran; I did not speak to them, yet they prophesied."[2] Rather, he was truly a prophet, transmitting the words from the Lord's mouth, filled with the Holy Spirit, and gushing with good things from his heart as from a good fountain. The tongue of the holy ones, after all, is not in the habit of telling lies.

The purpose of the prophecy was reproof of the two tribes in Jerusalem, namely, Judah and Benjamin; history tells us that they were impious, sacrilegiously devoted to the deceits of the idols, and ready to practice anything at all that was displeasing to God. A further detail helpfully provided is the period of the kingship when he raised such matters with the offenders, the purpose being that we might grasp the situation of that time and thus understand why and to what extent the movement of divine wrath was directed at them.[3]

I shall therefore outline in detail what is of benefit to the readers. At one time Hezekiah had reigned in Jerusalem, a man par-

1. Numerals in parentheses refer to the page numbers in the Pusey edition; see the select bibliography in this volume.

2. Ezek 13.3; Jer 23.21.

3. In a manner adopted by Antiochene commentators, Cyril identifies the historical situation of the prophet's ministry, or *hypothesis*, and its purpose or thrust (*skopos*).

ticularly devoted to God, a lover of piety, a custodian of righteousness, an enemy of deceit, who put a stop to the harmful effects of idolatry, sacred Scripture clearly testifying to such achievements of his. It was during his exercise of the kingly office in Jerusalem that the Assyrian tyrant Sennacherib went up, took Samaria, and deported Israel—that is, the ten tribes—to the territories of Persians and Medes. But though burning (169) innumerable cities of the kingdom of Judah, he did not gain control of Jerusalem, thanks to God's protection. As the account of the facts is familiar, there is need only to summarize it.

At the death of Hezekiah, Manasseh then succeeded to the kingship; despite his being Hezekiah's offspring, he proved so impious as to leave untried no form of depravity. The second book of Kings describes him this way: "He did what was evil in the sight of the Lord by way of the abominable practices of the nations that the Lord drove out before the sons of Israel. He reverted to building the high places that his father Hezekiah had overthrown, erected an altar to Baal, made groves as King Ahab of Israel had done, worshiped all the host of heaven, and served them. He built an altar in the house of the Lord, of which the Lord had said, In Jerusalem I shall put my name, and he built an altar to all the host of heaven in the two courts of the house of the Lord. He made his sons pass through fire, practiced soothsaying and augury, involved himself in wizardry, and multiplied mediums for doing evil in the sight of the Lord to provoke him. He set the image from the grove in the house of which the Lord had said to David and to Solomon his son, In this house and in Jerusalem, which I have chosen from all the tribes of Israel, I shall set my name forever."[4] The God of all was then angered by Manasseh's sacrilegious actions, and rightly so, and he clearly threatened to bring the effects of wrath on Jerusalem.

The text goes on in similar terms, "The Lord said by his servants (170) the prophets, Because King Manasseh of Judah has committed these abominations that are worse than all the Amorite did before him, and Judah has also sinned with his idols, thus says the Lord, the God of Israel, Lo, I am bringing such troubles upon Jerusalem and Judah that the ears of every-

4. 2 Kgs 21.2–7.

one hearing of it will tingle. I shall stretch over Jerusalem the measure for Samaria and the plummet for the house of Ahab, I shall wash Jerusalem as a jar is washed and turned upside down in their sight, I shall reject the remnant of my inheritance, I shall surrender them into the hands of their foes, and they will be a prey and a spoil to all their foes on account of all the evil they did in my sight."[5] This, as I said, is what God threatened to bring upon the inhabitants before long.

When Manasseh passed on, his son Amon came to the throne. Far from being inferior to his parent in sacrilegious behavior, he so rivaled him in impiety as somehow to surpass him. When he in turn departed this life, however, there came to the throne Josiah, who, despite being the son of Amon, imitated Hezekiah's godliness and was an ardent lover of his behavior. He destroyed altars and shrines, in fact, cleared the divine Temple of the abominations of Manasseh, and ordered the priests appointed by Law to perform the customary rites to the glory of God. In addition, he burned the chariot of the sun, drove out of Jerusalem the false seers, augurs, soothsayers, (171) and wizards as well. He slaughtered an innumerable horde of attendants, burned the altars of the idols, and overturned the altar of the heifers in Bethel that Jeroboam had made. Since he was so godly and upright, God stayed his wrath and inflicted none of what he had promised.[6]

When Josiah departed this life, however, Jehoahaz came to the throne, whom Pharaoh Neco conquered and put in chains, awarding the position of king to Jeconiah, second son of Josiah.[7] It was during his reign that Nebuchadnezzar invaded Judea; he plundered all the country, took Jerusalem, burned the divine Temple, and deported Judah and Benjamin as captives to his own country along with the sacred vessels. Now, there is need to be aware that the knavery of the Babylonian also crushed the cities of the Philistines—namely, Gaza, Ashkelon, and oth-

5. 2 Kgs 21.10–15. As usual, the PG editor has not reproduced all the biblical text of these citations.

6. 2 Kgs 22–23.

7. 2 Kgs 23.30–34. As in comment on the close of Mi 4, Cyril is (understandably) confused about the four kings that follow Josiah and the alternative names of Jehoiakim and Jehoiachin.

ers along with them—as well as Idumeans and Ammonites, and heavily taxed them, something mentioned as well by the text of the prophecy.

Let everything utterly disappear from the face of the earth, says the Lord. Let man and beast disappear, let the birds of heaven and the fish of the sea disappear. The ungodly will become weak, and I shall wipe the lawless from the face of the earth, says the Lord (vv.2–3). Here he expresses the prophecy by hyperbole as though their country would be completely desolate (172) and would perish along with all its inhabitants; after all, if we are in our right mind, we do not claim that the God of all inflicts his wrath on brute beasts and creatures that swim and fly. Rather, his intention is for the listeners to understand that there will be no sparing anybody; instead, just as when a ship founders no survivors are left, so when Judea is captured (he says) there will be nothing saved—no *man*, no *beast*, no bird, no fish. Since, however, it is very likely that there were some people in it living by the Law and observing an upright and praiseworthy lifestyle, consequently to avoid the impression that he vented his wrath on everyone as a whole indiscriminately, destroying good along with bad, and eliminating the pious along with the profane and ungodly, he makes clear who it was on whom he vented the effects of his wrath. He said, in fact, *The ungodly will become weak, and I shall wipe the lawless from the face of the earth*: they *will become weak* by being felled by the foe, and *be wiped out* likewise by dying and falling to the sword, or being deported as captives and in service to their captors.

If, on the other hand, you prefer elegantly to apply to behavior and morals *man and beast* and the rest, you would take *men* to be those living according to the flesh, with an earthly way of thinking and attached to things that pass, of which (173) the divine word also proclaimed, "I said, You are gods, and all sons of the Most High, but you die like mortals." In other words, the life of the holy ones is no longer mortal, but rather spiritual and divine, especially as it is true that though we tread the earth in the flesh, we do not live according to the flesh, according to Scripture, but have our citizenship in heaven.[8] Likewise, you would

8. Ps 82.6–7; 2 Cor 10.3; Phil 3.20. Unless otherwise noted, Psalm references in this volume utilize modern numbering.

take *beasts* to be those habitually addicted to deep folly and sluggish in their thinking, of whom he says in the words of David, "Though enjoying high status, the human being did not understand, becoming comparable to brute beasts and resembling them," and going on to adjure them, "Be not like horse and mule, which lack understanding."[9] By *birds* we shall understand people with conceited and, as it were, lofty attitudes, a mind carried away, scorning to be ranked with the lowly, such being the way with the arrogant completely in the grip of the failings of the haughtiness hateful to God. The *fish* in turn is to be taken as the irrational mob, the species of fish being completely mute; the general run of people are like this, living a life of confusion as though in some sea, feeding on the salty and bitter pleasure of its affairs, and caught in the nets of death, their life ending in annihilation. These people, then, *will disappear* when God imposes punishment on them and chooses to punish them for living a licentious and intemperate life without declining to offend him.

I shall stretch out my hand against Judah and against all the (174)
inhabitants of Jerusalem, and I shall remove from this place the names of the Baals, and the names of the priests, and with the priests those bowing down on the roofs to the host of heaven, those swearing by their king, those turning from the Lord, those not seeking the Lord, and those not attached to the Lord (vv.4–6). He now clarifies what had been said obscurely, clearly stating that the effects of wrath will befall the tribe of Judah and Jerusalem. He says, in fact, that his *hand will be extended* against it as though seizing and striking it, and subjecting them to the events expected to occur imminently, and bent on plunder and deportation of them when caught in the trap of slavery. He reveals their crimes, saying *the names of the Baals* will disappear from their midst, and those of *the priests* will depart along with them. In this he suggests that the number of devotees in their midst was vast, as well as various forms of error. The fact that they would be consumed by war, and the nations of the Jews would be reduced to such paucity that those using the name of the Baals or able to attend the shrines of the idols would no longer exist, he skillfully conveys, saying that *the names* of the idols and also of *the priests* would be *removed.* By *the*

9. Pss 49.13, 21; 32.9.

names he means (175) the memory or reputation; Solomon in his wisdom makes the same point, "A good name is preferable to much wealth."[10] He says that together with the priests and the names of the Baals *those bowing down on the roofs* would also be done away with; they would be the ones in the habit of bowing down to the moon, to Ursa Major, and to the rest of *the host of heaven.*

He says likewise that *I shall remove those swearing by their king and those turning from the Lord*; some of the victims of error were in the habit of taking oaths by heaven and phrasing their speech in terms of it, "By the king and lord sun" being an honorific form of exclamation. People opting to do this necessarily committed a serious breach of love for God in defiance of the clear direction of the Law, "You shall bow down to the Lord your God, and him alone shall you worship, and you shall swear by his name." The prophet Jeremiah, for instance, at one time confirmed to the people of Israel observance of the commandment of Moses, and said to God with a view to averting his wrath from them, "They say, As the Lord lives,"[11] By *those not seeking the Lord and those not* anxious to be *attached to the Lord* should properly be understood the ones living a depraved and shameful life and preferring a lifestyle at variance with the Law. After all, the God of all is sought by us not so much in places, in my view, but in actions, through true knowledge that is above reproach, through faith and (176) simplicity, and zeal and enthusiasm for everything that attracts holy admiration and is pleasing to him.

Now, it should be realized that these virtues were exemplified in the one who was king in Jerusalem—I mean Josiah—and it was in his time that the message of the prophecy was delivered. He was the one, in fact, who destroyed altars, shrines, and handmade images; he slaughtered their ministers, false seers, and augurs. It is likely that the prophet did not refer to the prevailing situation, or speak of what had already happened, instead foretelling that there would happen in due course the things done by Nebuchadnezzar, who was not acting for the glory of God—how could he, when he even burned the divine

10. Prv 22.1.
11. Dt 10.20; Jer 5.2.

Temple—but destroying and along with the idols burning those bowing down to them.

Be reverent before the Lord God, because the day of the Lord is at hand, because the Lord prepared his sacrifice, he sanctified his chosen (v.7). He helpfully interweaves exhortation with the threats, frightening them with terrors and bringing them to better ways, and instructing them to have respect (the sense, in my view, of *be reverent*) for the God of all, to strive to correct the ups-and-downs of life, and of course be converted to what is pleasing and acceptable to him. Now, he says that people must be seen as such *before the Lord God,* as is said in the statement of Isaiah, "Wash yourselves, make yourselves clean, remove from your persons evildoing before my eyes, cease (177) your evildoing."[12] Removing evildoing in human eyes, in fact, is not the same as *before the Lord God,* which is quite a different matter; sometimes an evil man, whose morals are not good, presents an appearance of reverence and creates a reputation for respectability, despite not being so in reality; Christ, for instance, says, "Beware of those who come to you in sheep's clothing, but within are ravenous wolves."[13] Such a person is reverent in the eyes of men, but not at all in God's sight, whereas the truly innocent person *before God* not only takes on superficial respectability and the appearance of being good, but has an irreproachable heart, and is also recognized as such. Solomon said somewhere, remember, "A man's ways are before God's eyes, and he examines all his ways."[14]

By *the day of the Lord* he refers to the time of capture, which he also says is *at hand;* he does not allow the more indifferent perhaps to ponder and reflect within themselves that there is a long delay in the coming of what was promised, and that by reaching the end of their life they would escape suffering it. Jews customarily thought and said such things, in fact, in regard to the prophecies of extreme calamities; God said somewhere to the blessed prophet Ezekiel, "Son of man, lo, the rebellious house of Israel is saying, The vision that he sees is for many years ahead; he prophesies for distant times. Therefore say to

12. Is 1.16.
13. Mt 7.15.
14. Prv 5.21.

them, The Lord Adonai says this, None of my words that I shall speak will be delayed any longer; (178) I shall implement the word I speak, says the Lord Adonai."[15] This is the case here, too, in my view, where he is confirming the nearness of *the day of the Lord, his sacrifice is prepared, and the chosen sanctified.* By *sacrifice* he refers to the slaughter of the impious to be effected by his will, by *chosen* to the Chaldeans, who he says are *sanctified,* not that they are made holy but that they are designated and called by God to set fire to Judea and destroy people in it to the exclusion of all pity. The sacred text says much the same in other places as well; the Persians and Medes and Cyrus's allies are called against Nineveh, the God of all saying of them, "They are consecrated, and it is I who bring them; giants are coming to vent my anger, rejoicing and exulting."[16] So in this case the *sanctifying* would suggest not a basis of depravity or a share in the Holy Spirit, but, as it were, the designation and appointment of some people to execute this business.

On the day of the Lord's sacrifice I shall take vengeance on the rulers, on the house of the king, and on all attired in foreign attire. I shall take vengeance openly on all in the vestibule on that day, those filling the house of their God with impiety and deceit (vv.8–9). There are three things contributing to the welfare of cities and countries: monarchy, ranks of officers under it, (179) and the celebrated priesthood. If these functioned well in a manner proper to each, their affairs likewise would, and the subjects would be safe; but if they chose the way of corruption and followed it, everything would immediately deteriorate and, as it were, topple into ruin. In other words, just as if an ailment strikes the body's head, the other parts necessarily are affected and become impaired, so too when the leaders take a turn for depravity and are afflicted with a tendency to worse behavior, the subjects are necessarily corrupted along with them. After all, the subjects are inclined to follow those appointed to leadership and are influenced by their views.

Accordingly, he says, *on the day of sacrifice* pleasing to God, that is, at the time when the slaughter of those committing dreadful

15. Ezek 12.27–28.
16. Is 13.3.

sins of all kinds takes place, the effects of wrath will fall on the very things that are ranked ahead of the others in importance and precedence. Namely, *the house* of the one on the throne; then the next in importance and prominence; and thirdly after them the minister of divine things who is promoted by God ahead of the others, being themselves rulers and leaders of the people in the category of priesthood. Now, he censures them severely for being *attired in foreign attire*, that is, descending to such a degree of ungodliness and choosing to scorn the oracles given through Moses, as no longer to maintain the trappings of priesthood when the time summons them to the obligation of celebrating sacred rituals. (180) Just as the sons of Aaron were consumed by fire for placing profane fire on the altar, which was held against them as a crime,[17] therefore, in the same way in my view the people referred to in the passage were called to account for dispensing with their due accoutrements and not being clad in priestly fashion in the manner acceptable to the lawgiver, and presuming to perform sacred duties dressed *in foreign attire*. This was an example of extreme scorn on their part and of setting no store by the Law; how would it then be possible for the others to give attention to observance of the Law if the leaders took no account of it?

Consequently, he says, *I shall take vengeance openly on all in the vestibule*, his meaning being something like the following. For sinning frequently and not responding to the words of the prophets he calls Israel to repentance, correcting them like a father by external afflictions, and sometimes also touching their bodies. For example, he struck the crops in the field with blight, or sometimes sent the young locust and the locust, or proceeded to the cutting locust, or the so-called rust; he also caused harm "with blight and mildew," in the prophet's words.[18] In inflicting them in times past he punished them secretly, as it were, whereas now *I shall take vengeance openly on them in the vestibule*, he says, that is, instead of inflicting the effects of wrath se-

17. Lv 10.1–2. Cyril sees the puzzling reference to foreign attire addressed to the priests, whereas the Antiochenes think of the general ban on wearing of mixed fabrics in Dt 22.11.

18. Hg 2.17; Jl 1.4; Am 4.9.

cretly, instead of young locust and rust affecting you, instead of bodily ailments, the sword of the enemy will be openly flashing, threatening with ruin those who have offended me, and cruelly annihilating at the very *vestibule* of the Temple *those filling the house of their God with impiety and deceit.* What *impiety*, then? What *deceit*? Another prophet makes it clear to us in speaking about Jerusalem, "Its leaders gave judgment with bribes, and its prophets (181) delivered oracles for money," and as well the wise Isaiah inveighs against it in saying, "Your princes are disobedient, companions of thieves, loving gifts, going after bribes, not judging in favor of orphans, and paying no heed to the case of a widow."[19]

The ministers at the divine altars should take care, therefore, not to be accused of such crimes. As a type, remember, priests of old received the vesture befitting their ministry; but when the time came for worship in spirit, let everyone called to service have for a kind of splendid garment and covering upright and blameless faith, life in keeping with the Gospel, a lifestyle that is reverent and law-abiding, upright behavior clear of any base gain, a mind fixed on virtue and placing God's will above all other considerations.

On that day, says the Lord, a sound of a cry will be heard from the gate of the torturers, lamentation from the second, and a great crashing from the hills (v.10). He clearly describes the calamities of war, and, as it were, presents people falling and dying and lamenting their fate, his purpose being that they may be influenced by the magnitude of the impending troubles to choose to repent and to feel the need to do what is better and more becoming, thus escaping the wrath. The Creator, after all, is kindly, and wishes not "the death of the one who dies[20] but his turning from his path of evil and living," in the words of the prophet (182) Ezekiel.[21] So at that time, he is saying, *from* one *gate of the torturers*, that is, those slaying the ones they encounter, there will come a fearful and dire cry; the enemy generally emit a frightening bel-

19. Mi 3.11; Is 1.23.

20. The LXX (Rahlfs ed.) has here τοῦ ἀνόμου ("of the lawless one"). Cyril's version, τοῦ ἀποθνήσκοντος ("of the one who dies") is not listed as a variant.

21. Ezek 18.23.

low when bursting into the cities being captured, striking fear in the inhabitants, and promptly inciting one another to cruelty, as it were.[22] From the other *gate,* on the other hand, there will be *lamentation* and weeping, with all the captives herded together, and everyone anxious to take leave of the city as from a sinking ship. There will, however, come *a great crashing from the hills,* perhaps referring by *hills* to the so-called citadel in Jerusalem, or Zion, or indicating something else; in their flight in time of war the inhabitants generally flee to the hilltops, thinking the difficult mountain terrain will prove an obstacle to the foe, and impede the charge of those pursuing them. Our Lord Jesus Christ, for instance, once predicted to the Jewish crowds, "When you see Jerusalem surrounded by armies, then let those in Jerusalem flee to the mountains."[23]

When God punishes and calls to account for their sins those who choose to be contemptuous, therefore, nothing will be of any benefit to the victims—not a city furnished with towers, not unshakeable ramparts and walls, not heights of mountains and roughness of rocks, not inhospitable approaches. Only repentance saves them, placating the judge, quelling his anger, and (183) readily winning over to the clemency befitting him the Creator, who is good by nature. While it would be better with all our strength to avoid offending him, yet since human nature always tends towards depravity and "we all fall many times,"[24] completely lacking a commitment to virtue, even if striving to bring our will to be directed to better behavior, let us also by repentance call to clemency the one who is kindly by nature, as I just said, the Creator of all.

Lament, you inhabitants of the stricken, because all the people resembled Canaan, all those taking pride in silver were destroyed (v.11). In this he implies that far from sparing anyone, the Babylonians' iron will utterly destroy the inhabitants of all Judea. He bids those remaining in Jerusalem bewail their fate, and those able

22. The references to quarters and occupations in the city in vv.10–11 of the Heb.—fish gate, second (new) quarter, quarry, (Canaanite) traders—are lost on the LXX, and so Cyril does his creative best.

23. Lk 21.20–21.

24. Jas 3.2.

to flee Jerusalem as already *destroyed,* and the city celebrated by them as already *stricken.* The reason was doubtless because all the people in it competed with the ways of the Canaanites and strove to be like them, and resembled them in everything so far as to surpass them and leave them behind. Now, the Canaanites were foreigners, godless, sacrilegious, idolatrous, and particularly profane because of their nefarious behavior. It would be a reproach to hear in the sacred Scriptures, for instance, "Offspring of Canaan, not Judah."[25]

Once again he points out that their wealth was futile, a pointless and unreliable resource, confirming that *those taking pride in silver* would perish, namely, those in the habit (184) of taking pride in wealth and possessions and adopting a conceited attitude to them. Since they succumbed to base gain, in fact, hankered after it and *filled the house of their God with impiety and deceit,*[26] as he himself said, consequently amassing wealth is condemned as ineffectual, pointless, and likely to save no one. So, as Scripture says, "A good name is to be chosen rather than great riches; instead of treasure benefiting the lawless, it is righteousness that will rescue from death," and "Truly better is a small portion with fear of the Lord than large income with injustice."[27]

At that time I shall search Jerusalem with a lamp, and take vengeance on the men who despise their protections, who say in their hearts, The Lord will not do good, nor will he do harm (v.12). God applies to his own person all that the enemy were due to do to the captives in venting their unmitigated fury—not that he personally would be the agent of such wrongdoing, but in allowing his wrath to take effect on the offenders. It is in fact as Solomon said obscurely in the Proverbs, "There is no wrong in nets being set for birds; by storing up troubles for themselves they share in their own slaughter."[28] In other words, while it is possible for those who prefer virtue to depravity to be proof against punishment and retribution, they brought wrath upon themselves, and by subjecting their souls to ruin of their own accord they would

25. Susanna 56, another deuterocanonical member of Cyril's canon.
26. 1.9.
27. Prv 22.1; 10.2; 15.16; 16.8.
28. Prv 1.17–18.

be overtaken by those who know how to make right judgments. He therefore *searches Jerusalem* (185) *with a lamp*; the Jews suffered a similar fate at the hands of the Romans, which befell them when Jerusalem was captured by Vespasian and Titus. As is recorded by Josephus, who at great length dramatizes the sufferings of the Jews, after the slaughter in the wars and the vast number who perished throughout the city, they sought out people hiding in caves and passages, brought them into the light, and cruelly and heartlessly slew them.

He says that he will *take vengeance on the men who despise their protections*, that is, either those who transgressed the laws prescribing everything to be observed, and offended by spurning their observance as of no value, or by *protections* he refers specifically to the priests' behavior, meaning the complete observance of the Law regarding clothing and appearance befitting priests and also sacrifices.[29] There was not a single way, in fact, for them to bring the victims to the altar; the difference in them you would learn by reading the Mosaic writings. No attention was given by them to the *protections*, however, doubtless on account of their descending to such a degree of frivolity and levity as to think and presume to say that the God of all takes no account of us, and is so uninterested in earthly affairs as not to commend the good and award them regard commensurate with their honesty, nor be provoked by sinners and inflict on them retribution in keeping with their unholy exploits. This in my view is the meaning of the saying, *The Lord will not do good, nor will he do harm.*

So denial of providence is simply an idle jest. It is such a vile and abominable idea as to be acceptable not even to the Greek (186) sages, who labeled its originator godless, by name Epicurus, one of those among them most fabled for wisdom. Accordingly, it is possible to claim that "a man's ways are before God's eyes, he surveys all his paths"; while he accords respect to those who practice virtue, he treats the sinner as deeply abominable, and repays everyone according to their deeds, as Scripture says.[30]

29. Cyril's explanation is the result of the reading by the LXX of a form similar to but different from the Heb. "dregs."

30. Prv 5.21; Ps 62.12.

So we should travel by the straight and narrow, follow a path pleasing to God, the Lord of all, and, by living such a lawful life and passing such a truly virtuous existence, enjoy the benevolent regard of the Lord of all, and by avoiding depravity not allow him to be provoked against us, and by repentance show zeal in correcting the faults of inertia and indifference.

Their power will become booty, and their houses disappear. They will build houses and not live in them; they will plant vineyards and not drink their wine (v.13). It will be timely for us even now to say, "Treasures will be of no use to the lawless."[31] Wealth is ever fleeting and has no permanence, in fact; rather, it totters and is inclined to depart, having itchy feet. Wanting also to take pride in it is very precarious; it hardly rescues those under God's wrath, nor would it rid anyone of blame if God assigns punishment and inflicts retribution befitting the crime. What, (187) then, is wealth? It cares only for the flesh, ministers to unholy and loathsome pleasure, is the father of arrogance, root and origin of conceitedness, and involves one in fleeting notoriety which deserts its possessor like shadows. It is true, in fact, that "all flesh is grass, and all human glory is like a flower of grass." The fact that zeal in gaining wealth on the part of the godless is therefore completely futile he conveys by saying that their power will become booty for the Chaldeans; it is to them, and rightly so, that there is reference in the verse in the Psalms, "See the one who did not make God his refuge, trusting instead in the abundance of his wealth, and was confirmed in his own futility."[32] Even if their houses were lavishly appointed, however, they would not belong to them, destined to be burned down; and if in addition they still were the possessors of vineyards, they would not drink from them. How so? They would go off as captives, leaving their possessions at home and bereft of everything that used to delight them. God makes this clear in the statement of Jeremiah to one of the rulers in Samaria, "You built yourself a comely house, spacious upper rooms, equipped with windows, paneled in cedar, and painted red. Surely you are not a king by the fact of competing with Ahab your father?

31. Prv 10.2.
32. Is 40.6; Ps 62.7.

They will not eat or drink. It would be better for you to practice justice and commendable righteousness."[33] (188)

Far from hankering after anything earthly, therefore, we should utterly reject a sense of satisfaction in passing pleasures and a claim to fleeting wealth that in a time of wrath is incapable of benefiting its possessor. Rather, we should boast of life in Christ and the ornaments of a special lifestyle, and should consider nothing better than relationship with God, crying aloud in the words, "Lord God of hosts, blessed the one who hopes in you," and further, "A single day in your courts is better than thousands. I would prefer to be abject in the house of God than dwell in the tents of sinners."[34]

Because the great day of the Lord is near, near and extremely swift. The sound the day of the Lord unleashes is bitter, harsh, and loud; that day is a day of wrath, a day of distress and pressure, a day of misfortune and ruin, a day of darkness and gloom, a day of cloud and fog, a day of trumpet blast and battle cry against the fortified cities and against the lofty turrets (vv. 14–16). Again he crushes the hope of those who in some cases are disposed to think that the prophecy will take effect only after a long delay; he presents retribution as being at the door, as it were, and the calamities of war advancing apace.[35] He calls the time when such things will occur the *day of the Lord,* referring to it as *swift* because coming without any delay and due to be seen before long. He says its sound is *harsh and loud,* suggesting in my view the shouting of the enemy; (189) and says it is a *day of wrath and distress, ruin and misfortune, a day of darkness and gloom.* After all, what fate of this kind will not befall people in such a predicament as to experience even the very terrors of death and be subject to extreme troubles? With the enemy taking the city, what will not befall the captives? What fate will they not experience? Will young men not be slaughtered before maturity, the corpses of maidens cast aside, dug up like plants before their time? Will not depression darken the heart of the captives like a kind of night and gloom so that they are at a loss

33. Jer 22.14–15, directed in fact against Jehoiakim of Judah.

34. Ps 84.12, 10.

35. Cyril, unlike Jerome, interprets the motif "day of the Lord" only as having a proximate historical fulfillment.

for planning and scheming? Instead, it will obscure each one's thinking like gloom and clouds, not allowing them to think where to turn.

Then, what room is there for doubt? The fact that the assault of the foe will be intolerable even on cities that are populous but devoid of maneuvers, and even on others that are encircled with ramparts, he conveys by proceeding to say that the day of the Lord will be *a day of trumpet blast and battle cry against the fortified cities and against the lofty turrets.* By *fortified* he refers, as I said, to their being well-manned and having a numerous fighting force, strongly walled with *lofty turrets;* in the surrounding walls *turrets* always rise up and are built into towers higher than the rest.

"It is therefore a fearful thing to fall into the hands of the living God,"[36] as Scripture says; no one can in the least resist him, (190) since he is the Lord of hosts.

I shall afflict people, and they will go about as though blind, because they sinned against the Lord, and I shall pour out their blood like dust, and their flesh like dung. Their silver and gold will not be able to rescue them on the day of the Lord's wrath, because in the fire of his zeal the whole earth will be consumed, because he will earnestly bring an end and haste to all the inhabitants of the earth (vv.17–18). Though the sense of the text is very clear, and in my view requires no comment for clarification, I shall give a cursory explanation. He threatens them, in fact, with surpassing troubles of all kinds and with darkness of mind, immediately supplying the cause by going on, *They sinned against the Lord.* It is as if you were to say, They would be guilty of provoking their brethren, flagrantly offending the Lord of all himself and infringing the divine glory. It is completely sacrilegious and unholy to deprive it of due respect and, as it were, rob it of its throne, and, as it were, install on it creation and the forms of brute beasts; while some accorded reverence to heifers, others did so to Astarte and Baal of Peor, and others to the moon and stars. Consequently, he now threatens to inflict on them the calamities of war, an *end* and *haste; end* would suggest the complete overthrow of the land of the Jews, and *haste* orderly and prompt enactment of what was forecast. The term *haste* often indicates in the divine

36. Heb 10.31.

Scriptures (191) a tumultuous attack as well; so sinning against brethren is therefore a dreadful thing. If, on the other hand, some people's sins reach such a degree of depravity as even to offend the ineffable nature itself, there would be no way of averting the effects of wrath.

It is therefore appropriate to deplore heretics, who are hateful to God in directing their speech against God the Son and claiming he is created and actually inferior to the Father. They even, as it were, fashion an idol according to their own thinking, and bid it be adored; if the Son completely falls short of being by nature God, and is generated, and is adored by us and the holy angels, how is it that we do not openly worship creation, as the pagans do under the form of the sun, or some other created thing, fashioning the idol out of foolish and vain imagining?

COMMENTARY ON ZEPHANIAH, CHAPTER TWO

Assemble and be bound together, untutored nation, before you become like a flower vanishing in a day, before the Lord's wrath comes upon you, before the Lord's anger comes upon you (vv. 1–2).

AFTER VERY clearly bringing out the ferocity of war and the magnitude of the coming disaster, he once again duly shifts attention to the call to repentance when it was an easy matter to convince them, probably because they were in fear. After all, sometimes when the mind is set firm in its perverse tendency to vile and profane behavior, we do not easily proceed to an option for repentance, whereas fear frequently forces people even against their will to do so. Accordingly, he urges them to relationship (192) with him. In other words, just as we claim that those who worship idols and devote their attention to their own passions are guilty of apostasy and keeping their distance, so in turn we interpret those who opt to adore him and him alone, and follow the oracles given by him, to be entering into a relationship with him. At any rate he describes the people of Israel as an *untutored nation* for the reason that they did not respect the ancient commandment, sacrilegiously rejecting the Law that was their tutor and capable of leading them to every form of goodness. As well, he threatens that unless *they were bound* to him in the ways just mentioned by us, they would differ in no way from *flowers* in the field that are transient and fading, and would definitely be subject to the effects of wrath.

So "while we have time, we work for the good of all." As long as the Lord, who as God is longsuffering, allows it, let us practice repentance, offer supplication, tearfully utter the appeal, "Do not remember sins of my youth and of my ignorance,"[1] at-

1. Gal 6.10; Ps 25.7.

taching ourselves to him through sanctification and sobriety. This in fact is the way *for us to be sheltered on the day of wrath* and wash away the stain of our sins *before the Lord's anger comes upon us*; he will come, you see, the judge will come in due course from heaven, and render to everyone according to their work.

Seek the Lord, all you lowly ones of earth, practice justice and seek righteousness, seek gentleness and respond to it, so that you may be sheltered on the day of the Lord's wrath (v.3). He makes clear mention (193) of the way for them to be *bound* to him, despite being a profane and *untutored* nation, bidding them *seek the Lord, practice justice and righteousness, and respond to it.* While God is *sought* by us, therefore, by hankering after what is pleasing to him through the removal of all indifference, we shall on the other hand *practice justice* by fulfilling his divine law and living virtuously without failing. Likewise, by zealously bedecking ourselves in the ornaments of good works we shall gain a reputation for *righteousness,* truly reputable and blameless in our reverence for God, and by treading the path of love for the brethren; as Scripture says, "love is the fulfilling of the Law."[2]

Now, in my view it is necessary to add to what I have mentioned *responding to it,* that is, addressing others and directing the brethren; this and no other is the way we shall be perfect in virtue. Our Lord Jesus Christ also said that the one who is proven in work and word will be called great in the kingdom of heaven, while the one who devotes himself to introducing it and is capable of it and bids others do it but cannot bring himself to do what he thinks is right is the least. Somewhere he also criticizes the leaders of the Jews in the words, "Woe to you, scribes and Pharisees, hypocrites, for loading heavy burdens on people that are difficult to bear, whereas you yourselves do not so much as lift a finger."[3] It is therefore surely proof of perfect reverence for God to practice virtue and also explain to others the means of becoming exemplary. (194) The fact that the effort involved is not without reward the disciple of Christ clarifies by saying, "The one who converts a sinner from the error of his ways will save that person's soul from death and will cover

2. Rom 13.10.
3. Mt 5.19; 23.4.

a multitude of sins." If, on the other hand, you were to think that *responding to it* means that one must pay attention to it, you could take this view; the Law of Moses also in reference to God's sayings ordered that "you are to recite them while seated and going about in public, lying down and getting up"; and David also sings, "I shall ever meditate on your ordinances."[4]

Because Gaza will be plundered, Ashkelon will disappear, Ashdod will be cast out at midday and Ekron uprooted (v.4). In God's providence the verse again foretells clearly for the encouragement and comfort of the people of Israel what will happen in due course; I shall recount what it is. After the sacking of Jerusalem and seizure of all Judea, the nearby Philistine cities gloated over the victims and mocked those despoiled; they also offered sacrifice to their gods in gratitude for the destruction of the race that was hateful to all. They presumed to say that trust in God had been proved in actual fact to be futile in their view, and they were convinced that the Babylonian forces were stronger and better even than help from on high. Should by chance anyone leave home in Judea and flee from his country in time of war and reach the neighboring countries in the expectation of being safe, he would be in a worse situation, falling in with people more cruel than the Babylonians, though obliged to show pity. The wretches therefore undermined the (195) glory of God, being hard-hearted and unmoved by those suffering misfortune, and declining to show sympathy; instead, they even aggravated the fate of the sufferers by their own knavery.

What, then, was the result? In due course the people of Israel later returned from captivity when the Lord finally permitted it, and on reaching Jerusalem they began fortifying the city, rebuilding the divine Temple itself, and to some extent had hope of enjoying prosperity with God's protection. When they learned that this was happening, however, the people of *Gaza, Ashkelon, Ashdod,* along with those from the so-called *Ekron,* Moabites, Idumeans, and Ammonites, and some other nations as well, were inflamed with the fire of envy and wanted to obstruct those encircling the city in a wall; they grouped together and advanced on the men called back from captivity. Battle

4. Jas 5.20; Dt 6.7; 11.19; Ps 119.117.

was joined in the valley of Jehosaphat; they were cut down and destroyed when God sided with Israel. They took by force the cities of the nations in such a way as to leave them completely desolate and turn them into sheepfolds. At this point he makes mention of this story, which contains a promise, firstly of the return from captivity, then of the future glory and the victory over them all, saying that *Gaza would be plundered, Ashkelon would disappear, Ashdod would be cast out at midday* (by *midday* meaning openly, not in the manner of brigands but blatantly by the norms of war), and as well *Ekron would be uprooted.* Now, he very subtly conveys the threat through the name, *Ekron* meaning "uprooting"; he says it will suffer the same fate, (196) containing in its name a reference to the disaster befalling it.[5]

Woe to the inhabitants of the cord of the sea, Cretan sojourners; the word of the Lord is against you, Canaan, land of the Philistines (v.5). After delivering considerable threats and foretelling what would befall the inhabitants of Palestine, namely, Gaza and Ashkelon, Ashdod together with the people of Ekron, he directs a similar message also to the Phoenician cities, especially those on the seacoast; consequently, he says, *Woe to the inhabitants of the cord of the sea.* Now, since many of the cities in Palestine also bordered the sea, to distinguish them, as it were, by their name he calls them in this case *cord of the sea,* for us to understand them from this to be residents of Phoenicia, whom as I said he also calls *Cretan sojourners* for the following reason. Cretans and Libyans are separated from one another by sea only by a very short distance; when the wind blows, so the story goes, sometimes the fragrance of plants travels from Crete and kills animals in Libya, namely, reptiles and venomous species. So Libyans and Cretans were ranked as a single nation. Hence at times they dispatched colonists, occupied Phoenicia, and built cities, as of course the Cappadocians also did the cities of Palestine. For instance, God said somewhere in Amos, "Are you not to me like the people of Ethiopia, (197) people of Israel? says the Lord. Did I not bring Israel up from the land of Egypt, the Philistines from Cappadocia, and the Syrians from Bothros?"[6] He calls the Palestinians Philistines,

5. Cyril derives the etymology from Jerome.

6. Am 9.7, where Cyril had earlier mentioned the variant readings (thanks

and the Phoenicians Syrians, whom he says he brought up from Bothros, referring to Libya as Bothros in my view on account of its being a country that is hollowed-out and low-lying; the sea digs out bays in it, as if the land were retreating and receding to southern regions in particular. Now, it should be noted that for "from Bothros" the other translators put Cyrene, because Libya is known to be a Phoenician colony, Cyrene being Libya's most famous city.

He is therefore saying, The word of the Lord is directed at you, *Cretan sojourners,* or Libyans (using *sojourners* for colonists or migrants), referring to them also as *Canaan.* All the inhabitants of the cities of Phoenicia were Canaanites, you see, even if initially they were colonists from Crete. Now, it should be noted that the other translators read, "The word of the Lord is against you, destructive nation." Since it was necessary to follow once again the text of the Seventy, however, we presented the account in the form which that version brings us, as the verse of the prophet also ratified as true.[7]

And I shall remove you from your habitation. Crete will be a pasture for flocks and a sheepfold (v.6). Lo, once again he is addressing migrants, as it were, and speaking to itinerants, (198) confirming the truth by the account; he says he will *remove them from their habitation,* that is, from the land which they colonized and occupied. He says that their cities will be reduced to such a state of desolation as to become *a pasture and sheepfold.* Again by *Crete* he means Phoenicia, or the people in Phoenicia, for the reason that they came from Crete, which is close to and a neighbor of Libya; in previous times they were one, and the races were combined in blood, customs, and laws.

The cord of the sea will belong to the remnants of the house of Judah, on them they will graze in the houses of Ashkelon, in the evening they will rest before the children of Judah, because the Lord their God watches over them and reversed their captivity (v.7). I mentioned above that all the nations became inflamed with envy, assembled together,

---

to Jerome), explicable by the mention of *bothros,* "ditch," for Libya (a distraction in this place). The attempt to identify Cretans and Libyans seems a further piece of creative commentary.

7. In other words, though Jerome makes available the alternative versions, the LXX is the *textus receptus.*

and advanced on Jerusalem after the time of captivity; battle was engaged; those sacrilegiously scheming against the redeemed people were defeated in the valley of Jehosaphat and cut down. When the people of Israel gained control, then, they grazed the fields of the Philistines, since they were deserted, and used the Philistines', or Palestinians', desolated cities for sheepfolds on account of the complete destruction of the people in them. Accordingly, he says, *The cord of the sea*, that is, the Palestinian cities on the sea, which once were inhabited, fearsome, and impregnable, will become grazing for flocks *for the remnants* (199) *of the house of Judah;* those saved from captivity and scarcely surviving, now that they are in control, *will graze in the houses of Ashkelon.* Towards evening, in fact, the shepherds will leave the herds of young in the folds. What, then, is the power of this kind? How will it happen, defying belief and all reason? *Because the Lord their God watches over them and reversed their captivity.* It would be like saying, He put an end to his wrath against them, he forgave their crimes, he takes up arms in conjunction with the people of Israel as of old, he grants them victory over the adversaries, and this without delay.

When God averts his gaze from us in our sin, therefore, we shall fall under the feet of the foe, and there will be no one to save or assist us. If, on the other hand, he observes us longing for virtue and wanting to live a lawful life, we shall prove superior to every foe and prevail very easily over the adversaries, and he will confirm in the case of every righteous person, "Because he hoped in me, I shall deliver him; I shall protect him because he knows my name. He will cry to me, and I shall hearken to him. I am with him in distress, I shall rescue him and glorify him. I shall fill him with length of days and extend to him my salvation."[8]

I have heard taunts of Moab and insults of the children of Ammon in mocking my people, and they made boasts against my territories. Hence, as I live, says the Lord of hosts, the God of Israel, because Moab will be like Sodom, and the children of Ammon like Gomorrah, Damascus abandoned, like a heap on the threshing floor, and disappeared forever. The remnant of my people will plunder (200) *them, and the remnant*

8. Ps 91.14–16.

of my nation will possess them (vv.8–9). The neighboring nations mocked Jerusalem in its sacking and the people of Israel in their miserable fate, as I said, convinced that the capture of Judea was the work of what were falsely named gods by them, since the hand from above that always helped them—namely, that of the God who had control of all—was completely reduced to nothing. It is not unlikely, in fact, that some of them reached such a state of folly as in their condition of error to worship sticks and stones and be ignorant of the one who is by nature and in truth God. I heard, he therefore says, the *taunts of Moab and insults of the children of Ammon*; there would in my view be no difference between someone striking with rod or stone and the one punishing with *taunts*, venting unrestrained abuse on them, blurting out and saying what would probably cause people pain by way of depression and grief, and feeling the onset of a worse disaster. Since, however, they were so unrestrained in their abuse as to call into question the divine and ineffable glory itself, he says, consequently they will suffer the retribution of *Sodom* and go to destruction, and by their misfortunes show the fate of *Gomorrah* to be slight, and eventually through their very fate come to know the power of the one who punishes.

Damascus was the capital of the Phoenicians, splendid and famous, in which there was the palace, but it will become a heap of straw, with no ears of grain; there will be no account of it, gone to utter incineration, or scattered to the wind. The blasts of wind winnow the heaps of chaff in all directions; in the same way the forces of the captors will scatter everywhere those apprehended in the cities (201), besetting them like fierce winds.[9] Now, the fact that correction will in due course come from none other than the victim of such troubles and the people insulted he indicates by saying, *The remnant of my people will plunder them, and the remnant of my nation will possess them.* By *remnant of the people,* as I said before, he refers to the people recovering from captivity, who gained power over the nations, captured their cities, and completely reduced them to devastation.

9. Damascus, clearly a rogue element in an oracle directed at Moab and Ammon, seems to have entered the LXX from a misreading of the rare Heb. term for "pile (of nettles)."

When, therefore, in the course of his plan the God of all tests the Church either by inflicting tribulations or allowing persecutions to be imposed through the onslaught on it of enemies, either pagans or unholy heretics, let no one mock it but rather await the outcome of every contest. Those who at times broadly mock it and, as it were, taunt Christ for not protecting his own or for, in their view, proving so weak, in fact, will suffer the fate of the Sodomites, become fuel for fire, and in addition will find prevailing those whom they thought vanquished.

This will be theirs in return for their insolence, because they taunted and boasted against the Lord almighty. The Lord will manifest himself to them, and will destroy all the gods of the nations of the earth (vv.10–11). *This will be their* part, he is saying, and this their lot; after all, the wretches had raged even against the ineffable glory itself, mouthing insults and uttering blasphemous remarks, (202) rebelling, as it were, against the one who surpasses all, and as well giving vent to vicious and unbridled audacity. Since they applied to their own gods the glory due to the one who is capable of everything, *the Lord will manifest himself to them,* that is, manifest his peculiar might to them by *destroying all their gods.* In fact, the shrines among them were destroyed and felled by Israel, and the captives' artifacts everywhere and in every nation became food for the flames. To where, then, had their gods' power gone? How could they save others when they were unable to help themselves? Or, rather, what are they but mute and insensate matter? "The idols of the nations are silver and gold," and not to labor the point, but rather to ask in the prophet's words, "What good is a carved image because they carved it? They made a cast figure of it, a figment of their imagination." And as the divinely inspired David says, "Those who make them are like them, as are all who trust in them."[10]

And they will worship him, each in his own place, all the islands of the nations. We are saying that the Lord was made manifest to them in destroying all their gods, in the first place in olden times by the resolute burning by the people of Israel of the shrines in the precincts and the altars within them in the Philistines' cities. And at the time of the Incarnation of the Only-

10. Ps 114.4; Hab 2.18; Ps 114.8.

begotten you could see this happening when the Word, who is God, became like us and was made manifest; the divinely inspired disciples, for instance, claimed to have touched with their hands and seen the one who is from the beginning, whom they heard. (203) The one who as God is too great to be seen, in fact, became manifest, and David also sings somewhere, "God will come in a manifest way, our God, and he will not keep silence." Now, when he became manifest, "appeared on earth," as Scripture says, "and lived with human beings,"[11] then it was that the loathsome and profane herds of the idols also perished. All the power of the devil was also done away with, and each of those who are brought through faith in Christ to the knowledge of the truth then offers through him and with him to the God and Father the *worship from his place.*

God is no longer known only in Judea; instead, the countries and cities of *the nations*, even if separated from Judea by an intervening sea, no less make their approach to Christ, present petitions, offer hymns of praise, and pay homage with unceasing benediction. While of old, in fact, it was "in Israel that his name was great," now it has become known to people everywhere, and land and sea are awash with his glory—the meaning of the statement, "As I live, says the Lord, and as all the earth will be filled with the glory of the Lord."[12] *Each one will worship from his own place,* therefore, he says; the Law built that ancient tabernacle to prefigure the beauty of the Church, and, as a type of it, that celebrated Temple was raised up in Jerusalem. The divinely inspired Moses—or God through him—gave orders to the people of old that those from the whole country of the Jews wanting to worship him should visit Jerusalem, and thus should sacrifice and worship God, death being the penalty for worshiping outside the Temple. When the time of the shadow passed away, however, and what acted as a type came to an end, (204), then it was that we came to know that the divinity is not confined to a place, nor does "the Most High dwell in temples made by hand," but rather fills heaven and earth and the nether regions. Consequently, those who believe, wherever each may be, that he

11. 1 Jn 1.1; Ps 50.2–3; Bar 3.37.
12. Ps 76.1; Nm 1.21.

is everywhere and in everything perform their worship there, having nearby the God who says, "I am a God who is nearby, says the Lord, not a God far off."[13]

Now, it should be realized that by *islands* the sacred text sometimes refers to the churches, situated in this world as if by the sea, surrounded by the bitter waters of its adversities, and stricken by persecutions like fierce billows, yet bearing up stoutly and borne on high without being submerged in the tribulations. Through Christ, in fact, the churches are unshakeable, "and the gates of hell will not prevail against them." If you therefore wanted to understand the *islands of the nations* as the churches from the nations, you would not miss the point; though beset with the turbulence of trials, they hold firm in Christ, to whom be the glory and the power forever. Amen.[14] (205)

Ethiopians, you are wounded by my sword (v.12). He mentions every race or nation in its fight against Israel and its jesting about the divine glory; so he passes from Idumeans and Ammonites to the Ethiopians, either those situated to the east and south who inhabit the country closest to the land of the Persians, or Egyptians as being close neighbors of the people of Israel. The land of the Egyptians is part of Ethiopia; at any rate the sacred texts normally refer to the rivers of Egypt as those of Ethiopia, since they draw from the Gihon, of which Scripture says, "It is the one that flows around the whole land of Ethiopia."[15] Accordingly, *You Ethiopians will be wounded by my sword,* referring by his *sword* to that of the Jews when he uses it on them for their sacrilegious treatment of his glory, as I said, and also of Israel.

Since, on the other hand, the inspired Scripture is in the habit of treating of spiritual *Ethiopians,* come now, let us deal also with them, though not proceeding beyond (206) the sense of the passage. Blessed David said in song somewhere, as though speaking to our Lord Jesus Christ, "You smashed the heads of the dragons in the water, you crushed the head of the dragon, you gave him as food for the Ethiopian peoples," and he said also somewhere else, "Ethiopians will fall prostrate before him,

13. Acts 7.48; Jer 23.23.
14. Mt 16.18. Cyril's first volume on Zephaniah closes at this point. The PG ed. does not include the final sentence.
15. Gn 2.13.

and his foes will lick the dust." And somewhere the character taking the role of bride in the Song of Songs admits to being "black and beautiful."[16] It is therefore to be understood that the Ethiopians are those who have a mind that is darkened and unenlightened, are not yet illumined, and lack the divine light. Those falling prostrate before Christ, by contrast, like the bride, of course, are illumined by him, and cry out in prayer, "Let the brightness of the Lord our God be upon us,"[17] whereas those with their impurity uncleansed, who persist in being darkened, will feast on the dragons' heads (the apostate dragon being food for them), but will fall to the *sword.* Now, in my view, the force of the verse applies particularly to the unclean spirits, whom Christ has *wounded* by canceling their tyrannical rule over us and destroying along with them the father of darkness, the inventor of all sin, who darkens "the minds of the unbelievers to keep them from seeing the light of the Gospel of the glory of Christ." This I think is what the divine Isaiah has also said to us, "On that day God with his holy and great and strong sword will strike the dragon, the twisting serpent, the dragon fleeing the serpent, and will destroy the dragon."[18] (207)

I will stretch my hand to the north and destroy the Assyrian, and will turn Nineveh into a waterless ruin like a desert. Flocks will graze in its midst and all the wild beasts of the earth, chameleons and hedgehogs will sleep in its mangers, wild beasts will cry out in its canals and ravens in its gateways (vv.13–14). I shall also touch the countries and cities to the east and north, he says, and destroy *the Assyrians* along with the others and the devastated cities, including even the celebrated *Nineveh,* capital of the Chaldeans. It will be *waterless,* like inaccessible and uninhabited lands. Once again the verse probably compares the vast number of the inhabitants to waters, which is customary with the sacred Scriptures. Another of the holy prophets, for instance, in foretelling the Assyrians' assault made on Jerusalem, said, "Lo, waters come from the north, and they will be like an overwhelming torrent."[19] So

16. Pss 74.13–14 LXX; 72.9 LXX; Song 1.5.
17. Ps 90.17 LXX.
18. 2 Cor 4.4; Is 27.1.
19. Jer 47.2, where in fact the fate of Gaza is in question.

when he says *Nineveh* will be *waterless,* I would say that he means it will be empty of inhabitants. He asserts that *flocks will graze in its midst,* giving a sign, in my view, of utter desolation and no one's inhabiting it, as rustic crops do not normally grow in cities; but if there should somehow be fodder in a city, it would be a clear indication that depopulation had occurred completely.

He proceeds to indicate a considerable horde of other things, saying that there would live in it *all the wild beasts of the earth,* and that *chameleons and hedgehogs will sleep in its mangers,* and as well *in its canals*—that is, pits or caves—wild *beasts will cry out, and ravens* even lodge (208) *in its gateways.* Now, no one in a right mind could doubt that hedgehogs do not live in houses, nor wild animals in the middle of the city, nor would ravens willingly take to gateways unless they enjoyed a complete liberty acceptable to their nature; wild animals, and in fact the others referred to, prefer not to lodge with human beings. In what way, then? Only if there were total desolation and a completely leisurely way of living would the extent of the desolation, as it were, provide security and expel all fear.

Now, if it is necessary to add something to this, let us make our own hearts secure and eschew completely with all our strength offending God, lest we become a dwelling for wicked and cruel *animals,* that is, the unclean spirits, when all our virtue is lost. This, in my view, is the meaning of the clear and wise statement in Jeremiah to Jerusalem, "You will be corrected with hardship and scourging, Jerusalem, lest my soul turn away from you, lest I make you a trackless waste which will not be inhabited."[20] When God removes virtue from us, in fact, he installs profane and unholy passions in our mind and heart, where, as it were, wild animals will come to live, and the savage horde of unclean spirits will enter.[21]

Because a cedar is its summit. This is the contemptuous city, dwelling in hope, saying in her heart, I exist, and after me there will be no one. How it has fallen in ruins, (209) *a pasture for wild beasts! All who pass by whistle at it and shake their fist* (vv.14–15). Nineveh is always represented as conceited, haughty, and arrogant; and

20. Jer 6.7–8.
21. The PG ed. does not reproduce this entire sentence.

that was in accord with reality, as it looked down on every nation and every government, and accorded little esteem to the power of others. The prophet Habakkuk also confirms this in speaking of the king of the Assyrians, "He will delight in kings, and tyrants will be his playthings; he will make fun of every fortification."[22] Accordingly, he again makes clear that the capital of the Chaldeans was very arrogant and conceited, and extremely inclined to be domineering, and he compares him to *a cedar's summit*, calling him *contemptuous*. Now, you would find this statement to be accurate and true from the words of the Rabshakeh, who on coming to Judea accosted those on the wall and showed contempt for the glory on high, saying, "Thus says the king, Do not let Hezekiah deceive you with words that will not be able to save you, and do not let Hezekiah tell you that God will save you." And a little later, "Surely none of the gods of the nations has rescued its land from the hand of the king of the Assyrians?"[23]

Accordingly, *this is the contemptuous city*, which thinks and says, *I exist, and after me there will be no one*. So since it was given to displaying such vile and accursed arrogance by way of outlandish boasting, consequently it will then be reduced to such a degree of misery that he will even say of it, *How it has fallen in ruins, a pasture for wild beasts*, the word *how* coming not from someone asking and wanting to know, but rather someone amazed (210) at the unexpected change. After all, far from severe and unexpected troubles not arousing amazement, they generally astonish those who see or hear of them. Likewise, everyone will *whistle at it and shake their fist*, involving one another in the astonishment, in my view, raising their hands in amazement, and emitting a vague sound from their stomach in a whistle. In this he conveys to us very well the effect of the unexpected disaster, as it were.

So "God really resists the arrogant," and this advice is wise and worth adopting: "Do not exalt yourself lest you fall," and again, "Whoever builds himself a lofty house is looking for col-

22. Hab 1.10, which Cyril there took to refer to the ruler of the Babylonians, and specifically Nebuchadnezzar.

23. Is 36.14, 18.

lapse."[24] In other words, just as buildings that tend to be built up to an exceedingly great height are more disposed to collapse, and run the greatest risk of falling to pieces, so too a person's soul that is swollen with arrogance by the vanity of its thoughts is unsteady and easily disposed to fall. If, on the other hand, things were done in a way pleasing to God, there would then be no obstacle.

24. Prv 3.34 LXX; Sir 1.30; Prv 17.19.

COMMENTARY ON ZEPHANIAH, CHAPTER THREE

O famous and redeemed city, the dove (v.1).

He immediately moves to remember the land of the Jews—Jerusalem, in fact—for the capture of which the Assyrians paid the penalty. The other nations were also punished for railing against the glory of God; but he grieves for its suffering a fate beyond expectations, as it were, and instead of attributing the cause of its unbearable misfortunes to anyone else, he says that it was rather the source of them. So he complains bitterly in the words, *O famous and redeemed city, the dove.*[1] (211) In other words, he is saying, why did you come to be completely dishonored, an object of pity and a captive, when you were so splendid and prominent, in control of every nation, effortlessly vanquishing your adversaries, ever harsh and impregnable to those who wished to oppose you, well-equipped for the fortunes of war? It was *redeemed* from the slavery of the Egyptians by many signs and portents, its neck released from unbearable oppression; on its account rivers turned to blood, hail and darkness damaged the land of the Egyptians, the sea joined in attacking it, submerging the pursuers, and countless other events occurred that were worth hearing.

O city, the dove, that is, most beautiful; the inspired Scripture takes this bird as a paradigm of comeliness, as of course in the Song the bridegroom wants to flatter the bride's appearance by the word *dove,* "Arise, come my friend, my lovely, my dove."[2] Now, Jerusalem was very beautiful, doubtless on account of being given luster by the divine Law, bedecked with the ornaments of priesthood, practiced in righteousness, a worshiper of

1. The PG ed. omits these opening sentences. The LXX had come up with "redeemed" for "impure," and "dove" for "oppressive."

2. Song 2.10.

the one who is God by nature, and performing his liturgy—all of which is spiritual beauty. On the other hand, you could on a different basis claim that Jerusalem is to be understood as a *dove.* It is the invariable custom of this bird, even if carried far away from the nest beloved by it, to make for home when given the opportunity and to reach its own place. This is what we shall (212) find happening in the case of Jerusalem as well; in possession of true religion from its ancestors it went down to Egypt, but it departed from the worship of its fathers and worshiped idols there. Summoned by Moses, however, it flew away from the error of Egypt in a way, and turned back to God again. But, he asks, what was the reason for its capture, and for then being redeemed from its subjection to others?

It hearkened to no voice (v.2). It heard the voice of God on Mount Sinai saying, "Listen, Israel, the Lord is your God, the Lord alone. You shall not make for yourself an idol, whether in the form of anything that is in heaven, or that is on the earth beneath, or that is in the water under the earth."[3] Bypassing what was commanded, however, it foolishly ran headlong into the error of polytheism. So *it hearkened to no voice* spoken to it on Mount Sinai; or we should understand the *voice* as commandment.

It did not accept correction. It ran riot over the Law that guided it and conducted it to righteousness, turning instead to "teaching and commandments of human beings,"[4] following its own instincts, straying from the straight and narrow, and persisting in being untaught and unacquainted with the divine instructions.

It did not trust in the Lord. When war brought tribulation, contest ensued, and (213) dangers befell them, it should have chosen to imitate the piety of its forebears and trust in the Lord as its only Savior. But "it called on Egypt," as Scripture says, "had recourse to Assyrians,"[5] and hired Syrians or Arabs, as though out of scorn for the divine power.

Its rulers within it are like roaring lions (v.3). It lists the crimes and parades the faults for which he is rightly moved and pro-

3. Dt 6.4; 5.8.
4. Is 29.13; Mt 15.9.
5. Hos 7.11.

voked to wrath, so that he may now be seen to be just in punishing the offenders for reaching such a degree of depravity that the offense is even intolerable to him. *Its rulers are like lions,* then, he says. What in fact do they do? Under pressure from hunger calling them to a desire for food, they vigorously scour hills and valleys emitting dire and fearsome roars. If they see something suitable for eating, they utter a bellow, as it were, and cause such fear that it seems frozen to the spot and, as it were, held fast in a trap, awaiting the diner. Now, this is what some of the leaders in Israel also did, in some cases threatening to impose the penalty of death, prescribed in the Law for transgressors, on those (214) not guilty unless they agreed to do what was to their satisfaction and liking, yielding to other people who accused them, and purloining the property of those who condemned them. He accuses them of such crimes in another prophet as well in these words, "They turned to pondering hardships and devising troubles on their beds, and at break of day they put them into effect because they did not raise their hands to God. They set their heart on properties, robbed orphans, took possession of houses, cheated a man of his house, a man of his inheritance."[6]

Now, the inventors of heresies also roar, so to say, at those opting to live a life of simple faith, opening their mouth, hateful to God, devouring, as it were, those who know nothing by making them more ignorant, imparting to them frigid and perverted ideas, spinning such fables, and persuading them so to accept what appeals to them that they give the appearance of being caught in their traps and perhaps lose their life, differing little from insensate stones. To them you might cry out, and rightly so, "Sleeper, awake, rise from the dead, and Christ will shine upon you." But, as blessed David says, "God will break their teeth in their mouth, the Lord has smashed the fangs of the lions."[7]

Its judges like wolves of Arabia, there was nothing left for the morning. They say that wolves in Arabia are inclined to ferocity beyond any other animal, suffering from an insatiable desire for (215) food, and so swift in flight as easily to outstrip any pursu-

6. Mi 2.1–2.

7. Eph 5.14; Ps 58.6.

er. Somewhere, in fact, in another prophet it said of the horses of Babylon, "swifter than the wolves of Arabia."[8] So he is taking the greed of wolves in the present instance as a figure of the judges, who consume the defendants, as it were, with wide-open mouth and insatiable teeth in the process of requiring by a perversion of justice everything possible even beyond possibility in their unholy effort to twist the intentions of the divine Law to others' satisfaction. It would, on the contrary, have been better for them to realize that "the ways of those who accept bribes under cover do not prosper." In fact, as Scripture says, "Bribes blind the eyes of the wise and subvert righteous words."[9] After all, what credit is there in accepting bribery? What good will base gain do to those addicted to it? Or, rather, what profit would come to them from it? Blessed Paul is in fact correct in saying, "Those who want to be rich fall into temptation and are trapped by many senseless and harmful desires that plunge people into ruin and destruction." So "a good name is preferable to great wealth,"[10] and the verse is surely very wise and correct.

Its prophets spirit-bearers, contemptuous men (v.4). He was right to add *its* to *prophets* here, because they were not God's, uttering deceptively what was "from their own hearts and not from the Lord's mouth," as Scripture says.[11] Now, the verse is being ironical in calling them *spirit-bearers,* not that they really had a share of the Holy Spirit, but that they presumed to feign the charism of prophecy, (216) and did not shrink from claiming that they were filled with the Holy Spirit. So in wanting to be both *prophets* and *spirit-bearers,* he says, they bedecked their own heads with an august title, and thus the wretches proved to be so *contemptuous* as not even to know what honesty is, instead destroying also others to whom they spoke what came from their heart, and this for trifling and insignificant profit, and, as the prophet Ezekiel says, "for a handful of barley and a crust of bread."[12] They were caught up in such a degree of madness as to claim for themselves the counsels of the ineffable glory, and to class as divine sayings words tossed up from their own thinking. In the state-

8. Hab 1.8.
9. Prv 17.23; Ex 23.8.
10. 1 Tm 6.9; Prv 22.1.
11. Jer 23.16.
12. Ezek 13.19.

ment in Jeremiah, for instance, he said of them, "I did not send the prophets, and they did not run; I did not speak to them, and they did not prophesy," the prophet himself clearly crying aloud in the words, "O Lord, Lord, lo, their prophets are prophesying and saying, You will not see the sword, nor will you have hunger in your midst, because it is truth and peace I shall give on the earth and in this place." And the God of all cried out, as it were, in the words, "The prophets are prophesying lies in my name: I did not send them, nor command them, nor speak to them, because they are prophesying to you false visions, oracles, augury, and preferences of their own heart. If they are prophets, and if the word of the Lord is in them, let them meet me. What has straw in common with wheat? It is like that with my words, says the Lord. Are not my words like a fiery flame, says the Lord, and like a hammer that breaks a rock?"[13] The word of God sinks deep into the mind, and, as it were, pierces the heart of the listeners, whereas (217) what comes from human counsels is frigid and powerless, like the one from the unholy false prophets.

Its priests profane holy things, and infringe the Law. Not even the chosen race—that is, that of the tribe of Levi—is found to be above reproach; he says that they *profane holy things, and infringe the Law.* Scripture says, in fact, "Because a priest's lips will preserve knowledge, and they will look for a norm from his mouth"; but as the Lord of all himself says somewhere, "The priests did not say, Where is the Lord?"[14] In my view, in fact, the phrase *infringe the Law* means not being prepared to clarify the Law for those unfamiliar with it, nor to show enthusiasm to bring the people in their care to what is pleasing to God. And far from stopping at those crimes, they even *profane holy things*; the Law given through Moses regarding sacrifices and offerings enjoys fullest observance when it must be performed in every single detail, whereas they probably offered sacrifices only carelessly and negligently, not bothering to observe times or forms, nor perhaps being purified or clothed in vesture appropriate to their priestly character or performing rituals with decorum. Instead,

13. Jer 23.21; 14.13–14; 23.28–29.
14. Mal 2.7; Jer 2.8.

they dishonored such an august and commendable ministry as though it were good for nothing.

Ministers of the Church ought therefore take care not to *profane holy things.* Now, there is not one single form of profanation, but many and varied; there is need for both soul and body to be purified, to eschew every kind of profane (218) pleasure, and instead to be conspicuous for works of beneficence, remembering the divinely inspired Paul's words, "Live by the Spirit, and do not gratify fleshly desire."[15]

The Lord is righteous in its midst, and will not commit injustice; morning by morning he will deliver his judgment, and not allow injustice to prevail (v.5). Justice and injustice can never be reconciled, nor would what is pure have anything in common with what is profane. After all, "what does light share with darkness?"[16] In fact, such things are at odds, and you would find them quite at variance. So since God, who controls all things, loves righteousness and has no truck with injustice, how were the awful crimes of the Jews likely to prevail or attain their goal without being nipped in the bud? It seems, however, that it is somehow a form of injustice not to subject the sinner to punishment, and not call to account the one who opts for a licentious and sacrilegious life, paying no heed to the laws, and being so inclined to injustice as to set no store by better behavior, and take as a credit and a boast what should be found a source of shame. Accordingly, since *the Lord is righteous in its midst, and will not commit injustice,* showing no tolerance for those in the habit of being unjust, *morning by morning he will deliver his judgment,* that is, at daybreak, in the open and, as it were, in daylight he will no longer postpone the effects of wrath, instead, bringing them forth, making them obvious, and, as it were, putting what he promised in full view. In fact, he will not *allow injustice to prevail.* (219) Now, by *prevail* he means achieve complete victory; when wrongdoers are punished, the form of *injustice* will cease, there being no one to engage in it any longer.[17]

It therefore behoves people of truly sound mind to consid-

15. Gal 5.16.
16. 2 Cor 6.14.
17. The versions of the text of this phrase differ, as the PG ed. also differs.

er well the fact that the Lord loves justice and could not bear those who sin incorrigibly. If, on the other hand, someone has recourse to repentance and sheds tears for his sins, he will find him most tender, will win forgiveness, and escape from the snares and the need to be punished. If, on the other hand, he should be inflexible and retain his intention of resisting the need to opt for a more fitting way of life, he will persist in his sins, or rather perish in them, and be subject to the Lord's response, because he does not put up with sinners indefinitely.

I brought down the arrogant with corruption, their corners were demolished; I shall make their roads desolate so that there is absolutely no traveling them; their cities were too wasted for anyone to live there or dwell there (v.6). Since, as I said, the priests profaned holy things, and some even broke the Law itself, *the Lord is righteous in its midst, and morning by morning he will deliver his judgment.*[18] What does that involve? *He brought down the arrogant with corruption;* that is, he consigned to destruction the haughty and insolent. After all, are they not haughty who are given to opposing God and (220), as it were, resisting his will expressed in the oracles given through Moses, paying very little heed to the divine laws but inclined towards extreme obduracy, and saying to the Lord, "Depart from me, I do not wish to know your ways"? Next, there is no doubt that the poor in spirit and humble of heart, as Scripture says, is the person who is well-disposed, compliant, and ready to obey, and it is he whom he accords his supervision. In one of the prophets, for example, the God of all said, "On whom shall I cast my gaze if not the humble and peaceable person who trembles at my words?"[19] So the conceited race was therefore drawn down to its destruction, and *their corners were demolished,* by *corners* referring in my view to the walls and the cities' ramparts, *corners* generally being uplifted, with prominent towers. It is perhaps therefore as if to say, The cities among them will be bereft of walls.

Now, in addition he threatened also to *make their roads desolate,* namely, Israel's, *so that there is absolutely no traveling them.* He seems to me to mean something like the following. The Law

18. 3.5.
19. Jb 21.14; Mt 5.3; 11.29; Is 66.2.

given through Moses gave orders that if in due course the festival of Tabernacles should be celebrated, they should come up from all Judea to Jerusalem and perform the prescribed rituals there.[20] When the cities were *brought down*, therefore, and the people in them perished, it was then we claim that *the roads were made desolate* so that no one any longer came by them and traveled as before to perform the festival prescribed for them. The Jews' good order had in fact reached such a state of deterioration that there was no one to celebrate festivals and hardly any survivors or remnant from the war to be in a festive mood. (221) The prophet Jeremiah, for instance, composed part of the Lamentations in the words, "The roads to Zion mourn the lack of anyone coming to the festival."[21] Once again the passage itself establishes the truth of the verse, proceeding immediately, *Their cities were too wasted for anyone to live there or dwell there.*

"It is therefore a fearful thing to fall into the hands of the living God."[22] By provoking him, in fact, through opting to offend him without restraint, then it is that, very rightly for being caught up in crimes of arrogance, as it were, we are *brought down to corruption*, shall be bereft of the rampart from on high, shall find the heart within us to be, as it were, vulnerable and unprotected, and furthermore shall not find the *roads* of righteousness. On the other hand, the person choosing to follow the Lord's wishes and subjecting to him the indulgent neck of their soul would easily avoid such troubles.

I said, Only fear me and accept correction, and you will not disappear from her sight as a result of everything for which I took vengeance against her (v.7). He tries to convey the fact that once again they would be guilty of bringing upon their own heads the effects of wrath. He had in fact given advice by frequently ordering them to live their lives in fear of God, and conveying the fact that they needed to *accept correction*, namely, from the Law and the Prophets, this being the way, and no other, to avert the wrath and avoid their fate. Since, however, Israel was unresponsive, obdurate, and inflexible, and failed to accept correction, that is, it did not succeed in being wise, as it were, it *disappeared from*

20. Dt 16.16.
21. Lam 1.4.
22. Heb 10.31.

her sight despite being always obliged to abide by sound correction and readily to accept (222) whatever was pleasing to God; in this way it could have avoided *everything for which I took vengeance against her.*

Accordingly, when we dismiss fear of God from our mind, when we decline to accept *correction,* and set no store at all on being wise, then it is that we shall definitely suffer the fate that befits those given to showing contempt. Then it is, too, that God will *take vengeance* and require an account of sacrilegious behavior. There is consequently need to remember the one who says, "The fear of the Lord guarantees life," "The fear of the Lord is our glory and boast." It is also "pure," that is, it makes one pure, and "abides forever," according to the verse of the psalmist.[23]

Get ready, rise early, all their gleanings are spoiled. Since you did not accept correction from me, he says, instead rejecting and abhorring a life lived in fear and simplicity, prepare yourself to meet a fate that could have been avoided if you were virtuous and wise. He bade him *rise early,* suggesting that the time had arrived for calamity to be at the doors, as it were, coming next day, arriving at break of day. Now, this was the warning of someone thwarting the hope of delay and not permitting them to think that there would be a truce or postponement, and that a long interval would intervene, perhaps transferring the effects of wrath to their successors. *Get yourself ready,* therefore, as for an urgent appointment, and *rise early* for flight; you will go off to the foe as a captive, will leave your country behind, and will be an object of pity to others. (223)

The God of all then says to the prophet, as if grieving for the captives, *All their gleanings are spoiled.* What he means we shall explain as far as possible. The Babylonian tyrants had plundered Samaria and other cities of Judea as well—firstly Pul, then after him Shalmaneser, and thirdly Sennacherib.[24] As though harvesting a vineyard, they proceeded to return to their own country, leaving Israel like scarce remnants and bequeathing to them mere *gleanings,* as it were. By *gleanings* we refer to the smallest

23. Prv 19.23; Sir 1.11; Ps 19.9.

24. Again Cyril uses terms like Assyria and Babylonia, Israel and Judah, interchangeably, with predictable effects on dating the prophet's ministry.

bunches, few of them containing grapes, which often escape the notice of the harvesters because they are concealed under leaves. Another of the holy prophets says something similar: "Woe is me for becoming like someone gathering stubble in the harvest and gleanings at the picking, there being no bunches available for eating the first-fruits." Whereas it was they who did the harvesting, therefore, Nebuchadnezzar arrived after them, destroyed even the gleanings, gathered the insignificant remnant of Israel, and went off home, continuing to boast. The prophet Jeremiah, for instance, mourns the captive Jerusalem, saying in reference to those left desolate, "Let all their evildoing come before you, and glean them as they gleaned me," and again, "Look, O Lord, and consider whom you have gleaned in this way. Do women eat the fruit of their womb? A cook did the gleaning."[25]

When we provoke God, therefore, then it is that we are deprived of all assistance, bereft of mercy, and given (224) over to the foe, with no remnant of virtue or goodness left in us. Satan harvests everything of good in us, and collects as *gleanings* even the very desires in our mind that lead it to make a choice to practice virtue.

Hence wait for me, says the Lord, on the day of my rising in witness (v.8). Since they were given over to the foe for despising the divine commandments, and fell into the hands of the one who even destroyed the very gleanings, he then bade them *wait* and endure, putting up bravely with servitude, until he should come to their aid, of which he had, as it were, given *witness* and clearly foretold through the holy prophets that it would come in due course. So by *the day of my rising in witness* he suggests the time of giving aid, which he testified in advance would surely come.

So much for the account of the facts. We claim that the spiritual meaning of the passage took effect in the mystery of Christ,[26] and conveyed the time of the total and universal redemption—namely, through Christ. In former times, remember, the God of all at the expiration of the seventy years arose

25. Mi 7.1; Lam 1.22; 2.20.

26. The mention of "rising," plus the obscurity of the passage, encourages Cyril to pass quickly from *historia* to *theōria* in terms of resurrection.

to the aid of those suffering that fate, whereas at the end of the age the Only-begotten became man, not only to rescue Israel, but to lead out all the nations from slavery to the devil, make them free, rid them of corruption, defilement, and sin, and, in advance of the others, of adoring creation instead of the Creator. When he became (225) man, "he endured the cross, disregarding the shame," so that by his own blood he might acquire for the God and Father both those still living and also those whom "death had swallowed" in advance, as Scripture says. "For to this end Christ died and lived again, so that he might be Lord of both the dead and the living."[27] It was therefore rightly said to the former generation, *Hence wait for me, says the Lord, on the day of my rising in witness.* Now, Christ's coming to life again is *witness,* as it were, that death is canceled, because in him we too are personally raised, being justified through faith, and escaping along with death the mother of death, namely, sin.

Because my judgment is on assemblies of nations, to receive kings, to pour out on them all the wrath of my anger, because all the earth will be consumed in the fire of my ardor. He threatens the nations of the Chaldeans with the devastation that occurred through Cyrus and all his allies and fellow attackers, who would overrun the cities of the Babylonians and conduct a frightening assault on all. Accordingly, he says that *my judgment will be on assemblies of nations* so as also *to receive kings*—that is, those named—and through them to punish them and *assemblies of nations,* quite divested of their power and strength and enduring every form of cruelty. In fact, I shall *pour out on them all the wrath of my anger*; it is true that God punishes serious and enormous sins with considerable responses, yet the retribution he imposes is completely commensurate with whatever sins one commits. Now, the fact that (226) the Chaldeans' fortunes were, so to say, consumed by fire he makes clear by saying, *All the earth will be consumed in the fire of my ardor.* What this *ardor* was, and on whom it was fully vented, the prophet Zechariah clarifies by saying, "The Lord almighty says this, I am extremely jealous for Jerusalem and Zion. I am extremely wrathful towards the nations who have con-

27. Heb 12.2; Is 25.7; Rom 14.9.

spired, the reason being that while I was slightly wrathful, they conspired with evil intent."[28]

While such is our factual understanding of the passage, it would have a different meaning when the interpretation is applied to the mystery of Christ. He said, remember, in what was predicted already, *Hence wait for me, says the Lord, on the day of my rising in witness. Because my judgment is on assemblies of nations, to receive kings, to pour out on them all the wrath of my anger.* In other words, Christ came back to life after plundering Hades because it was not possible for the one who is life by nature to be under the power of death, as Scripture says.[29] Far from allowing those who professed faith in him to be subject to diabolical powers, he delivers a holy and godly *judgment on assemblies of nations,* that is, the herds of the demons, seizing and confining those very ones who once exercised power and rule over the deceived, and plunging them into the very depths—Hades, that is—and *pouring out on them all his wrath* and, as it were, incinerating them by his ineffable divine power under the influence of great *ardor.* While he in fact was somewhat wrathful on account of the transgression by Adam, "they conspired with evil intent," in one fell swoop separating from God the whole earth under heaven and stifling the mind of those under their control with the enticements of sin. Accordingly, the Word of God was ardently concerned (227) for the spiritual Zion, that is, the Church; he rescued it and "presented it to himself," as blessed Paul writes, "without spot or wrinkle or anything of the kind, instead being holy and blameless."[30]

Because I shall at that time change the speech of peoples for their generation so that all will call upon the name of the Lord and serve him under one yoke. From the reaches of the rivers of Ethiopia they will offer sacrifices to me (vv.9–10). He is saying that when the city of the Babylonians is plundered and the arrogant are brought to destruction, the nations will recognize God's power, which brought them down. Those who mocked Israel at its fall and ruin, on seeing it going home in splendor and returning to the holy city while those who formerly ravaged it are completely ruined, will

28. Zec 1.14–15.
29. Acts 2.24.
30. Eph 5.27.

then *change* their *speech* and in future make offerings with blessings to God, despite previously shaking their heads, thinking and saying that Judea was captured, doubtless on account of the ruler of the Babylonians prevailing over their helper, namely, God. So when they see the reversal of fortunes, then they will *change* their *speech* in the case of each of their *generations*, or tribe by tribe and race by race, by way of praising God. In my view they would also choose to *serve under one yoke* and offer sacrifices, even if at a distance by the location of the countries and inhabiting the country of the Ethiopians.

While this may suffice for the literal sense for the time being, (228) we claim the Word fulfilled it at the time of his coming, and provides a clear sign of the change of languages. In the Acts of the Apostles, remember, it is written that on the day of holy Pentecost everyone was gathered "in the one place and, lo, there came a sound from heaven like the rush of a violent wind, and it filled the entire house where they were sitting. And, lo, divided tongues as of fire appeared among them and rested upon each one of them. They were all filled with the Holy Spirit and began to speak in different languages, as the Spirit gave them ability to speak." So it will be at that time, he is saying, that I shall change *the speech of peoples*; all heard them speaking in their "native language, Parthians, Medes, and Elamites" and the other nations.[31] But note the precision: he said he would change *the speech for their generation*, that is, remaining in those who spoke it once to the end of their life, or *generation*. The sign came, in fact, to those on whom the sacred text says the tongues rested; hence he says, I shall change *the speech for their generation*—it did not continue to happen to those after them. Let Paul in his wisdom explain the reason; he said, "And so the tongues are a sign not for believers but for unbelievers; it is written, By people of strange tongues and by the lips of foreigners I shall speak to this people, yet even then they will not believe."[32]

In what way there is benefit, therefore, in changing *the speech for its generation* he himself clarifies for us in saying, *so that all will call upon the name of the Lord and serve him under one yoke. From the*

31. Acts 2.1–4, 8–9.
32. 1 Cor 14.22, 21; Is 28.11.

reaches of the rivers of Ethiopia they will offer sacrifices to me. In other words, when they saw the apostles speaking in foreign tongues, considerably (229) marveling at the extraordinary event, they came to faith in Christ, and large numbers beyond counting then *called upon the name* of the one who by nature and in truth is God, submitting their neck to the Gospel oracles and entering the service of Christ. They also *offer sacrifices from the reaches of the rivers of Ethiopia.* He extends the race of the Ethiopians from east to west, and they drink from the Gihon, "the river that encircles all the land of Ethiopia."[33] The verse of the prophecy then closes with the reality; the Gospel not only was preached throughout the Roman Empire but also spread at that time to the barbarians. There are churches everywhere, for instance, flocks and teachers, leaders, spiritual guides, and altars to God, and the lamb is sacrificed spiritually by the holy ministers even in the Indies and in *Ethiopia.* This is surely the meaning of the statement of another prophet, "Because I am a great king, says the Lord, my name has been glorified among the nations, and in every place incense is offered to my name and a pure offering."[34]

On that day you will not be put to shame for all your pursuits by which you offended against me, because at that time I shall remove from you your insolent scorn, and you will no longer continue to boast on my holy mountain (v.11). The God of all once more speaks here from two points of view; there is need, in my view, to consider the statements in detail, thus finding the meaning in them without confusion. He promises the people of Israel, then, cancellation of their sins and (230) forgiveness of past faults, confirming it by saying that they would no longer be *put to shame for their pursuits* and former impious behavior against God. On the other hand, he threatens the Babylonian, as it were, saying that he would *no longer continue to boast* of having devastated the holy city dedicated to him—namely, Zion—which he also calls *mountain*; after the return—from captivity, I mean—Jerusalem remained intact and no longer under threat of the Babylonians' inhumanity.

33. Gn 2.13.
34. Mal 1.14, 11.

Now, there would be no doubting that it was at the time of his coming that cancellation and forgiveness were granted to all the believers; we have been justified, "not because of any works of righteousness that we had done, but according to his great mercy." We are also rid of shame; the one who gave us the honor of faith said somewhere to us, "Do not be concerned that you have been disgraced, or be worried that you have been mocked." We have in fact been led to have confidence by the one who for us was among the dead and for our sake ascended to heaven in the sight of the Father; for our sake Christ ascended as a forerunner, "now appearing before God."[35] On the one hand, therefore, he removed the faults of all, and rid the believers of the failings of *shame* and disgrace, while on the other hand it is also said by him to Satan, who formerly dominated us, *I shall remove from you your insolent scorn, and you will no longer continue to boast on my holy mountain.* That is to say, you will no longer scorn people on earth for being severely affected by impotence, nor show insolence for the consecrated ones by easily bringing them to submit to your will. The old has passed away, in fact, and things have been transformed to a new state,[36] (231) since Christ has achieved this renewal of them, making strong what was weak, confirming in piety what was subject to sin, and making firm what was unstable. So the *insolent scorn*—that is, the devil's—has been removed, and he would no longer show his conceit against the *holy mountain,* that is, the spiritual Zion, "which is the Church of the living God," founded as it is on a "rock, and the gates of hell will not prevail against it." Now, the prophet Isaiah also told us the Church has the name *mountain,* saying, "In the last days the mountain of the Lord will be conspicuous, and the house of God on the peaks of the mountains; it will be uplifted over the hills, and to it will come all the nations. Many nations will come and say, Come now, let us go up to the mountain of the Lord and to the house of the God of Jacob, and he will announce to us his way, and we shall travel in it."[37]

I shall leave in your midst a people gentle and lowly, and the remnant of Israel will reverence the name of the Lord; they will not be guilty

35. Ti 3.5; Is 44.4 LXX; Heb 9.24.
36. 2 Cor 5.17.
37. 1 Tm 3.15; Mt 16.18; Is 2.2–3.

of iniquity and will not say idle things, nor will deceitful talk be found in their mouth (vv.12–13). Again he addresses Zion, or the holy city—I mean Jerusalem—in which he also promises will be left the *gentle and lowly people.* Though in fact the synagogue of the Jews had raged against Christ the Savior of all, and had turned murderer of the Lord, and of it he requires an account, yet not all perished; the remnant was preserved and the survivors saved, a great number of them coming to faith. (232) These were the *gentle,* not venting on Christ their rage like a bull, like of course those who at that time brought him before Pilate, crying out in the words, "Away with him, away with him, crucify him," and adding to this the cry, "If you do not kill him, you are no friend of Caesar's." In fact, what could be more cruel than such people, and more fierce than their anger? They brought innocent blood upon their own heads in saying without a thought, "His blood be upon us and upon our children." So the *people* who had no share in their savagery were *gentle,* therefore, and likewise *lowly* in their subjection to Christ, submitting the neck of their mind to his yoke, and willingly heeding his loving call, "Come to me, all you who are weary and are carrying heavy burdens, and I shall give you rest. Take my yoke upon you, and learn from me, for I am gentle and lowly in heart, and you will find rest for your souls."[38]

They are therefore also conformed in this to Christ, who for our sake made himself poor,[39] as though unconcerned for the glory proper to God and his pre-eminence by nature, in order that in the divine plan he might endure the condition proper to a slave. Let those who enjoy spiritual guidance from his laws therefore model themselves on him. It is they who will also *reverence the name of the Lord*; the divinely inspired disciples, who before others also have the role of light of the world,[40] are among those who have particular love for God. Now, those who love God, and are good, will avoid *iniquity* and idle words, he says: *they will not say idle* things, nor will their *talk* be false, the meaning of *deceit.* By contrast, this is spiritual adornment, highly befitting the ornaments of virtue like a kind of crown: where there are

38. Jn 19.15, 12; Mt 27.25; 11.28–29.
39. 2 Cor 8.9.
40. Mt 5.14.

gentleness and lowliness, as well as (233) a longing for righteousness, and *talk* that is unacquainted with idle tales, not at all sinful in its speech, but instead an upright instrument of truthfulness, there it is that virtue appears that is altogether resplendent and perfect. Now, such deportment would befit those in Christ, because the beauty of piety is not found in the Law; rather, it shines forth in the force of the evangelical teaching.

Because they will graze and lie down, and there will be no one to cause them fear. Formerly, the scribes and Pharisees ministered to the needs of the masses of the Jews in a lethargic manner, being assigned by the Law to leadership of the people, doubtless through being promoted by the priestly elders. While they were shepherds, therefore, they were nonetheless hirelings, as it were, appointed over flocks not their own, and on seeing the wolf coming they abandoned the sheep, in the Savior's words.[41] The fact that they were quite indifferent to the rational flock and guilty of abandoning them to wild animals, or rather became wolves themselves, you could easily discern in statements of the prophets. One, for instance, said, "Woe to the shepherds who scatter and destroy the sheep of their pasture," and another likewise, "Thus says Lord the Lord, O you shepherds of Israel, surely shepherds do not feed themselves? Do not shepherds feed the sheep? Lo, you consume the milk, clothe yourselves with the wool, and slaughter the fatlings, but do not feed my sheep. You have not strengthened the weak, bound up the injured, brought back the strayed, and searched for the lost, (234) instead treating the strong with hardship. My sheep have been scattered as a result of there being no shepherds, and have become food for all the wild beasts of the field and birds of heaven." And somewhere he says to the shepherds themselves, "Shepherd the sheep of slaughter. Those who acquired them killed them without repenting, and those who sold them said, Blessed be God, we are rich."[42]

The shepherds ruined the flocks of the rational sheep, therefore, not frightening off wild animals, but themselves imitating the wild animals. When Christ shone forth, however, the good

41. Jn 10.12.
42. Jer 23.1; Ezek 34.2–6; Zec 11.4–5.

shepherd who gave his life for the sheep, we grazed on gardens and were shepherded even among lilies, as Scripture says. We also *lay down* in folds, being lodged in churches and holy temples, with no one to frighten or ravage us, no bounding wolf, no creeping lion, no burglar breaking in, no one else advancing on us "to steal, kill, and destroy."[43] Rather, we live in security and stability, enjoying every good, with the Savior of all as our protector—Christ, I mean. The God and Father made this clear to us in the statement of Ezekiel, "The Lord says this, I shall save my sheep, and shall judge between ram and ram. I shall set up over them one shepherd, my servant David, and he will be their shepherd."[44]

Rejoice exceedingly, daughter Zion; proclaim, daughter Jerusalem; be happy and glad with your whole heart, daughter (235) *Jerusalem. The Lord has removed your crimes, he has redeemed you from the hand of your foes; the Lord will reign in your midst, you will witness troubles no longer* (vv.14–15). As far as the factual account goes, he clearly promises them peace after the return from Babylon, when their former faults are forgotten and God promises to accompany and protect them. On the other hand, as far as the deeper meaning goes, he necessarily ordered them to *rejoice exceedingly*, and as well to *be glad with their whole heart* at the removal of their sins—through Christ, obviously. That is to say, the spiritual and holy Zion, that is, the Church or vast company of the believers, has been justified by Christ and by him alone; we have been saved through him and by him, escaping harm from the unseen foe, with him as our mediator appearing in a form like ours as God and King of all, the Word of God the Father. Because of him, we shall *witness troubles no longer*, that is, we shall be liberated from everyone able to do harm; after all, he is the instrument of benevolence, he is peace, the wall, the provider of immortality, the dispenser of crowns, who repels war waged by the spiritual Assyrians and annuls the schemes of the demons. He it is who allows us to "walk on snakes and scorpions and on every power of the foe"; through him we trample on asp and basilisk, and tread underfoot lion and dragon;[45] through him we

43. Jn 10.11; Song 6.2–3; Mt 6.20; Jn 10.10.
44. Ezek 34.22–23.
45. Lk 10.19; Ps 91.11.

enjoy sound hope of incorruption and life, sonship and glory; through him we shall *witness troubles no longer.* (236)

At that time the Lord will say in Jerusalem, Have confidence, Zion, let not your hands grow slack. The Lord your God is in your midst, a warrior, and he will save you; he will bring joy to you, and renew you in his love, and he will rejoice in you with satisfaction as on a festival day. I shall assemble those of you who are oppressed (vv.16–18). The prophecy of the need to *have confidence* is clear, and the one who makes the promise is reliable. We also heard Christ himself saying this, and, as it were, renewing the ancient oracle, or rather bringing what was promised into sight. He said, remember, "In the world you will have tribulation, but have confidence: I have overcome the world"; when he came in our midst, then our hands were no longer slack, our knees not frail. Rather, we directed ourselves to the effort and labor of good deeds, which are described and in fact are "renowned fruit."[46] Then it was that we became confident, because Christ in us is strong, God as he is, and rescues and saves those believing in him; he dwells in our hearts through the Spirit, and brought us this acceptable *joy*—of a spiritual kind, obviously. After all, what is a share in the Holy Spirit other than satisfaction, happiness, and every kind of *joy*? So when he brought us joy through the Spirit, then it was that he also *renewed us in his love,* namely, at the time of his coming in the flesh, when as "one who died for all" he was correct in saying, "Greater love than this no one has, for someone to lay down his life for his friends."[47]

Now, when he lay down his life and joined the dead for us, being life by nature he came to life again, reforming human nature in newness of life and reforging it to its original state. (237) Scripture says, remember, "If anyone is in Christ, he is a new creation"; the God and Father was pleased to "restore all things" in him, as Scripture says.[48] Now, "restoring" means in a way taking up again and, as it were, reshaping to the original state. When he *renewed* us, Christ then also *brought joy* to us as though *with satisfaction as on a festival day*; how would the divinity not be likely to take satisfaction in our situation when we

46. Jn 16.33; Heb 12.12; Wis 3.15.
47. 2 Cor 5.15; Jn 15.13.
48. 2 Cor 5.17; Eph 1.10.

were rid of sin, had prevailed over death and corruption, and enjoyed a share in the Spirit and in sanctification? At that time he also *assembled those who were oppressed*; as Paul in his wisdom writes, "Christ came into the world to save sinners," and he himself says somewhere, "I came to call, not the righteous, but sinners to repentance." So Christ *assembled* those whom Satan had *oppressed* through sin and had rendered *slack*, not knowing how to tread the straight and narrow or follow the paths of righteousness. But even if Satan had *oppressed* them, Christ bound them up, curing those afflicted and "removing our infirmities," as Scripture says.[49]

Woe, does anyone bear reproach for it? If we choose to adopt the right attitude, we declare that the cross of the Savior, which was raised for the sake of the life of the world and for incorruption, is the boast of the Church; Paul in his wisdom also makes this confession in writing, "May I never boast of anything except the cross of Christ, by which the world has been crucified to me, and I to the world." But it was he who likewise said that the cross was "a stumbling block to Jews and foolishness to Gentiles";[50] the wretches broadly (238) ridicule it, completely unaware of the power of the mystery, and yet they will not escape retribution. How so? They will not mock Christ or the churches; instead, they will become food for the fire that is ignited, and will fall to the flames that are insatiable and long-lasting. Some of those among the Greeks reached such a degree of frenzy and knavery in their thinking, in fact, as to direct sacrilegious words against the divine Gospel preaching, and to deliver a written curse on it, the result being that their sins not only bring them to judgment, but even follow them after death,[51] doubtless on account of their leaving behind a sin that is, as it were, alive. He therefore rightly deplores those who deliver a *reproach* against the holy churches; to them the *Woe* is very applicable.

Lo, I am taking action in your midst on your behalf on that day, says the Lord: I shall save the distressed, welcome the outcast, and make them something to boast of, famous throughout the land, and they will not be ashamed at that time when I do the right thing by you, and at the

49. 1 Tm 1.15; Mt 9.13; 8.17.
50. Gal 6.14; 1 Cor 1.23.
51. 1 Tm 5.24.

time I welcome you (vv. 19–20). The verse adopts the point of view of Zion again, and promises what was achieved against the odds by Christ in regard both to the masses from the nations and to Israel in its rejection, saying, *I shall take action in your midst.* That is to say, when some were reduced to intoxication as a result of oppression, while others were ignorant of the God who became man for the salvation of all, the Lord of all generously showered his mercy on both, (239) and worked wonders among us *on our behalf.* In fact, *the distressed were saved,* that is, the vast number of those in error who suffered tribulation, and then were brought to such a degree of hardship by Satan's distressing behavior as to lose all life-giving fluid, the mind in error being a corpse. The *outcast* synagogue of the Jews will also be welcomed back; it had raged against Christ, after all. Consequently, it was dismissed, had forfeited hope, and was despoiled of relationship with Christ; but even it has had mercy shown it, being called to repentance and cleansing through faith in the end-time. They will therefore be *a boast, made famous* and rid of shame.

Now, these are the ones, the two peoples, who are no longer separated, with mutually exclusive attitudes and divided in their views about God, as of yore. Instead, by the unity of the Spirit they are closely related in fellow-feeling and shared belief; Scripture says, "The multitude of believers had one heart and one soul." Christ also "created one new humanity of the two, making peace, and reconciling both in one spirit," as the text says.[52] If they emulate each other, therefore, the enemy will then be completely *ashamed,* astounded at the magnitude of the *fame* accorded them, the permanence of the satisfaction, and the reliability of the hope. Now, you would see the truth of the promise from the actual outcome: the Church of Christ has become glorified, and is admired by all for its being bedecked with splendid achievements. But he specifies also the time when such things will happen: *at the time I welcome you;* that is, what comes after faith should rightly be understood as not before faith, but after it. (240) So we have been called in the times of the Incarnation of the Only-begotten; then it is that the fulfillment of the promise has taken effect in reality.

52. Acts 4.32; Eph 2.15–16.

Because I shall make you famous and something to boast of among all the peoples of the land when I cancel your captivity in your sight, says the Lord. In this he clearly suggests to us the way in which he "restores" the purpose of the liberality that is proper to God, which the believers will completely enjoy; he says they will be celebrated, bedecked with splendid ornaments, and in a better condition than any nation. He likewise proceeds to mention at what time such things will happen, referring at all points to the Incarnation of the Only-begotten, when, as I just said, the proof of every good and everything that is marvelous came into effect for us. Then it was, in fact, then it was that to great astonishment he rescued those in the devil's power and yoked to the passions of the flesh; then it was that he rid them of the error of polytheism and allowed them to participate in truth; then it was that he rescued them from the bonds of death, giving himself as a ransom for them and acquiring for the God and Father the earth under heaven. It is through him, in fact, that we have been called, and we have been enriched with access and relationship in the Spirit through him—I mean Christ. Through him and with him be the glory to the God and Father together with the Holy Spirit, now and forever, for ages of ages. Amen. (241)

COMMENTARY ON THE *PROPHET HAGGAI*

PREFACE TO THE COMMENTARY ON HAGGAI

THE PURPOSE of the prophecy of Haggai we would take as different from some others', nor would you regard his words as similar to those from the others. The divinely inspired Hosea and those after him up to Zephaniah, remember, foretold what would befall the Jews in due course, and with the time of the captivity still in the future they endeavored to frighten Israel, mentioning here and there the columns of the enemy, the overthrow of cities, the burnings, the plundering, and helpfully predicting the devastation of the whole country to those inclined to be contemptuous. Their conviction was, in fact, that even if they did not elect to perform what was pleasing to God voluntarily, as it were, and to show zeal for better ways, such people would still be scared by the enormity of the calamity.[1]

Haggai, at any rate, when the time of the captivity had passed (242) and Israel returned to the holy city from the land of the Persians and Medes, delivered his message on themes like the following.[2] Cyrus had in fact released them from captivity, and ordered them to go home together with the sacred vessels, to rebuild the divine Temple in Jerusalem, and in addition to this, if they wished, to fortify the city. When this was done, and the foundations of the Temple were laid, some of the people in Samaria—Beltethmus and those in his company—out of envy reported the people of Israel, making a pretense of loyalty to the leaders of the Babylonians, and claiming that Jerusalem had

1. Cyril shows his resemblance to the Antiochenes in his interest in determining the *skopos* of the different authors.

2. Though we have seen Cyril insecure in his grasp of the events, peoples, and personages referred to in the texts of the previous prophets, as also the time of their ministry, he is provided with unmistakable data in the opening of Haggai and also in the deuterocanonical work 1 Esdras.

become warlike and hostile, and was intolerant of the very kings of the Persians. They then persuaded them to order the Jews to cease operations, and not to continue building the Temple or be involved in work on the city. After the lapse of a short time, however, when Darius had come to the throne and was in his second year of kingship, some of the Jews in Babylonia made their approach and begged him to allow them to rebuild the divine Temple. Darius gave an order and wrote to those who administered the whole of Phoenicia with instructions not to obstruct the Jews if they wanted to rebuild the Temple; instead, they were to be generous in supplying resources and to allow them to have the cedars in Lebanon brought down by them unopposed so that nothing useful for them would be lacking for the easy accomplishment (243) of the task for the honor and glory of the God who has control of all things.

Now, since the facts have been told clearly and in detail in the first book of Esdras,[3] I consider it superfluous to trace the course of it minutely at present. Though it was possible, however, for the people of Israel now to go to work, build the divine Temple, offer sacrifices and prayers, and live life in ways corresponding to the Law, the people of Israel became slothful, doing their own thing, completely inclined to whatever suited and appealed to them, and paying extremely little attention to the glory of God. So they once again suffered hardship, with God punishing them, not with war but with famine, infertility, and loss of livestock; he wanted to bring them around, not by subjecting them to penalties commensurate with their faults, but both out of pity for their weariness and likewise from a wish to reform them out of love. This, in a nutshell, is the basis of the prophecy of Haggai; the message is a mixture, the spiritual and interior meaning that is suited to spiritual people being combined with what was done and said factually.[4]

3. 1 Esdras 2; 4.

4. The procedure will be as before, a movement from what is *historikos* to what is *mystikos* for the benefit of a reader who is *pneumatikos*.

COMMENTARY ON HAGGAI, CHAPTER ONE

In the second year of King Darius, in the sixth month, on the first of the month, the word of the Lord came by means of the prophet Haggai in these terms (v.1).

I SAID ABOVE that the lack of enthusiasm of the people of Israel for building the Temple was excusable for the reason that the authority for it had been removed owing to the envy in its regard by the people in Samaria and their extreme criticism of Jerusalem to (244) those in power in Persia. In the second year of his reign, however, Darius gave them full authority and free rein for the work, ordered them to do as they wished and to continue with their holy endeavors, and assigned them resources for doing so. Far from lack of enthusiasm being excusable any longer, therefore, it seemed unreasonable and could claim no excuse. Accordingly, *the word came by means of Haggai,* the phrase *by means of* meaning with his conveying it or serving the message from God and performing the ministry of prophecy. Now, he helpfully indicates also the actual time when Darius gave these orders, disallowing the unreasonable pretexts of the Israelites' inclination to laziness.

Say to Zerubbabel son of Shealtiel of the tribe of Judah, and to Joshua son of Jehozadak, the high priest, as follows. The Lord almighty says this: This people says, The time has not come to rebuild the house of the Lord (vv.1–2). Shealtiel was the son of Jeconiah, who was of the tribe of Judah and the line of David. Accordingly, when the latter was administering the kingdom of Judah in Jerusalem, the city was plundered and all of Israel was deported in captivity; at that time Nebuchadnezzar also burned down even the divine Temple; Jeconiah himself was captured and went off into captivity along with the others. Zerubbabel was *son of Shealtiel;* (245) hence on Israel's return to Jerusalem he became king over Judah as being a descendant of the tribe appointed to reign.[1] Joshua, on the other hand, was of the tribe and lineage of Levi and a descendant of Aaron, and so with the loss of the others he gained the chosen position and *was high priest.* The Law, remember, nominated the one appointed to head the priestly ranks, forbidding them to hand over fugitives in the cities of refuge; they were all to remain where they were "until the death of the high priest,"[2] that is, the chief priest.

The word came to both, therefore, namely, the king and the one presiding over the priestly ranks; it was appropriate for him to communicate the oracle to them before all the others. In my view, it was not to men ignorant of the people's pretexts that the God of all bade him report it; instead, it was by way of mockery of their lapse into indifference at that time, when they probably had responsibility for the enterprise but were gravely neglectful of it. After all, they should have known better that since the things of God were entrusted to them by way of precedence, it was altogether by his mercy and grace that they were commissioned to serve well and passed their life in prosperity and wealth, enjoying an abundance of the necessities of life. It is as if he adjures them, therefore, by the statement of the prophet that Israel in an unholy manner was neglecting what was particularly useful to it and had relevance to the glory of God; by dressing up their crimes with specious excuses, as they believed in their own minds, they claimed that *it was not the time to rebuild the house of the Lord.* On the contrary, the time really had arrived to decide to do it, (246) and it is always in the power of good and honest people to discharge duties for the glory of God. Since, on the other hand, an apparent obstacle and impediment seemed to have disappeared, delay was then difficult to excuse, and the crime was then laziness and utter unwillingness to work, no matter what pretext was offered. This, in my view, is what is meant by the statement of David, "Do not turn my heart to evil words to make excuses for sin."[3]

1. Like Theodore, but unlike Jerome (and Theodoret, who challenges Theodore's position), Cyril, against the evidence of the text, speaks of Zerubbabel returning as king, not simply as "governor," an unfamiliar Akkadian term for which the LXX reads "of the tribe" (of Judah).

2. Nm 35.28.

3. Ps 141.4.

The word of the Lord came by means of Haggai the prophet in these terms: Is it a time for you to live in your paneled houses while this house is in ruins? (vv.3–4) A second oracle from God to Haggai condemns Israel with a clear accusation, presenting them as opposing their own tardiness and satisfaction to the glory of God. Has not the time yet arrived, he asks, to honor the God of all with the raising of the Temple instead of your treating *time* and importance in such a way as to indulge yourself with lavishly built dwellings and *live in paneled houses*? Does it not seem to you burdensome and intolerable to see the Temple so dishonorably violated, left in ruins in such an ugly aspect, and, as it were, crying out in protest at the unholy behavior of the Babylonians and the former burning? Would it not be better to see it in good condition with its former appearance? (247) It would then be possible to sacrifice to God and offer prayers for whatever you choose. Now, he mentions *paneled houses*, which had doorposts, or door jambs, hollowed out with iron, the result of artisans' etchings, in my view, and filigree created by the skill of the craftsmen—an indication of people given to luxury and boasting of their wealth. The lavish display in furnishing houses that surpassed what was necessary would be a very clear proof of affluence.

It would therefore be a terrible thing, involving inexcusable sin, for us to put the things of God in second place behind human things.

The Lord almighty now says this: Bring your hearts into keeping with your ways. You sowed much but harvested little, you ate but not to satisfy, you drank but not to inebriation, you had clothes to put on but did not warm yourself; the one collecting a wage collected it in a bag full of holes (vv.5–6). Neglecting prior claims, as I said, and paying no attention to what redounded to the glory of God, the people of Israel directed themselves to their own interests, erecting houses that were lavishly furnished, then stupidly claiming, *The time has not come to rebuild the house of the Lord.* Although they should have proceeded to the building of the divine Temple, in fact, and were unwilling to do so, consequently they pleaded lack of resources and claimed that they had to amass (248) them, and, as it were, wipe out poverty by farming for a while or trading or assembling herds of livestock or pursuing other such business.

It would have been better to have confidence in God, however, who finds means where there are none, and is able to enrich and shower blessings on farmers and the one searching for paths of upright endeavors.

Since you were bereft of plans for religion, however, had forfeited benevolence from on high, and did nothing in an upright fashion, consequently he has no choice but to say, *Bring your hearts into keeping with your ways.* It would be like saying, Consider in detail the paths you followed in life, or what avaricious pursuits you followed in doing what you wished. *You sowed much but harvested little;* it would instead have been better with God's blessing to sow little and reap much, but since what was necessary was lacking, the labors are many and the fruits very little. *You ate but not to satisfy.* It is a terrible thing, a proof of extreme need and hardship, if much is sown and yet the yield is such that the laborers are met with the punishment of famine, and food falls short of satisfaction. *You drank but not to inebriation*: instead of the vineyard being fruitful, there was the same deficit of flourishing plants as of the crops. *You had clothes to put on but did not warm yourself,* perhaps because pestilence also affected the herds of sheep to such an extent that even owners of large herds suffered a need of clothing.

The one collecting a wage collected it in a bag full of holes. In this he suggests those involved in trading, who in a way amass a wage from trading, (249) consistently practicing extortion in everything sold, fattening their wallets by increasing the price. Not even they, however, could satisfy their avarice; they perhaps fell foul of unexpected losses and shipwreck, and seemed to be no different from people putting money into *a bag full of holes.* It would have been a wise and better thing to do, therefore, to seek blessing from God, who provides us with everything; this would also have easily accrued to those who choose to adopt his attitudes and prefer to their own affairs what redounds to his glory. The Savior himself also spoke to us in those terms, "Do not worry about your life, what you will eat, or about your body, what you will wear. Seek first the kingdom of God and his righteousness, and all these things will be given to you as well."[4]

4. Mt 6.25, 33.

That suffices for the factual account, in my view; so come now, let us apply our minds to the spiritual interpretation, considering the fact that the fate of the Jews would be a very clear type of the overall and universal divine plan brought into effect through Christ. Some were held in the yoke of unwelcome slavery in Babylon, remember, paying the penalty for their own sins; though they were the victims of this guilt and laboring under the control of the enemy, they were redeemed in due course by God's mercy, went back home, and occupied the Holy Land under the leadership and presidency of Zerubbabel and Joshua. Though he was still devoted to the worship of the idols, Darius gave orders that the divine Temple had to be rebuilt, (250) and supplied timber from Lebanon and sources of supply, whereas they continued to be lazy and slow in doing what God wanted. They were also guilty of claiming excuses, saying, *The time has not come to rebuild the house of the Lord.* Now, the whole earth also lay under the control of the deceptive and tyrannical Satan, and was his captive, snared into this condition by sin and through not knowing the one who by nature and in truth is God and Lord of all. But God in Christ rescued it by breaking the bonds of slavery; we followed his guidance, abandoned our stay among the enemy, left behind the error of polytheism as though some foreign land, and hastened back to Zion—the spiritual one, that is, or the Church.

Consider, in fact, how Christ is prefigured for us in Joshua and Zerubbabel. Zerubbabel was, remember, as I said, from the tribe of Judah,[5] and from it our Lord Jesus Christ also sprang. Consequently, he had also reigned over Israel, saying as much somewhere in the statement of David, "I have been appointed king by him on Zion, his holy mount, to tell of the decree of the Lord."[6] Joshua in turn was from the tribe and lineage of Levi, and nominated high priest; Christ too became our chief priest, sacrificing himself for us as a spotless victim, offering himself as a true lamb for an odor of sweetness to the God and Father. The actual explanation or translation of the names confirms this sense for those interested in a detailed examination of it; (251)

5. Cf. note 1 above.
6. Ps 2.6–7.

Zerubbabel means "flow that is changed," and Shealtiel "God's turning away." Christ also said somewhere, "Lo, I turn away to them like a river of peace, and flood the glory of nations like a torrent"; he is admittedly a torrent of delight,[7] and like a flow of peace. But he turned away to us, and, as it were, he underwent change, abandoning Israel; he went, as I said, to those called from the nations, generously conferring an abundant outpouring of spiritual goods from on high. Joshua in turn means "Yah salvation," and Jehozadak "Yah righteousness," Yah being the God of all. Now, Christ was both salvation and righteousness for us from the God and Father; we have been saved by him in fleeing the wiles of death, and are made righteous through faith, shaking off sin that exercised tyrannical control over us.

Therefore (I return to the original theme), in Zerubbabel we shall consider him[8] as king, and in Joshua as chief priest. Let the serious student likewise take note, however, of the Jews' fall into indifference and their option to work at the fabric of the divine Temple,[9] that is, the Church of Christ; let him in addition consider the enthusiasm of the nations and their ardent involvement in the work. Darius, in fact, as I said, ordered the erection of the Temple and its completion for the glory of the God who controls all things, whereas the former were reluctant and lazy, preferring their own interests to what was pleasing to God, and being much (252) more inclined to earthly things, building *paneled houses*, as he says. Accordingly, the divinely inspired David says of the nations, "You hearkened to the desire of the poor, O Lord; your ear readily attended to their heart";[10] while those from the nations were more ready to believe, the people of Israel were very reluctant. Now, you would see what I mean also in the evangelical writings, or parables; while those with invitations to the banquet ran off to bring guests to the wedding, some declined to come, and concocted "sinful ex-

7. Is 66.12; Ps 36.8. As a second "spiritual interpretation" Cyril makes a foray into etymology. For Zerubbabel Jerome offers a range of derivations, Cyril preferring "flow that is nearby" (which he alters) to the more likely "branch of Babylon."

8. That is, Christ.

9. The PG ed. reads, "option not to work."

10. Ps 10.17.

cuses," one claiming, "I have bought a field," and another, "I have got married," and still others went off to their business. So people found in the street and by the wall were called and came running to the wedding, and in truth the first became last, and the last first. Christ also said in the words of David about both the people of Israel and the nations, "A people I did not know served me; on hearing the report it hearkened to me; foreign sons were false to me; foreign sons grew old and went limping from their paths."[11]

Thus says the Lord almighty, Bring your hearts into keeping with your ways. Climb the mountain, cut wood, and build the house, and I shall take pleasure in it and be glorified, said the Lord. You looked for much, and little happened; it was brought into your home, and I blew it away (vv.7–9). He delivers frequent exhortation, (253) aware that it is for the good of the listeners. The divinely inspired Paul also writes to some people in this vein, "To write the same things is not troublesome to me, and for you it is a safeguard."[12] So give a thought, he is saying, to *your own ways* which you are treading now. What they are he immediately explains, *You looked for much, and little happened; it was brought into your home, and I blew it away.* In other words, the expectation of those working the soil was disappointed; they exerted much effort, but gathered only a little. They have been deprived even of this, however; it was *blown away,* that is, became other people's, not theirs, instead being consumed by domineering people. Their effort and labor was therefore in vain, because they preferred not to carry out the Lord's will, and gave attention by preference to base and earthly things rather than hard work for better things. Surely, then, he did not leave Israel without admonition, or fail to point out to the deceived the way to reform? We shall in fact see this happening immediately; he said, *Climb the mountain, cut wood, and build the house, and I shall be glorified in it* again *and take pleasure;* that is, I shall welcome and commend the effort and enthusiasm of those laboring to that end.

It is therefore surely a fine thing pleasing to God to exert

11. Ps 141.4; Lk 14.16–24; Mt 22.5; 20.16; Ps 18.43–45 (not all of which is cited in the PG ed.).

12. Phil 3.1.

oneself to perform everything which would seem useful and necessary to the fabric of the Church and its upbuilding. Now, this we shall do with great prudence (254) by gathering material that is necessary, and *chopping* as *wood* from a forest the spiritual meanings in the inspired Scripture. Through them you would render secure and reliable glory to God, or recognition of him, and you would ensure that the manner of the Incarnation in the flesh is eminently conveyed. In addition, you would convey as well a precise knowledge of spiritual lore, and the goodness found in manners and behavior. These are surely the ways in which we claim that *the house of God is rebuilt* and the fabric of the Church created.

I shall also go on to say that each of us could be considered a temple and house of God; Christ dwells in us through the Spirit, and we are temples of the living God, according to the Scriptures.[13] So let each of us also build up his own heart through right faith, and have Christ the Savior of all himself as the truly precious foundation. Let him also add to this a different material, namely, obedience, compliance in every respect, fortitude, endurance, self-control; thus "knitted together by every ligament with which we are equipped, we shall grow up into a holy temple and a dwelling place for God in the Spirit."[14] Those, on the other hand, whose faith is limited, or who, though believing, are somehow still reluctant to separate themselves from passions, sin, and worldly pleasures, for that very reason cry out, as it were, *The time has not come to rebuild the house of the Lord.* Consequently, they also fall victim to the lack of heavenly goods and to spiritual sterility as the mind within them wastes away like a kind of soil that produces neither grain (strength, that is) nor wine, (255) which is a symbol of joy. Scripture says, remember, "Bread strengthens a man's heart, and wine gladdens a man's heart."[15]

Hence the Lord almighty says this, Because my house is in ruins while you are occupied with your own houses, accordingly heaven refrains from giving dew, and the land withholds its seed from you. I will inflict a sword on the land, the mountains, the grain, the wine, the oil,

13. 2 Cor 6.16.
14. Eph 4.16; 2.21–22.
15. Ps 104.15.

and all that the land produces, on human beings, on cattle, and on all the effort of their hands (vv.9–11). He does not allow people who are wrongfully slothful about divine things to pursue their own goals successfully and to give more earthly things priority over what redounds to his glory. Rather, he urges them to consider that unless what is incomparably superior is given proper ranking, neither would what is of less importance or of interest to them succeed. Consequently, he says, *Because my house is in ruins while you are occupied with your own houses, accordingly* such and such a fate will befall you, by which crops in the field will fail, *heaven* no longer sending *dew, the land* losing its force, and a *sword* or wrath being inflicted,[16] drying up *oil* along with crops and vines, and consuming in addition *human beings and cattle.*

For those reluctant to discharge what redounds to the glory of God, and the means of his house being built up—that is, (256) the Church—neither would spiritual *dew* fall, namely, comfort from heaven that enriches souls and hearts. Neither would there be fruitfulness from the *land,* namely, bodily achievements, nor *grain, wine,* or the use of *oil;* everything would be completely impotent, far from bringing joy, with no means of enriching with the spiritual oil of gladness—in a nutshell, they would remain tasteless and without a share in the blessing that comes from Christ. In addition, they would fall to the *sword,* and sustain an effort that goes entirely unrewarded, even if some form of goodness is explored by them; after all, no one wins a crown "without competing according to the rules,"[17] as Scripture says. Let us therefore regard enthusiasm for a better life desirable and highly esteemed, and let our concerns enjoy less importance and be placed after what redounds to the glory of God—and not only dwellings and possessions and vainglory, but also family and brethren and parents. Christ also, in fact, speaks in these terms, "Whoever loves father or mother more than me is not worthy of me, and whoever loves son or daughter more than me is not worthy of me, and whoever does not take up his cross and follow me is not worthy of me."[18]

16. Jerome had mentioned that the LXX says "sword" where the Heb. has "drought."

17. 1 Tm 2.5.

18. Mt 10.37–38.

Zerubbabel son of Shealtiel, of the tribe of Judah, and Joshua son of Jehozadak, the high priest, and all the remnant of the people listened to the voice of the Lord their God and the words of Haggai the prophet, because (257) *the Lord their God had sent him to them, and the people were afraid of the presence of the Lord* (v.12). You could easily discern from this that, far from making threats in vain, fear is not without benefit to people addicted to indifference. Note, in fact, note that when they heard the divine words, they immediately fell to work, now responding to those appointed to lead them—I mean Zerubbabel and Joshua—and showed great respect for the words of the prophet and were in awe at his mission, despite previously according his words very little regard. The saying is therefore true and established by the facts themselves, "The one whom the Lord loves he corrects, he chastises every son he accepts."[19] In other words, dread of being punished sometimes prompts our mind to better thoughts, and the onset of problems spurs us to fear of God. We can trust the saying in the book of Proverbs, "The one who fears the Lord prospers," and again, "Fear of the Lord gives life to a man"; and in the book of Wisdom likewise, "Fear of the Lord is our glory and boast," and, "Fear of the Lord will delight the heart, and will furthermore give joy and gladness and long life."[20] Consider in what a kindly manner befitting him God punishes us: instead of straightway inflicting the effects of his wrath on human bodies, he prefers to scare us with some slight external fears, and by the loss of foodstuffs he brings us around to better ways and the choice of then discharging his work. (258)

Haggai the messenger[21] *of the Lord said to the people, I am with you, says the Lord* (v.13). Observe lovingkindness immediately accompanying the change for the better; the God of all changes, as it were, in a fashion with those who opt to repent, and promises to be with them—what could compare with that? When God is with us, after all, every harm facing us disappears, allowing good things to approach; different forms of prosperity will develop and manifest themselves, and everything pleasing will befall us. Now, even if the sacred text says, *Haggai the messenger of the Lord,*

19. Prv 3.12.

20. Prv 13.13; 19.23 LXX; Sir 1.11–12.

21. Greek: *angelos.*

no one should think that he is an "angel" by nature, since he is instead a man like us, born of a woman; such an idea would be quite silly. Rather, we shall take the view, provided we are of sound mind with an eye to the truth, that the terminology and reference to "angel" derives from the verb "to give a message."[22] If we are to be guilty of no error in adopting another absurdity, we may admit that those who reported to Job what happened in the field at the hands of the horsemen, and as well the fact that his children died when the house was shaken down, were by nature angels. The Word of God is also called "Angel of Great Counsel";[23] he reported to us the will of the God and Father. So "angel" comes from the verb "to give a message," and even if the term should be applied to human beings, it does not mean they are by nature what they really are not. (259)

The Lord stirred up the spirit of Zerubbabel son of Shealtiel, of the tribe of Judah, the spirit of Joshua son of Jehozadak, the high priest, and the spirit of the remnant of all the people. They went in and began doing the work on the house of the Lord almighty their God on the twenty-fourth day of the sixth month (vv.14–15). Though *the people of Israel were afraid of the presence of the Lord,* consider once again, I ask you, that they would not have made a move to do what was pleasing to God unless he had first been with them and *stirred up their spirit.* So we realize from this that even if you were to opt for doing good, and even if you were enthusiastic in such an endeavor, you would still not in any way achieve it unless God were with you to prompt you to your resolution, stir you to endurance, and dispel reluctance in the good work. Consequently, the divinely inspired Paul says in reference to those believing the divine message, "I worked harder than any of them," and in his wisdom he proceeded, "It was not I, but the grace of God that was with me." The Savior himself also said to the holy apostles, "Apart from me you can do nothing"; it is he who is our desire and enthusiasm for every good work, he who is our

22. Cyril profits from Jerome's comment that, though the status of an angelic being was accorded by some people to the Baptist, Malachi, Haggai, and others, in the lemma the term *angelos* means simply "messenger." He helpfully proceeds to relate the term to the verb *angellō*. He therefore avoids the ruse, adopted by Theodore, of omitting the term from the lemma.

23. Jb 1; Is 9.6.

strength, and when he is with us, we shall be held in esteem, building ourselves "into a holy temple, into a dwelling place for God in the Spirit."[24] But when he leaves and forsakes us, who could doubt that we would be overcome by laziness and timidity, showing revulsion for hard work as if a waste of time? (260)

Nonetheless, notice those who were formerly subject to wrath on account of their grave unbelief now entering *the house of the Lord* and setting to work, accompanied by *Zerubbabel and Joshua the high priest.* This would likewise be a type of the calling of Israel due to occur in the end-time. While formerly they refused to believe, and consequently remained fruitless as well, lacking dew, grain, wine, and also oil, falling victim to the sword as well, at the time when they *are afraid of the presence of the Lord* and show regard for the words of the holy prophets, they will have the God of all accompanying them, their *spirit will be stirred up,* and they too will work on the temple of the Lord, that is, the Church. Now, this too happens in Christ, who is, as it were, prefigured in Zerubbabel and Joshua, being both king as God and likewise chief priest as man, and mediator between God and men, since the priest is mediator.[25]

Now, it is of necessity that the phrase *on the twenty-fourth day of the sixth month* is added, the purpose being to give a very clear indication of the wavering mindset of the people of Israel. Though the word came to them by means of Haggai in the second year of the reign of Darius on the first day of the sixth month, they set to work on the Temple *on the twenty-fourth day of the sixth month;* so in the meantime there was a period of twenty-three days of delay, or deliberation.

24. 1 Cor 15.10; Jn 15.5; Eph 2.21–22.
25. 1 Tm 2.5.

COMMENTARY ON HAGGAI, CHAPTER TWO

In the second year of King Darius, in the seventh month, on the twenty-first day of the month, the Lord spoke by means of Haggai (261) *the prophet, saying, Tell Zerubbabel son of Shealtiel, of the tribe of Judah, and Joshua son of Jehozadak, the high priest, and all the remnant of the people in these words: Is there any of you who saw this house in its former glory? How does it look to you now: is it not as nothing in your sight?* (vv. 1–3)

WHEREAS THEY had entered the house of God and set to work on the twenty-fourth day of the sixth month, directly afterwards on the twenty-first day of the next month, the seventh, the word of the Lord came to the blessed prophet Haggai. So what we are to think of it in this case, too, and what the occasion was, there is need to explain. On beginning to feel weariness, and undertaking responsibility for the divine Temple, they kept going till the twenty-seventh day, when they were found to have lost heart, grumbling among themselves or to one another that their work was in vain; even if the rebuilding of the Temple was completed, it would in no way resemble the former one. Whereas that one was in fact very splendid and furnished lavishly, and was bedecked with gold and silver offerings, this one is ugly, bereft of every adornment, and lacking generous expenditure. Though those reigning at various times in Jerusalem, especially Solomon, had liberally decorated that former one so that it still glittered with riches, they had been ordered to build the latter one when they had just returned, were still dripping with the sweat of captivity, and had absolutely nothing at home.

While they kept working, beset and depressed with such arguments, (262) they were guilty once again of lack of enthusiasm and reluctance. Consequently, God strengthens them in their weakness, and proposes a very useful question to them, whether there was anyone among them who had seen the former Temple in its original glory. Now, they were very few and elderly; the Temple had been plundered by Nebuchadnezzar, and Israel had been taken captive and just restored after the lapse of seventy years. It was therefore very difficult to find an old person who was there before the devastation, had lived in captivity, and returned to Jerusalem. Hence he asks, *Is there any of you who saw this house in its former glory,* and then will see the one that is to come and is so new as to be almost non-existent? Now, there is a rebuke in the question, suggesting that they should not think that, even if they were in difficulties and short of resources, God was at a loss, but rather that he would again be capable of producing his own Temple as required, namely, celebrated and famous.

Be strong now, Zerubbabel, says the Lord, and be strong, Joshua son of Jehozadak, the high priest, and let all the people of the land be strong. Get to work, because I am with you, says the Lord almighty. My agreement, which I made with you when you came out of the land of Egypt, and my spirit are in your midst. Have confidence (vv.4–5). He does not allow them to fall into dejection, nor to be reduced (263) to laziness by apprehension; instead, he arouses them to activity, and imparts to them vigor and enthusiasm. At the same time he tests their faith, and makes them rely on him, bidding them *have confidence* and making them a promise which even surpasses that and is truly desirable, that he would be with them, proceeding to tell them in what way: *my spirit is in your midst, have confidence.*[1]

Now, no one with good intentions and in a right mind would doubt that to those laboring for the upbuilding of the divine temple—that is, the Church—he grants strength and gives *confidence* that he is both with them through the Holy Spirit and will achieve everything for them to make them capable of living their lives in a splendid and upright way. Our Lord Jesus Christ also spoke in these terms to the holy apostles, who were des-

1. At this point Theodore delivered a lengthy and spirited rejection of the possibility of the Holy Spirit being known to people in the Old Testament. Cyril, under no such pressure to exclude a New Testament dimension to his interpretation, finds the reference instead a spur to inclusion of NT texts referring to the Spirit.

tined to build the Church and summon the believers into the holy temple, consequently saying, "Lo, I am with you all days, even to the end of the age." He likewise personally clarifies the fact that he meant also to be with them through the Spirit, saying at one time, "I shall not leave you orphans, I am coming to you," and at another making clear the manner of his coming by saying in turn, "It is good for you that I should go away, for if I did not go away, the Advocate would not come to you, whereas if I go, I shall send him to you."[2] He is therefore with those who build his house, but likewise leaves and (264) completely abandons those who undermine it. These people would similarly include those who by Beelzebul say "Anathema" to Jesus,[3] overturn everything that is upright, and pour the venom of destruction on the souls of simple people.

Because the Lord almighty says this: Once again I shall shake heaven and earth, sea and dry land. I shall shake all the nations, and the treasures of all the nations will come, and I shall fill this house with glory, says the Lord almighty. Mine is the silver and mine the gold, says the Lord almighty (vv.6–8). He redirects attention to the Church from the nations and to the time of our Savior's coming. At that time he promises to cause the trembling of *heaven and* earth, and also the sea, and in addition *all the nations,* saying, *Once again I shall shake* them. Now, what he is suggesting is, to the best of my thinking, something like this. When he decided to liberate Israel from its service to the idols, therefore, and its being reared on the ways and laws of the Egyptians, and wanted to bring them instead to the knowledge of the truth, he is found, as it were, causing everything to tremble: the waters were turned into blood, the sky sent down hail, the sea was divided and its waves fixed in the manner of walls, and heaven (265) dripped with manna. The psalmist suggests something of the kind in saying, "O God, when you went forth in the sight of your people, when you traveled in the wilderness, the earth was shaken and the heavens were dripping."[4]

Now, we say the earth was then shaken, not that it was affected by a normal earthquake, but that the exodus of the peo-

2. Mt 28.20; Jn 14.18; 16.7.
3. 1 Cor 12.3.
4. Ps 68.7–8.

ple of Israel was so remarkable, going unnoticed by no one on earth. He is saying that there will similarly be such a shaking at the time of the coming of our Savior that no one will be likely to be unaware of what is achieved by it. On the one hand, heaven was aware of the mystery, as Paul testifies in the words, "So that through the Church the wisdom of God in its rich variety might now be made known to the rulers and authorities in the heavenly places in accordance with the eternal purpose that he has carried out in Christ Jesus our Lord." On the other hand, the whole earth also was similarly aware, as well as the sea, that is, the islands; after all, is there anyone at all left without a share in this knowledge—any sea, any nation, any part of heaven? The Gospel has been preached "to all the nations," in the Savior's words.[5] Accordingly he says, *Once again I shall shake heaven and earth, and then the treasures of all the nations will come, and I shall fill this house with glory.* That is to say, a great number of believers from every nation have become illustrious and chosen, assembled in God's *house* like illustrious offerings, thus contributing to his glory, (266) making it famous and celebrated, and themselves glorified by Christ. They have learned, in fact, how to pray in these words: "The brightness of the Lord our God will be upon us," and again, "We are blessed by the Lord, who made heaven and earth."[6]

Now, the fact that God needs not lifeless matter but a spiritual array he suggests in saying, *Mine is the silver and mine the gold, says the Lord almighty.* It would be like saying, Do not consider the Temple inglorious because it happens to lack gold and silver and the splendor of wealth; I need nothing like that. How so? *Mine is the silver and mine the gold, says the Lord almighty:* I look rather for sincere worshipers; it is with the splendor of such people that I shall gild my Temple. In other words, just as when he relieved Israel of the obligation of sacrifices according to the Law, he necessarily said, "I shall not accept calves from your house, or goats from your flocks, for all the beasts of the countryside, cattle on the mountains, and oxen are mine,"[7] so too here he declines to accept adornment of a material kind,

5. Eph 3.10–11; Mk 13.10.
6. Pss 90.17 LXX; 115.15.
7. Ps 50.9–10.

and seeks rather the spiritual kind, saying, *Mine is the silver and mine the gold.* In other words, I am content and satisfied, and have no need of any such thing; instead, let someone come who has an upright faith, is distinguished for ornaments of virtue, resplendent with love for me, pure in heart, poor in spirit, compassionate, and kind. When they assemble in my temple, in fact, (267), that is, the Church, they will make it glorious, the cynosure of all eyes.

Because the final glory of this house will be great and will surpass the former, says the Lord almighty. And in this place I shall give peace, says the Lord almighty, and peace of soul as a possession to every builder for raising up this Temple (v.9). At the time of the coming of our Savior the divine temple emerged as incomparably more glorious, so much better and more eminent than the former as you would think worship in Christ and according to the Gospel differs from that according to the Law, and the reality from what is in shadows. Furthermore, I think that this claim, too, could usefully be made: the former Temple was one, and was only in Jerusalem, and the people of Israel were the only nation performing sacrifices in it. By contrast, when the Only-begotten became like us, God as he is, and "the Lord shone upon us," as Scripture says,[8] the earth under heaven has since been filled with holy houses and innumerable worshipers, who venerate the God of all with spiritual sacrifices and immaterial fragrances. This, in my view, was foretold in the statement of the prophet Malachi made in the person of God, "Because I am a great king, says the Lord, and my name has been glorified among the nations, and in every place incense is offered to my name, and a pure sacrifice."[9] The verse is therefore truthful in saying that the *glory* of the final temple—that is, the Church—*will be* greater. (268)

Now, the fact that, to those bent on building it, Christ will be given as a kind of present from the Father and a gift from heaven, since he is peace for everyone and through him "we have access in one Spirit to the Father," he makes clear by saying, *In this place I shall give peace, and peace of soul as a possession to every builder for raising up this Temple.* Christ himself, in fact, also said some-

8. Ps 118.27.
9. Mal 1.14, 11.

where, "My peace I give you, my peace I leave with you." How this is of benefit to those who love him Paul likewise conveys in writing, "The peace of Christ, which surpasses all understanding, will guard your hearts and your bodies," and Isaiah in his wisdom also prays somewhere, "Lord our God, give us peace, for you have rendered everything to us"[10]—in other words, for those once thought worthy of receiving the peace of Christ, it is an easy matter to save their own souls and direct their minds to the practice of virtue. So he says, *peace* will be given *to every builder,* either someone building up the Church and appointed spiritual guide for the house of God, or benefiting his own soul by presenting himself as a living and spiritual stone "for a holy temple, a dwelling place for God in the Spirit,"[11] such a one succeeding in saving his own soul without the slightest difficulty.

On the twenty-fourth day of the ninth month, in the second year of Darius, the word of the Lord came to the prophet Haggai (269) *in these terms: The Lord almighty says this, Ask the priests for a ruling in these words: If someone takes consecrated meat in the fold of their garment, and the fold of their garment touches bread, or stew, or wine, or oil, or any other food, will it become holy? In reply the priests said, No. Haggai said, If someone personally defiled from any of these things touches someone, will they be defiled? In reply the priests said, They will be defiled. Haggai replied, It is like that with these people, and like that with this nation in my sight, says the Lord, and it is like that with all the works of their hands: whoever approaches there will be defiled* (vv.10–14). This is another oracle through the prophet to Israel, and we claim that it was delivered for this reason. It was in the second year of the reign of Darius, in the seventh month, after God had reproached those redeemed from captivity and accused them of laziness—namely, in their duty of working on the Temple—that they finally exerted themselves and then got involved in laborious work. God then commended them for doing so, promised to be with them and bless them, and bade them have confidence that the Spirit would be present in their midst.

10. Eph 2.18; Jn 14.27; Phil 4.7; Is 26.12.

11. 1 Pt 2.5; Eph 2.21–22. Cyril is right to be tentative in this interpretation of the final clause of the lemma in the LXX, which, as Jerome mentioned, does not occur in the Heb. or in any alternative version (but is a part of the Antioch text).

They were no less lazy and slipshod, however, and after the lapse of scarcely two months they relapsed into indifference, and once again were guilty of bitter complaints. They were, in fact, (270) culpably and wrongfully inclined to commercial dealings and uncontrollably disposed to making money, and they experienced regret for not being able to devote a great deal of time to commercial concerns. They then offered sacrifices and claimed that that would suffice for the need for purification, even though the divine Temple was not yet completed. The prophet is therefore bidden to goad them with suitable reproofs, and inform them that even if they chose to perform prayers and sacrifices, but were guilty of indifference in completing the house of God, it would be of no use to them. Rather, the refusal to perform animal sacrifice at the appropriate time and to approach the divine altar would incur wrath and condemnation. In addition he makes clear that by associating with evil foreigners in the course of their commercial dealings they definitely incurred extreme defilement also from idolatry.

Now, though the question is a very legalistic one and difficult to interpret, I shall as far as possible clarify it by presenting the meaning in words I can muster. The prophet, then, by Law puts the question to the priests; Scripture says, remember, "The lips of a priest will maintain justice, and from his mouth they will look for the Law."[12] What is the question? *If someone takes consecrated meat in the fold of their garment, and the fold of their garment touches bread, or stew, or wine, or oil, or any other food, will it become holy? In reply the priests said, No.* By *consecrated meat* he refers to what was taken from an animal presented as an offering to God. His intention is to teach them the following. Sometimes when the priests were performing the sacrifices according to Law, they touched with their clothing the (271) meat destined for burning. So, he asks, if sacred attire that is perhaps sanctified by *consecrated meat* touches something else not offered to God, surely the latter will not also become holy? The priests denied that this would be in accordance with the Law.

Well, then, let us proceed from the example to what is more

12. Mal 2.7.

in keeping with the reality: surely the person who offers sacrifice though offending God in other ways is not sanctified by it? Far from it: he is condemned for offering sacrifice without being cleansed. For proof that the statement is true, listen to what the lawgiver says in Leviticus: "Meat that touches any unclean thing shall not be eaten; it shall be burned by fire. All who are clean may eat meat; but those who eat of the meat of the sacrifice of well-being, which is the Lord's, while in a state of impurity, shall be cut off from their kin. If any one of you touches any unclean thing, whether human uncleanness or unclean animals or any unclean abomination, and eats meat from the sacrifice of well-being, which is the Lord's, that person shall be cut off from kin."[13] Do you see how foolish it is, or rather a cause of wrath and death, to offer sacrifices with unclean hands? Just as the priests' garments, therefore, even if sanctified by the meat of sacrifice, did not sanctify anything touching them, so he is saying that sacrifice to God would not make holy those offending him in another way and refusing to perform what is pleasing to God. (272)

Now, the fact that, as I said, for the sake of commerce and its gains they were completely involved with profane people and themselves became profane from them, he makes clear through another question. He proceeded to ask, *If someone personally defiled from any of these things touches someone, will they be defiled? In reply the priests said, They will be defiled.* The Law given through Moses, in fact, bade people already purified not to touch a corpse nor approach anyone dead; it said, for example, that priests must not defile themselves except in the case of father or mother or brethren, and the leader presiding over the ranks of priests should not do so even in their case.[14] Now, what was commanded was obscure, the Law being a shadow; the corpse, to be sure, would once again be a type of dead works and worldly uncleanness. In my view, people who have adopted a sacred and quite pure way of life must decide to take leave of dead works and be separated from worldly corruption. But if they should then have happened to touch the corpse of someone else, or

13. Lv 7.19–21.
14. Lv 21.1–2, 10–11.

a person or clothing, by Law this would definitely have been a defilement. The prophet therefore asks whether anyone, on happening to touch a corpse, and while still unwashed touching someone else, would definitely contaminate him. On their replying, He contaminates him, God then proceeds, *It is like that with these people, and like that with this nation in my sight, says the Lord, and it is like that with all the works of their hands, says the Lord: whoever approaches there will be defiled.* In other words, when he touches dead works, he is saying, it is not only that he himself is defiled; (273) he reaches such a degree of depravity as consequently to have the capacity also to defile others very severely.

There is therefore need for us to give attention to good works, and we should be zealous in performing what is particularly dear to God, and sacrifice in such a spiritual manner. Then it is, in fact, that he will accept us, and our prayer will become not a curse but an advantage and a blessing. Let us also shake off dead lusts and, as it were, lifeless pleasures and worldly uncleanness; God, after all, is with people who are cleansed in this way and sanctified.

For their morning profits they will grieve when confronted by their wickedness, and you hated their reproof in the gates. They say that neither the Hebrew text nor the other translators include or show knowledge of this;[15] yet the thought seems to correspond with what went before. Since, as I said, they involved themselves in profiteering and avarice, which emerged as the basis of their indifference, despite their being ordered to rebuild the divine Temple, consequently he now accuses them of it. He mentions *morning profits,* doubtless because morning appearances and early business happened for no other reason than this, namely, a longing for profits. He says that *they will grieve* when their intentions do not attain the desired outcome. Without God's guidance, in fact, and his smoothing for us the course that actions should take, people's efforts in any direction prove absolutely futile and pointless; (274) Scripture says, remember, "Unless the Lord builds the house, in vain do its builders labor."[16]

15. Cyril gets the information from Jerome; to him, however, the key consideration as often is not the integrity of the LXX text but its potential for moral and spiritual development.

16. Ps 127.1.

Since they placed greater importance on *morning profits* made at dawn than on erecting the divine Temple, and ranked base considerations ahead of better ones, they were found to suffer another ailment in addition to this: *they hated those who reproved them in the gates*, by *in the gates* meaning "openly." Why did they *hate* them? To people once in the grip of wicked pleasures and incorrigibly guilty of doing what was improper, those brave enough to reform them could not appear welcome, only burdensome and odious. After all, what else could they think of such people?

It is therefore a fearful thing to have an ailing mind, a proclivity to vile behavior, a loathing of people in a position to help, and being so deranged as to welcome with joy whatever happens, even though it should prove to be extremely disordered. Far better and wiser to repel with fortitude the harmful influences that flood the soul and mind from outside, and, if we must suffer, speedily to seek out physicians and love those who *reprove* us, on the one hand, and on the other to throw ourselves at the feet of God, as it were, and say, "Heal me, O Lord, and I shall be healed, save me and I shall be saved, because you are my boast."[17]

Now ponder in your hearts from this day forth: before laying stone upon stone in the Temple of the Lord, what condition were you in when you put twenty measures of barley into a chest, and there were ten measures of barley, and you went into the vine vat to draw fifty measures and there were twenty? I struck you with sterility, with windblast and (275) *with hail all the works of your hands, and you did not turn to me, says the Lord* (vv.15–17). He convinces them with irrefutable arguments that they have done the right thing in choosing to rebuild the divine Temple, and are better off than before in showing enthusiasm for it. Consider and recognize, he says, in fact, *what condition were you in*, that is, how you were situated, *before laying stone upon stone in the Temple of the Lord.* At that time, remember, he says, the produce of fields and threshing floor, *twenty measures of barley*, were collected with difficulty after lengthy exertion (a *measure*, I think, being an amount),[18] which you put into a *chest* (to be understood also as a kind of deposi-

17. Jer 17.14.

18. Jerome does not help Cyril with the Heb. term *sata*, which he finds in his LXX text.

tory of crops). But *there were ten measures of barley*, clearly because the weevils had consumed the crops and reduced them to dust as a result of divine wrath. And if you went to the wine vat, to draw out *fifty measures* in jars, you were then astonished to find the level unexpectedly reduced. And, he says, you were *struck* with other plagues, *sterility, windblast, and hail*; but you were still hard-hearted, for *you did not turn to me*, he says.

So what shall we learn from this? It is obvious that for those unwilling to build up the house of the Lord—that is, the Church—or for those culpably lazy in turning their own souls into a temple of God, whatever good they have previously acquired will come to nothing. In addition, the harmful effects of the unclean spirits will also affect them, sterility and *hail;* that is, the intolerable onset of temptations will reduce them to every form of trouble, and the effects of divine wrath will befall them.

Set your hearts to think from this day (276) *forth, from the twenty-fourth day of the ninth month, and from the day the foundation stone of the Temple of the Lord was laid. Ponder in your hearts whether it will be recognized on the threshing floor, and whether I shall bless the vine, fig tree, pomegranate, and olive trees that are bearing no fruit from this day* (vv.18–19). After firmly convincing them in what has just been said to us, that an extreme onset of dreadful troubles had befallen them when they were guilty of laziness regarding the divine Temple, in his knowledge that a joyful fate awaited them he says that they would enjoy prosperity as the fruit of their enthusiasm for what was pleasing to him, and would be completely gratified by a reward for their generosity shown towards his house. He promises in particular to provide them with such a good yield from the fields as to beggar belief; the heaps of grain from the *threshing floor* would exceed expectations, the *vine* would be found to be laden with grapes thanks to the produce of the trees in the orchard, *fig tree and pomegranate* and, in short, everything in season would abound for them, and as well the *olive* would yield its own *fruit* for them in unexpected abundance, doubtless because of blessing from God.

In other words, just as for those guilty of indolence in building up the Church, or in presenting themselves as a holy temple to Christ, everything takes a turn for the worse, and as well the fate befalls them of being quite overwhelmed by temptations and spiritual infertility, so too it is likewise true that to those willing to do the upbuilding and give priority to the effort of good living the gift will be given of enjoying every good, being enriched with fruitfulness of mind, and, as it were, having an interior orchard bedecked with various ornaments of virtue. It would be like (277) blooming into fruits in season so as then to be able to utter the forthright cry in the Song of Songs, "Let my nephew come down into his garden, and eat the fruit of his fruit trees,"[19] the shoots of the virtues being, as it were, food for God, like the grace of fruitfulness of mind.

The word of the Lord came a second time to Haggai the prophet on the twenty-fourth day of the month in these terms, Speak to Zerubbabel son of Shealtiel, of the tribe of Judah, thus: I shall once and for all shake heaven and earth, sea and dry land. I shall overthrow kings' thrones, destroy the power of kings of nations, overturn chariots and riders, and horses and their riders will each fall on the sword of their brother (vv.20–22). Our prophetic text consistently involves a development from particular details and from events under consideration to universal and generic matters. Should it, for example, make reference to the redemption of some people, it often moves on from there to that achieved by Christ. The prophetic text in this case, too, suggests something of the kind; to what was already stated, a sequel is necessarily appended that includes a detailed reference to the mystery of Christ obscurely and in shadow. The prophet is sent, note, to Zerubbabel, of the tribe of Judah, saying that *heaven and earth* and as well *sea and dry land will be shaken*, and the *thrones of kings overthrown.* Paul in his wisdom also refers to the meaning of the passage, using the term *will be shaken* (278) to mean that there will be a movement of what is shaken "so that what is not shaken may remain." This had to be perfected through Christ, however, for in him all things have become new and "the old have passed away,"[20] namely, what is staggering and shaken, whereas things in him have become new in the sense of being made stable, firm, and permanent. Note, therefore, the divine plan implied in the pas-

19. Song 4.16.
20. Heb 12.27, citing Hg 2.21; 2 Cor 5.17.

sage: after promising them an admirable fruitfulness, and saying that he would generously provide everything needed for satisfaction and enjoyment, he immediately introduced the moment of true fruitfulness, namely, the generous supply of spiritual blessing from on high. I did shake the earth under heaven, in fact, he is saying, when I led Israel out of Egypt; but *I shall once and for all shake*, that is, once more I shall do something illustrious and celebrated throughout the earth, as it were, by shaking everything.

And I shall destroy *kings' thrones*, abolish all their *power*, deprive, as it were, of their oppression of everyone *riders* coursing across the earth under heaven, and raise up other riders or warriors drawing their *sword* against family and brethren. In this he is probably suggesting to us the evil and hostile powers destroyed by the strength of our Savior, principalities and powers over which he has triumphed by his cross,[21] and by depriving them of their oppression of everyone he has assisted the wronged, namely, ourselves. The holy and immaculate Virgin, for instance, when pregnant with Christ, and with her mind filled with the Holy Spirit, cries aloud in prophecy in these words, "My soul magnifies the Lord, and my spirit has rejoiced in God my Savior"; and further on (279) likewise, "Holy is his name, and his mercy is upon generation to generation for those who fear him. He exercised power with his arm, he scattered the proud in the thoughts of their heart, brought down the powerful from their thrones, and exalted the lowly. He filled the poor with good things, and sent the rich away empty. He helped Israel his servant, to remember his mercy, as he said to our fathers, to Abraham and his offspring forever."[22]

While the powerful have been brought down, therefore, and toppled from their thrones, the achievements of our Savior's coming did not stop at that; a kind of array of *riders* was created, men of war skilled in the art of fighting and making war, and in general hostile to the antagonism of the devil. These would be the divinely inspired disciples, who in a spiritual manner brandish the sword of the Spirit, that is, the word of spiritual guid-

21. Col 2.14–15.
22. Lk 1.47, 49–55.

ance that is living and active and sharp.[23] They advanced on every person and race and *brethren*, not causing a deadly blow but disposing of their ignorance, putting the world to death, as it were, and causing sin to die so that they might live for God, loving a glorious and blameless life, that is, according to the Gospel. Now, there is no doubt that for the sake of love for Christ sons were destined to be at odds with their fathers, daughters with their mothers, and brethren with one another; the Savior clearly said, "Do not think that I have come to bring peace to the earth; I have come to bring not peace but a sword. I have come to set a man against his father, a daughter against her mother, a daughter-in-law against (280) her mother-in-law, and one's foes will be members of one's own household."[24] So while foes are people of a different way of thinking, friends are not those of longstanding so much as sharing a fellowship of faith, unity in the Spirit, and love in Christ.

On that day, says the Lord almighty, I shall take you, Zerubbabel son of Shealtiel, my servant, says the Lord, and make you a seal, because I have chosen you, says the Lord almighty (v.23). Such a statement is really not directed to Zerubbabel; rather, it was made to our Lord Jesus Christ as clearly prefigured in Zerubbabel, because he was of the tribe of Judah, and a king to boot, leader of those redeemed from captivity, and a kind of foreman of those building the house of the Lord. *Taking you, my servant,* accordingly, means the one who appeared in the form of a servant but is free by nature.[25] At the time when I choose to bring down the mighty ones from their thrones and expel the principalities, *I shall make you a seal,* the Son being the seal of the God and Father, bearing a complete and perfect likeness to him, and in his beauty reflecting the nature of the one who begot him.[26] By him God also sets the seal of his peculiar likeness on us as well; by being conformed to Christ, we acquire the image of God, as it were. The Son is therefore the precise stamp of the God and Father, and he chose him, that is, made him eligible and select.

23. Eph 6.17; Heb 4.12.

24. Mt 10.34–36; Mi 7.6.

25. Phil 2.7.

26. The mention of Zerubbabel as God's seal prompts Cyril, Jerome, and Theodore to consider possible Christological implications of the verse.

For instance, at the Jordan River he confessed him to be such in saying, "This is my Son, (281) the beloved, in whom I am well pleased; listen to him." The God and Father was in fact well pleased to reform all things and restore them to their original state, as the divinely inspired Paul also writes, "to restore things in heaven and things on earth" in Christ,[27] through whom and with whom be glory to the God and Father with the Holy Spirit, now and forever, for ages of ages. Amen.

27. Mt 3.17, plus the words spoken at the Transfiguration, 17.5; Eph 1.10.

COMMENTARY ON THE PROPHET ZECHARIAH

COMMENTARY ON ZECHARIAH, CHAPTER ONE

In the eighth month, in the second year of Darius, the word of the Lord came to Zechariah son of Berechiah son of Iddo the prophet in these words (v.1).

BLESSED ZECHARIAH was prophesying in Jerusalem at the same time, in my view, as Zephaniah. After the return from captivity, in actual fact, Israel no longer lived in divided fashion, some in Judea and some in Samaria; instead, they all gathered in one city—namely, Jerusalem—and throughout Judea. Zerubbabel of the tribe of Judah reigned over them, and Joshua son of Jehozadak was the leader of the priesthood as chief priest.[1] Now, he framed (283) the delivery of his prophecy very artfully. The majority of the people who had been taken off into captivity from Judea or Samaria, remember, were returning from there, and were aware of all the crimes committed by the Babylonians against Jerusalem at the time. They were not unaware, in addition to that, of God's resentment at those crimes. Others, on the other hand, who had been born in the country of the Persians and Medes, had no knowledge of what Jerusalem was like, and were ignorant both of Judea and of the punishments inflicted on their forebears as a result of the divine wrath as well as any of the reasons for their paying such severe penalties, except perhaps from casual reports.

Consequently, the God of all appointed for them at the time of ransom blessed Zechariah as the kind of tutor we assign to the very young and as a governor. He was in the priestly line, that is, of the tribe of Levi, sprung from Berechiah according to the

1. Cyril begins commentary with reference to the historical situation of the prophet (though the connection with Zephaniah in the time of Josiah is unusual), citing key figures in the returned community mentioned in Ezra 3. The royal status of Zerubbabel derives from the LXX's misreading the Akkadian term in the Heb. of Hg 1.1, "*governor* of Judah," as "of the tribe of Judah."

flesh, but according to the spirit styled son of Iddo the prophet—in other words, he was probably reared by his standards and proved an imitator of his exploits to the same degree.[2] It is therefore appropriate to give a brief account of the drift of his prophecy and the stages by which it proceeds. He lectures the ransomed, in fact, on the sentence to which they were subject for gravely neglecting the divine commandment and being in the habit of disregarding what had been communicated through the all-wise Moses. He instilled no little fear into them, and persuaded them to change their allegiance in the direction of choosing rather the right way to gain a reputation for obedience and responsiveness in everything. He proceeded to state that if some of them were not good, compliant, and well-disposed to the divine laws, they too would suffer a harsher fate than that which befell their forebears. (284) Developing his theme in the manner of educational discourse, he tried to bring out, on the one hand, what were the pursuits of their forebears in former times and for what crimes the divine anger befell them, and on the other how they were in turn laid waste, as well as the way they were also released, delivered from the yoke of captivity, and brought back to Judea. In addition to this, he declared, as I said before, that they would suffer a worse fate than their forebears by following the pattern of their lack of love for God. He stresses at every point the redemption that would come through Christ in due course, and describes for us in many ways the mystery occurring in his case.

Those willing should therefore give careful attention to each part of the prophecy, not treating its contents as repetitious or as an idle account of what happened in the past. They should rather remember that for those returning from captivity to Judea the account of what had happened in the past was most needful. On the one hand, you see, he recalls to remembrance those aware of their previous sufferings, while on the other he provides those who were very young and ignorant of the

2. Cyril is obviously puzzled, as are modern commentators, by the statement (in the Heb. text) that Zechariah is said to be "son of Berechiah son of Iddo" (as though father and grandfather) whereas in Ezr 5.1 and 6.14 he is called only "son of Iddo"—so which was his father? Cyril offers a plausible explanation; Didymus had referred to mention of Berechiah in Lk 1.5.

past with security against falling victim to similar troubles by becoming fond of a profane and lawless life.

The Lord was extremely angry with your forebears (v.2). You will notice how he startles them with his narrative, presenting for explication even to the very young the events that happened before their time, and scaring them into amendment. It was as if he were threatening them that they would undergo similar or even harsher (285) troubles and lament bitterly unless they sensibly chose to abjure their forebears' behavior and give every care and attention to God's anger. He says the God who is omnipotent *was extremely angry;* far from letting the accuracy of his statement go without proof, he demonstrates from what they had already experienced and suffered that he is not a liar. After all, it was an index of no slight indignation that the whole of Judea and with it Samaria was attacked and plundered, the actual holy places set on fire, and Jerusalem overturned; Israel, the chosen one, became a refugee, suffering a miserable and wretched servitude in foreign parts, enduring intolerable privation. On the one hand, it could no longer perform sacrifices, unable to enter the sacred courts, unable to offer thanksgiving rites or tithes or first-fruits according to the Law. On the other hand, it was excluded by necessity and fear from duly celebrating the festivals sanctioned and beloved by it. So *the Lord was extremely angry with their forebears.*

Now, you would be able to relate such events even to the Jewish population if you chose to give an introduction into the mystery of Christ. Since they killed the prophets, remember, and crucified the Lord of glory himself,[3] they were taken captive and plundered, and the famous Temple itself was reduced to ruins. Then was fulfilled in their case what was said in the verse of Hosea, "The children of Israel will remain many days without king or ruler, without sacrifice or altar, without priesthood or insignia."[4] Who would doubt that they are captives, in the devil's hands because giving offense to God and rejected by him, and beyond all mercy from on high? (286) If, however, they were freed in due course after embracing the faith and confessing

3. 1 Cor 2.8.
4. Hos 3.4.

Christ to be God, King, and Lord, at that time in fact, at that time and quite properly you could apply to them that wise advice in these words opportunely, *The Lord was extremely angry with their forebears.*

You will say this to them, The Lord almighty says this: Turn to me, says the Lord of hosts, and I shall turn to you, says the Lord almighty. Do not behave like your forebears, whom the prophets in the past upbraided in the words, The Lord says this, Turn away from your evil ways and from your evil pursuits. They did not give themselves to hearkening to me, says the Lord (vv.3–4). They were called back from captivity, as I said, and returned to Judea; but they proved indifferent to God's will, and though for a time not worshiping idols or adopting the former error, they were still found to be provoking God in other ways. As is written in the book of Esdras, in fact, they had relations with foreign women, introducing them from the neighboring nations and fathering foreign children despite the Law's veto of this as unlawful.[5] They also neglected to celebrate festivals and perform sacrifices, and even proved to be unenthusiastic in their duty to rebuild the divine Temple. As a result, as is written in Haggai, he struck them by affecting all the works of their hands with blight, mildew, and hail; when they put twenty measures of barley in a chest, (287) there turned out to be ten, and when likewise they went in to draw fifty measures, there turned out to be twenty.[6] So he promised them that if they chose to make a change for the better and turn to him by opting to do what was good and pleasing to him, then he for his part would also turn to them—that is, he would desist from his anger with them, have rapid recourse to mercy again, and deign once more to show pity and compassion. He went as far as forbidding them to choose to emulate their forebears' deeds, as productive of ruin, which was an appeal and recommendation made frequently by him through the holy prophets summoning them to desist from their shameful pursuits. But the appeal was quite unsuccessful and fell on deaf ears.

Those who followed their forebears' stupidity, therefore, were ridiculous, constantly adducing the hereditary addiction as an

5. Cf. 1 Esdras 9.7.
6. Hg 2.17, 16.

irrefutable excuse, despite being reprehended for their extreme vices. This, however, is the way particularly with people who serve idols: though summoned to an acknowledgment of the truth, they persisted in the error of their forebears, and by embracing their stupidity like some ancestral inheritance, they remained blind. Now, it is my view that, even if someone were to advise the circumcised to abandon their shameful attitude and have regard for salutary options, they too would have recourse to their forebears' habits. Hence the relevance of the declaration to those in error, *Turn to me and I shall turn to you, says the Lord almighty,* and further, *Do not behave like your forebears,* that is, those in error, persisting utterly in ignorance. (288)

Your ancestors and the prophets—where are they? Surely they will not live forever? Only accept my words and my laws, which I give in my spirit to my servants the prophets, who restrained your forebears. They replied in these words, As the Lord almighty has ordained to treat us according to our ways and according to our behavior, so has he treated us (vv.5–6). Before the capture of Judea and likewise of Jerusalem, some people applied to themselves the name of prophet as though a sort of mask and addressed the people of old "from their own hearts and not from the mouth of the Lord," as Scripture says.[7] They were deceitful in claiming that the holy city would never be taken, nor would Israel ever be vulnerable to those bent on plundering it; instead, it would enjoy continuing prosperity and would experience uninterrupted delights under the protection of God, who ever had regard and love for his chosen one.

Now, as I said above, the wretched liars made these claims, rendering Israel still more lax when it was already indifferent, despite their obligation to urge it to appease God, abjure the crimes with which he had for so long been distressed, and have a change of heart in favor of his will. They set little store by the truth, however; a prey to petty and grubby bribes, they deceived Israel. The prophet Jeremiah for one censured them severely in these words, "O Lord, you who are, lo, their prophets prophesy, saying, You will not see the sword, and (289) will not experience hunger, because I shall give you true peace in the land and in this place. And in response to this, God said, The prophets are

7. Jer 23.26.

giving false prophecy in my name; I did not send them, I did not command them and did not speak to them, because they are prophesying to you false visions and oracles and divinations and the wishes of their own hearts." And elsewhere he says further, "I did not send the prophets, yet they ran; I did not speak to them, yet they prophesied."[8]

So Israel was deceived, as I said, unwisely beguiled by the lies of the false seers. It would not have been taken by the enemy at that time, however, or experienced such a harsh and burdensome servitude if it had given heed to the prophets from God, who both forecast to them that such things would happen, and openly declared that they would definitely be punished by experiencing misfortune unless they chose to do what pleased God. Consequently, he invites them to remember the scoundrels who gave false prophecy and told lies: *Your ancestors and the prophets—where are they? Surely they will not live forever?* It is just as if he were saying, Your ancestors perished, and pitiably, too, in captivity, and with them those who lied and deceived you, those who traded on the name and practice of prophecy. If they were still alive, however, perhaps they would have reformed you by constantly lamenting what had happened and raising a loud outcry against the false prophets who had been among them.

While they received the wages both for their indolence and for their disobedience by being wiped out along with those they deceived, however, you must accept the message of the holy prophets and set great store by their utterances. They said this also to them before your time, remember, *The Lord almighty has ordained to treat us,* namely, by captivity and the (290) hardships it would involve. They censured you by saying openly, *According to our ways and according to our behavior, so has he treated you.* The God of all, of course, does not punish without reason, nor does the divine verdict deliver a sentence on anyone prior to examination, being just and proof against error. Instead, after showing extraordinary patience, then and only then it repays the sinners in the most commensurate way possible. Obedience is therefore wise; we shall be freed from all trouble by obeying the divine laws, by respecting the prophecies of the holy ones

8. Jer 14.13–14; 23.21. Only fragments exist of a work by Cyril on Jeremiah.

and receiving the statements of the Spirit in faith, considering that all the predictions will be completely fulfilled, by making a change for the better and having recourse to repentance. This, in fact, is the way we shall divest ourselves of the effects of wrath and don the protection of the gentle Lord; he justified the ungodly,[9] remember, and discharges from judgment those who have fallen into sin from ignorance or weakness.

On the twenty-fourth day of the eleventh month, which is Shebat, in the second year of Darius, a word of the Lord came to the prophet Zechariah, son of Berechiah son of Iddo the prophet: I saw by night and, lo, a man riding a red horse, and he stopped in the middle of the shady mountains, and behind him horses, red, bay, piebald, and white. I asked, What are they, Lord? The angel who was speaking in me said to me, I shall show you what they are. The man standing amidst the mountains replied, (291) *saying to me, They are those whom the Lord sent to roam the earth. They replied to the angel of the Lord standing amidst the mountains, saying, We roamed all the earth, and lo, all the earth is inhabited and is at peace* (vv.7–11). God gave visions to the holy prophets separately and at set times; we do not claim that the favor of a vision of God and the revelation of the future was granted them constantly and in frequent and indiscriminate incidents. Rather, it was at set times appropriate to the particular situation and in the judgment of the one who was revealing hidden things. They were instructed in one thing at one time, in another at another time, in many and various ways. Sometimes they received a simple insight, as the Holy Spirit inspired them; sometimes, in addition to that, they were part of the action in the visions themselves when at various times and in various ways God gave shape to sacred realities and revealed them obscurely. Blessed Isaiah, for instance, says he saw "the Lord of hosts seated on a lofty and elevated throne," with the seraphim attending on him and praising him in turn. The divinely inspired Ezekiel says he saw him above the firmament, with the seraphim situated below; he said that the being he saw seated on the throne took two forms: the part below the loins, as it were, seemed clearly to take the form of fire; the upper part in the vision was in the form

9. Rom 4.5. Cyril closes comment on the opening verses of the chapter with a doxology and some parenesis.

of gleaming amber.[10] The description in each case would prove banal and extended if you ventured to pry into the reasons why the visions they had from God were multifarious.

Likewise, therefore, in the case of Zechariah: he is specific about the time in terms of day and month, saying he saw the (292) Lord in a form like ours: *Lo, a man riding a red horse.* In this he suggests, as it were, that the man was skilled in martial arts and procedures: he is seated on a *horse*, which is *red* as if of the color of blood. His meaning, in my view, is something like this: the God of all fights against those who resist him, and like a warrior he takes up arms against those rearing against him a rebellious and haughty neck of their mind. Now, that is what was done, and very wantonly at that, by the natives of Israel, inhabitants of both Judea and Jerusalem itself, as well as the occupants of the land of the Samaritans—in other words, the ten tribes. They turned to polytheism, and in paying homage to objects made by human hands they acclaimed the golden calves by saying, "These are your gods, Israel, who brought you out of the land of Egypt."[11] In addition to this, they completely set at naught the decrees of the Law and heedlessly devoted themselves to doing what each one pleased. Consequently, the God of all now pays them a visit on horseback mysteriously in a form like ours.

And he stopped in the middle of the shady mountains. In my view *the shady mountains* refers to those of Judah—namely, Zion—and of Samaria; of them God said, remember, "Alas for those who despise Zion and trust in Mount Samaria."[12] Both are *shady*, to be sure, for the possible reason of their being crowded by the immense multitude of inhabitants and resembling dense and spreading timber. Behind the rider of *the red horse*, in fact, there were likewise other horses, not of the one color but *red,* (293) *bay, piebald, and white.* Now, they actually represent kings, or warlike and contentious nations, not only desirous of having their own country, but scattered throughout the earth, as it were, and anxious to bring under their power the land under heaven, as do the Babylonian kings—firstly Pul, who seized the

10. Is 6.1–2; Ezek 1.25–27.
11. 1 Kgs 12.28.
12. Am 6.1.

tribes beyond the Jordan; then Shalmaneser, who plundered Samaria; thirdly Sennacherib, who savagely ravaged what was left of Samaria, also burning many cities of Judah; fourthly Nebuchadnezzar, who took Jerusalem itself and took Israel into captivity.[13] His seeing the horses in a range of appearances perhaps suggests the difference in each man's attitude; and you might take the difference in color among them to convey obscurely each one's mentality, and rightly so.

The prophet, therefore, was at a loss, and asked for an explanation. He learned that *They are those whom the Lord sent to roam the earth.* Those who were sent reported that they had roamed the entire earth and could confirm that it was in fact at rest, unable to resist their greed, bearing their yoke not willingly but of necessity.

The angel of the Lord replied in the words, Lord almighty, how long will you have no mercy on Jerusalem and the cities of Judah, which you have overlooked these seventy years? (v.12) With the dispatch (294) of the horses—that is, the nations and kings roaming the whole earth—and their report that it was inhabited, at peace, and bearing the imposition of the yoke, the blessed angel, who was perhaps assigned by God to watching over the Jewish nation, turns at once to entreaties for Jerusalem and Judah. Now, we shall find that when they fled from the land of Egypt, Pharaoh was thunderstruck and, armed to the teeth, instilled terror into them and was bent on pursuing them, but the angel of the Lord stood between them, the text says, "and one did not come near the other all night."[14] Paul too, on the other hand, versed in the Law, said that the Law itself was communicated by angels.[15] And the force of the Gospel parable also conveys something similar: Christ somewhere said in reference to the assembly of the Jews, with the intention of forecasting obscurely what was destined to happen to it, "Someone had a fig tree planted in his field," but when it bore no fruit, he wanted to cut it down, and actually gave orders to the vinedresser, "Cut it down: why should it even take up the ground?" He said in reply, "Sir, leave it be for this

13. Under "Babylonian kings" Cyril includes both Assyrians and Babylonians.
14. Ex 14.10
15. Heb 2.2.

year as well for me to dig around it and manure it; maybe it will yield in the future, but if not, you shall cut it down."[16]

In other words, what else does the figure of the vinedresser suggest to us than that of the protective angel, who was bidden guide them, as I said? God determined the length of the captivity as *seventy years,* and before that period was complete, he had to keep silence lest he seem to be in opposition to the Lord's decrees. But with the expiration of that period, he makes entreaties, and with (295) the removal of the suspicion of transgressing, and in his knowledge that the Lord is not false to his word, he thinks fit to inquire whether there is an end to the wrathful punishment of the sinners in terms of the ancient decree *for seventy years,* or whether there will be a prolongation because of the further sins, and their hardships will continue still further. Hence his asking, *How long will you have no mercy on Jerusalem and the cities of Judah, overlooked these seventy years?*

For those who reverence God, therefore, there is sound and certain hope, to be sure, that should they happen to offend God through weakness, they still have suppliants with God on their behalf, not only human beings but also the holy angels themselves, who render God mild and benign, appeasing his wrath with their peculiar purity and, as it were, making the Judge ashamed of his indignation. While at that time it was an angel who was making appeals for the assembly of the Jews, we who are believers and are now sanctified by the Spirit "have an advocate with the Father, Jesus Christ the righteous, who is the atoning sacrifice for our sins, and not for ours only but for those of the whole world." As the divinely inspired Paul writes, it is he whom "God put forward as a sacrifice of atonement through faith,"[17] freeing from sin those who approach him.

The Lord almighty replied to the angel talking in me, with fine words and consoling expressions. The angel talking in me said, Cry aloud in the words, The Lord almighty says this, I am extremely jealous for Jerusalem and Zion. I am extremely wrathful towards the nations (296) *who have conspired, the reason being that while I was slightly wrathful, they conspired with evil intent* (vv.13–15). It is true to say, in the words

16. Lk 13.6–9.
17. 1 Jn 2.1; Rom 3.25.

of the psalmist, "The Lord shows compassion and mercy,"[18] and experience itself would proclaim that this is so and not otherwise. I mean, observe how he immediately accepts entreaty on the part of those maltreated and crushed in a foreign land and enduring the yoke of captivity; he not only anticipates the prayer of the petitioner and immediately replies with *fine words and consoling expressions—consoling,* I say, because capable of reviving and consoling those in trouble. While he perhaps uttered no kindly word all the time of their captivity, in fact, and regaled them with nothing else likely to give consolation, he begins to speak in kindly manner and shows the signs of mildness towards them. It is with great joy, therefore, that the divinely inspired angel bade the prophet then cry aloud and communicate to everyone everything said by God. *I am extremely jealous for Jerusalem,* he says, not showing jealousy for it as when beforehand it had strayed into foreign worship, but on its behalf to the plunderers, with whom he was also angry (he says), not with some simple and chance movement of anger, but as though with unmitigated and unrestrained anger. While I corrected my own, he says, and meant them to suffer nothing beyond measure, they of their own choosing inflicted cruelty in a foul manner and without restraint, omitting no form of cruelty and inhumanity.

This, I think, is the meaning of the verse, *While I was slightly wrathful, they conspired with evil intent:* while the God of all corrects sinners out of love, (297) and inflicts chastisement and hardship in measured fashion, thus frightening them into reforming, they took to it by force, sometimes in the manner of wild beasts ravaging those corrected. But God *was extremely wrathful towards them:* whereas his intention was to reform them with chastisement like a father, they vented unrestrained attacks on the weary victims, as it were, with all their might. When the Church suffered this treatment, the persecutors were unaware that they were rendering themselves liable for their ferocity towards it, and would pay a harsh penalty at the hands of God its protector.

Hence the Lord says this, I shall return to Jerusalem with compassion, and my house will be rebuilt in it, says the Lord almighty, and a measuring line will still be stretched out over Jerusalem (v.16). He

18. Ps 103.8.

emphasized the fact that by experiencing the alienation of the one capable of bringing salvation, it was reduced to that degree of misfortune and misery. Yet quite simply and without effort it would return to the situation it formerly enjoyed with the change to benignity in the one who had been provoked. Now, it is clear that God is capable of everything; it was as if he returned to that attitude by once more bestowing clemency and love, holding no grudge and condoning their faults. He promises, in fact, to raise up the Temple and make Jerusalem stand tall, the Temple having been burned down, the very walls of the city destroyed so as to give the impression of being tiny and dismantled, and its inhabitants few in number. But, as I just mentioned, he guarantees to restore it (298) to its former condition, which actually occurred: Cyrus released them from captivity; Darius actually gave orders for the rebuilding of the very Temple and allowed the city itself to be fortified with walls.

Now, we observe that sometimes God exercises the faith of his holy ones and the love of those devoted to him by letting the Church be persecuted at times. He immediately restores it, however, after a short period of suffering, and once more reinforces it with his assistance, crowning his own house with grace from on high. Now, each of those committed to religious living is a city and a house of God; often it is put to the test when fleshly pleasures and worldly care stimulate it to follow base conduct so that the soul of the sufferer gives the impression of being on fire and remaining bereft of walls, or protection. But God has pity on it and, thanks to the prayers of the holy ones, changes his attitude to one of mildness; so once more it is rebuilt to become "a holy temple, a dwelling place for God in the Spirit."[19] With all impurity removed as well, it is fortified by God and becomes a city of the great King, that is, Christ.

The angel speaking in me said to me, Cry aloud in these words: The Lord almighty says this, Cities will yet overflow with good things; the Lord will have mercy on Zion and again choose Jerusalem (v.17). With the extension of the period of captivity, the cities of Judea became completely desolate, and no less those of Samaria: the houses had been burned and, as it were, cried to high heaven

19. Eph 2.21–22.

about the Babylonians' ferocity; the very appearance of the cities was defaced and completely destroyed. (299) Among the number of inhabitants easily counted, it was impossible to find a man of distinction or otherwise conspicuous, nor were some people still prosperous—all were dejected, suffering starvation and need. He promises there would be an end to all this: *Cities will yet overflow with good things;* that is, they would enjoy their former good fortune, with good things accruing to them in abundance; their appearance would change and they would return to the condition they wished again: *the Lord will still have mercy on Zion and again choose Jerusalem.*

Now, observe how the drift of the prophecy is communicated to us in a skillful manner: he does not guarantee to *have mercy* on it all, or to *choose* it for all time. Rather, he says *again,* as if promising a specified period of mildness. It was destined, you see, to be caught up in worse troubles when condemned for its abusive behavior towards Christ. So the term *again* means that he determines the period of mildness, since it contains a veiled threat of what would befall it at the time of our Savior's coming.

I raised my eyes and looked and, lo, there were four horns. I said to the angel speaking in me, What are they, sir? He said to me, These are the horns that scattered Judah and Israel. The Lord showed me four artisans. I asked, What are they coming to do? He replied to me, These are the horns that scattered Judah and Israel, and none of them raised their head. They came in to sharpen with their hands the four horns, these being (300) *the nations that lifted up their horn against the Lord's land to scatter it* (vv. 18–21). The prophet moves to another vision not long after, the purpose being for him to be instructed about the future, not only in word but by enjoying an insight into the actual future events, and thus he may keenly and precisely see what they mean. What the sense of the vision is, therefore, I shall to the extent possible try to explain. In the inspired Scriptures the word *horn* is always used as an image or figure of power or kingship; often it also has the meaning of arrogance, as in blessed David's statement, "I said to the transgressors, Do not transgress, and to the sinners, Do not raise up your horn, do not lift up your horn on high or make unjust statements against God." Somewhere he also sings in reference to Christ,

"His horn will be lifted in glory,"[20] that is, his kingship, power, and authority to rule over all.

So the prophet sees *four horns,* that is, four nations, harsh and strong, easily capable of reducing both cities and towns to kindling wood. Some commentators claim, on the one hand, that they are the kingdom of the Assyrians, and further the kingdom of the Babylonians, the third the Macedonians (Antiochus, remember, given the name Epiphanes, was a Macedonian and devastated Judea); to this number they add the kingdom of the Romans, which after the crucifixion of the Savior took Jerusalem by force. Since, on the other hand, the divinely inspired angel in interpreting the vision to the prophet said in reference to the horns that *these are the horns that scattered Judah* (301) *and crushed Israel,* I think it necessary to pass these over and rather come to the nations that crushed Israel. So there were in fact four powers at whose hands we find Judah suffering this fate: Pul was the first to conquer the two tribes beyond the Jordan River, then after him Shalmaneser, third Sennacherib, and finally in addition to them Nebuchadnezzar. Consideration would more properly be given to them, therefore, as the four *horns that scattered Judah and Israel.*

Next, with God demonstrating and explaining the vision to the prophet, *four artisans* were seen. Once more he inquired what their purpose was in coming. Then *the angel who spoke in him* said that they are the four *horns that* crushed and *scattered Judah and Israel* and *came to sharpen them.* So what shall we say is meant in turn by this as well? Surely those who had already plundered Israel were not provoked, nor did God render more savage those who had attacked them out of anger? Admittedly, it emerges that he cried aloud and said, "I am extremely jealous for Jerusalem and Zion. I am extremely wrathful towards the nations who have conspired, the reason being that while I was slightly wrathful, they conspired with evil intent."[21] How could the one who showed a slight and moderate wrath and manifested jealousy to the plunderers for committing crimes

20. Pss 75.4–5; 112.9. The commentator helpfully explains obscure terms for the reader.

21. Zec 1.15. The word "sharpen" appears in the LXX where (our) Heb. reads rather "terrify."

beyond measure against the captives bid the horns *be sharpened* against them?

So it is not against Israel but against themselves that they are sharpened; they rebelled against one another, in fact, and when Cyrus came to the throne, Persians and Medes waged war on Assyrians and Babylonians, as I mentioned before. (302) So unless the horns had been *sharpened* and Babylon devastated, Israel would not have been freed from slavery; it would not have been released from bondage and unbearable hardship. Accordingly, the *four artisans* that give an edge to *the horns with their hands,* that is, while they hold them or control them, for us to understand them as kings reigning over the Persians, should be understood as angels appointed to carry out to perfection God's will. This involved the subjugation of the Babylonian empire and its coming into the control of Persians and Medes, of whom the Lord God of all says somewhere else, "They are consecrated, and I lead them; giants come to execute my anger, rejoicing and exulting."[22]

22. Is 13.3.

COMMENTARY ON ZECHARIAH, CHAPTER TWO

I lifted up my eyes and saw and, lo, a man with a measuring cord in his hand. I said to him, Where are you going? He replied to me, To measure Jerusalem to see what its breadth and its length are. Lo, the angel speaking in me was at hand. Another angel came to meet him and said to him, Run and say this to that young man, Jerusalem will be inhabited as fruitful on account of the number of people and cattle in its midst. For it, I shall be, says the Lord, a wall of fire round about, and I shall be as glory in its midst (vv.1–5).

THE FACT THAT THE SHARPENED HORNS were not against Israel but rather against those who captured and plundered Jerusalem and Judea the above vision would indicate, and rightly so. The prophet, note, raises his eyes again, not at all those of the body—the kinds of things in the vision are not visible to eyes of the flesh—but the interior and spiritual eyes, namely, those in the heart and mind.[1] He then says he saw someone in the form of a man holding a measuring cord, and in turn he asked him where he was going and what he intended. When he replied, *To measure Jerusalem to see what its breadth and its length are, another angel* in turn bade the former angel go and tell him, *Jerusalem will be inhabited as fruitful on account of the number of people and cattle in its midst.* You see, since Jerusalem had been devastated,[2] the divine Temple itself burned down, and the houses throughout the whole of Judea and the cities overthrown, hope that it could ever be restored had vanished. God makes plain, however, that with the sharpening of the horns—that is, the nations or kingdoms—and their waging war on one another, Israel would be restored,

1. Cyril seems to be adopting the position of Didymus that such visions were interior only rather than physical.

2. This clause and the preceding sentence Joannes Aubertus (in the sixteenth-century edition adopted by Migne for PG 72) found missing from the manuscript he was using.

and Jerusalem given increased population and fortifications by divine power, and saved by benevolence from on high as though by an invincible flame. So the angel runs to *measure Jerusalem,* and, as it were, determine its width and breadth.

While this is the factual sense, it would seem that the (304) vision could rightly be taken to refer also to the Church of Christ.[3] Satan, you see, had ruled as a tyrant over all beings on earth, and we were in thrall to him, subject to his yoke. But the grace of the Savior had smashed his horn in pieces and crushed his arrogance; he triumphed over the rulers, the powers of the cosmic authorities, and opposing forces.[4] He rescued us and loosed the devil's bonds; for us he raised up the Church, the truly holy and celebrated city in *its breadth and length,* which we have inhabited *fruitfully, men and beasts* together—that is, those already exercising reason and those not yet at this stage but in readiness and preparing for admission. We have inhabited the city which Christ himself fortifies, consuming the adversaries with flames of unspeakable power and filling it with his own glory; standing in the midst of its inhabitants, as it were, he gave this promise: "Lo, I am with you all days even to the end of time."[5] The prophet Isaiah also made mention somewhere of this holy city in the words, "Your eyes will see Jerusalem, a wealthy city, with tents that will never be shaken; the pegs of its tabernacle will not be moved, nor its cords broken." He also says to it, "Broaden the place of your tent and your courts; set it firm, show no hesitation, extend further to right and to left."[6] The Church of Christ is in fact expanded and extended to limitless dimensions, always admitting those who adore him beyond number.

O, O, flee from the north, says the Lord, because I shall gather you from the four winds of heaven, says the Lord. Escape to Zion, you inhabitants of daughter Babylon (vv.6–7). He expresses sorrow, as it were, for those experiencing captivity because of their suffering intolerable hardship, and actually even bids them retreat then

3. As elsewhere in this commentary, Cyril attends first to the factual interpretation of verses (*historikōs*), and then gives them an ecclesiological or Christological sense, or both.

4. Cf. Col 2.15.

5. Mt 28.20.

6. Is 33.20; 54.2–3.

from the land of the Chaldeans—something possible for them to do at that time when no one forbade it, and he assembles from every place those scattered by the enemy's assault. By the phrase *daughter Babylon* and land of *the north* he refers to the country of the Chaldeans; the major cities precede the other cities as mothers, and the country of the Chaldeans was somewhat to the north and east.

Again let this suffice for us in reference to the factual meaning; the passage has a different sense by way of spiritual interpretation. There is some suggestion of the person of the Savior speaking, in a way grieving and, as it were, weeping for people on earth because of everyone's betaking themselves to the service of Satan's tyrannical rule and enduring such harsh servitude as to seem oppressed by his wishes. He therefore urges them to escape *from the land of the north,* that is, from the freezing country, his purpose being that we may recognize indirectly in this some worldly attitude or moral condition; if anyone had it and seemed to dwell in it, they would not be spiritually ardent or have the word of God as a flame dwelling in them. Blessed David, remember, somewhere sings to God, "Your saying is tested in a very hot furnace, and your servant loves it." (306) God himself somewhere said to the blessed prophet Jeremiah, "Are not my words like a burning fire, says the Lord, and an axe cutting stone?"[7] The one who does not have the living and flaming word of God, therefore, would be freezing and lifeless; blessed Paul also said that the love of the general run of people will grow cold owing to the growth of wickedness.[8] Sin has been called *daughter Babylon,* and rightly so, if it is true that Babylon means "confusion"; sinning would be the fault, not of a firm and set mind, but of one that is confused and, as it were, under the influence of tendencies to depravity. There should consequently be a departure from such things, the mind leaving a foreign land, as it were, that is freezing and lifeless to transfer to Zion—that is, the truth. As a result, we may see reference to the Church of Christ, and when we are in it, we shall have a vision of God's will

7. Rom 12.11; Ps 119.140; Jer 23.29.

8. Not Paul in fact (unless the reference is rather to Rom 5.20), but Jesus at Mt 24.12.

and grasp the doctrine of the Trinity, holy and one in being,[9] and shall find Christ himself bringing us together from every direction and binding us together in harmony in a spiritual manner. He said in reference to us, remember, "I have other sheep, too, that are not of this fold; I must bring them in as well, and there will be one flock, one shepherd."[10]

For the Lord almighty says this, In the wake of glory he has sent me to the nations despoiling you, because the one touching you is like the one touching the apple of his eye (v.8). Of the fact that Christ assisted and redeemed also the (307) peoples of old no one would be in doubt, at least if their mind were fond of precision. I mean, if he it is who is the rock that gave water to Israel when thirsting in the desert, and he it is from whom everything comes from the God and Father, how is there any doubt that it is from him that also every redemption comes at the right time, and every form of assistance is provided? It is on this basis at least that we claim to propose him to those justified by faith and sanctified by the Spirit, and to indicate the manner of the Incarnation. *In the wake of glory he has sent me*, the text says, and it would never lie: if the one in the form of the God and Father is God the Word, who is from him and in him, and "he did not regard equality with God something to be exploited," as it is written, instead coming "in the form of a slave and humbling himself," how could he not be *in the wake of the glory* particularly appropriate to him?[11]

What reason was there, then, for his having to suffer dishonor for a while? He came, in fact, to despoil the plunderers who subjected the people on earth—namely, us—to their own yokes when the wicked and hostile powers brazenly ravaged us. They are now despoiled when Christ the Savior of all gathers us through faith to himself, and makes those burdened by them with greed his own worshipers, extending to us such security that the one wanting to harm us is, as it were, *touching the apple of his eye*, with the achievement of their efforts ever being frustrated. To each of the persecutors of the Church the verse in the Psalms could be recited, "He made a pit and dug it out, and

9. Cyril cites the term *homoousios* from the formula of Nicaea and Constantinople.

10. Jn 10.16.

11. 1 Cor 10.4; cf. Nm 20.11; Phil. 2.6–7.

he will fall into the hole he made; his trouble will reside upon his (308) own head, and his wickedness will come down on top of him." So, the text is saying, the one who schemes against the souls of those who believe in me will *touch* himself. This, to be sure, is the meaning of the psalm verse: "Do not touch my anointed, do my prophets no harm." After all, if we "are the body of Christ and individually members of it,"[12] how would he expose his own body to those who love sin? Or how could Christ's members be filled with evil? Or, rather, how could those who scheme against his subjects fail to pay the ultimate penalty?

For this reason, lo, I raise my hand against them, and they will be booty to their slaves, and will know that the Lord almighty sent me (v.9). Christ *touched* the cosmic rulers of this age, in fact, crushed the heads of the baleful dragon with his unbearable hand, and allowed us to "walk on snakes and scorpions and on all the power of the foe."[13] Those who once were fearsome and utterly harsh, and whose onslaught was irresistible, have become *booty to their slaves.* In other words, we who formerly were in thrall to sin are made righteous in Christ and have already attained to such a degree of spiritual vigor as to be capable of displaying the luster of every virtue and of living the evangelical life in Christ. We shall then be filled with the gifts of grace from (309) him, given authority over unclean spirits, and inflict punishment on the unholy demons, with Christ prostrating and crushing under the feet of the holy ones Satan himself and the wicked powers subject to him.[14]

There is also another way you could make booty of those once in power: when we resist our own passions and give the highest priority to controlling worldly and fleshly pleasures and every improper and vile desire, then it is that we have vanquished those once in power. Even if we do not see ourselves involved in this, then it is, I say, then it is that we shall know by experience itself that the Word, who is God, has been sent in the flesh into this world by the God and Father, and has come *in the wake of glory* for no other purpose than to bind what has been

12. Pss 7.15–16; 105.15; 1 Cor 12.27.
13. Ps 74.13; Lk 10.19.
14. Mt 10.1; Rom 16.20.

crushed, give strength to what has been weakened, raise up what has been cast down, strengthen what is feeble, heal what is ailing, so that what is lost may be saved.

Rejoice and be glad, daughter Zion, because, lo, I am coming, and I shall dwell in the midst of you, says the Lord. Many nations will take refuge in the Lord on that day, and will be a people for him, and will dwell in your midst, and you will know that the Lord almighty has sent me to you. The Lord will inherit Judah as his portion in the holy land, and will still choose Jerusalem (vv.10–12). From this, too, you would come to realize that the coming of the Savior will be an occasion of the greatest satisfaction for those on earth. In fact, he consequently gave orders for joy and gladness to the (310) spiritual Zion, "which is the Church of the living God,"[15] or the sacred multitude of those saved by faith. He promised that he would come and would really be *in its midst;* the divinely inspired John said, remember, "He was in the world," and the Word who is God did not abandon his own creatures; rather, he it is who gives life to what has a share in life, and who holds all things together for growing and living. But "the world did not know him," adoring creation rather than him. He was with us, however, when he took upon himself a likeness to us and was born of the holy Virgin. Then it was that he was also "seen upon earth and lived with human beings," the divinely inspired David also giving witness in the words, "He will come in visible manner, our God, and will not keep silence."[16]

Then it was that he also proved a refuge for the nations: he no longer gave instruction only to the race of Israel by that ancient commandment—rather, the whole world under heaven was gilded with the proclamation of the Gospel, and "his name was great among every nation" and in every country. He it was, remember, who was "the expectation of the nations," in the words of the inspired author, and to him "will bend every knee of those in heaven, on earth, and under the earth, and every tongue will confess that Jesus Christ is Lord to the glory of God the Father." People from the ends of the earth betook themselves in faith to him, in fact, and dwell with him in the holy

15. 1 Tm 3.15.
16. Jn 1.10; Bar 3.37; Ps 50.3.

and spiritual Zion, and realize clearly that "God so loved the world as to give his Only-begotten Son, so that all who believe in him may not perish but have eternal life."[17] The Father sent us from heaven the Son, you see, (311) as Savior and Redeemer, so that we might believe in him, admire the Father in him, and by seeing the one who proceeds from him by nature as an exact image, as it were, of the one who begets him, we might grasp the archetype.

Then it was, indeed, then it was that Judah became Christ's *inheritance*, that is to say, everyone confessing and glorifying him, Judah meaning "confession"; as Paul says, remember, "Not everyone is a Jew who is one outwardly, nor is true circumcision something external and physical—rather, a person is a Jew who is one inwardly, and real circumcision is a matter of the heart, spiritual, not literal; such a person receives praise not from others but from God." So all of us who are enriched with circumcision of the spirit are *his portion in the holy land*, so that we understand the city on high, the spiritual Jerusalem, "whose architect and maker is God,"[18] who renders it lovable and chosen (the text saying *he will still choose Jerusalem*). Now, it would also not be unreasonable for you to choose to think of *Jerusalem* as now referring to the Church, since the divinely inspired David also calls it the city of God in saying, "As we have heard, so we have seen in the city of the Lord of hosts, in the city of our God."[19]

Let all flesh show reverence before the Lord, because he has roused himself from his holy clouds (v.13). This is a fine saying of value, and a good recommendation for those willing to give it a hearing, whether it comes from Christ himself or from the person of the prophet. It should be given careful consideration; he bids them *show reverence*, as though those not giving it credence are completely and totally lost. Christ himself also made this statement to those from Israel not arriving at faith in him: "Amen, Amen I say to you, if you do not believe that I am he, you will die in your sins," and again, "The one who

17. Mal 1.11; Gn 49.10 LXX; Phil 2.10–11; Jn 3.16.
18. Rom 2.18–19; Heb 11.10.
19. Ps 48.8.

believes in the Son is not judged, but the one who does not believe has already been judged, because he has not believed in the name of the Son of God," and consequently "the stumbling block and rock of scandal" is the name belonging to Christ.[20] In other words, just as crowning him in faith is by common consent a fine and salutary thing, so it is a source of destruction not to show reverence to the one who for our sake has taken on our condition, and for no other reason than to save what was lost, bring back what had strayed, give life to what was corrupt, enlighten what was in darkness, purify from fault what was encumbered with sins, and make healthy and strong what was ailing.

We shall in turn consider him *rousing himself from his holy clouds* in the sense of moving from the former solitude and silence to caring for us, at least in that he is descended from the *holy* men Abraham, Jesse, and David and those in their line, whom he calls *clouds* on account of the mind of the holy ones being lifted on high, abjuring things on earth and a debased attitude, and instead seeking what is above in the heavens, and bedewing others with spiritual rain in the manner of clouds. Now, the fact that it is not unreasonable to consider the rising mentioned here as the movement of the ineffable nature to caring the Savior himself will again confirm (313) in speaking in the verse of the psalmist, "Because of the tribulation of the poor and the groaning of the needy I shall now arise, says the Lord."[21] So *he has roused himself;* that is, he has now moved to give assistance to the victims of distress on earth. He is the solution to all problems, the termination of the ancient curse, source of every good, and giver of hope in the world to come.

20. Jn 8.24; 3.18; 1 Pt 2.7. The latter half of the next sentence is missing from the PG text of Aubertus.

21. Ps 12.5.

COMMENTARY ON ZECHARIAH, CHAPTER THREE

The Lord showed me Joshua the high priest standing before an angel of the Lord, and the devil standing at his right hand to oppose him. He said to the devil, The Lord rebuke you, devil, and the Lord who has chosen Jerusalem rebuke you (vv. 1–2).

ON THE ONE HAND, the report is a vision, though having an historical basis; it makes obscure references, and depicts Joshua as though in an image again. On the other hand, it should be understood that since the happenings in the visions have already come to pass, the prophet is delivering his statement in reference to them. It is not without purpose, however, nor does it come after the event and assemble a heap of stories of no use to us. Instead, as I said in the beginning, he makes a point of conveying what was seen before the event with the purpose of making Israel wise and secure lest it fall into similar mistakes and be captured a second time, aware that they were saved with difficulty and that redemption and grace came to them even through the care, as it were, of the angels in heaven. (314)

So he said that he saw the angel standing, and before him the high priest Joshua son of Jehozadak.[1] While the angel is an image and type of Christ, the priest should be understood as representing all the people, the way a priest is taken in the divine Scriptures. God said to Moses, for example, "Lo, I have taken the Levites to represent all the sons of Israel, given to me as a gift."[2] So in taking the priest to represent all the people, the verse comes to us without violating the nature of Scripture.

1. While Didymus had denied any historical basis to the vision, and taken Joshua to represent Jesus, Cyril allows such a basis and sees Joshua representing the people, the angel acting as a type of Christ.
2. Nm 3.12, 9.

Israel, you see, had served idols and even scorned the Law itself given by Moses, and was banished from God's presence; but when his righteous anger had been vented on them, they were invited once more into his sight. This, I believe, is the obscure suggestion in the clause *the priest was standing before an angel of the Lord:* in anger he turned away and directed his eyes from those in the habit of showing scorn, whereas in forgiveness he regards them and looks at them. The divinely inspired psalmist, for his part, prayed in the words, "Do not hide your face from me, nor in anger turn away from your servant," and again, "Look upon me and have mercy on me."[3] While God, who is naturally kind and merciful, was in the habit of freeing Israel from sin, there was *standing* there Satan, who drove them into it, still their *opponent* and adversary, and continuing to accuse them and, to the extent of his power and will, prevent their being pitied because of their persistence in sin, their being guilty of impious faults and having nothing to recommend them. He was, in fact, *standing at his right hand,* (315) somehow disabling commendable deeds; it is not our useless actions he opposes but those that are commendable and praiseworthy. This is the experience blessed David requested for anyone who acted impiously towards Christ, saying, "Let the devil stand at his right hand."[4] So Satan opposed him, but was rebuked by the voice of an angel; note what it says, *The Lord rebuke you, devil, and the Lord who has chosen Jerusalem rebuke you.*

Observe, in fact, how he immediately presented him as an adversary of God, sacrilegiously resisting decrees from on high; while God shows pity and is now freeing Israel from sin, welcoming Jerusalem and now in some way making it an object of choice, Satan does not cease accusing it and presuming to condemn those who have been shown mercy. God therefore censures him for his insatiable wrath in the words, *Lo, is it not like a brand snatched from the fire?* (v.2) It is as if he were saying, Admittedly Israel has sinned, and is obviously deserving of your censure; but it has paid no slight penalty, sustained calamities, and has barely been *snatched from the fire* like a half-burned

3. Pss 27.9; 119.132.
4. Ps 109.6.

firebrand. He had not yet depicted the effects of the captivity, you see; Israel had only just escaped the flame of insupportable hardship. So cease your censure of those shown mercy: "Since God justifies, who is to condemn?"[5]

Joshua was dressed in filthy clothes and standing before the angel, (316) *who said in addressing those standing before him, Take the filthy clothes off him. He said to him, See, I have taken away your iniquities. Put on him a long tunic, and place a clean turban on his head. They clothed him in garments and put a clean turban on his head* (vv.3–5). Now that the one assigned the role of priest had been presented in the role of the whole people, it is in my view sufficient to say that *the filthy clothes* are an unambiguous symbol of the people's impurity. Clad in their own sins, as it were, and bearing the indelible stain of impiety, they lived in captivity, subject to punishment and paying the penalty for their unholy transgressions. When God had mercy, he ordered them to be freed from sin, rid of the *filth,* and in some fashion clad in grace that justifies. He promises them an end to hardship and release from what had befallen them. In the place of God, therefore, the blessed angel bade the ministers in attendance to remove the filthy vesture from them, and he actually says, *See, I have taken away your iniquities.* He next says he must be given *a tunic* and *a turban on his head,* the purpose being for us to understand in this that the glory of priesthood always goes hand in hand with the condition of the people.

You see, (317) the purity of those under them is the boast of priests, and they consider the good repute of the priesthood as one of their greatest distinctions, when the people enjoy a good reputation, are amenable to doing God's will without fault, delicately submitting their minds to decrees from him, and consequently finding God benevolent and loving. By contrast, indifference and a heedless tendency to sin are a charge and a stain on subjects; you see, just as in the case of the people committing sin the priest's clothing was also *filthy,* so if they enjoy a good reputation, the impression given by the priesthood will be pure and resplendent, and they will enjoy great confidence with God. The divinely inspired Paul,

5. Rom 8.33–34.

therefore, in ministering the Gospel of Christ to the nations and observing the impressive developments in their growth and their sound faith in him, writes in these words, "Brethren, you are certainly the boast I have in Christ Jesus," and again, "You are my joy and crown."[6]

The angel of the Lord was standing by. The angel of the Lord assured Joshua, The Lord almighty says this, If you walk in my ways and keep my commandments, you will make decisions in my house. If you guard my halls, I shall give you those living in the midst of these attendants (vv.6–7). While we have taken the high priest Joshua as an outline of Christ the Savior of us all, (318) Aaron, remember, being appointed to this role in the beginning, in the present text, however, we claim there is reference to the son of Jehozadak in the verse, *If you walk in my ways and keep my commandments, you will make decisions in my house,* and so on. Such a statement would not refer to Christ: he is the way, he is the ordinance of the God and Father, he *made decisions in his house,* exercising authority as Son. While the divinely inspired Moses was faithful in serving "in the whole house of God, Christ was over his house as a son, and we are his house."[7] Let us take such references as made to the son of Jehozadak, therefore, not to Christ. God promised that he would be in charge of the priesthood according to the Law even after the period of captivity, and so the priests ruled Israel and governed the holy tabernacle. You see, when the captivity occurred, the holy places burned down, and sacrifices were no longer offered, some people thought that the Mosaic provisions would be completely overthrown and the Law no longer observed, although the time had not yet come when it was necessary for the Only-begotten to become man and be manifested. Consequently, to persuade them that Israel would once again be subject to the ancient customs and would live under the control of the priests, he necessarily says that if Joshua was a sincere observer of the Law, he in turn would *make decisions in his house* and enjoy the former glory, with even the holy angels ministering along with him. We nowhere claim, in fact, that the old Law was devoid of the force of reason: even

6. 1 Cor 15.31; Phil 4.1.
7. Jn 14.6; Heb 3.5–6.

if (319) the provisions of the Law came as types and shadows, they were nevertheless observed for the glory of God.[8] This, I think, is suggested by the phrase *I shall give you those living in the midst of these attendants*, that is, angels ministering and serving together, as it were.

Now, observe how at all points the sacred text says the holy angels are *standing*, suggesting by the mention of standing that they have not succumbed to sloth but retain an attitude that is ever upright, as it were, and cannot bear to be slack, instead standing with God. This is the way we find the text expressing it also in Ezekiel in reference to the cherubim, that "their legs were straight"; the human mind very easily relaxes and is inclined to want to fall victim to sloth, whereas he was *standing* like the holy chorus of the spirits on high. Consequently, it is said by God also in reference to Zion, "Stand up, Zion."[9] Blessed David also somewhere offers thanksgiving songs in these words, "He made my feet stand on a rock"; in these words the inspired author suggests by the word "stand" the level and fixed character of mind.[10]

Listen, Joshua the high priest, your intimates, and those seated before you, because the men are seers. Because, lo, I bring my servant, Dawn by name. Hence the stone which I have set before Joshua, and on the one stone are seven eyes (vv.8–9). In what was just told us, he promised (320) Joshua, or at least, as is closer to the truth, the priesthood according to the Law, the role of making decisions in his house, continuing to rule peoples and fulfilling the types of worship according to the Law. Note, I ask you, the management and the great finesse of the divine oversight. God was on the point of transferring before long the provisions in the Law to worship that is true, and of transforming the shortcomings of the types into a way of life that is desirable and spiritual. The vinedressers who murdered their master were on the point of being driven out of the vineyard, and the place given to others[11]—namely, the holy apostles and evangelists, who were likely to render it

8. An endorsement of the abiding value of the Old Testament.
9. Ezek 1.7; Jer 21.21.
10. Ps 40.2, the psalmist being declared "inspired," *pneumatophoros*.
11. Cf. Mt 21.39–41.

fruitful and luxuriant by bestowing on it solicitous attention. "A righteous king" was about "to reign," and "rulers to rule with justice," in the verse from the prophet;[12] some other high priest was about to rise up, not in the order of Aaron but "in the order of Melchizedek," "a minister in the sanctuary and the true tent that the Lord and not any mortal has set up." Our Lord Jesus Christ entered the holy of holies, you see, "obtaining redemption, not with blood of goats and calves but with his own blood," and "by a single offering perfecting for all time those who are sanctified" in conscience.[13]

Lest God give the impression of telling false and frivolous stories, therefore, by promising the priesthood according to the Law that it would always and forever supervise and judge his house, he consequently delivers a prophecy of the mystery of Christ, that the provisions in the Law will come to an end and instead he will judge his own house through his begotten, that is, the Son. Consequently, he (321) adjures Joshua in person, his *intimates and those seated before* him, whom we may take to be Levites and priests; the levitical order, remember, attended on the high priest when he celebrated,[14] whereas the senior priests, being still higher and more sacred than they according to the Law, also had ranking in the assembly. He actually calls them *seers,* that is, constantly searching to see signs and hankering after portents, which is what the nation of the Jews is naturally always like. For instance, when Christ "made a whip of cords and drove all of them out of the Temple with the words, Take these things out of here, do not turn my Father's house into a marketplace," they approached and said, "What sign do you show us for doing this? Who gave you this authority?" We shall find also other people making their approach and saying to him, "Teacher, we want to see a sign from you."[15]

So since *the men are seers,* the text says, let them learn about what will happen to you and about the all-powerful one who will bring to fulfillment the signs for which you ask. Who is he? *Lo, I bring my servant, Dawn by name.* The Only-begotten appeared, then, by nature God and from God the Father, and in that

12. Is 32.1.
13. Heb 8.11; 9.2, 12; 10.14.
14. Nm 3.6.
15. Jn 2.15–18; Mt 21.23; 12.38.

capacity a free agent; yet "he emptied himself,"[16] according to the Scriptures, taking a form that had not existed and being styled a servant on account of his humanity, though as God he was Lord of all. But even so, he was *Dawn*, too—that is, "Sun of Justice": he rose and shed light on us as though living in darkness, awoke us to sobriety when we were overcome, as it were, by night and sleep through the pleasures of this world, (322) and made us shine with grace from him. Paul in his wisdom, therefore, also writes to us, making the same point, "The night is far gone, the day is near; let us then lay aside the works of darkness, and put on the armor of light, let us live honorably as in the day"; and again, "Sleeper, awake, rise from the dead, and Christ will shine on you."[17] He thus forecasts the splendid achievements of the coming of our Savior.

Now, he speaks of him as a *servant*, assuredly on account of his coming "in the form of a servant," and as *dawn* because he is the true light, brightness, and daylight, clear morning star that rises on our minds and brightens our hearts. In addition to this he also calls him *stone*, and says he is set *before Joshua*, and is well equipped with *seven eyes*. There was need in particular, you see, for the priesthood according to the Law, for which we have cited Joshua as a type, constantly to have before its eyes as if *before him* the chosen *stone*, the cornerstone, precious as it is, meant as the foundation of Zion, the pearl of great price—namely, Christ—gazing on all things with many eyes (*seven* always meaning completeness: the barren woman has seven children, remember).[18] Now, no one would doubt that the divine and ineffable nature of the Son gazes on all things with countless eyes and oversees our situation: "The word of God is living and active," remember, "sharper than any two-edged sword, piercing until it divides soul from spirit, joints from marrow, able to judge thoughts and intentions of the heart. (323) Before him no creature is hidden, everything being naked and laid bare to his eyes," as Scripture says.[19]

16. Phil 2.7. Where our Heb. speaks of "branch," the LXX reads "dawn."
17. Mal 4.2; Rom 13.22–23; Eph 5.14.
18. Is 28.16; Mt 13.46; 1 Sm 2.5.
19. Heb 4.12–13.

Lo, I am digging a pit, says the Lord almighty, and I shall get a grip on all the injustice in that land in one day. He presented our Lord Jesus Christ as light and *dawn,* and the fact that he will illuminate like daylight those in darkness and the shadow of death,[20] that is, in error. But it was also necessary to forecast the fulfillment of the divine plan, namely, death for the sake of us all, which he willingly underwent by surrendering his own body to the cross, because the Jewish race had also offended and forfeited their relationship with him. You see, since the wretches did not understand the mystery of the Incarnation and became murderers of the Lord, consequently and very properly they were deprived of hope and perished miserably as miserable people, caught up in terrible and ineluctable calamities. So he actually likens the cross of the Savior to *a pit,* since those who shed the Lord's blood fell into a pit, as it were, even presuming to give over to crucifixion the Author of life.[21]

Now, if the Father himself spoke of *digging a pit,* let no one be scandalized, but consider rather that the expression is redolent in some way of the Incarnation; it is like what is said wisely and precisely by Christ, "I came into this world for judgment so that those who do not see may see, and those who do see may become blind."[22] Admittedly, while there is truth in claiming that he did not come for this reason, for some people to become blind, nevertheless it was not only the fault of uncomprehending people that misrepresented the manner of the wonderful Incarnation; they refused to see, in fact, despite having access to the divine light. This is the way to take it here, too: while the Father sent the Son "so that the world might be saved through him,"[23] on account of the folly of those who failed to understand, he who was sent became *a pit* and a trap for those who crucified him. Perhaps it was the one who sent him who is somehow thought to have *dug the pit;* so he actually says, *I shall dig a pit, and I shall get a grip on all the injustice in that land in one day,* by *digging a pit* meaning, I shall seek it out and carefully pry into it.

You see, they killed the holy prophets, and like hunters they

20. Lk 1.79.
21. Acts 3.15.
22. Jn 9.39.
23. Jn 3.17.

assailed those sent at various times, abusing some, maltreating others, killing still others.[24] God was still tolerant, however; the victims were servants and fellow slaves of those who committed the murders. Since in their unrestrained assaults they went to extremes, and contemplated such an unholy outrage as audaciously to do violence to the Son himself, and fell into the pit by crucifixion, he no longer forgave their unbridled sin. He sought out the offenders and submitted them to punishment, decreeing the destruction of the whole of Judea *on one day* when they paraded him before Pilate and cried, "His blood be upon us and upon our children."[25] Even if the effects of divine wrath did not immediately befall them, even if the penalty was not sought without delay, nevertheless the just sentence from God took effect on them, destruction gripping the land of the Jews, as I said. (325) While the Savior was taken off to crucifixion, therefore, women followed him, weeping and wailing; he then turned and said to them, "Daughters of Jerusalem, weep not for me: weep for yourselves and for your children." They were, in fact, delivered to destruction and slaughter, and there happened to them what was said in the verse of Isaiah, "Your land is desolate, your cities are burned, foreigners consume your very land before you, and it is devastated and overwhelmed by foreign peoples."[26]

On that day, says the Lord almighty, each of you will invite your neighbor under your vine and under your fig tree (v.10). On the one hand, he clearly foretold that once their sin was grasped, those who fell into the pit, as it were, by crucifying Christ would be involved in every trouble. On the other, he makes the positive prediction that the event would not be without benefit to believers and those who love him, instead proving conducive to happiness and seemly enjoyment. Blessed Simeon also testifies to this: when he saw the divine child and held him in his arms, he made the following prophecy, "Lo, this child is set for the fall and rise of many in Israel, and as a sign to be contradicted."[27] It was in fact those who brought down innocent blood on their own heads who fell, as though thrust to the ground and lying there, under the devils' feet, while those from the nations were

24. Cf. Mt 21.35.
25. Mt 27.25.
26. Lk 23.28; Is 1.7.
27. Lk 2.34.

lifted up. And Christ himself in one place foretells to the holy disciples the (326) suffering on the cross; when he notices their becoming dejected, he encourages them in the words, "A woman has pain when giving birth to her child because her hour has come; but when she has borne the child, she rejoices greatly because a human being has come into the world. Though you have pain, later you will see me and your heart will rejoice." Similarly also when he rose from the dead, he said to the women weeping in the garden, "Be glad."[28] It would behove each of those who love him to say both at the crucifixion and the resurrection, "You have turned my mourning into joy, you have torn up my sackcloth and clad me in happiness." After all, how would grief not take its leave and "all tears be removed from every face," in the words of the prophet's statement,[29] when Christ is risen and the power of death overcome? Life, after all, is his by nature as God, even if he appeared in the flesh.

So *on that day*, that is, at the time when he came back from the dead and the crucifiers went down into the pit, *let each of you invite your neighbor under your vine and under your fig tree.* If, on the one hand, you wanted to take such a statement in the obvious sense and at face value, you would assert that the terms stand for spiritual enjoyment. On the other hand, I claim that it is not unreasonable to say that in addition to this there is the other sense, a customary reference in *fig tree and vine* to the Church, to which the divinely inspired psalmist also refers in speaking obscurely of the heavenly bridegroom from on high, namely, Christ: "Your wife as a vine flourishing in the recesses of your house." (327) It was also he who in one place said, "The vines blossom, they give forth fragrance, the fig tree bears figs out of season."[30] In other words, with the churches already beginning to release the fragrance of faith in the world, he says the vines are blossoming, and even fruit out of season is appearing, which should be understood as the large number of those who have recently come to faith, sweet though not yet mature but shortly to become so, destined to produce yields in greater amounts. They are ripening, in fact, and "coming to maturity, to the

28. Jn 16.21–22; Mt 28.9.
29. Ps 30.1; Is 25.8.
30. Ps 128.3; Song 2.13.

measure of the full stature of Christ,"[31] sweet as if we were fruit for God, as though growing up for the Church like some mother.

With the churches understood in *fig tree and vine*, therefore, we shall be *under* them and lodge in them, reciting to one another encouragingly the prophetic verse, "Come, we shall go up to the mountain of the Lord and to the house of the God of Jacob; he will tell us his way, and we shall travel by it."[32] If it should be our good fortune to attain this, we shall give every credit to those who called us to it, saying yet again, "I rejoiced in those who said to me, We shall go up to the house of the Lord," which could, in fact, be rightly taken as the fruit of our enjoyment on high. We shall say once more, then, in the words of the holy psalmist, "One thing I asked of the Lord, this I sought, to dwell in the house of the Lord all the days of my life, to behold the enjoyment of the Lord and visit his holy temple."[33] (328)

31. Eph 4.13.
32. Is 2.3.
33. Pss 122.1; 27.4. At this point the first volume of the Zechariah commentary comes to a close.

COMMENTARY ON ZECHARIAH, CHAPTER FOUR

The angel speaking in me turned back and woke me in the way a person is woken from sleep, and said to me, What do you see? I replied, I see and, lo, a lampstand all of gold, on top of it the lamp, seven lights on top of it, seven spouts of the lights on top of it, and two olive trees above it, one on the right of its lamp and one on its left (vv. 1–3).

THE PHRASE *turned back* here we shall interpret not in a local sense, which would be very naïve; rather, we shall take it as an immediate movement from the present vision to another one related to it, namely, a spiritual one. Since there was need of unimpaired attention surpassing human understanding, however, in these matters in particular, God instills in the prophet a keen state of alertness, with the angel speaking in him as the means, so that he had the impression of *waking from sleep.* Such is our state of mind, in fact, far inferior to that (329) of the holy angels such that you could claim that whereas they are awake, we are asleep, as it were.

Now, when the divinely inspired angel perceived that he was disposed in mind and will for the purpose of having a sufficiently clear understanding of the vision, he asked him what he thought was being shown to him. The prophet then gave an accurate account of the vision, saying he saw *a lampstand, all of gold, on top of it a lamp,* and actually *seven lights* and an equal number of *spouts, and two olive trees, one on the right of its lamp and* the other actually situated *on its left.* While the very clear explanation of what was shown would not differ from this, my view is that there is need to try very hard to look into its innermost purpose, and skillfully relate it to what was said above. The God of all had said, then, that he would both dig a pit and lay hold of all the iniquity of that land in one day, and he recommended others as well to invite one another under vine and under fig tree. In clarifying the purpose of the prophecy,[1] we said that, for those who chose to disbelieve and ignorantly dishonor the salvation coming through Christ, a kind of pit had been dug that would convey them to destruction, namely, the folly having to do with the cross and the criminal murder of Christ. The wretches guilty of the unholy murder of the Lord did, in fact, perish, whereas to "those who have really longed for his coming"[2] there was enjoyment and delight: what was actually not in store for such people? After all, they were in the churches as though under fig tree and vine. (330)

But, lo, the prophet discerns the force of the mystery in another form as well; again we claim that the *golden lampstand* is the Church for the reason of its being honored throughout the world, conspicuous for virtue, and raised to the very heights by the teachings of the true knowledge of God. On it is the *lamp*, that is, Christ, of whom the God and Father says, "For Zion's sake I shall not keep silent, and for Jerusalem's sake I shall not rest, until my righteousness emerges like a light, and my salvation burns like a lamp."[3] This lamp, which enlightens everything under heaven, the God and Father placed on the lampstand "so that everyone on entering may see the light, and that it may shine on everyone in the house."[4] There were *seven lights;* instead of their having light of themselves, it comes to them from an outside source, and is fed by the supply of oil. These also refer to the holy apostles and to the evangelists as well, and to the Church's teachers at various times, who receive illumination from Christ into their mind and heart like a kind of *light* and keep it fed with the Spirit as the source, which provides light to those in the house; they also illumine the believers with the lamp.

Note that the seven lights had *spouts* through which oil was provided to them, whereas the lamp did not have a spout. For what reason? You see, the Son is the true light, which is not from another source, nor is it brought to him, nor is his ability to illumine something assigned by another. Instead, he

1. An example of Cyril's accent on the author's *skopos* as a basic hermeneutical criterion.

2. 2 Tm 4.8.

3. Is 62.1.

4. Lk 11.33; Mt 5.15.

is by nature the light; the share in it given to the saints comes from him. The wise John confirms the prophecy in saying, "Of his fullness we have all (331) received." The Son, who is the true light, referred to those sharing in his brightness as "light of the world," saying to the holy apostles, "You are the light of the world."[5] The *two olive trees*, situated *one on the right and one on the left* of the lamp, refer to the two peoples, as if surrounding Christ; as objects of mercy they are honored by having this position. One group was from the cultivated olive tree, that is, from the synagogue of the Jews; the other grew from the wild olive tree, that is, from the vast number of the nations, but was grafted onto the cultivated olive tree and made sharers in the richness of the root, in the words of blessed Paul.[6]

Note how on the lampstand are the seven lights and the two olive trees together with the lamp; Christ is with us in the Church, and the vast number of believers that are the object of mercy shine with light from him, but are also illuminated by lights which also have a share in the light from him. Now, it should be realized that in the furnishings of the holy tabernacle as well there stood in the Holy of Holies a golden lampstand with seven lights. God gave directions to Aaron, "Seven lights shall burn before the lampstand on one side";[7] in other words, the illumination from the lights was not given to those behind it but to those brought before Christ, as it were, by faith. Jews, for example, are positioned behind him at his back, with mind darkened, whereas those who have come to the faith from the nations have the lights in their face, since the illumination came to them through the saints and is free and unshackled. Now, there was also one light burning in the first tabernacle, (332) this fact suggesting to us that the light of the Law gave way to the teaching of the Gospel. Note, in fact, how only one light burned for those in the first tabernacle, whereas to those who entered the Holy of Holies seven lights and the lamp burned as though emitting extraordinary brilliance.[8]

5. Jn 1.16; Mt 5.14.

6. Rom 11.24, 17.

7. Nm 8.2.

8. By sustained use of allegory, Cyril maintains the ecclesiological interpretation of the passage.

I put a question to the angel speaking within me in these terms, What are these things, Lord? The angel speaking within me replied to me, asking, Do you know what they are? I said, No, Lord. The angel replied to me in these terms, This is the word of the Lord to Zerubbabel, Not by great power, nor by strength, but by my Spirit, says the Lord almighty (vv.4–6). From this you would also learn that the understanding of the spiritual powers is greater and more sacred than the mind we have, surpassing our capacity with an excellence beyond comparison. "The angel speaking in me turned back," the prophet said, remember, "and woke me in the way a person is woken from sleep." If you wanted to compare the limits of human thinking with the understanding enjoyed by the powers above, you would find the former to be defective to the extent that the insubstantial bogeys we see in dreams are inferior to the thinking of people awake. The prophet was woken up, therefore, but being in that condition and very dull he was no less slow to succeed in understanding what was shown him. Consequently, and quite properly, he inquires and asks to learn from the angel instructing him. The latter (333) was astounded, as it were, that he did not grasp it, asking him if he really did not know. When he openly confessed his ignorance and was not ashamed of his failure to grasp it, he then clarified the riddle of the vision, and as if from a clear and visible picture he interpreted the purpose lying concealed in it. *This is the word of the Lord to* Zerubbabel, he said, *Not by great power, nor by strength, but by my Spirit, says the Lord almighty.* It is as if he were to say, The sense of the vision and the purpose of what was revealed proclaimed, as it were, and gave voice to what was said by God to Zerubbabel, that all this vision will in due course be fulfilled, not achieved by human *power* nor fleshly *strength,* but by the power of the Holy *Spirit* and as a result of divine decrees.

You see, while the Only-begotten became a human being like us, yet he did not take up arms in fleshly fashion for the purpose of presenting the Church to the world as a lampstand. Instead of employing material weapons and troops of warriors and presenting the two peoples to himself, or in other words placing the two spiritual lights on the lampstand, by the power of his Spirit he commissioned in the churches "first apostles, second prophets and evangelists,"[9] and the rest of the whole band of the saints, filling them with divine charisms and enriching them abundantly with the outpouring of the Spirit. So it was not *by great power, or by* fleshly *strength* that Satan was plundered, but by the force of the Spirit from Christ, and with him there fell also the cohorts of the opposing powers. Called to the knowledge of God through faith were those from Israel and also those who of old served creation instead of the Creator. (334)

The lights, that is, the saints, were made visible also in the churches, shining together with the lamp—Christ, that is; they became, as for instance the most wise Paul writes, "luminaries in the world, offering it the word of life."[10] The fact that he saved the world under heaven, not with human hand but with his own powers as God the Emmanuel, is given verbal confirmation also in the words of Hosea as follows, "I shall have mercy on the children of Judah, and save them by the Lord their God; I shall not save them with bow, with sword, with war, with chariots, with horses, or with riders."[11] Now, the verse was very applicable to Zerubbabel, who was of the tribe of Judah and at that time was conducting the seat of the kingdom in Jerusalem. You see, in case he should think that, with such conspicuous and praiseworthy achievement forecast to him, he would in due course engage in wars and battles, he consequently discouraged him from thinking such flawed and human thoughts, and instead bade him be of the view that the force that belonged to God and the power that was not human for bringing such things to a conclusion was Christ's. We recall that we said that Zerubbabel himself, being from the tribe of Judah and a king, stood for the person of Christ, and Joshua son of Jehozadak was connected with him, so that Emmanuel should be understood as both king and high priest in one and the same person.

Who are you, mighty mountain before Zerubbabel, to achieve anything? I shall bring forth the stone of the inheritance, its grace an equality of grace (v.7). The meaning of the text is very difficult to arrive at; but we shall state (335) what seems the best and most correct sense. The verse, then, is probably censuring the

9. Cf. 1 Cor 12.28.

10. Phil 2.15–16.

11. Hos 1.7.

mighty mountain, namely, Satan, who is Christ's adversary and is raising in opposition to him the power of his perversity, as was described by us in obscure fashion also in what went before. The prophet, remember, said he had seen "Joshua the high priest standing before an angel of the Lord, and the devil standing at his right hand to oppose him."[12] After all, you would not doubt that as far as lay in him and was in his power he had fought and struggled in vile fashion against the Incarnation of the Savior, who was inviting the world under heaven to salvation, since you understood that he first made his approach to him while he was fasting in the desert; on seeing him saving the world under heaven, he wanted him to present himself as his worshiper, displaying to him "all the kingdoms of the world"[13] and saying that everything would be his if he chose to bow down and worship him. Then he went further and actually snatched the treacherous disciple from the actual band of the holy apostles,[14] persuading him to become an instrument of the Jews' ferocity.

So the verse actually rebukes him in these words, *Who are you, mighty mountain before Zerubbabel, to achieve anything?* The question *Who are you?* is not to be taken as though he wanted to find out who he was and where he came from, since as God he was not unaware. Rather, it is as if he were belittling him and giving him no importance, even if he were *a mighty mountain,* irresistible and blocking the way of Christ in his wish to achieve such things, Zerubbabel being a type of him, as we remarked above. You see, even though the rebellious dragon offered implacable resistance, (336) it was trampled underfoot by Christ without trouble or difficulty, since he was by nature God, who overcomes everything. So we either address ourselves to the words in some such way, or even in a different way if it is acceptable. We said, remember, that it would not be by human power that life would be restored to the world, the lampstand would be upright that holds the lamp—Christ, that is—the lights would shine, and the two olive trees would take their position to the right and left of the lamp, signifying two peoples. Then it is as if someone were asking the question, *Who*

12. Zec 3.1.
13. Mt 4.8.
14. Cf. Jn 13.27.

are you who promise in this way to perform great deeds without any fighting or effort? The God and Father replies in the words, I am the *mighty mountain before Zerubbabel, to achieve,* that is, I am the nature surpassing everything, which to an extent proper to God surpasses everything in the glory it emits, and is destined in due course to effect the fulfillment of the promises even *before Zerubbabel.* Christ, of course, far from being ignorant of his own Father, made him, as it were, an associate in his own achievements in the words, "I do nothing of myself; rather, the Father who sent me abides in me, and it is he who does the works."[15] In other words, it was as if in his own power that he acted through the Son, through whom also in the beginning he is rightly admired for bringing everything into being.

Now, we mentioned that the God and Father is given the name *mountain* likewise by the most wise Daniel, and it is from him that "a stone was cut without human hands, and it crushed the gold, the silver, the bronze, the (337) iron,"[16] and it too was a type of Christ, the Son coming from God the Father in a manner surpassing word or thought, and crushing all kingdoms so that now their control is in his hands. Scripture says, remember, "To him every knee will bend, and every tongue confess that Jesus Christ is Lord to the glory of God the Father." So it was from the *mountain* of the God and Father that the Son was cut as cornerstone and chosen stone,[17] and came as our *inheritance;* we were called to sonship through him, and became heirs of the living God, gaining *an equality of grace* for *grace.*

What is the actual sense of that expression? *Grace* was given to Israel, in fact, that ancient and celebrated grace: they were ransomed from Egypt in a physical sense, to their own advantage they shook off the slavery imposed on them, they passed through the sea, they ate the manna in the desert, they thus crossed the Jordan, they entered the land of promise. So this was really the first grace. But in both *equality* and similarity to that ancient grace another grace has been given to us by Christ, who proved to be for us a stone, a foundation or cornerstone, and likewise an inheritance, for through him we are God's

15. Jn 8.28; 14.10.
16. Dn 2.45.
17. Phil 2.10–11; 1 Pt 2.6.

heirs.[18] So how does the second grace bear an *equality* to the first? That which was done for those people in a fleshly or material way Christ performed for us both spiritually and immaterially.[19] He rescued us from the slavery of the devil as though from mud and brick, he freed us from passions in the world and from fleshly impurities, he made us pass over as if through the sea—in other words, we escaped the flood of the (338) present life and the bitterness of its cares—we ate bread from heaven (in a eucharistic sense), we were transported over the Jordan, we received circumcision in the Spirit, we inherited the city on high, the truly holy land, which Christ himself also mentioned in the words, "Blessed are the meek, for they will inherit the land."[20]

Now, in my view, the most wise evangelist John intended to convey the same point in saying of Christ, "Of his fullness we have all received, grace upon grace; the Law was given through Moses, grace and truth came through Jesus Christ."[21] That is, while Moses was minister and mediator of that former grace, Christ is in fact the source of the latter, bearing a likeness to it. There were types of the reality, or at least giving birth to the beauty of the reality, which, however, is as much better and more outstanding as what is spiritual properly surpasses what is material. Paul also confirms this in writing, "Jesus has become guarantor of a better covenant."[22]

The word of the Lord came to me saying, The hands of Zerubbabel laid the foundations of this house, and his hands will complete it. You will acknowledge that the Lord almighty has sent me to you (vv.8–9). Lo, he conveys to us under material things once again what is spiritual, presenting what was completed at that time by *hand of Zerubbabel* as a type of what was performed in remarkable manner through Christ. You see, when the city of Babylon was taken by the Persians and Cyrus, and the people of Israel were released from the bonds of captivity (339) and actually even returned to Jerusalem when Darius took control of the Chaldeans and then the throne, God ordered the returned

18. Rom 8.17.
19. Cyril's terms are *pneumatikōs* and *noētōs.*
20. Mt 5.5.
21. Jn 1.16–17.
22. Heb 7.22.

exiles to rebuild the divine Temple straightway, with Zerubbabel as king and the high priest Joshua son of Jehozadak acting as priest. Whereas they set to work, and the project reached the first layers of the foundations and the walls had reached a certain height, there then intervened opposition from some people and obstacles arising from the envy of the neighboring nations, and an interruption occurred in their enthusiasm and a delay in their work. When God allowed them once more the ability to finish the work, the Temple was completely finished, with Joshua as priest and Zerubbabel in charge and on the throne.

With this summary there is sufficient treatment of the facts. Since, on the other hand, Zerubbabel is presented to us as a type of Christ, being from the tribe of Judah, come now, let us explain how and in what way he began to build the Temple of the Lord, and again how he performed the task immaterially and spiritually. In fact, he restored the house as it was originally as a dwelling suitable for him and the Father, the assembly of the Jews; this was the way God spoke of it through the all-wise Moses: "If one of you is a prophet for the Lord, I shall make myself known to him in a vision and speak to him in a dream. Not so with my servant Moses, who is faithful in all my house. With him I speak face to face, in bodily form, not in riddles."[23] So it was founded as a house through Christ, but destroyed in the meantime. The prophet (340) Jeremiah, for instance, lamented it as fallen and shaken, "The house of Israel has fallen, there is no one to restore it."[24] You see, since they vented their rage on Christ, it fell on that account, and there was no longer anyone to restore it. But it was raised again through Christ, and fitted out in a better way, with the entrance of the nations and the appearance in the world of the Church, "the house of the living God,"[25] of whose beauty the Lord and God of all has become fond. The fact that the temple raised up in the last days—that is, the Church—is incomparably better than the former temple God confirmed in the words of Haggai the prophet, "Is there a person among you who saw this house in its

23. Nm 12.6–8.

24. Am 5.1–2 (not Jeremiah).

25. Cf. 1 Tm 3.15.

previous glory? How do you see it now, as though not existing in your sight?" And later, "The latter glory of this house will be greater than the former, says the Lord almighty."[26]

You would be in no doubt of the folly of taking such references in a factual sense, however, if you were to wonder how the glory of the Temple in the latter times could be considered more wonderful than the former when Nebuchadnezzar the Babylonian burned and plundered it; and though it was rebuilt later after the period of captivity, the Romans no less fiercely put it to the flames and ravaged the actual city of Jerusalem and the Jews' whole country along with it. The factual interpretation, therefore, does not measure up to the reality; instead, the final glory is greater and more wonderful, where the Church is taken as "a holy temple, as a dwelling of God in the Spirit." We are, in fact, built "upon the foundation of the apostles (341) and prophets, joined and knit together with every ligament with which it is equipped for the working of each part," and, as it were, entering a union of faith and love with one another through the Spirit to build a holy temple, being living stones.[27] The divinely inspired Paul, for instance, speaks of the community of believers in one place as "God's field," again in another as "God's building," and says that he laid "the foundation stone like a skilled master builder,"[28] namely, Jesus the Christ, by whom we are all supported, through whom we all stand firm and are styled temples, with him as our mind and heart dwelling and abiding through the Spirit.

Because who was scornful for a short time? They will rejoice and see the tin stone in the hand of Zerubbabel. These seven eyes are the Lord's, looking down on the whole earth (v.10). The vision is not in reference to what would immediately happen, but rather of what would bear on the future, at the time of the coming of Christ the Savior of us all. While this coming happened in the last times of the present age, it was not a long period after the events of the prophecy before us, or the rebuilding of the Temple erected by *the hand of Zerubbabel.* So if anyone was really *scornful,* he is saying, *for the short time* in between, which was easily calculated, and considered the delay brief, they would not be depressed by this, but would be

26. Hg 2.3, 9.

27. Eph 2.20–22; 4.16; cf. 1 Pt 2.5.

28. 1 Cor 3.9–11.

filled with satisfaction of every kind, *rejoicing and seeing the tin stone in the hand of Zerubbabel.*

Now, by *the tin stone* he referred to (342) Christ; if you wanted to learn the reason, I would quickly state what some people think and what is the correct opinion on our part as well. Some commentators, in fact, say that tin is an amalgam of bronze and lead, and for this reason it is not completely devoid of toughness nor is it found to be without softness. For our part, too, we speak of Emmanuel in some such way as being composed both of unbreakable divinity and of a humanity that is, as it were, vulnerable to suffering.[29] Now, it should be realized that they also claim that a diamond can easily be cut with lead, although resistant to this effect from any other material. So we claim that although Christ is very kind and all-powerful and shows no severity as God, like a diamond he fractures Satan, of whom it is written, "His heart is immovable like stone, set firm like a steady anvil."[30] Other commentators as well are actually of the opinion that tin, or lead, is required to be used in purifying other materials by fire, and this practice is in particular both helpful and necessary for silversmiths. God somewhere says through the prophet Jeremiah again, for instance, in making the same point obscurely, "In vain was the blowing with fire, in vain lead, to no purpose the silversmith worked the silver, their vices were not eliminated."[31] He therefore compares Christ to tin or lead as eliminating impurities, getting rid of superfluities, as purifying in a spiritual sense.

So, he is saying, if anyone is indifferent to the interval of the intervening period, and considers of no importance (343) the short time in between, *they will rejoice and see the tin stone in the hand of Zerubbabel.* What is the actual meaning of *in the hand of Zerubbabel?* The divinely inspired Scripture takes *hand* in the sense of power and authority.[32] It is therefore by the power and authority of Zerubbabel—that is, Christ—that *they will see the tin stone,* Zerubbabel being from the tribe of Judah, as I said,

29. In this passage there is repeated use of dyophysite expressions about Jesus.

30. Jb 41.24.

31. Jer 6.29 LXX.

32. Author and text of Scripture are *theopneustos,* Cyril frequently reminds us.

and king over Israel. In just the same way our Lord Jesus Christ also sprang from the blood and tribe of Judah according to the flesh, and he too was king over Israel, not in our fashion of having a limited and chronologically determined kingship, but as God in true fashion of having a kingdom that extends for ages without end. The blessed Gabriel will confirm this in speaking to the holy Virgin about him, that she will bear a son and call him Jesus; he continued, "The Lord God will give him the throne of his father David, and he will reign over the house of Israel forever, and his kingdom will have no end."[33] It is in *the hand of Zerubbabel*, therefore—that is, in the power and authority of Zerubbabel—that the *tin stone* will be seen in due time.

Immediately following on this is the verse from the prophecy, *These seven eyes are the Lord's, looking down on the whole earth.* What would these in turn be? Either the seven lights which he saw with the lamp and now calls *eyes of the Lord*, for us to take them as the saints through whom the whole earth is illumined and is seen to be accorded a visit from God. Or I think we shall say it has the following meaning: that (344) the God and Father of all would not neglect his own creation, instead surveying everything with many unsleeping eyes, as it were, and granting those on earth the *tin stone*, that is, Christ, through whom he came to us in a manner of visitation or contemplation; "the dawn from on high has broken in upon us," in the scriptural text. And since we are "the body of Christ and individually members of it,"[34] I do not think it unlikely that he means that the spiritual guides act as eyes in seeing better and more eminently than others, and consequently are called bishops, as I believe. It is through them that our Lord Jesus Christ contemplates those who believe in him.

Actually, our Lord Jesus Christ could be understood as the *tin stone* in another fashion as well: tin binds together things that are separated, having a naturally adhesive quality. Now, Christ had an effect like that on us, too, if this is true, so that "he creates one new humanity in place of the two peoples, making

33. Lk 1.31–33. The parallel of the two kings, of course, as noted above, rests on the faulty designation of Zerubbabel as king in the LXX of Hg 1.1.

34. Lk 1.78; 1 Cor 12.27.

peace and reconciling both in one body"[35] to achieve unity in the Spirit. Hence his also being called "cornerstone," binding the two peoples into one, as I said. He also related people on earth to angels, and related us to the God and Father in himself by destroying the sin that lay between us and of old cut us off.

In reply I asked him, What are these two olive trees on the right of the lampstand and on its left? I asked a second time and said to him, What are the two branches of the olive trees in the hands of the two golden pipes that (345) *pour out and bring back the golden cups? He said to me, Do you not know what they are? I said, No, Lord. And he replied, These are the two sons of plenty, who stand in attendance on the Lord of all the earth* (vv.11–14). The mind of the saints is very anxious to learn; accordingly, the prophet passes over nothing revealed in the vision, instead being very curious, and he asks precisely about each item as to its meaning. It was therefore necessary for one of this attitude to declare through the voice of the prophet[36] what meaning was conveyed by the position of the olive trees on the right and left of the lamp—hence his curiosity and wish to find out.

Now, observe how he proposes the question a second time, and actually changes the form of the question to obtain certainty. At first, you see, he spoke of *two olive trees;* but directing the mind's eye somewhat more precisely to what was seen, he no longer spoke of *olive trees* but rather *branches of the olive trees.* So the blessed angel now skillfully makes a clear response to his question, saying, *These are the two sons of plenty, who stand in attendance on the Lord of all the earth.* By *sons of plenty* he definitely meant the two peoples, that of Israel and the one from the nations, in that they are brought to spiritual plenty.[37] Consequently, he says he saw them in the *pipes* of the lights, rejoicing and luxuriating in the oil from Christ and richly nourished by the grace of the Spirit; we are the object of mercy, you see, "justified by his grace as a gift," and consecrated as "sharers in the divine nature" (346) through participation in the Holy Spirit.[38] Hence in both the oil and the lights there

35. Eph 2.15–16.
36. Here Pusey reads "prophet" for the "angel" of the PG ed.
37. This sentence does not appear in the PG ed.
38. Rom 3.24; 2 Pt 1.4.

is recognized the establishment and the attendance of the two peoples: in the light there is our calling, as it is also in the oil, which is from God, since it is true to say that we were shown mercy and freed from death and sin, and our necks were loosed from the ancient slavery; we were also illumined, acknowledging the one God who is divine by nature, and emerging from the darkness of the error of polytheism.

Come now, however, let us investigate the sense of the observation, and what the blessed prophet understood by not needing to continue to say "olive trees," but *branches of the olive trees*. The synagogue of the Jews had been styled a cultivated olive, and the vast number of the nations a wild olive; this is the way blessed Paul mentioned them, saying to the believers from the nations, "If you have been cut from what is by nature a wild olive tree, and grafted contrary to nature on a cultivated olive tree, much more will these natural branches be grafted back into their own olive tree."[39] So the synagogue is a cultivated olive, as I just said, and the flock of the nations a wild olive: the former, though instructed by the Law, remained fruitless, whereas the latter were a hive of wild wasps, their minds full of demons and completely fruitless. It was not the whole Synagogue of the Jews, however, that accepted faith in Christ, nor in fact did all the vast number of the nations; instead, a great number were shown mercy as though snatched from each group, and were called through faith into illumination by the Spirit. So those who were snatched could rightly be called olive trees, because they were shown mercy through (347) grace, and found themselves, as it were, in the light of the lamp, that is, Christ, and of the seven lights shining together, that is, the vast number of the saints.

Now, observe how the divinely inspired angel takes the lamp as a type and image of Emmanuel: with the branches placed to right and left of him, and being called *the two sons of plenty*, he says they *stand in attendance on the Lord of all the earth*, their standing suggesting very clearly spiritual relationship and the readiness of the free will to submit to duty and serve him. This is the way, in fact, that Christ would be understood presenting to himself the Church,[40] which is composed of two peoples. In my

39. Rom 11.24.

40. Eph 5.27.

view, it was in this fashion that the divinely inspired Moses was also honored with the mention of standing, God saying to him, "But you, stand here with me": instruction through the Law was not abrogated by the God who knows everything. For what reason? It gives guidance to Christ, and, as by types and shadows, it gives birth to the truth itself in us. The Son himself will confirm this to us in saying to the unbelieving Jews, "If you believed Moses, you would believe me, for it was about me that he wrote."[41]

41. Dt 5.31; Jn 5.46.

COMMENTARY ON ZECHARIAH, CHAPTER FIVE

I turned around, lifted up my eyes and looked, and, lo, a scythe flying. He said to me, What do you see? I replied, I see a scythe flying, twenty cubits in length and ten cubits in breadth. He said to me, This is the curse that issues forth on the face of all the earth, because every thief will be punished from this point to the moment of death, and every perjurer (348) *will be punished from this point to the moment of death. I shall bring it forth, says the Lord almighty, and it will enter the house of the thief and the house of the one swearing falsely in my name; it will cause destruction in the middle of his house and topple it, its timbers and its stones* (vv. 1–4).

AGAIN IN THIS CASE, in my view, you would not take the phrase *I turned around* in reference to place, but rather to a change to another vision. After identifying the first vision, remember, and when his sight turned to the next, he used the term *turned around* to suggest what took place. So he lifts *the eyes* of his mind on high, and then sees a *scythe* like a bird raised on high and, as it were, darting across the whole earth. It was very long and broad, twenty cubits long and half that number in breadth. Now, when he proceeded to ask what it was and admitted to not knowing, he said, *This is the curse that issues forth on the face of all the earth,* inflicting upon *the perjurer* the punishment befitting him and upon *the thief* along with him. There is no difficulty as far as a more obvious explanation of the revelation goes: a divine *curse* will in all its gravity and without reprieve be directed at thieves and in addition to them at those in the habit of taking false oaths; by shearing the violators with a scythe, as it were, it will turn them into thatch for roofs, and feed them as fuel for the fire, *enter the house* of such a man, proceed to topple and shake it severely. (349)

I think it is necessary to busy ourselves in scholarly fashion with the reasons why the present vision in the text before us is included with the others. Why is it, a fair-minded person might ask, that of the huge number of faults in daily life and as well the actual involvement of the Israel of that time in different crimes, it says that the punishment of the scythe is imposed only on thieves and perjurers, or at least the curse will enter, cutting down those it catches and completely *toppling* them? Our reply to such questions is that God through the holy prophets makes a response that fits each occasion, always benefiting in some way the current situation. It was therefore necessary for the people of the time in particular that the vision be clarified; we shall provide the reasons, and demonstrate that it was timely.[1] The people of Israel had just left Chaldea, remember, had laid aside the yoke of slavery, had returned to Judea, and were in Jerusalem. They should have abandoned those ancient faults, reformed past behavior with recourse to better ways, and given joy to their Redeemer by opting to perform what was pleasing to him; but they continued the same as ever, heedlessly violating the prescriptions of the Law. Though Moses had forbidden them to have relations with foreign women,[2] in fact, they paid little attention to his decrees, involving their daughters with the neighboring nations, fathering children to foreigners, and once again filling the holy city with unholy offspring.

There were also, however, some of the more conspicuous among them who (350) remained aloof from such faults; Ezra deplored the events, occupying the divine house and offering prayers for the offenders. There then occurred something which we know from what was written by him,[3] as follows: "When Ezra was praying and making his confession, weeping and lying on the ground in front of the Temple, there gathered around him a very great crowd from Jerusalem, men and women and youths, for there was great weeping among the multitude. Shechaniah son of Jehiel, one of the men of Israel, called out and said to Ezra, We have sinned against the Lord

1. On this passage, as on some others, Cyril finds grounds for detecting the historical situation that prompted the vision.

2. Dt 7.3.

3. For the churches of Alexandria and Antioch at this time, 1 Esdras is perhaps a canonical work. We find Cyril citing it occasionally and Theodoret (alone in Antioch) also citing it three times in his OT works.

and have married foreign women from the nations of the land, and all Israel is now beyond hope. Let us take an oath to the Lord about this to banish all our wives from foreign nations with their children, in your judgment and that of all who obey the Law of the Lord. Rise up and take action: it is up to you, and we are on your side in adopting strong measures. Ezra rose up and made the leaders of the priests and Levites of the whole of Israel swear to do this, and they swore."[4]

When they swore to perform the decrees of the Law, therefore, it was necessary to hang the *curse* harshly over the heads of those who normally broke the oath, the purpose being for them to prove observant of what was sworn. In the rebuilding of the divine Temple, however, there was a collection of a great deal of money, Darius contributing some and the people providing the rest. Then it probably happened that some of the people (351) appointed to administer it embezzled some of what had been provided for the glory of God. Consequently, he was very right to say also that a *curse* was directed at thieves so that they too might forfeit their base profiteering and keep their hands off the sacred funds instead of spending it for their own needs.

This, then, was the occasion of the vision. I claim that those in the habit of stealing and breaking oaths had to dread the curse and the blade of the scythe in the realization that God would unquestionably bring to fulfillment all his decrees, and would not spare thieves or in fact other criminals. He never fails, you see, to render abominable those who scorn his divine glory and those who with insatiable greed hanker after what does not belong to them.

The angel speaking in me came out and said to me, Raise your eyes and see what it is that is issuing forth. I replied, What is it? He answered, It is a measure that is issuing forth, and he said, This is their injustice in all the earth. Lo, a leaden weight lifted, and, lo, a woman seated in the middle of the measure. He said, She is iniquity. He pushed her into the middle of the measure, and thrust the leaden weight into her mouth (vv.5–8). I originally began the clarification of the prophet by saying that after the return from Babylon he helpfully explained to those released what he saw in the period

4. 1 Esdras 8.91–96.

of captivity. That is to say, he had seen them very indifferent about needing to discharge the requirements of the Law, (352) and unrestrainedly inclined to what was enjoyable and pleasing to themselves while on the other hand little concerned about the laws given through Moses. For instance, they had had relations with foreign women, and some even had completely exceeded customary practices by worshiping idols and in addition committing sins it is not proper to mention. Consequently, the prophet gave an explanation of what was seen so that those just released might understand that despite all the prayers of human beings and holy angels to which they were indebted for the event, they were once more inciting the God of all against them and involving themselves in their former injurious faults.

He said, then, *The angel speaking in me came out.* Came out from where? Where was he, anyhow? There has thus been something of an exit from the time of the revelation of the scythe to the present vision, namely, the one to do with the measure. The prophet in fact *raises his eyes,* which would normally be appropriate for observing the divine mysteries in the case of those concerned to traverse the heights. He accordingly asked the meaning of what was revealed. He replied to him, *It is a measure that is issuing forth. This is their injustice in all the earth.* The meaning of the measure we must consider. We claim, in fact, that the Lord of all is by nature good and kind, showing forbearance to those who sin, being tolerant to those who transgress, awaiting each person's repentance. If, however, you were to go on sinning at length and thus reach the limit of the tolerance allowed you, then you would be subject to punishment, no excuse would be given you for protracted indifference, nor would you be excused from the need to pay equal dues for what you were shown to have committed. (353) Christ said somewhere, for instance, to the Jewish populace who with unrestrained folly betook themselves to all kinds of unseemly behavior, "Fill up the measure of the ancestors."[5] The measure that was seen, therefore, had the purpose of bringing out the accumulation of the sins of the peoples against him.

Now, seated in the measure was *a woman* who acted as a type

5. Mt 23.32.

of *injustice*, filling up, as it were, by herself the capacity, perhaps even over the limit, and peeping out from the overflow. And, the text says, *Lo, a leaden weight lifted, and he thrust it into her mouth.* Now, the vision properly conveys to us in some fashion *iniquity* under the guise of a woman, the woman acting as a type of pleasure and as well, to be sure, of weakness. All iniquity is committed in no other fashion than as a result of some pleasure enticing us to depravity, with weakness affecting the mind in addition to it. Had the mind been firm and virile of itself, in fact, it would not have chosen to experience the influence towards depravity, whereas when it is beguiled and entranced in the direction of pleasure, it comes to grief. The woman is described, then, and very accurately, as *iniquity*.

The *leaden weight lifted up* and actually blocking *her mouth* should, in my view, be taken as nothing other than our Lord Jesus Christ, who was lifted up by the precious cross, "bore our sins in his body on the tree," and canceled the record against us, so that, in the words of the divinely inspired melodist, "every iniquity blocked its mouth."[6] Now, he is likened to *lead* as well; lead is used, as I remarked, by silversmiths for purifying what is being (354) molded—something like the force of Christ in us: if he is found in our mind and heart, he completely expunges every stain. Now, it is the opinion of some commentators that *the leaden weight was thrust into the mouth of iniquity* as though God were blocking it and not allowing sinners to cry aloud beyond measure any more. Consequently, it is roped in by a *measure*, God, in my view, in his mercy for everything measuring the penalties for each one by the sins committed.

I lifted up my eyes and saw, and, lo, two women issuing forth, and wind in their wings. They had wings like a stork's wings. They lifted up the measure between earth and heaven. I said to the angel speaking in me, Where are they taking the measure? He replied to me, To build a

6. 1 Pt 2.24; Col 2.14; Ps 107.42. Cyril's hermeneutical process is clear in comment on this vision: first he sketches the historical background of the exiles, and then he adopts a procedure of interpretation-by-association, searching for other (OT and NT) occurrences of terms like "lifted up," "iniquity," "measure," "blocking the mouth," all of which encourages or allows him to introduce a Christological dimension. He does not dogmatize in arriving at the interpretation: it is "in my view."

house for it in the land of Babylon and furnish it; they will set it down there on its furnishings (vv.9–11). What meaning is intended by the pair of women, or of what they are a type, I think it necessary to explain even before anything else. The God of all said to the prophet Ezekiel, then, "Mortal, there were two women, daughters of one mother. They played the whore in Egypt, they played the whore in their youth, their breasts fell there." To clarify the story, he proceeds from that point to add, "As for their names, Oholah is Samaria, and Oholibah is Jerusalem."[7] (355) In other words, one was the assembly of the Jews in former times; at the time of the reign of Rehoboam the ten tribes were torn away from the others and occupied Samaria, where they played the whore with the golden calves, which Jeroboam son of Nebat had made. But the other, namely, Jerusalem, was not free of blame,[8] itself also playing the whore in many ways: some worshiped idols and sacrificed to Baal, Astarte, the hills, the sun, the moon, and the other stars; others gave themselves eagerly to every form of impurity, and set no store by the decrees of the all-wise Moses.

The vision also makes a comparison, therefore, of the two communities of Israel to *two women,* who it says had *a stork's wings,* the purpose being to make a very clear suggestion that the will in them was impure and readily inclined to every form of unseemly behavior. The stork, you know, is an ostrich, known for being fond of mud and dung, venting its fury on heaps of worms, and accustomed to make extreme impurity its food. Idolaters have a mind rather like this: instead of making directly for what is seemly, it departs from the normal, has no knowledge of the divine law, is full of every uncleanness, and takes delight in every form of depravity. Consequently, the account of the vision said that *a stork's wings* were fitted to the women, conveying the fact that the same attitude resided in it and them.

Now, they *take up the measure* full of iniquity. (356) Every soul, after all, has to be burdened with its own weight—of sin, that is. Since the crimes of the sisters—I mean Samaria and Jerusa-

7. Ezek 23.2–4.

8. While the PG ed. suggests there is a lacuna at this point, Pusey retains this form of the text, though noting discrepancy in the manuscripts.

lem—were common to both and of equal gravity, consequently they were loaded in the same way with both measure and iniquity, *the wind* striking *their wings*, and they moved with rapid and unfettered course towards the land of the foreigners—clearly, that of the Babylonians.[9] You see, with the impure wind propelling them into sin, and being burdened with iniquity, they were transported into captivity and fell under the feet of the foe. Since the blessed angel says that *they will take the measure to build a house for it in the land of Babylon*, however, we must take this as a sign of the prolonged residence of the people of Israel among the foe, namely, both the building of a house for iniquity and its seat and station, as it were, being among the foe. This is what actually came to pass: at the very expiration of their seventieth year they were released from the bonds of captivity.

9. Cyril is trying to maintain a connection with the situation of the exiles.

COMMENTARY ON ZECHARIAH, CHAPTER SIX

I turned around, lifted up my eyes and saw, and, lo, four chariots coming out between two mountains, and the mountains were mountains of bronze. In the first chariot were red horses, in the second chariot black horses, in the third chariot white horses, and in the fourth chariot piebald horses of dapple-grey. I asked in reply to the angel speaking in me, What are they, Lord? In reply the angel speaking in me said, They are the four winds of heaven issuing forth to attend on the Lord of all (357) *the earth. The chariot with the black horses issued forth to the north country, the white issued forth after them, the piebald issued forth to the south country, the dapple-grey issued forth and searched where to gaze and roam the earth. And they roamed the earth. He cried out and spoke to me thus, Lo, those issuing forth to the north country have set at rest my anger with the north country* (vv. 1–8).

HE PREVIOUSLY showed that, snared in their own nets and constrained by the cords of their own sins, as Scripture puts it, they were deported to a foreign land and dwelt among the foe, bearing the unfamiliar yoke of slavery. It was necessary, however, to mention also the time of release, and he actually does suggest it, interweaving other things; the prophet had been given overall instruction in everything that would happen to the nation in due course.

The *four chariots between two mountains*, then, we claim again to be the kingdoms that were more famous than the others and located in the four quarters, or winds, under heaven, which are highlighted at different times. In my view, the *bronze mountains* refer to the two halves of the world, some people dividing the whole earth into Europe and Asia. Its halves are *bronze*, doubtless on account of their stability on all sides, their immobility, and being proof against any damage. The divinely inspired David, remember, also sings to the Lord of all, (358) "You established the earth, and it abides."[1] So these kingdoms are, as it were, *from*

1. Ps 119.90.

the four winds, stouter than the others, as I said; they enjoyed a higher reputation and *issued forth to attend on the Lord of all the earth.* Their *attending* suggests to us the manner of their servitude: they serve his wishes, and if they are strong and famous, this advantage accrues to them through him. If they performed any deed and plundered countries and cities, it was again only with his permission that they achieved this degree of force. After all, if what the prophet says is true, "There will be no evil in the city for which the Lord was not responsible" (where we speak of trouble as "evil"),[2] how would they prevail over nations and countries without once more his granting the power as part of his plan?

Now, it is time to explain as well which in fact are the kingdoms. *In the first chariot were red horses,* it says, then, representing the cruelty of the kingdom of the Chaldeans, red appropriately suggesting bloodshed to us. The Babylonians, in fact, were very bloodthirsty, capturing Judea and the cities in Samaria, with no quarter given. *In the second chariot black horses,* probably suggesting the kingdom of the Medes and Persians, that is, under Cyrus, black being the color in which they were invested, doubtless on account of the exorbitant and immeasurable slaughter they inflicted on the nations of the Chaldeans, in my view, and the great grief they caused the country; so their appearance would symbolize mourning and death. *In the third chariot* there were *white horses,* he says, perhaps suggesting the rule of Greeks and Macedonians, or (359) the kingdom of Alexander—*white* both because of effeminacy and because the nations of the Greeks were clad almost entirely in white clothing, and because they were clear in their speech, not having the darkness, as it were, of the barbarians' language. *In the fourth chariot* there were some *piebald horses of dapple-grey.* Now, it should be realized that the Hebrew text and some of the other translators put "strong" for *dapple-grey.* But we also claim that this is the kingdom of the Romans, which constantly has among its rulers at various times a variety of skill and a seriousness of purpose; they were and are very intelligent and in addition very powerful, controlling as they did the might of the Roman rule. They are also placed last after the preceding ones in chronological order.

2. Am 3.6.

Now, let us see also the departure of each of the chariots, or kingdoms, where it headed and in which direction it went; in this way the explanation of the meanings would become clearer. While the prophet said there were four, in fact, he mentions the departure of three and says nothing of the fourth.[3] I shall briefly repeat what I said. Whereas he said there were *red* horses in the first chariot, he begins with the second, saying, *The chariot with the black horses issued forth to the north country, the white issued forth after them, the piebald issued forth to the south country;* but although he adds *the dapple-grey*, this does not total four chariots, for we quoted them as the same as the piebald, saying, *in the fourth chariot piebald horses of dapple-grey*. So he has mentioned three, saying nothing of the fourth. So what the basis is of the (360) whole arrangement, come now, let us explain to the more studious as far as we can. We confirmed that the *red horses* are the bloodthirsty rule of the Chaldeans, which completely devastated Judea, burned its cities, and deported Israel into captivity. We took the *black* ones to be the kingdom of the Persians and Cyrus. In the expression *the white horses* are contained Alexander and Macedon; both of them attacked the land of the Chaldeans and took it by force, firstly Cyrus and then after him Alexander, who even overpowered Darius himself around the so-called Issus, a city of Cilicia, killing countless numbers of Persians; at any rate, they say a mighty pile of bones was heaped up of those who fell there, and an inscription was made to this effect:

> By the walls of Issus near the stormy billows of Cilicia
> We lie, countless hordes of Persians,
> The work of Alexander of Macedon,
> Following former king Darius on his last journey.[4]

Since it was likely, you see, that Israel would grieve to hear mention of the kingdom of the Chaldeans, under which they had been ravaged, consequently, lest they seem to be moved to grief,

3. Cyril notes this textual peculiarity. Our Heb. text has only three groups of horses going on errands; the LXX in vv.6–7 also loses sight of the errand of the red horses from v.2 and instead divides the fourth group of piebald and dapple-grey into two.

4. Though Aubertus in the PG ed. is silent about the origins of the epigram, Pusey identifies it as Antipatria Sidonii. It was Darius III who was defeated at Issus in 333.

and that at an untimely moment, the prophet graciously passes over reference to them. On the other hand, what cheered them up in particular he elaborated on conspicuously—namely, the reference to the kingdom of Cyrus and also of Alexander, who were sent, as it were, to requite the arrogance of the Chaldeans in showing cruelty to Israel itself. (361) Hence he proceeded to say, as if in God's person, *Lo, those issuing forth from*[5] *the north country have set at rest my anger with the north country,* the land of the Chaldeans being to the north, and the God of all being enraged with the Babylonians. This would likewise be clear as well from his openly stating, "I am extremely jealous for Jerusalem and Zion, and am extremely wrathful towards the nations who have conspired, the reason being that while I was slightly wrathful, they conspired with evil intent."[6] Since the land of the Chaldeans paid the penalty with the devastation of it, firstly by Cyrus with Persians and Medes, and after that by Alexander, he consequently says, *Those issuing forth to the north country have set at rest my anger with the north country.* The prophet from his overall standpoint, however, says nothing of the Chaldeans' attack, bypassing the red horses, whereas he did mention the events of the Roman rule, saying, *The piebald issued forth to the south country.*

Now, note how he skillfully and, as it were, in passing gives an explanation of the statement. After the crucifixion of the Savior, you see, Vespasian and his son Titus overran the land of the Jews, stripping it bare and setting fire to the holy city itself. The prophet, however, cleverly states, *They issued forth to the land of the south,* the land of the Jews being the most southern. Again, *the piebald and dapple-grey* were ordered to *roam the earth,* and in fact *they did roam:* they took control of the earth under heaven and dominated the whole earth, since God permitted it and invested with conspicuous glory those who administered Roman rule in this case, (362) as though God knew in advance the greatness of their future piety.

A word of the Lord came to me saying, Take from the rulers among those in the captivity, from its useful ones and those familiar with it. On that day enter the house of Josiah son of Zephaniah, who comes

5. This preposition does not occur in the lemma or below, but in Pusey's view is the correct reading here.

6. Zec 1.14–15.

from Babylon. Take silver and gold, make a crown, put it on the head of Joshua son of Jehozadak the high priest. You will say to him, The Lord almighty says this, Here is a man, Dawn by name, and it will rise beneath him, and he will rebuild the house of the Lord. He will receive virtue, will be seated and rule on his throne; the priest will be at his right hand, and a counsel of peace will be between them both. The crown will be for those who endure, its useful ones and those familiar with it, and as a gift for the son of Zephaniah and as a psalm in the house of the Lord. Those far distant from them will come and rebuild in the house of the Lord; and you will know that the Lord almighty has sent me to you. It will happen if you really hearken to the voice of the Lord your God (vv.9–15). The word from God was addressed to the blessed prophet Zechariah, or through him to everyone in the company of Zerubbabel, who was from the tribe of Judah and in charge of Israel, since the royal tribe summoned him to the role. As to the reference to him by God, we must say something by way of introduction. (363) He had said, then, "The hands of Zerubbabel laid the foundations of this house, and his hands will complete it."[7] But accompanying him in laying the foundations of the house and finishing it was also *Joshua son of Jehozadak the high priest.* Consequently, the God of all bade the divinely inspired prophet, *Take from the rulers among those in captivity, from its useful ones and those familiar with it.*

Now, who they were and what was *from the captivity* we shall properly explain. The people of Israel were brought back from Babylon, not in a confused mass, but with orderly decorum by clan and tribe, bringing with them associates and leaders, as is written in the book of Esdras.[8] When they then reached Jerusalem, and God obliged them to erect the Temple, they established a treasury so that the financial collections should fund the work, garments for the priests and the sacrifices determined for them by the Law. Josiah son of Zephaniah was appointed treasurer. The God of all, therefore, gave orders that from what had been brought *by the leaders from the captivity,* which had also been deposited with Josiah, *silver and gold be taken,* then *crowns* be made and placed by them *on the head of Joshua son of Jehozadak the high priest,* and the words said to him about

7. Zec 4.9.

8. Cf. 1 Esdras 2.

Zerubbabel, *Here is a man, Dawn by name.* Now, the Hebrew text conveyed the sense of *Dawn* by the word "shoot": *and it will rise beneath him;* that is, (364) a great deal will spring up from his root. *He will receive virtue,* that is, comeliness or glory, the way the other translators rendered it.[9] From this he proceeds to say that both Joshua and Zerubbabel will sit on the same throne, with the result that there will be sharing of kingship with the one who is entrusted with priesthood, and of priesthood with the one appointed as king. To both there will be *a counsel of peace,* such that there would be no difference of opinion at all.

He next ordered the *crowns* be made and brought as a splendid offering to God in his house to be a grace or boast of those making the offering—namely, Josiah, *the useful ones of the captivity and its rulers.*[10] They were to be offered, not without purpose but as an occasion for singing by the Temple singers and psalmists. Then it is, he says, that *those far distant from them*—namely, those from the other nations—*will come* and adore the Lord. Such things will happen, he says, if they choose to lend themselves the attraction of obedience, and *hearken to the voice of the Lord God.* Then, with the prophecies fulfilled, *you will know* in all clarity that the prophet was sent to make God's will clear, and not (as some of those claim who are addicted to lying) to speak from his own heart[11]—rather the truth, not as a false messenger.

While this is the obvious and superficial interpretation of the factual events, it is clear that no one would doubt that, if interpreted closely, the event has to do with the mystery of Christ.[12] We confirmed (365) at the beginning, remember, that

9. Cyril apparently has found in Jerome information (not provided at 3.8) that behind the "Dawn" of the LXX lies a Heb form that can be rendered "branch." He could have learned this from Symmachus (we learn from Theodoret), but only turns to these alternative versions for the next phrase. But, he concludes, both the Heb. and the faulty version are compatible.

10. This time the LXX version, though clearly puzzling Cyril (he will rationalize it below), does not lead him to look to Jerome for the meaning of the Heb., where there occur the proper names Heldai, Tobijah, and Jedaiah, rendered in the LXX as personal attributes. The Antiochene text—typically—includes both, though its commentators are also unaware of the doublets. Cyril is trying hard to relate the text to the historical situation.

11. Cf. Jer 23.16.

12. Having stayed for a considerable time with the face value of the text, Cyril develops a fuller meaning. This is not the Pauline sense of the term "mystery of Christ," which suggests rather the divine plan in which Jews and Gentiles

Christ has taken physical form at least in Zerubbabel and of course also in Jesus, individually in each and together in both as one. In the same person, in fact, there is both king of Israel and great "high priest, holy, blameless, undefiled."[13] But since those of the tribe of Judah administered the resources of the kingdom while those from the tribe of Levi were appointed to priesthood, and oversight of both kingdom and priesthood was not given to the one, consequently by a wise arrangement Christ takes single form in the two. If God were to say of Zerubbabel, therefore, "The hands of Zerubbabel laid the foundations of this house, and his hands will complete it," you would understand it of him in a rather factual sense, whereas you would refer to Christ the force of the mystery in an immaterial way, he being our foundation and all of us being built up spiritually in him into a holy temple. He it is who is our beginning and end; he presents us sanctified in spirit, a splendid and sacred dwelling place for himself and the Father, with sin completely erased and corruption eliminated. Jesus is the one, as I said, who is the high priest. On the one hand, "Jesus" means "salvation of the people"; the divinely inspired Gabriel also said somewhere to the holy Virgin, "Lo, you will conceive and bear a son, and you will call him Jesus, for he will save his people from their sins."[14] On the other hand, Jehozadak means "God's righteousness"; in him we have been justified through faith, and are washed clean of the stain of former sins. He rescued us when we were captives, (366) delivered us from spiritual slavery, and, as though from a strange land and the devilish error of foreigners, he brought us to the knowledge of God and to the beautiful city of the saints, the holy city of the true Jerusalem, which is the Church.

For this reason he is awarded *a crown* for our firm and unblemished faith, the credit of our virtue, and both hymns and thanksgiving. While the crowns at that time were *of gold and silver*, made from corruptible material, those plaited and awarded to us contain nothing earthly, being composed rather

---

together are included (cf. Eph 3). Cyril is rather thinking of the degrees to which figures like Zerubbabel and Joshua, and even Jesus, represent and even achieve some of the goals of that divine plan—liberation, sanctification of the people—and thus can claim to have the form of Christ (the verb *demorphousthai* thus having a sense roughly equivalent to "being incarnate").

13. Heb 7.26.

14. A conflation of Lk 1.31, Mt 1.21.

of the glory befitting God. What we offer him as gold, in fact, is the undistorted understanding of the doctrines about him, and as silver the spiritual splendor coming from good works. The crown and glory of Christ, on the other hand, can be taken in a different sense as the salvation of those saved by him; it was not a single nation that was saved, as Israel of course was saved formerly by Moses—rather, the whole world under heaven is now saved.

Now, consider how the materials for the making of the crowns are provided by *the rulers among those in captivity, by its useful ones and those familiar with it.* Those in charge of peoples, you see, and appointed to such offices by God, and those familiar with the manner of our former captivity and useful to the ransomed people in the role of guides and teachers in prescribing and providing adequately for a life in accord with law—these are the ones who offer gifts for everyone, thus supplying for the shortcomings of the disabled.[15] (367)

With the crowns placed *on the head of Joshua,* words are addressed to him in reference to Zerubbabel, *Here is a man, Dawn by name, and it will rise beneath him.* Having had a vision of Jesus crowned as priest, he now sees him excelling in the person of Zerubbabel in royal glory as well. Realize that it is he who is *Dawn,* that is, "branch," of whom the divinely inspired Isaiah says, "A shoot will spring up from the root of Jesse, and a bloom will spring up from the root."[16] It is we who blossom *beneath him:* Christ is the root of humanity, or those called in faith—the second root, not in the style of the first, namely, Adam, but incomparably better. We no longer blossomed to corruptibility and death because of the curse, you see, but to life and incorruptibility, since for our root we have life, that is, Christ. Just as he is "the vine, we the branches,"[17] attached to him through spiritual participation, so too he is shoot and branch, or growth and *dawn;* we have sprung up *beneath him,* grown and blossomed to incorruptibility and life, as I said.

It was he who *built the house of the Lord.* He is filled with every virtue, that is, glory most befitting God: "His virtue covered the

15. Apparently unaware that the LXX is offering occupational skills for the proper names in the Heb., Cyril rationalizes them.

16. Is 11.1.

17. Jn 15.5.

heavens, and the earth was full of his praise," according to the prophet Habakkuk. The wise John also wrote somewhere, "And we have seen his glory, (368) glory as of the Only-begotten of the Father, full of grace and truth."[18] It is he who *is seated on a throne:* he is enthroned with his own Father, and with him he rules all things. Now, the fact that Zerubbabel and Joshua are associated with one another, as it were, in a unity that very nicely suggested Christ, he brought out by proceeding to say in reference to Zerubbabel, *The priest will be at his right hand,* that is, in honor and glory, *and a counsel of peace will be between them both.* He is the one, you see, as I remarked earlier as well, who is both king and high priest, represented as Emmanuel, as one in two. The effort of those who assign the crown to Christ is not without reward, however: for them the yield will extend to everlasting remembrance. That the statement is true he establishes by adding, *The crown will be for those who endure, its useful ones and those familiar with it, and as a gift for the son of Zephaniah and as a psalm in the house of the Lord;* that is, it will be a gift for those who consecrated the offerings, and will also be an occasion for giving praise, the piety of the leaders proving to be for the others a path to love of God.[19]

With Christ crowned by us, it is then that the flock of the nations will betake themselves to knowledge of him, *and those far distant* on account of error will be called through faith and *will come and rebuild in the house of the Lord.* What will they rebuild? Themselves, obviously, by being attached to the saints, and joined by faith in unity with those from Israel, Christ being the cornerstone and joining together in a like mind through himself what was once divided. He caused "the two peoples to become one new person, making peace and reconciling in his body all things to the Father."[20] (369) When this comes to pass, we shall confirm the truth of the holy prophets, and have a clear realization that God was speaking in them and foretelling to us the mystery of Christ. (370)

18. Hab 3.3; Jn 1.14.

19. The version of the LXX continues to trouble Cyril.

20. Eph 3.20, 15–16. Because of Cyril's ecclesiological and Christological bent, Ephesians is a favored text. Comment on this chapter of Zechariah closes here, as does Cyril's second tome.

COMMENTARY ON ZECHARIAH, CHAPTER SEVEN

In the fourth year of King Darius the word of the Lord came to Zechariah on the fourth day of the ninth month, which is Chislev. He sent Sharezer and Arbeseer the king to Bethel, and his men with him, to placate the Lord, asking the priests in the house of the Lord almighty and the prophets, Has sanctification entered here in the fifth month as they did for many years in the past? (vv. 1–3).

AFTER THE occurrence of the visions, other words came from God at short intervals. Before the visions, for instance, the text says, "On the twenty-fourth day of the eleventh month, the month of Shebat, in the second year of Darius, the word of the Lord came to Zechariah son of Berechiah son of Iddo the prophet in these terms,"[1] whereas in the visions before us a different (371) time is specified after that: *In the fourth year on the fourth day of the ninth month, which is Chislev*—a Hebrew term, obviously—some kind of apparition came to the prophet. What the occasion was is very clearly explained by the account of the factual situation. Some commentators, in fact, would take no other view of it than what is in keeping with the form of the text in hand.[2] That is to say, it is obviously necessary to learn first of all the identity of *Sharezer and Arbeseer, and his men with him*, the nature of the *sanctification in the fifth month*, likewise the actual manner of interrogation, and the purpose of the speakers.

Hoshea son of Elah, then, was king of the ten tribes in Samaria, and very inclined to infidelity, worshiping idols and bringing God's wrath on Israel. Next, Shalmaneser king of the Assyrians invaded the country, took Samaria, deported Israel, and caused

1. Zec 1.7.

2. One problem for Cyril and other commentators is that the text of Heb. and LXX is suspect, the sense depending on division of Heb. words and recognition of proper names.

some of those from the country of the Chaldeans to occupy the land so that it might belong to the Persians through having occupants from there in future. You have a factual account in the second book of Kings: "In the twelfth year of King Ahaz of Judah, Hoshea son of Elah became king in Samaria over Israel, reigning nine years. He did what is evil in the eyes of the Lord, though not like the kings of Israel who were before him. Shalmaneser king of the Assyrians came up against him, and Hoshea became his vassal." And further on, "Israel was exiled from its own land until this day. The king of Assyria brought people from Babylon, (372) Cutha, Avva, Hamath, and Sepharvaim, and settled them in the cities of Samaria in place of the people of Israel; they took possession of Samaria and settled in its cities."[3] These people took the inheritance of the Samaritans, therefore, occupied the land, perhaps became parents of children and adopted the ways of the Jews, being in fear of attacks from the lions. Among them were *Sharezer and Arbeseer,* the latter being styled *king,* presumably because of his leadership at the time of those settled in Samaria from Persia.

So much for the men; as to the *sanctification,* come now, let us once more say what the likely scenario is. Before the capture of Judea by Nebuchadnezzar, then, the blessed prophet Joel had prophesied what would happen, and in fact bade the priests and, further, the peoples under them to grieve at the prospect of Jerusalem falling under the enemies' feet and even the divine Temple itself going up in flames. He spoke this way, "Gird yourselves and lament, you priests; mourn, you who serve at the altar; go, pass the night in sackcloth, you ministers of God, because your sacrifice and libation are withheld from the house of God. Sanctify a fast, preach a message of service, summon the elders and all occupants of the land to your God's house, and cry at length to God, Alas, alas for the day!"[4]

So much for the prophet; in what way the predictions took effect (373) I shall make clear by once more citing the sacred text itself. In the second book of Kings it reads this way: "In the fifth month on the seventh day of the month, which was the

3. 2 Kgs 17.1–3, 23–24.
4. Jl 1.13–15.

nineteenth year of Nebuchadnezzar king of Babylon, Nebuzaradan the captain of the bodyguard, who had a position before the king of Babylon, came to Jerusalem and burned down the house of the Lord, the house of the king, and all the houses of Jerusalem; the captain of the bodyguard burned down every house." He next appointed Gedaliah in charge of the populace of Israel; but in the seventh month Ishmael son of Nethaniah son of Elishama of the royal family won his confidence, and overcame and killed him, Scripture tells us.[5] Since, therefore, it happened *in the fifth month* and on the seventh day that Jerusalem was captured and the Temple was burned, and furthermore that Gedaliah had been killed in the seventh month, perhaps the remnants of the Jews were brought to remember the saying of the prophet and decreed that *in the fifth month* and on the seventh day of the month everyone from the surrounding district should go up to Jerusalem, observe a fast, exhibit grief as at a bereavement, in some way bewail the Temple, and shed tears in hindsight for the burning of the city. They thought they had thus most wisely come upon a manner of worship acceptable to God; but they still lived under the yoke of the captivity that had been imposed, no thought being given to the divine Temple.

When they returned after leaving the land of the Persians and Medes, (374) occupied the holy city, and then rebuilt the divine Temple, the practice no longer seemed to them to be appropriate and seemly. There was need, in fact, rather to move away from the past and in the direction of celebration, to perform the festivals and offer hymns of thanksgiving to the one who had called them to freedom. So the men referred to in the passage, *Sharezer and Arbeseer,* sent some people to ask *the priests and the prophets, Has sanctification entered here in the fifth month as they did for many years in the past*—that is, had those in the habit of grieving assembled in Jerusalem and adopted the practice performed in the manner of *sanctification* despite the rebuilding of the divine Temple and ending of captivity? As I said, they observed a fast, in fact, as they had done for many years; while Israel was in captivity, they continued to mark the time for griev-

5. 2 Kgs 25.8–9, 22, 25.

ing, and to observe the fast, as I remarked. It was therefore a question by people unsure whether they still had to perform the sanctification and the grieving, even after the rebuilding of the Temple, or abstain from grieving now that the reason did not apply.

The word of the Lord of hosts came to me: Say to all the people of the land and to the priests, If you fasted and lamented in the fifth and the seventh month, and this for seventy years, surely you did not fast for me? If you eat and drink, is it not for yourselves that you eat and (375) *drink? Are not these the words the Lord spoke by means of the prophets in former times when Jerusalem was inhabited and prosperous along with the cities round about, and the mountain country and the plains inhabited?* (vv.4–7) Some people were asking the priests and the prophets, as I mentioned before, about the so-called sanctification. God then replied when the priests and prophets were offering prayers as normal, and were anxious to give a clear reply to those asking to find out about such matters. What was the word that then came from God? Short and to the point, with no complications—instead, knowledge of its benefit was accessible and open to scrutiny, so to say. What was the good, he is saying, in fact, if perhaps *you fasted in the fifth and the seventh month?* What virtuous achievement was there in doing your mindless wailing over rubble and charred wood? How on earth would God take satisfaction in what was done by you when, after performing nothing for your benefit of what was required, you take the view that you have actually done the best possible? After all, if I require such fasting, and if wailing fit for a woman is deserving of commendation, what was the reason that for seventy years (he asks) you persisted in not fasting? (When they still lived among the Babylonians, in fact, they did no public fasting, nor would they have been found showing zeal in performance of any other of their customs and ways prescribed by the Law of Moses.) How is it that I then showed mercy, he says, (376) and rescued you from the hand of those in power? I therefore have no need of such fasting,[6] just as, of course, even if you chose to eat and drink (he says), it is not I whom

6. Pusey's text at this point supplies words admitted by Aubertus to be missing from the PG ed.

you gratify but yourselves. So your fasting is in vain and of no benefit, and your sweat and tears pointless and without reward. *Are not these the words the Lord spoke by means of the prophets in former times when Jerusalem was inhabited and prosperous,* overflowing with good things, taking pride in its own still unharmed *cities and the mountain country and the plains?*

The prophet Joel, in fact, had said that it behoves both priests and people to lament and, in addition to that, to sanctify a fast.[7] And the purpose of the exhortation was to summon them to repentance. His wish, you see, was not for them to wait to experience events so as to mourn the Temple after its burning, but before experience, as I have said, to placate God with weeping and wailing and thus escape the troubles. *Are not these the words of the prophets in former times,* then, of which you were ignorant when you lamented to no avail, shedding tears of ignorance over strewn stones, when you ought to have reformed the way of your own living and trodden the straight and narrow, clearly discerning the way to perform the decrees of the Law?

The word of the Lord came to Zechariah: Thus says the Lord almighty, Deliver a just judgment, show mercy and pity, each one to their brethren. Do not oppress widow and orphan, sojourner and poor person, (377) *and hold no grudge in your hearts, each of you against your brethren* (vv.8–10). After declaring grief anathema in being useless and of no benefit, and scoffing at their futile weeping, he now summons them to beneficial observance, rendering clear and obvious the way of life acceptable to him, and illuminating the sense of both Law and Prophets as his own. The lawgiver, you see, takes satisfaction in upright and blameless *judgment;* he honors with great enthusiasm *mercy* and mutual love, and regards as commendable the love for *orphans* and pity for women suffering the burden of widowhood. He outlaws greed and oppression of the weak, and wishes those of his mind to be kind and forgiving. Christ himself also said somewhere, "Forgive and you will have forgiveness," and actually taught them in their prayer to say, "Forgive us our debts as we forgive those indebted to us, and lead us not into temptation, but deliver us from evil."[8] The merciful

7. Jl 1.13–14.

8. Mt 6.12–14.

God, you see, forgives faults to others who forgive; "the ways of the unforgiving lead to death," according to the text of the book of Proverbs. Now, how could you doubt that love contains the fulfillment of the whole Law when the divinely inspired Paul writes to this effect?[9] The aforementioned are the fruit of love, and the one who performs them is a diligent observer of the Law.

They refused to give heed, they stupidly turned their backs, (378) *they blocked their ears against hearing, and made their hearts resistant to hearkening to my Law and the words the Lord almighty issued in his Spirit by means of the prophets of old. Great wrath came from the Lord almighty. It will happen this way: just as he spoke and they did not listen to him, so they will cry out and I shall not listen to them, says the Lord almighty. I shall expel them to all the nations that they have not known. And the land behind them will be bereft of anyone passing or abiding; they turned a chosen land into a wilderness* (vv.11–14). There is confirmation in this: that they did not desist from provoking the hostility of the judge of all against them. Though in fact they had the possibility of obeying the words of the holy prophets, generously rejecting as vigorously as possible opposition to the wishes of the lawgiver, embracing a peerless life in strict adherence to the Law, and treading a blameless path, they remained obdurate, set their teacher at naught, and kept their heart inflexible and unbending. They never ceased outrageously insulting the divine sayings and those who transmitted them and who exercised the role of prophecy, abusing them in a vile and unholy manner, even though they spoke through the Holy Spirit. They had already descended to such a degree of ferocity and lawless nonsense that they did not opt for repentance until the prophecies had taken effect on them and they became victim of what befell them through divine wrath.

Now, if in this text God says, *I shall expel them to all the nations,* (379) *and the land will be bereft of anyone passing or abiding,* let us take such words again as a case of inspired prediction.[10]

9. Prv 12.28 LXX; Rom 13.10.

10. It may be from Theodore that Cyril (like Theodoret) notes the future reference in these verses, arising from a common confusion by the LXX of tenses and moods in the Heb. These commentators sense there is a past reference in future forms, and that it is "the ancients" (as Cyril proceeds to say) who are

They were in fact driven out to the Persians and Medes, and they had already experienced captivity, their land was made desolate, and the best country of all *left bereft,* as the text says, with no one *passing or abiding:* some were wasted in war, others were subjected to the yoke of slavery and went off to captivity. So let us take this text to be recited like the others in the manner of prophecy. Now, the fact that disobedience to the divine sayings is disadvantageous or, rather, productive of ruin you could see even from what befell the ancients; and you would not need lengthy statements to prove it—instead, the facts are totally obvious, once a person knows the good results of obedience.

---

in focus. For them, of course, prophecy is always prospective, not involving commentary on present or past.

COMMENTARY ON ZECHARIAH, CHAPTER EIGHT

The word of the Lord almighty came to me saying, The Lord almighty says this: I am jealous for Jerusalem and Zion with a great jealousy, and am jealous for it with a great anger (vv. 1–2).

AFTER SUFFICIENTLY DEPLORING the people's former disobedience and recalcitrance and what resulted from it, and revealing that it was the source of all their troubles, he shifts his focus to the good that emerges from mildness. He then makes it his business to promise them times of prosperity and shower them abundantly with the good things they prayed for, now that they had paid the penalty for their unholy provocation, and were cleansed, as it were, from the charges of the former depravity through (378) punishment by foes and suffering the yoke of slavery. He decries, as it were, the cruelty of the Babylonians, who completely exceeded the bounds of audacity and committed against them what even the divine anger did not intend. He had said clearly, in fact, "While I was slightly wrathful, they conspired with evil intent."[1] Hence his saying, *I am jealous for Jerusalem*—that is, I show jealousy for it—*and am jealous for it with a great anger.* It is as though he were to say, It will be the Babylonians' lot in turn to suffer a worse fate than they delivered, and I shall vent on the plunderers the effects of my wrath.

Christ fulfilled this prophecy: distressed at our being lost in misery, and, as it were, jealous for the Church, which was foreknown to him though not yet revealed in the world, he crushed the hordes of demons and expelled the leader of their folly from his hegemony over us. By submitting him to the surging of his wrath, he has now liberated the mass of his worshipers from his ill-omened sway.[2]

1. Zec 1.15.
2. After an attempt to relate the verses to the historical situation, Cyril feels

The Lord says this: I shall turn back to Zion, and dwell in the midst of Jerusalem; Jerusalem will be called a true city, and the mountain of the Lord almighty a holy mountain (v.3). God fills everything, and all things are full of his ineffable nature. Yet sometimes he is said to depart from sinners, though not separated from them by distance in a local sense, such a notion being extremely naïve; rather, it means by his no longer (381) wishing to be well disposed or accord them pity and love. We refer to this as a display of wrath. When Israel turned to false worship, then, and Jerusalem prostituted itself, God departed, as it were, from them, and submitted them to the troubles resulting from apostasy. But when he finally had pity on them, the text speaks of his *turning back,* that is, I shall put an end to my wrath, I shall make it worthy of a visit, and shall make it my home once again. Just as, with his turning away, the *holy mountain*—that is, the Temple in Jerusalem—no longer seemed to be something venerable to those who saw it burned, so, with God's choosing to dwell in it again and rebuild it, reverence for it will return and be renewed. Jerusalem will once more be *true,* no longer offering worship to gods made by human hand as of old and to images of false gods, but adoring the one true God, divine by nature, in simplicity by choosing now to live by the Law and by obedience in every way.

You would be right to apply such terms to the Word, who for us became like us; though he was in the form of the one who begot him and equal to him in everything, "he emptied himself, taking the form of a slave," and "became poor for our sakes so that by his poverty we might become rich."[3] So the one who rightly turned away on account of the transgression in Adam and "the inclination of the human heart towards evil from its youth"[4] has now turned back to us as though from natural kindness, dwelt in the Church, and made the sanctified ones his city and august dwelling. (382) Of it—the Church, that is—he said somewhere, remember, "Here shall I dwell, because I chose her"; blessed David also sings, "Glorious things are said of you,

---

it is time to explore some further levels of meaning—as usual, Christological and ecclesiological.

3. Phil 2.6–7; 2 Cor 8.9.

4. Gn 8.21.

city of God." The prophet Isaiah also referred her to us in the words, "The mountain of the Lord will be conspicuous, and the house of God on the peaks of the mountains; she will be elevated above the hills, and to it will come all the nations."[5] That is to say, the Church of Christ will be the cynosure of all eyes, and known to people in all directions as though set on a mountain. She will also be called *true* because she is not in thrall to types and shadows, but rather welcoming the truth, who is Christ, and performing the worship that is "in spirit and in truth."[6]

The Lord almighty says this: Old men and women will again sit in the streets of Jerusalem, all with their sticks in their hands from their advanced age. The streets of the city will be filled with boys and girls playing in its streets (vv.4–5). Since the nation of the Jews had been wasted by war, the inevitable consequence was that the cities among them were empty of inhabitants, and the houses and their furnishings seen to be in ruins. But, lo, he promises to grant them lengthy and desirable peace, which the Greek writers very appositely call "nursing mother";[7] it rears its offspring to puberty, and for those already (383) in their youth it stretches out a kind of road to old age, with no one to lay waste, no oppressive warfare, no consuming battles. So it is presumed, and very correctly, that cities in peacetime, though broad and wide, give the impression of being cramped and reduced in size owing to the vast numbers of inhabitants. The present text likewise gives rise in us to such an interpretation, saying that *old men and women will sit in the streets of Jerusalem,* gaining scant comfort *from a stick* in their old age, and using a cane as a support. Yet that fact is a tribute to times without war and profound peace, which, as I said, rears infants to puberty, and brings to old age those already in manhood, passing the whole period of their lives without fighting. If the boys were destined to play in the city, and the girls to dance in the streets, this also could supply a clear proof that no bitter concern troubled them; they would

5. Pss 132.14; 87.3; Is 2.2–3.

6. Jn 4.24.

7. The term *kourotrophon* is found in Homer and later in Euripides. Kerrigan, *St Cyril of Alexandria,* 9, remarks that Cyril "was anything but a total stranger to the humanities." Russell, *Cyril of Alexandria,* 5, assumes that Homer, Euripides, Menander, and Demosthenes would have figured in his classical education.

not have allowed some to play if it were a time of foreboding.

Christ became our peace, too, and by quelling every war he caused the Church to be full of the saints. In it are found people venerable for their wisdom and elect souls beyond counting, to whom the wise John also writes in these words, "I write to you, fathers, because you know him who is from the beginning,"[8] whereas children, like adolescents and young girls, are the more immature mass of those recently converted, beautifying with their spiritual antics, as it were, the truly holy city, (384) the Church. To them you could also apply the saying, "Come, let us rejoice in the Lord, let us cry aloud to God our Savior."[9] If, on the other hand, the old people were perhaps described as leaning on a stick, you could understand that Christ supports both small and great, being the rod from Jesse, synonymous with power, which the God and Father sent us from the Zion on high for us to rejoice in him and say, "Your rod and your staff have consoled me."[10]

The Lord almighty says this, If it will be impossible in the view of the remnant of this people in those days, surely it will not be impossible also to me? says the Lord almighty (v.6). Great and extraordinary events somehow invite disbelief, and run their course to fulfillment without arousing amazement. It was out of disbelief, for example, that Sarah laughed at the promise in the case of Isaac,[11] noting her old age, and pitting the unlikely event against the laws of human nature; yet against all hope she gave birth, God rendering the event possible for her. It was therefore very likely that those released from captivity would be in two minds and not particularly confident that events would bring such prosperity for them that Jerusalem would be full of elderly people, groups of boys and dancing by girls would be seen in it, and the fruits of profound peace would ensue. After all, they observed (385) walls broken down, houses burned, all the surrounding cities turned into lairs of wild beasts, doubtless because of their being completely empty of inhabitants, fields that had previously been fertile and blooming now full of thorns and with nothing ripe, and the whole rural landscape utterly ruined. So

8. Eph 2.14; 1 Jn 2.13.
9. Ps 95.1.
10. Is 11.1; Pss 110.2; 23.4.
11. Gn 18.12.

it was likely, as I said, that there was on these grounds disbelief that the promises would take effect for them. Consequently, God did not allow them to be in two minds, bidding them have confidence and providing confirmation in the words, *If it will be impossible in the view of the remnant of this people in those days, surely it will not be impossible also to me? says the Lord almighty.* After all, what is beyond our devising is very easily accomplished by God, who is omnipotent. He is the Lord of hosts, remember, fulfilling by his will even what is quite extraordinary, and bringing his decision to fulfillment without delay.

The God and Father somewhere said to the Jews in foretelling the wonders of the coming of our Savior, "See, you scoffers, look on and disappear, because I am doing a work in your days that you would not believe if anyone described it to you."[12] That is to say, as far as our words to you are concerned, the actual mystery of the Incarnation surpasses admiration and description; no less are the wonders that come to us from it. After all, how could it not beggar belief that the Word sprung from God was united with human flesh, came in the form of a slave, endured the cross, and underwent insult and injury and the effects of the Jews' stupidity? Or how could anyone not admire the outcome of the Incarnation, whereby sin is canceled, (386) death abolished, and corruption dispelled, and the human being, once a fugitive, is now seen to be resplendent with the grace of adoption? So let there be reference to Christ in this actual verse, *If it will be impossible in the view of the remnant of this people in those days, surely it will not be impossible also to me?* For him, in fact, everything is light and easy, and whatever he needs and wishes to do, in my view there would be no resistance.

The Lord almighty says this, Lo, I shall rescue my people from the land of the east and from the land of the west. I shall bring them in and shall dwell in the midst of Jerusalem, and they will be my people and I shall be their God in truth and righteousness (vv.7–8). In former times also God saved those in the line of Israel who were scattered in war, assembling them in Jerusalem and dwelling among them, at least by rebuilding the divine Temple and permitting them once more to placate him with sacrifices according to the

12. Hab 1.5; cf. Acts 13.41.

Law, offer prayers, and celebrate festivals. But to say *rescuing his own people from the east and the west* would rightly be applied to Emmanuel,[13] who called all of earth under heaven, landed by faith those from the end of the earth as his catch, and gathered the whole flock of the nations into the truly holy and celebrated city, "which is the Church of the living God" and heavenly Jerusalem. How is it not a simple claim that *he dwelt in its midst?* After all, he became like us, and "dwelt among human beings" (387) in the flesh. God foretold this to us through another prophet: "Be of good cheer, Zion; do not let your hands grow weak. The Lord your God is in your midst; as a warrior he will save you. He will bring joy upon you, and will renew you in his love."[14] He is with us still, however: far from leaving us orphans, he sent us in his place the Paraclete, and through him he is with those who love him, as he will confirm in the words, "Behold, I am with you all days until the end of the age."[15] Accordingly, we have become his people, after once being no people,[16] only worshipers of stones; abominating the ancient and loathsome error, we have chosen him as *our God, in truth and righteousness.* Far from adhering to types and shadows, like those in love with the letter, we instead welcome into our mind and heart the splendor of the evangelical preaching and perform the true worship, and, holding fast the righteousness acceptable to him, we perform the worship in the spirit. "God is spirit," as the Son himself says, remember, "and those who worship him must worship in spirit and in truth."[17]

The Lord almighty says this, Let your hands be strong, you that have been listening in these days to these words from the mouth of the prophets from the day the foundations have been laid of the house of the Lord almighty and the Temple has been rebuilt (v.9). The God of all often makes to those who love him promises surpassing all hope while

13. Cyril finds support for his Christological interpretation in the use of *anasōzein* in the Zechariah text, "re-saving" instead of the saving that God had done previously.

14. 1 Tm 3.15; Bar 3.37; Zep 3.16–17.

15. Mt 28.20.

16. Mt 28.20; Hos 1.10; 1 Pt 2.10.

17. 2 Cor 3.6; Jn 4.24. Though in practice Cyril does not abjure a fondness for the letter of Scripture (such as he rebuts here), he has twice in these verses (cf. note 6 above) upheld the value of worship in spirit.

never being deceptive; instead, by his peculiar force and certain ineffable powers he brings to pass in (388) due course whatever he wishes without effort. On the other hand, it becomes us not to be weak in faith, but to testify in definite terms to his ability to fulfill every promise easily, and to be valiant in the deeds through which we shall be conspicuous and earn the glorious crown of simplicity. It also becomes us to believe the words coming from him, and be careful to take as our guides those who would in due course be honest ministers to us of the divine oracles.

Our Lord Jesus Christ also promised through the holy prophets the good things stemming from the Incarnation, and, in explaining the magnitude of the gifts to the extent possible for the human intellect, he delivered a well-nigh incredible discourse, as I said. Through faith, however, we have rendered acceptable what is beyond nature, and, in directing our minds to the marvelous actions, we have allowed the neck of our minds to become compliant and docile, as it were, to the instructors in religion. Now, the time befitting the provision of the good things and submission on our part is the revelation of the Church; note how the God of all ordered even what pertains to us to *be strong*, take action and obey the words of *the prophets from the day the foundations have been laid of the house of the Lord almighty and the Temple has been rebuilt.*

Because before those days people's wages will be of no benefit, there are no wages for cattle, and (389) *there will be no relief from distress for the one leaving or the one arriving. I shall dispatch everyone against their neighbor* (v.10). The Hebrew text does not have the verb in the future tense, citing it in the past: *Because before those days people's wages were of no benefit, there were no wages for cattle,* and further, *there was no relief from distress for the one leaving or the one arriving;* and instead of saying, *I shall dispatch everyone,* they put, *I dispatched everyone.*[18] Now, the verse is very convincing, and the force of the description will highlight its truth. His intention,

18. Probably influenced by Jerome, Cyril notes the incompatibility of tenses rendered by the LXX as future when past in the Heb. (as they are mostly in the past in the Antiochene text in this case) and accepts that his version has made an error.

in fact, was to suggest something like the following. The people of Israel came from Babylon to the holy city; but there was no place of sanctification for them, now that the Temple of old was overthrown; there was no sacrifice or libation, and no altar standing. Then the God of all urged them to show the care that had been devoted to what was previously necessary for them, to rebuild the Temple and erect the divine altar in it so that they might be able to perform properly what was required by Law and to appease the God of all. But they put it off for various reasons, some citing dearth of resources, some using as an excuse the opposition of neighboring peoples to rebuilding. Then, since they offended God by this, they were struck down with frequent calamities in quick succession—infertility, blight, incursions, and assaults by the neighboring nations. (390) The God of all leveled against them the charge of indifference, saying as much through the voice of Haggai the prophet: "These people claim that the time has not yet come to rebuild the house of the Lord. Is it a time for you to live in paneled houses when the Lord's house is not rebuilt?"[19]

Now, as I said, since they had relapsed into indifference, they frequently fell victim to shortage of necessities and war with the neighbors. When they had rebuilt the Temple, on the other hand, the effects of wrath ceased, they had an abundance of everything, and there was a general feeling of satisfaction. Consequently, he says, *Because before those days*—that is, before the rebuilding of the Temple—*people's wages were of no benefit, and there were no wages for cattle;* the farmers got no return, they harvested nothing, they abandoned the fields along with oxen equally fatigued. And *there was no relief from distress for the one leaving or the one arriving:* sometimes, he says, people left one city to go to another, either to ply their trade or even for other things. *There was no relief* even for them, he says, since the nations nearby fought against Israel, and everybody regarded as a particular enemy one who was close to him, whether relative, family, or neighbor.

Now, it should be realized that before the Incarnation of the

19. Hg 1.2, 4. Cyril relates the verse (after correctly seeing in it a reference to the past) to the situation of the restored community, citing Haggai in support.

Only-begotten and the revelation of the Church, there were *no wages for people* or for cattle. In other words, in this life some individuals were rather rational and had a reputation for intelligence, and would be considered *people,* (391) but in their language showed no interest in what is useful or helpful, put nothing in writing that was of value, and were incapable of thinking or communicating anything to others. Likewise, by contrast, some lived the life of cattle or sheep, going *without wages,* not being involved in anything that would win commendation from God. There was absolutely no *relief* on earth, either, the herd of demons confusing everything, and rendering the earth full of disturbance, the result being that everyone's affairs and thoughts were subject to tossing and turning, devoid of stability.

At this time I shall not deal with the remnant of this people as in former times, says the Lord almighty. Instead, I shall let peace emerge: the vine will yield its fruit, the land will yield its produce, and heaven will give its dew. I shall give all this as an inheritance to the remnants of my people (vv.11–12). He makes a change from his wrath and the effects of it, saying that punishment will disappear along with the time of the offenses. Sin had in fact come to an end—or, rather, Israel had already paid the penalty for it—and so he promised to bring to a close the calamities, and rightly so, and to desist from imposing disasters. His decision in their regard was not related to the former one, but had reference to mildness. This was an outcome of *peace,* an abundant supply of what they liked, seeing their *vine* covered in fruit and their *land* fertile and covered in crops, (392) rewarding the efforts of the farmers, obviously with the cooperation of *heaven,* which clearly *gives its dew* to the fields and what is in them. Heaven and earth and creation as a whole, in other words, will definitely respond to the will of the Lord. This is Israel's *inheritance,* with God directing their prosperity, and every *producer* free of trouble.

The verse in this case would be applicable to Christ the Savior of us all: before the time of his coming we all went our own way, living the life of cattle and brute beasts, and in thrall to the deceit of the demons. But when we were undone, as it were, toppled to the ground and under the feet of the foe, the Father had pity and no longer treated us *as in former times.* Instead of ignoring our being disadvantaged, subjected to the cruel tyrant and carried off into disgusting behavior of every kind, he gave us *peace* from heaven—namely, Christ—who has bestowed on us also an abundance of all spiritual fertility. We have in fact been filled with grain and wine, and "the true vine"—namely, Christ—has given us his own *fruit,* which "gladdens the human heart," as Scripture puts it.[20] He is the grain of wheat and the sacred sheaf, made into bread of life for us; he has also gladdened us greatly, giving us *dew from heaven*—namely, dew that is immaterial and of the Spirit, which the divinely inspired David mentioned, "Like dew of Hermon descending upon the mountains of (393) Zion."[21] This comes to us by way of *inheritance* and goodly allotment from God, since to be sure we have become Israel, that is, "mind seeing God," since in the Son we have a vision of the Father.[22]

Just as you were a curse among the nations, house of Judah and house of Israel, so I shall save you and you will enjoy blessing. Have confidence and be strong in your hands (v.13). The people of Israel were made captives and fell victim to abuse by their captors; so they were given the name "accursed," as some claim, in the likely formula "May I not become like Israel." But since the compassionate God saved them and they enjoyed the former good things, they threw off the calamities and the appearance of being accursed. They were in fact blessed, and became no less devoted than before, God gladdening them with good things from on high, and bestowing on them a share in complete satisfaction.

This same experience can be easily discerned in our own case as well. We were accursed, after all, in thrall to the herds of demons and subjected to every form of depravity through their perversity. But when we came to know God as Creator of all, and were known by Christ, then it was, in fact, then it was that we learned to celebrate in our own case, "Blessed are we by the Lord, who made heaven and earth."[23] Since we have been called

20. Jn 15.1; Ps 104.15.
21. Jn 12.24; Lv 23.10–11; Jn 6.35; Ps 133.3.
22. Jn 14.9. Cyril could have found the etymology of "Israel" in Didymus.
23. Ps 115.15. The mention of "knowing" and "being known" seems to be a relic of the long digression Didymus indulges in at this point.

to such a degree of honor and glory, however, we must be committed to good works and do battle with the passions, declare sin anathema, and excel in practice of the evangelical laws so as to be devoted to doing what is pleasing to Christ. We have heard him saying to us, in fact, *Have confidence and be strong in* (394) *your hands,* and we have accepted from Christ the need to be confident; he overcame the world for our sakes, trampled down the foe, proved his own temple to be superior to death, and stopped the mouth of lawlessness,[24] so that we too might profit from that on his account. It was not for himself that he has conquered, after all, as I said, but to achieve benefits for us in our weakness from his conquest.

Because the Lord almighty says this, Just as I planned to afflict you for your fathers' provocation of me, says the Lord almighty, and I did not relent, so I am ready and I plan in these days to treat Jerusalem and the house of Judah well. Be confident (vv.14–15). The fact that there is no resisting the divine considerations or intentions, then, emerges also from these verses; what God would intend and actually choose to effect would clearly emerge and be brought to fulfillment. He says this somewhere also in Isaiah to highlight his natural omnipotence, "I said, My purpose will stand, and I shall carry out all I intended."[25] From what they happened to suffer when the divine wrath befell them, therefore, it is possible to understand quite clearly that the way of happiness was opened up for them when he wished and allowed them to enjoy it or, rather, when in kindness he offered them the enjoyment of every good thing. In other words, he is saying, just as nothing prevented my maltreating you for grave sin when I wanted, so too when I want to be kind and (395) intend to show compassion for those who have suffered enough, there will be no obstacle. In fact, *I am ready to treat Jerusalem and the house of Judah well.* Now, the text is very definite: it is not simply that, as the text says, I intend *and plan,* but I have moved to such a degree of willingness and mildness towards you that *I am ready,* which is a clear indication of a deliberate consideration. And he con-

24. Jn 16.33; Ps 107.42. Cyril is not reading the same text of v.13 as Didymus (adopted also by Jerome), where "heart" replaced "hands." Antioch's agrees with Cyril's on this.

25. Is 46.10.

firms the truth of the promise by adding the words *Be confident.*

In like manner Christ brings us to a secure knowledge of truth after we have been called to it through faith: just as before the call we had descended to every form of depravity, and he gave us over to a reprobate mentality and punished us for our impurity, so too *he is ready and he plans,* as he himself says, *in these days to treat* the Church *and the house of Judah well,* that is, ourselves who make our confession to him and honor him with praise as Lord, as Savior, and as Redeemer ("commendation" being the meaning of *Judah*). Now, *the house of Judah* should be taken in no other way than as the Church: it has been styled Christ's house, "which sprang from Judah," and is given that name also by the divinely inspired Scripture. The patriarch Jacob, remember, likewise refers to it in saying, "Judah, your brethren will praise you," and again, "You have sprung, my son, from the shoot of Judah." Christ was descended from the root of Jesse, and, as though from the shoot of the holy Virgin, he is "a distinguished staff and rod of greatness," according to the prophet's statement. So the words *Be confident* are doubtless addressed to us, therefore, and rightly so: (396) the Father crowned us with a "shield of favor" by the salvation and grace coming through Christ.[26]

These are the directions you will carry out: speak the truth each of you to your neighbor, deliver a peaceable judgment in your gates, do not ponder evil in your hearts each of you to your neighbor, and do not entertain a false oath, because I loathe all this, says the Lord almighty (vv.16–17). To those unwilling to be disobedient and not in the habit of adopting an unproductive way of life—or, rather, to those fond of following the straight and narrow and opting for a spotless life—God promises to give the reward of his characteristic mildness, and actually to be ready to be beneficent to them.[27] He bade them, in fact, not to give the impression of being liars, and instead to speak their words truthfully, love uprightness in their *judgments,* deliver a judgment on every matter that is fair and completely transparent, uninfluenced by base motives, with no eye for base profit or tipping the verdict for

26. Heb 7.14; 3.6; Gn 49.8–9; Jer 48.17; Ps 5.13.
27. Pusey's text differs in several respects at this point from the PG ed.

the sake of a bribe. Instead, they should have an eye solely for what is pleasing to God, forgiving their brethren in cases where they failed in action or speech, and furthermore carefully avoiding taking *false oaths;* such offenses he encourages them to hate.

Now, observe how he instructs them to do nothing by way of shadows or types; he does not give instructions on the need to sacrifice oxen or show reverence by libations. Instead, he wants them, as it were, to practice the evangelical life, like some carefully rehearsed pattern. You see, since in these instructions no little reference is made regarding the coming of our Savior, consequently and of necessity a commandment is introduced that speaks of the oracles coming through him: if there is need for us who follow the divine sayings to speak the truth, we shall completely discuss the story of Christ, for Christ is the truth. Hence the all-wise Peter bade us to be quite ready "to make our defense to anyone who asks an accounting for the hope that is in us."[28] Now, those who are used to telling the story of Christ, and have him always on their lips and meditate on him in mind and heart, would be righteous in every way, conspicuous for upright behavior of every kind, *peaceable* and gentle and patient as well, not given to taking false oaths, but rather avoiding oaths altogether. They remember his words, "Let your word be Yes, Yes, or No, No; anything more than this comes from the evil one."[29]

The word of the Lord almighty came to me: The Lord almighty says this, The fast of the fourth, the fast of the fifth, the fast of the seventh, and the fast of the tenth will be an occasion of joy and happiness and of joyous festivals for the house of Judah; be glad, love truth and peace (vv.18–19). I feel it is necessary to outline once again for studious readers the reasons for the fasts mentioned here, and what are the (398) *fourth, fifth,* and those following them, *seventh and tenth;* in this way we shall then proceed to supply as well in due course and proper order the force of the directions. After the capture of the holy city, then, the burning of the Temple, and the deportation of captive Israel along with the sacred vessels, the survivors and those left behind in Judea considered as un-

28. 1 Pt 3.15.
29. Mt 5.37.

mentionable and oppressive the days in which their lot was to suffer such trials; assembling in groups they kept weeping and wailing, and subjecting themselves to fasting. Now, what actually transpired on each of the days just mentioned to us, come now, let us explain from the sacred text.

Blessed Jeremiah, then, said, "In the ninth year of his reign (that is, Zedekiah's), in the tenth month on the tenth day of the month, Nebuchadnezzar king of Babylon came with all his might to Jerusalem, building ramparts around it and besieging it with a ring of squared stones. The city was surrounded till the eleventh year of King Zedekiah in the fourth month on the ninth day of the month, when famine was extreme in the city and there was no food for the people of the land. A breach was made in the city walls, and all the warriors came out by night by way of the gate in the middle of the wall and the fortification by the king's garden." Then, after mention of the killing of Zedekiah's sons and his blinding, he went on, "In the fifth month on the tenth day of the (399) month, Nebuzaradan the lieutenant, who had a position before the king of Babylon, came to Jerusalem, burned the house of the Lord, the house of the king, and all the houses of the city, and put to the flames every great house in the city. The forces of the Chaldeans accompanying the lieutenant destroyed the whole wall surrounding Jerusalem."[30] You hear how in the tenth year Nebuchadnezzar besieged Jerusalem, then in the fourth month of the eleventh year, it says, the city was laid low, and in the fifth month the Temple itself was burned and all the city disabled by the lieutenant. They therefore declared sacrosanct the *fourth, fifth, and tenth* days, transferring the numbers from months to days.

As for the *seventh,* it is necessary to explain once more. When the lieutenant took Jerusalem, he appointed Gedaliah as governor of the remnant of the Jews in Jerusalem; after doing so he left for Babylon. But when the survivors from the Jews learned this had been done, they converged on Jerusalem, hoping still to occupy the land. In the seventh month, however, as Scripture tells us, Ishmael slew Gedaliah; then the whole people scat-

30. Jer 52.4–14.

tered, took refuge in Egypt, and perished there.[31] So they also declared the *seventh* day sacrosanct, and the month itself for this reason. This, then, is the basis of the fasts. But since it was logical, at the cessation of the effects of the wrath, the return of Israel to Jerusalem, and the end of hardship, to fast and grieve no longer, (400) he bids the mourning be changed to rejoicing, and satisfaction be taken in what they were in receipt of from God, or a memorial be held of what they had been punished for on occasion, sinning without check and descending into every kind of shameful excess.

Now, Christ also did this for us: "he turned our mourning into joy, removed the sackcloth, and clothed us in joy," according to the verse of the psalmist.[32] We are no longer accused of not knowing God, adoring creation instead of the Creator, falling under the feet of the foe, and adopting a reprehensible attitude. Instead, we give thanks for being granted mercy and salvation, rescued from the hand of the foe, inhabiting the holy city—that is, the Church—being thought worthy now of venerating him in prayers and spiritual sacrifices, *loving peace and truth,* and being taught by the inspired Scripture to consider the event the basis of satisfaction from on high. "He is our peace,"[33] in fact, he is the *truth,* and thanks to him we enjoy sound hope and ought to rejoice, now that all dejection has been removed.

The Lord almighty says this, Many peoples shall yet come, the inhabitants of many cities. The inhabitants of five cities[34] *will assemble in one city, saying, Let us all go together and entreat the favor of the Lord and seek out the favor of the Lord almighty; I too shall go. Many peoples and many nations will come to seek out the favor of the Lord almighty* (401) *in Jerusalem, and to win the favor of the Lord* (vv.20–22). When Christ transforms our grief into joy, festivity, and true happiness, and changes mourning into satisfaction, the approach of those called to salvation through faith and their relationship with God through sanctification will not now occur singly, he is saying. Instead, the *cities* encourage one another to do so, and

31. 2 Kgs 25.22–26.
32. Ps 30.11.
33. Eph 2.14.
34. With the LXX Cyril (as does Theodoret) reads "five cities" where our Heb. (like Theodore's reading) has "one" (Didymus reading simply "cities").

the nations will come in large numbers, late arrivals exclaiming to those preceding them, *I too shall go*. Scripture says, remember, "Iron sharpens iron, and one person sharpens the face of another"[35]—in other words, the enthusiasm of some always proves a stimulus to others in the need to perform good works.

Now, what is the purpose of the cities or the nations? To *win the favor* and seek out *the favor of the Lord*, that is, Christ, who is the unchanging image of the God and Father, "the exact imprint of his being and the reflection of his glory," as Scripture says; of him the divinely inspired David also says, "Make your face shine upon your servant."[36] The image and favor of the God and Father has shone upon us, as I said; finding him benevolent and propitious, we cast off the harmful effects of sin, being justified through faith, "not because of any works of righteousness that we had done, but according to the abundance of his mercy," compassionate and kind as he is, forgiving the faults of those who approach him. By seeking him out studiously (402) we shall find him by complete performance of his requirements, and through him we shall cling to the God and Father, since "he is our peace," in the words of Scripture.[37]

The Lord almighty says this, In those days ten men of nations of all languages will lay hold of the hem of a Jewish man and say, We shall come with you because we have heard that God is with you (v.23). He once again clarifies the way the approach of those seeking the face of the Lord will happen in the case of both cities and nations. It will happen, he says, note, *in those days*, that is, at that moment of time when *ten men will lay hold of a Jewish man and say, We shall come with you*. Through the word *ten*, then, you should understand the perfect number of those approaching, the number ten being a symbol of perfection. Now, he makes clear that it is to the holy apostles that those from the nations attached themselves and endeavored to tread the same path as they did, being justified by faith in Christ, and he cites a visual example that is well developed by way of an image from our own experience. Little children, remember, sometimes choose to follow their parents, clutching their hem and, as it were, sup-

35. Prv 27.17.
36. Heb 1.3; Ps 119.135.
37. Ti 3.5; Eph 2.14.

ported by the contact and hanging from the garments, and they thus make their way safely and securely. In just the same way, in my view, those who had worshiped creation rather than the Creator of all (403) enlist as their own parents the expositors of the evangelical doctrines, and, clinging to them in fellow-feeling, they follow them, being still at the infant stage. They travel the same path, proving themselves imitators of their pattern of life in every detail, and with constant growth in better ways they "advance to maturity, to the measure of the full stature of Christ."[38]

Now, what is the reason for their following? They are convinced that *God is with them*—Emmanuel, that is, the name meaning "God is with us." The fact that the call at that time will be not only for those descended from Israel, but rather for all the nations throughout the entire world, he mentioned when he said that those grasping the hem will be *from nations of all languages.* But when were the nations called to the knowledge of the truth, and when did they decide to seek out the Lord's favor, appease him, and feel the need, as it were, to follow the same path as the holy apostles, if not when the Only-begotten became like us? He is "the expectation of the nations"; it is of him that the divinely inspired David sings, "All the nations you have made will come and bow down before you, Lord."[39] After all, the whole mass of the nations is also saved through him.

38. Eph 4.13. The ecclesiological thinking of Ephesians makes it a favorite text of Cyril's.

39. Gn 49.10 LXX; Ps 86.9.

COMMENTARY ON ZECHARIAH, CHAPTER NINE

An oracle of the word of the Lord in the land of Hadrach and Damascus its rest, because the Lord surveys human beings and all the tribes of Israel, and Hamath in its borders (vv. 1–2).

WHILE THE text is not without problems, and the actual series of expressions very difficult to grasp, it will receive comment by us as far as possible. (404) There is naturally need to explain the references we think we find,[1] this being the way the sense of the prophecy should be understood.

When in due course, therefore, Israel emerged from the bonds of captivity and was set at liberty, and they finally returned to Judea and tried to fortify Jerusalem, then it was that the neighboring nations that inhabited Samaria and occupied the cities of Palestine and even Phoenicia were overcome by envy.[2] At the same time they were afraid that with the restoration of the former situation, and the growth of the race to excessive proportions, they would then have a city that was so fortified and impregnable that they would attack them again and raise their well-nigh invincible hand against them, as in the past. Consequently, they wanted to hinder their wish to build fortifications by hatching insidious plots and even conducting piratical raids against them. They reached such a degree of resentment and envy as to write to the king of the Persians at the time what is

1. Cyril has noted a break in sequence and tone in the book of the kind that has led commentators since Joseph Mede in 1653 to think in terms of a difference in authors—not an option for these ancient commentators. Following his customary procedure, he will try to plot historical "references" first before having recourse to another level of interpretation.

2. With a keener eye to ancient geography than Didymus's, Cyril is able to detect the sequence in the author's movement from cities of Syria (Damascus, Hadrach, and Hamath) and then to the Phoenician coast (Tyre and Sidon) and Philistia. Like Theodoret, he will offer the readers their current names, at least in some cases.

written in the book of Esdras, as follows: "To King Artaxerxes our lord, your servants Rehum the scribe, Shimshai the scribe, the remaining members of their council, and the judges in Coelesyria and Phoenicia. Let it now be known to the lord the king that the Jews who came up from you to us have gone to Jerusalem, (405) and are rebuilding that rebellious and wicked city, repairing its market places and walls and laying the foundations for a temple. If this city is built, then, and the walls finished, they will not only refuse to pay tribute but will even resist kings. Since the building of the temple is now going on, we think it best not to neglect such a matter."[3]

Since they had mocked Israel without restraint when it was captured and suffering captivity, and again had no less harassed it when it was scarcely rescued and its bonds released, and inflicted countless hardships on it, scheming in various ways, not allowing the divine Temple to rise or the holy city to be fortified, God was naturally provoked against them and surrendered them into the hands of Israel. At the completion of work and the raising of the Temple, they plundered all their cities and took control of their occupants, and became masters of wealth beyond counting.

He therefore says, *An oracle of the word of the Lord in the land of Hadrach and Damascus.* That is to say, the text before us from God will be directed against Hadrach, Damascus, and also *Hamath,* which is *in its borders*—namely, those of Damascus. Now, *the land of Hadrach* lies to the east, and is a neighbor of Hamath; it is now called Epiphaneia, which is a little above Antioch. Damascus is the capital of Phoenicia and Palestine. The cities under them will obviously be subject to the capitals. Why, then, is the *oracle* directed at them? (406) Because in them also was *its rest,*[4] that is, the God who controls everything: he was resting because he saw them punished. The one who surveys everything, remember, had not kept silence, bestowing pity and consideration to the chosen race, namely, Israel. The God of all, in fact, has been surveying human beings and considering each one's ways, inflicting on wrongdoers the effects of his wrath, and rescuing the wronged.

3. 1 Esdras 2.17–20.
4. The LXX diverges from the Heb., offering "its sacrifice" at this point.

Now, it should be recalled that in what preceded he introduced treatment of the four chariots and the kinds of horses, going on to say further, "Lo, those issuing forth to the north country have set at rest my anger with the north country."[5] The Lord's anger, as though hating evil, comes to rest when those who offended him with extreme and unrestrained sin have paid the penalty.

Tyre and Sidon, because they were very proud. Tyre built itself a rampart, stored up silver like dust, and amassed gold like dirt of the streets. Hence the Lord will take possession of it, will strike its might into the sea, and it will be consumed by fire (vv.2–4). Consistent with the verse was the fate of the cities against which the *oracle of the Lord* was directed. He begins with Tyre and Sidon, which had the highest reputation of all, holding (407) the others in subjection, as it were, and being more famous than its neighbors.[6] Since Sidon and Tyre adopted a conceited attitude, therefore, thought themselves high and mighty, put their trust in fortifications—namely, encircling ramparts or other such things by which a city would be safe and secure—and were also proud of their great wealth, consequently *the Lord will take possession of it.* In other words, by saying *the Lord will take possession of it* he means it would be sacked by the people of Israel, or at least by Vespasian and Titus; it was the Lord who surrendered it into the hands of its captors. The Romans, in fact, in subjecting the whole world to their control, were mild and benign to those yielding peaceably, but harsh and warlike to those bent on resisting. So he says it will be set on fire once its fortifications are brought down *into the sea,* and its wealth plundered as if its *gold* were *like dust* and *its silver like dirt of the streets.* The occupants of Tyre, remember, were very mean and greedy traders, a topic developed at great length in the writings of the prophet Ezekiel.[7]

No benefit will come, therefore, to those who offend God at any time by mocking the saints if they happen to be suffering some trial, or ridiculing them extremely if God is testing the

5. Zec 6.8.

6. The statement of these cities' pre-eminence is briefer in Pusey's text than in the PG ed.

7. Cf. Ezek 28. For Cyril, Ezekiel is a writer.

faith of his own. Every *rampart* of theirs and every kind of security will tumble. There will be no wealth at all; instead, it will be a stimulus for war and (408) rather a motive for enthusiasm for those involved in pillage.

Now, you could recognize in this case also pagan scholars who take pride in their worldly wisdom and the errors of complicated arguments like *ramparts,* as it were, fortifying with the force of eloquence their own deceitfulness, and gilding the display of their speech as though it were *silver* and the precious nature of their ideas as though *gold.* Christ *will take possession* also of such people, however, having destroyed the *rampart* and plundered the *gold* and the *silver.* Those presiding over the Church at times, in fact, men of eloquence and wisdom, have made their own the power of those people's winning speech and have dedicated it to God, applying in the contest the doctrines of faith, and giving a full and truthful refutation of the deceitfulness coming from them. This was the kind of thing done by the people of Israel: making use of the Egyptians' objects of *gold and silver;* taking possession of them from the greedy owners, they offered them to the all-holy God in the desert by the furnishing of the holy tabernacle and the sacred vessels within it.[8] Those who thus manage the Church by means of worldly wisdom and attractive speech, robbing the pagan scholars and, as it were, enriching themselves with their *gold and silver* in great fairness, make it God's *inheritance,* communicating to others what is for his glory, (409) overturning those people's *ramparts,* and building up in spiritual fashion the holy city, that is, the Church.

Ashkelon will see it and be afraid, Gaza too, and feel intense anguish; Ekron too, because its hope was frustrated. A king will perish from Gaza, and Ashkelon will not be inhabited. Foreigners will dwell in Ashdod, I shall destroy the arrogance of Philistines (vv.5–6). When the onset of war and fighting befall a region, the cities in it become more confident and sometimes hopeful, believing they will overcome the foe either by the vast number of its inhabitants or by fortifications and military strategies. If it happens, on the other hand, that one of their number is captured, especially

8. Ex 12.35; 25.1–9.

if it has a claim to being the most powerful, then most of all the whole region collapses in fear, loses its hope—in the ability to escape, I mean—and takes to mourning as though already fallen. When Tyre was taken, therefore, despite being so splendid, robust, and adorned with wealth, *Ashkelon will be afraid, Gaza will feel anguish,* and *Ekron too,* these being cities of Palestine. It will *feel anguish, because its hope was frustrated:* they thought that the power of Tyre would suffice for their own protection. The leader of Gaza will pass on, he is saying—that is, will perish—and *foreigners will dwell in Ashdod,* probably because the original occupants have been wasted in war. (410) To this he adds, *I shall destroy the arrogance of Philistines,* by the term ἀλλόφυλοι, meaning as usual Philistines or Palestinians.[9]

Now, it would be possible, if you preferred, that the mention of those wronging Israel refers also to other nations, who were nearby and neighbors to the Jews. But let it suffice for our explanation of the literal sense of the text. It should be realized, on the other hand, that when the Church is at times persecuted by foes, as I said, the foes cruelly harass and mock them, perhaps by crying, "Aha, aha,"[10] in the scriptural phrase. But Christ gives assistance, shatters all their might by raising his own temple, inflicts on the schemers the effects of his unmitigated anger, and overturns the assemblies of the heresies like cities, as it were, and in addition to them the unholy covens of the idolaters.

And I shall remove the blood from their mouth and their abominations from between their teeth. And they too will be left for our God, and will be like a commander in Judah, and Ekron like the Jebusite (v.7). They too devoured Israel, and like wild animals their mouth was, as it were, stained with blood. Since they were idolaters and given to the worship of worthless gods, they always had the names of their own abominations on their tongues (or in *their teeth*), hither and (411) yon calling their handmade idols gods, and saying to lifeless stones, in the words of the prophet, "You are my god, you gave me birth."[11] But they paid the appropriate

9. Probably with Jerome's assistance, Cyril clarifies the meaning of the ambiguous term that might also mean simply "foreigners."

10. Cf. Ps 35.21, a mocking taunt by the psalmist's foes.

11. Cf. Jer 2.27 (where other forms of the LXX read, "You are my father").

penalty due to them for sinning harshly against Israel. They did not perish as one, however; God foretold their conversion to Christ that would eventually come. So he says, *I shall remove the blood from their mouth,* that is, even if they greedily devoured Israel like wild animals, yet the time will come when they would be pure and cleared of responsibility for this; they will be justified by faith, and lose the stain of their former depravity. *I shall also remove* the names of *their abominations from between their teeth:* they will no longer mention what are falsely called gods or refer to them as such. Instead, *they too will be left for our God,* as of course Israel will do as well, who will be saved as his remnant,[12] even if guilty of impiety towards Emmanuel himself.

Now, the vast number of the nations who were called were united spiritually to those who came to faith from Israel, with Christ bringing them into unity: "He is our peace, having made the two one and broken down the dividing wall, creating one new humanity from the two peoples and reconciling both with the Father in one Spirit."[13] Consequently, he says, *they will be like a commander in Judah;* that is, they will progress to such a degree of sincerity arising from faith and simplicity that from them will emerge leaders of Israel. Also, *Ekron*—that is, the foreigner, the one from the land of Philistia—*will be like the Jebusite;* that is, once more it will (412) be the people inhabiting Jerusalem. Jerusalem was formerly known as Jebus;[14] so by *Jebusite* here is understood the resident of Jerusalem. Now, many *commanders*—that is, leaders and presiders of the people—came from the nations, and are now scattered throughout the world. By *Judah* you are to understand those in the habit of "praising," namely, ourselves, who are called in faith and have the custom of crowning with unceasing hymns of praise the one who gives us our name, Christ.

I shall provide my house with an elevation to prevent going and coming; no one will invade them any longer to drive them off, because now I have seen with my eyes (v.8). Lo, he clearly refers to Christ as *elevation* and wall, through whom and in whom we are exalted, obviously by the good will and pleasure of the God and Father.

12. Cf. Is 11.11.
13. Cf. Eph 2.14–18.
14. Cf. 1 Chr 11.4–7.

We who believe, you see, are the spiritual house and dwelling of God, in Paul's terms, if it is true that he dwells in our hearts through the Spirit, and dwells with those who love him. It was he, remember, who said through the voice of the prophet, "I shall live in them and walk among them, and I shall be their God and they will be my people."[15] So Christ is the *elevation* raised up for the Church by the will of the Father to prevent the *going and coming* of some people, moving to and fro as of old, treading, as it were, a barren path and filling our hearts with every evil. (413) He said as much, on the one hand, of the people of Israel, remember, who were the beloved's ancient vineyard, "I shall remove its fence, and it will be ready for stealing; I shall destroy its wall, and it will be open to be trampled."[16] To us who acknowledge his coming, on the other hand, Emmanuel it is who is the wall and fence raised up, surrounding us with ineffable force and scaring away the unclean demons from our thoughts, and not letting them be trodden under their feet. Hence the prophet also said to him, "You will be called builder of fences, and you will put an end to crossroads":[17] just as those involved in fencing uncultivated vineyards put an end to crossroads so as not to allow them to be trampled down by people going hither and yon, so too Jesus Christ our Lord surrounded us with himself as a kind of impregnable wall, and by hemming us in with angelic powers he made us safe from being trampled on.

In addition to this he said, *No one will invade them any longer to drive them off.* Of old, you see, we were vulnerable, easily led, and quite ready for any wrong behavior, with Satan pushing and pulling us, and, as it were, driving us in one direction and another. Christ, however, put an end to that as well: the robber will not come against us; he will not make an assault at his pleasure as in the past. We are fixed firm in Christ, you see, our heart secure and firm, no longer under pressure to go where it should not; we do not stray into polytheism, we are not driven into error—instead, we have set our course in faith and love towards God so as to rejoice in saying of him, "He set my feet upon a rock." By saying, *Because* (414) *now I have seen with my eyes,* he

15. 1 Cor 3.9; 2 Cor 6.16; Lv 26.12. 16. Is 5.1, 5.
17. Is 58.12.

clearly declared that the time of the Savior's coming was a time of visitation: "The dawn from on high has visited us," and as David says, "The Lord looked down from heaven on earth,"[18] although in former times on account of the sin in us he did not consider us worthy of oversight, of compassion or love, of anything else of the kind at all, but, as it were, he turned his back on us. Consequently, we were dismayed, as blessed David testifies by saying, "When you turn your face away, they will be dismayed and return to their dust."[19] But since he has now—that is, at the time of his coming—*seen with his eyes*, we are both saved and pitied; what have we not gained of the things that defy description and are truly admirable? (415)

Rejoice exceedingly, daughter Zion, proclaim, daughter Jerusalem: lo, your king comes to you righteous and saving; he is gentle, riding on a beast of burden and young foal (v.9). Obviously in this he now proclaims the revelation of our Savior, the result being that there is no sign of any problem, the consequent order given to the spiritual Zion necessarily being to *rejoice* for the reason that all our sadness has also been removed. After all, what continuing basis of sadness could exist, and on what grounds could sorrow be our lot, now that sin has been driven off, death trampled underfoot, human nature called to the dignity of freedom, the gift of sonship conferred as a decoration and given added luster with the heavenly graces from on high?

Now, observe that in giving the good news of our Savior's coming he immediately summons *daughter Zion*. So it was quite right for him to bid her *rejoice exceedingly* and to urge *Jerusalem* to announce that *her king* will be coming and be revealed in the flesh, *righteous and* (416) *saving*. In other words, Christ has justified us and directed in the path of salvation those who approach him. Furthermore, he is *gentle*, not proposing the severity of the Law nor punishing with death those who transgress its commandment, but rather *saving* by his mildness and raising up the lapsed, even be they sinners, since he has come in person as an advocate with the God and Father.[20] We read that

18. Ps 40.2; Lk 1.78; Ps 102.19.
19. Ps 104.29. Cyril's fourth volume begins with v.9.
20. 1 Jn 2.1. This final clause does not appear in the PG ed.

"the letter kills but the spirit gives life," the letter being the Law that punishes, which is a shadow and a type, whereas the spirit that gives life is Christ. We have, in fact, been taught to worship him in spirit and truth;[21] you need no lengthy treatment by way of proving that *he was riding on a young foal* and in this way entered Jerusalem—the divinely inspired evangelist's writing to this effect being sufficient for our faith. Christ was seated on the foal, remember, while its mother followed; what happened also gave us an indication of a most important reality.[22] That is to say, Christ rested upon the new people, namely, the one called to the knowledge of the truth after formerly worshiping idols; it was like a kind of foal, as yet untamed, not in the habit of taking the right path—in other words, it lacked guidance in the divine law—yet he who leads everyone to spiritual proficiency destined the foal for himself. On the other hand, it also gave us to understand by mention of the ass which followed that the assembly of the Jews followed in due course, although being the elder in its vocation in terms of time, having been previously called through Moses and the prophets. But since it offended against (417) *the saving king*, not having accepted the faith, consequently it was right that it should come behind the foal, bringing up the rear, taking second place to those from the nations, the first becoming last.

Now, consider how the one "who knows minds and hearts"[23] showed human nature being reduced to extreme irrationality: the assembly of the Jews is likened to the extremely irrational ass, and the vast number of the nations are, too, While in fact the latter worshiped creation instead of God its Creator, the former spurned the Law which gave it instruction, thus forfeiting good sense and inclining to every form of depravity, "comparable to brute beasts and resembling them,"[24] as the psalmist says. Now, in another sense an ass is a symbol of uncleanness: it is an unhallowed animal, carrying a curse by law.[25] This is the way with people who are in error and addicted to sin.

21. 2 Cor 3.6; cf. Jn 4.23.

22. The evangelists unanimously speak of Jesus riding a foal on the occasion of his entering Jerusalem, Mt 21.5 and Jn 12.15 citing this verse.

23. Mt 19.30; cf. Ps 7.9.

24. Ps 49.20.

25. Ex 13.13.

He will destroy chariots from Ephraim and a horse from Jerusalem; a war bow will be destroyed, a multitude and peace from nations. He will rule waters from sea to sea, and to the outlets of the earth's rivers (v.10). The prophetic text conveys to us obscurely that in becoming man the Only-begotten intended to put under the feet of those who love him "principalities and powers and the cosmic powers of this present darkness"[26]—that is, the loathsome columns of the demons—to subject to them every foe seen and unseen, to crush every enemy (418), and to bring gladness through the good things stemming from *peace.* At one time the Babylonians invaded Jerusalem; and as well in fact some other neighboring nations, mounted on horses and chariots and armed with bows, as Scripture has it,[27] attacked and inflicted severe suffering. On the basis of what normally happens, he suggests the splendor of Christ's achievements: the righteous and gentle King who saves will come before long—not equipped with a great cortege of bodyguards, not having at his disposal countless skilled personnel. Instead, he will exercise such moderation in behavior as to be seated on a mere foal. Yet he will be so conspicuous for virtue and bring such benefit to those who believe in him as to prevail over *chariots from Ephraim,* remove a *horse from Jerusalem, destroy a war bow,* and bring a deep *peace from all the nations.* Now, by *Ephraim* he refers to the ten tribes in Samaria, and by *Jerusalem* those dwelling in it, these being Judah and Benjamin.

The prophetic text, therefore, introduces also a promise of security and *peace* for us: the holy city would not be so easily overrun by those bent on harming it—that is, the spiritual Zion or Jerusalem, "which is the Church of the living God."[28] Instead, he who saves his kingdom will so govern it as to rule all Judea *from the sea to the rivers,* these being *the earth's outlets* or limits. The divinely inspired David somewhere also sings (419) in referring to the assembly of the Jews as a vine, "It spread its branches to the sea, and to the rivers its shoots";[29] in other words, the country of the Jews extends to the sea to the south and the Indian

26. Eph 6.12. By "obscurely," *ainigmatōdōs,* Cyril admits that, with the text conveying no clear historical reference, the commentator is obliged to seek meaning at some other level.

27. Ps 78.9.

28. 1 Tm 3.15.

29. Ps 80.11.

Ocean, and to what is called Mesopotamia. Christ's kingdom, on the other hand, is not contained in these boundaries: far from it. The verse proceeds from a particular example to the whole and the generic; in fact, he rules not only Judea but everything under heaven, and has under his governance everything from end to end.

And as for you, by the blood of the covenant you dispatched your captives from a waterless pit. You will take your place in a fort as prisoners of the assembly, and for one day of your sojourn I shall repay you double (vv.11–12). The text now moves to the righteous and saving King himself, who is also gentle—namely, Christ—and clearly presents the distinguished and commendable achievements of his coming. The Only-begotten Word of God, remember, emptied himself in becoming man, endured the cross, despising the shame, gave his life as a ransom for many, and acquired for the God and Father the world under heaven *by the blood of* an everlasting *covenant.* As a type of this, blood was sprinkled on the ancients by the all-wise Moses; taking blood (Scripture says), Moses "sprinkled it on the book and on all the people, saying, This is the blood of the covenant which God has made (420) with you." While they were types, however, and an outline of the reality, now the reality itself is Christ,[30] who bought us all *by the blood of the covenant;* we have been ransomed, as his disciple says, "not with perishable things like silver or gold, but with the precious blood of Christ, like that of a lamb without defect or blemish."[31]

So you, O most righteous and gentle King, he is saying, those who have become your *prisoners,* that is, those whom you shackled with bonds of love and whom you persuaded to submit to your yoke and clearly bind the neck of their minds, *you dispatched*—that is, withdrew, or released, or lifted out *from a waterless pit,* either meaning by this Hades itself, where there is no life, taking water as a type of life, since it is life-giving, or taking *pit* very properly as the deceit involved in the false gods. It really is a deep shaft, in fact, and if you were completely drawn into it, you would lose all share of life for the age to come. Now, the fact that Christ at his death emptied Hades and opened the

30. Phil 2.7; Heb 12.2; 13.20; 9.20–21; Ex 24.8.
31. 1 Pt 1.18–19.

gates of the lower world for the spirits in prison is clear to everyone.[32] The God of all somewhere said through the voice of Jeremiah about the people of Israel who abandoned him and stupidly turned to the foolish deceit of the idols, "Heaven is appalled at this, and greatly shocked, says the Lord, because my people have committed two evils, leaving me, the fountain of living water, and digging themselves leaking pits that will be unable to hold water."[33] In other words, just as correct and truthful knowledge of God is a life-giving spring of life, (421) so the diversions of idolatry are to be taken as a kind of waterless and leaking pit.

Then he addresses the *prisoners* themselves, and encourages them to have sound hope, saying, *You will take your place in a fort as prisoners of the assembly.* In my view, by *fort* he means the Church as fortified by Christ and being unshakeable. He says the seat he takes is made firm in faith; Scripture says of God, remember, "You are seated forever";[34] that is, your nature is firm and unshakeable. So you will enjoy security, he is saying, with stability in faith, *O prisoners of the assembly*, these being the holy congregation of those justified in Christ. Now, the fact that they will not go unrewarded for their endurance in all their exploits, as also their constancy in loving God, he indicates by saying, *And for one day of your sojourn I shall repay you double.* His meaning is something like this: all the saints are sojourners and aliens in the land, and every human being's bodily life is very brief; if you compare it with the life to come, you would so lament its extreme brevity that it would resemble *one day.* So *for one day of your sojourn,* he is saying, that is, for the brief and limited period of bodily life, *I shall repay you a double* reward in excess. Christ also said somewhere, "A good measure, pressed down, shaken together, running over, they will put into your lap":[35] (422) the recompense we look forward to, far from being of equal measure to what we have achieved, is much more besides, since the Giver is generous with his gifts.

Hence I have stretched you, Judah, my bow; I have filled Ephraim

32. 1 Pt 3.19. Cf. W. J. Dalton, "1 Peter," *NJBC* 907.
33. Jer 2.12–13.
34. Bar 3.3.
35. Lk 6.38.

(v.13). In this he explains the name that will be given to the flock from the nations, how they will gain entry through faith, the hardships awaiting the one who formerly ran riot—namely, Satan—now that he is deprived of the worshipers he had acquired in his greed. He directs his words, in fact, as though to the holy apostles in their capacity as Israel's teachers who also travel the countryside of the nations, calling them to knowledge of the truth and by that means making them part of their haul. *O Judah,* he says, therefore, *I have stretched you, my bow;* that is, through you I shall strike down the adversaries; and you, *O Ephraim, I have filled.* What that means I shall in turn explain. When the archers hold the iron part of the bow and pull the string to their chest, they are then said to *fill* the bow, and in this way they release the arrow, something dire and unerring, traveling with irresistible force and discharging venom. So the one meaning is expressed differently: I have made you *my bow, O Judah,* and *I have filled you, O Ephraim,* Judah and Ephraim referring to the whole race of Israel. Before the others, therefore, I have made the believers from the Jews a *bow,* as it were,[36] going in advance with the intention of guiding the nations, repelling the herds of the demons that deceive them, and striking down Satan and, in a nutshell, the opponents of the divine (423) teachings and assailants of the initiation achieved through them. In similar terms the divinely inspired David also says somewhere to God, who is Savior of all, "Your arrows are sharpened, O warrior; peoples will fall under you in the heart of the king's enemies"[37]—that is, the arrows of the warrior (namely, Christ) will strike the enemies of the God and Father in their heart and entrails.

Now, those in error, who do not know the one who is God by nature and in reality, are struck down by his "arrows," the guides in initiation, though not unto death; instead, they bring them to love in Christ, so that they may also be subject to him.

36. Cyril, whose text does not contain the word "like" (a bow), though not finding an historical reference to Zechariah's situation, pursues the factual detail of the bow's operation. He is probably deriving this from Theodore, who speaks in similar terms, but unlike Theodore he sees an eschatological meaning in reference to believers from Israel and the nations.

37. Ps 45.5.

This resembles what the bride who is described in the Song of Songs says with clarity, "I am wounded with love."[38] Now, the fact that the divinely inspired disciples are both strong and sturdy the wise psalmist confirms in referring to them in the Spirit, "Like arrows in the hand of a warrior are the sons of those shaken," by "shaken" referring to those from Israel who fell victim to divine grace as a result of being inebriated in Christ; their sons, at any rate, became arrows, as it were, discharged from the hand of a warrior. Habakkuk also said somewhere as though to Emmanuel himself in reference to the divine apostles, "Your shafts will travel in the light of your weapons' gleaming."[39]

I shall stir up your children, Zion, against the children of the Greeks, and stroke you like a warrior's sword (v.13). See, he clearly refers to the spiritual guides from the Jews as his own bow; (424) I mean, what is meant by *the children of Zion* ranged against *the children of the Greeks* if not the divinely inspired disciples and the leaders of the churches in their time, correctly teaching the word of truth?[40] After all, what is to be understood as the spiritual Zion if not the Church? They oppose *the children of the Greeks*, and are ranged against the victims of error, God wielding them *like a warrior's sword.* This is the way the divinely inspired Paul also sees the spiritual soldier equipped by Christ: he clothes him in a "breastplate of righteousness," and a "helmet of salvation" as well, then gives him "the sword of the Spirit, which is the word of God." By use of this sword against *the children of the Greeks*, then, they shear off the error springing up among them, and bring against them the penetrating word of God, living and active,[41] and thus cut away the evil and unclean spirit, so that they may then be able with a pure and free mind, rid of the demons' arrogance, to accept the word of the true knowledge of God.

The Lord will appear over them, and an arrow will go like lightning (v.14). In this he indicates that the Lord God will be with them, accompany them, and join them in destroying the adversaries. *The Lord will appear over them*, the text says—namely, those bent on opposing the ministers of his Gospel. Every *arrow*—that is, guide or apostle, a comparison of them with a shaft or arrow

38. Song 5.8.
39. Ps 127.4; Hab 3.11.
40. 2 Tm 2.15.
41. Eph 6.14, 17; cf. Heb 4.12.

dispatched by God (425)—will fly *like lightning* in the sense of illumining and effortlessly falling on the eyes of everyone. The divinely inspired disciples, you see, the heralds of the Savior's good news, and after them the leaders of the peoples and governors of the churches, were so conspicuous that no one was unaware of the brilliance of the virtue abiding within them. The Savior himself said as much, "No one lighting a lamp hides it under a jar or puts it under a bed, but on a lampstand so that those who enter may see the light." And likewise in another place, "Let your light so shine in people's view that they may see your good works and glorify your Father in heaven."[42]

The Lord almighty will sound a trumpet blast and issue forth brandishing his threat. The Lord almighty will protect them. They will consume them, overwhelm them with slingshot, drink their blood like wine, and fill the altar like bowls. The Lord will save them on that day, his people like sheep (vv.14–16). The text presents the God in charge of all as a comrade in arms, as I said, and fighting alongside them, deployed and choosing to join the contest in such a way as already to give the impression of hostile engagement and, as it were, readiness to advance against them, employing all his might and the resources within (426) him. He is very properly engaged in battle, the text says, not with those taken as a catch through faith for justification, but with those locked in unholy conflict with the divine preaching, whom Paul also indicated to us in saying, "A wide door for effective work has opened to me, and there are many adversaries."[43] *The Lord will sound a trumpet blast,* then, the text says; in other words, Christ has spoken the Gospel message, which spread throughout the whole world under heaven, for the mystery of Christ can be heard everywhere. Moses, remember, was softly spoken and slow of speech,[44] and consequently was heard only throughout Judea alone, whereas the word of Christ is not confined to these boundaries: he gave voice like some long and echoing trumpet, and uttered a piercing sound for all ears.

Now, *he will issue forth* as though *brandishing his threat,* and *will protect* his bodyguard in such a way that his adversaries will be

42. Lk 8.16; Mt 5.16.
43. 1 Cor 16.9.
44. Ex 4.10.

consumed by fire, as it were, and in a fashion *overwhelmed with slingshot* and totally smitten. They will also *drink their blood;* that is, by attacking them like wild animals they will easily prevail and leave them dead. They will offer *bowls filled with their blood,* like some libation on the *altar.* The death of those not allowing people in error to be saved is a sacrifice pleasing and acceptable to God;[45] after all, if those who slay bodies do not deserve mercy, and instead they are subject to punishment, what would you say of those who are destroyers and corrupters of souls? (427) The pagan elite with a high reputation for worldly wisdom are they who apply the name "gods and goddesses" hither and yon, and urge people to adore creation instead of the Creator, giving the glory due to God to each of the elements. They have kept the world in error, not only in their own lifetime, but also in subsequent ages. Countless numbers have been lost over the ages by being in thrall to these people's falsehood, and adhering to their incredible old wives' tales. Such people have therefore now disappeared: the profanity of their writings is no more, their fables have achieved nothing, their *blood has been drunk,* as it were, they have been struck down by the teachings of truth like stones and *overwhelmed with slingshots,* and the loss of their babbling is acceptable to God, as I said.

The Lord has saved his people like sheep. In other words, since he is the Maker of everything, those formerly in error could also be called *his people.* Christ, on the other hand, saved them like a flock driven off by brigands; he expelled the false shepherds, and brought the human race under his own control. He is the "good shepherd," after all, who gave his life for his sheep.[46]

Because holy stones roll on his ground. Because anything good is his, anything beautiful is from him, grain for young men and fragrant wine for maidens (v.17). We claim that the *holy stones rolling on* God's *ground* refer to the saints in the churches at times, who (428) are spiritual guides and teachers. They are conformed, you see, to that chosen and esteemed stone, the cornerstone, laid by the God and Father as the foundation of Zion. If the foundation is a stone, however, those who are joined and knit together and

45. Phil 4.18.
46. Jn 10.14–15.

erected as a holy temple to God are arguably called *stones* after him.[47] It very properly says they *roll*, by this indicating in my view their readiness and celerity in turning to anything holy; round or spherical stones, you see, offer no resistance and are more ready for movement than other stones if you want to move them, and the mind of the saints is very disposed to pleasing God. This being the way with stones, it behoves us to be similarly disposed.

Because anything good is his, and anything beautiful is from him, obviously because God awards us everything conducive to piety and life. Such as? *Grain for young men and fragrant wine for maidens:* to people of vigor and a youthful attitude, who acquiesce in his will and choose to perform good works, still further strength will be given by way of spiritual *grain*, since bread strengthens a person's heart. To people already purified, who have a mind unstained, and who can be properly likened to venerable and holy maidens, there will be given spiritual *wine*, which is obviously clear and undefiled knowledge of God, which gladdens a person's heart.[48] *Young men and maidens*, then, are those who, according to the explanation just given by us, will be called to an ample and abundant share in the good things from on high, and will in fact listen to God's (429) words, "Eat and drink, become drunk, you who are near."[49] Such people, in fact, are near God, not in a local sense, which would be silly to imagine or declare, but by a resolute frame of mind, by a longing for every fine thing, and by love for him. In other words, just as depravity disorients us and carries us, as it were, to a long distance from him, so virtue brings us close, causing what divides and comes between us to be withdrawn, by which I mean sin.

47. Is 28.16; 1 Pt 2.6; Eph 4.16; 2.21.
48. Ps 104.15.
49. Song 5.1.

COMMENTARY ON ZECHARIAH, CHAPTER TEN

Ask from the Lord timely rain, early and late (v.1).

THAT IS TO SAY, just as without labor there would be no grain in the fields or a fruitful vineyard producing wine, so too there would be no spiritual fertility in us unless God shed the revelation of his own sayings like rain on mind and heart, and, as it were, bedewed us with knowledge of the old and new Scriptures, namely, the Law and the Gospels, such being *early and late rain.* Now, the fact that knowledge and spiritual appreciation of the Law is not without benefit the Savior himself confirms by saying to the Jewish crowds, "Do not think that I shall accuse you before the Father; your accuser is Moses, on whom you have set your hope. In fact, if you believed Moses, you would believe me, for he wrote about me."[1] He also said somewhere in reference to the scribes (430) and Pharisees, on the grounds of their being called from the teachings of the Law to something better, namely, the Gospel, "Therefore, every scribe trained for the kingdom of heaven is like the master of a household who brings out of his storehouse new things and old."[2] So in seeking from God knowledge both of the Law and of the Gospel, and presenting ourselves in a condition worthy to receive it, we shall definitely receive it and fill the storehouse of our mind, amassing both old things and new, and stocking our minds with the greatest degree of spiritual fruitfulness.

The Lord caused visions, and will give them winter rain, to each one a plant in the field. Because the diviners spoke of trouble and the seers spoke of false visions and false dreams, they offered empty consolation. Hence they dried up because of having no rain, and were abused like sheep because there was no healing (vv.1–2). The text is preg-

1. Jn 5.45–46.
2. Mt 13.52.

nant with a hidden meaning, and in my view requires clear explication; studious readers would understand the drift of the prophet's words in the following way.[3] His statement, you see, had reference to the saints, whom he called "holy stones" and said that "grain" was particularly appropriate for them for their vigor as "young men," and as well sweet-smelling "wine" on account of their being "maidens," that is, holy and sacred. "Those who belong to Christ Jesus," remember, "have crucified the flesh with its passions and desires," as the divinely inspired Paul says.[4] (431) Now, he bade them *ask for early and late rain;* then, after inserting a reference to those who had gone astray, as it were, he gives an explanation of why they had neither grain nor wine, instead being bereft of spiritual rain with the result that they lacked *a plant in the field.*

While the passage pretends to deal with material things, these contain a very subtle and refined level of meaning. It says, in fact, that God *causes visions,* that is, lightning flashes, and sheds *winter rain* on the soil, which is beneficial, and *to each one*—of the beasts in the field, obviously—*he gives a plant. The diviners*—that is, those that were lying and fraudulent—delivered oracles from their own hearts; they *spoke of trouble,* that is, what was not conducive to rest for the people believing them, instead obliging them to suffer for offending God and being ignored by him. *The seers* and the *false dreams offered consolation,* making comforting sounds and exciting them with lavish promises, but saying nothing true. Instead, they led them into deceit and error, giving them hardly a glimpse of the giver and source of spiritual gifts, urging them to seek contentment rather from the false gods—hence his remark, *They dried up because of having no rain, and were abused like sheep.* That is, there was no *plant, there was no healing:* there was no one among them to bind up what was broken, to restore what was fractured, to revive what was abused.

Notice should be taken, therefore, not of those *practicing empty divination,* (432) liars, flatterers, and seers, but rather of

3. While it is typical of Cyril to direct his more studious readers to the *skopos* of a text so as to plumb its meaning, he himself is handicapped in this case by the LXX's seeing "visions" for the "(thunder) clouds" of the Heb., "dried up" for "wandered," and "healing" for "shepherd."

4. Gal 5.14.

God, who flashes into our mind the light of the true knowledge of God, and who sheds spiritual rain—meaning consolations from the Holy Spirit—and produces a plant for those *in the field,* meaning once again the one who provides us, as it were, with ample fodder, the flawless knowledge of the inspired Scripture. "Despite his dignity, the human being did not understand, he was comparable with the brute beasts and resembled them."[5] If you preferred, on the other hand, to turn your mind to the knowledge of the divine sayings and partake of spiritual nourishment, then by dispelling sluggishness you would again be held in honor, under the control of sound thinking, and adopting an attitude befitting a human being.

My anger is roused against the shepherds, and I shall have regard for the lambs (v.3). By *shepherds* here, in my view, he refers to the false prophets and false seers, and to the peddlers of error, who have proved a plague and snare to some people who are deficient in a true opinion about God and attribute to creation the honor and worship due to him, "adoring the works of their own hands," as Scripture says.[6] It is not implausible to relate the false seers to the pagan elite, who in their sophistry have deceived their adherents with their grandiloquence, and who, unlike good shepherds, pasture their flock in thorns and the extreme futility of idle thoughts. What contribution, in fact, could be made by them to the knowledge of the truth? On (433) them would fall also the effects of divine wrath, and very properly: they ruined not only their own souls, but also those of others as well, deceiving them with their high-sounding talk as though to gild the falsehood and turning the value of language into chicanery.

He will have regard for the lambs, in the sense of pitying them, bringing them from deceit to the knowledge of the truth, and leading them to the straight and narrow after being deceived. In other words, just as it was logical for those wronging them to pay a penalty fitting the crime, so likewise it would be a mark of the mildness befitting God and of a fair verdict that the judgment on the sufferers would not be bereft of clemency. It was

5. Ps 49.13.
6. Jer 1.16.

necessary, you see, necessary for the wronged to be saved, with God forgetting the past and freeing from punishment those who perhaps involuntarily had been under the influence of those people's arrogance.

The Lord God almighty will visit his flock, the house of Judah, and will make them like his handsome warhorse. From it he looked down, from it he drew up, from it his bow in anger, and from it will issue forth everyone driving forth in it. They will be like warriors trampling mud in the streets in time of war and will be deployed, because the Lord is with them (vv.3–5). The way he will inflict on the shepherds the effects of his wrath, and will visit and rescue the lambs, he makes (434) clear: after bringing to the fore from the Jews the world's spiritual guides, the holy apostles and evangelists, through them he engaged in combat the pagan sages, rescued the lambs from their grandiloquence, and, after freeing them from the snares of deceit, transferred them to the true and flawless knowledge of God. So the text says, *he will visit his flock, the house of Judah.* He will also make it like *a handsome horse* ready for war, and, as it were, riding on it in a spiritual sense, he will engage in combat the language of the pagans, as I said, and refute the deformity and stupidity of the artfulness within them. You see, no one could doubt the fact that the divinely inspired disciples were to be found among the widely scattered pagans like horses of a kind, as it were, neighing against their garrulity and erroneous hatred of God. We have Christ's words to Ananias about blessed Paul, "Go, for he is an instrument I have chosen to bring my name before nations and kings and the people of Israel." Habakkuk also said somewhere as if addressing our Lord Jesus Christ, "You will ride your horses, and your cavalry will bring salvation."[7] Hence his saying, *He will make it like his handsome warhorse, and from it he will look down,* as if to say, God surveyed those suitable for ministering the Gospel teachings, and made a choice of *those from Judah, and will make appointments from it*—that is to say, he chose them to be servants and ministers of his will, and, as it were, mediators and conveyors of the grace coming from him. Now, he says, it is *from it,* that is, from Judah, that his *bow* is drawn *in anger* against the adversaries. (435) Likewise

7. Acts 9.15; Hab 3.8.

from it will issue forth everyone driving forth in it, meaning by *driving forth* the one who ravages and takes captives.

Now, this is what the divinely inspired disciples also did, snatching some from the pagans and bringing them to the great king—Christ, I mean—for them to be subject to him and choose to adopt his sentiments, at this late stage shaking off the yoke of the devil's arrogance. The divinely inspired disciples struggled against the sophists among the Greeks to such a degree as already to give the impression of trampling on *dust* scattered *on the street.* In fact, *the Lord was with them,* he who does "what is great and unsearchable, marvelous, extraordinary, and beyond counting." Christ also proclaimed somewhere to those believing in him, "Lo, I have given you power to walk on snakes and scorpions and over all the power of the foe."[8]

Now, it should be realized that it is in our effort to develop a spiritual interpretation that we are making comments like this, whereas Jews do not think this is the right way, taking it rather in a historical sense and claiming that after the time of the captivity Antiochus Epiphanes had waged war on them, accompanied by a massive assembly of fighters from the country of the Greeks and ranged against them with allies from those peoples.[9] But Israel was victorious, they claim, and covered themselves in glory exceeding his fury; that was the time in history when those members of the Maccabees furnished proof that the crown of a good reputation had been awarded. In confirmation of their views they adduce what was said just now by us and in fact the verses (436) just above, namely, "Hence I have stretched you, Judah, my bow, I have filled Ephraim. I shall stir up your children, Zion, against the children of the Greeks, and stroke you like a warrior's sword. The Lord will appear over them, and an arrow will go like lightning. The Lord almighty will sound a trumpet blast and issue forth brandishing his threat. The Lord almighty will protect them."[10]

And the cavalry will be confounded. I shall strengthen the house of Judah and save the house of Joseph, and shall settle them, because

8. Jb 5.9; Lk 10.19.
9. Interestingly, Cyril cites the "Jewish" view without condemning it.
10. Zec 9.13–15.

I loved them (vv.5–6). Those who advocate Jewish explanations likewise claim that, with the battle joined against the Greeks, their horses perished, and people belonging to Israel prevailed, with the result that they occupied the country—namely, Judea—rid of all fear, with no one at all deported or taken captive. We, on the other hand, are anxious to adopt an interpretation of the ideas that is consistent and related to what went before; so we claim that *the cavalry* that is *confounded* is nothing else than the proponents of the pagan teachings who were in the habit of arguing the erroneous case that is in opposition to God, whom *Judah* cast down and overcame, and *the house of Joseph was saved.* In this there is reference to the line and race of Israel, or at least the mass of those justified in Christ, who are Jewish in mind and heart, share in circumcision of the spirit,[11] with a mind that "sees God," (437) which is the meaning of "Israel." But since they are *loved* by God, consequently they are also *settled,* that is, in possession of an established residence among all the best things; Scripture says, remember, "The Lord settles the solitary in a house." The divinely inspired Isaiah also said somewhere about the one who practices a special way of life, "Walking in righteousness, speaking in an upright way, hating lawlessness and iniquity, keeping one's hands free of bribes, stopping one's ears from listening to bloodshed, shutting one's eyes from seeing iniquity, this person will dwell in a lofty cave in a rocky fortress."[12] It is not implausible that the giving of the house by God to the saints refers to the Church, or at least the heavenly mansions; blessed David actually declares it worthy of complete admiration when he says to God, the Savior of all, "Blessed are all who dwell in your house; they will praise you for ever and ever," and again, "Better one day in your courts than thousands; I would prefer to be cast aside in the house of my God than dwell in the tents of sinners."[13]

They will be as though I had not turned them away. Because I am the Lord their God, and I shall hearken to them. They will be like the

11. The justified person, as Paul says in Rom 2.29, is a Jew inwardly. Again there is no scorn for the Jewish interpretation, certainly by comparison with pagans. The following (faulty) etymology of Israel Cyril had offered previously.

12. Ps 68.6; Is 33.15–16.

13. Ps 84.4, 10; the PG text does not cite the second of these verses.

warriors of Ephraim (vv.6–7). With the confounding of the sages among the pagans, who were also called *cavalry*, he promises to strengthen and settle (438) those who had been pitied, adding, *because I loved them.* What they will gain through being loved by God he likewise explains: as he says, *I had not turned them away*, not having overlooked them at all but rather visited them when in danger, *because I am the Lord their God*, God not only of Jews but also of nations,[14] being Creator and Lord of all; consequently he says as well, *I shall hearken to them*, that is, I shall render their prayers acceptable. *They will be like the warriors of Ephraim*, as if he were to say again, Those who formerly through weakness of mind and intellect were exhausted and laid low will be brought to such a degree of spiritual strength as already to seem to be of equal ranking with the heroes *of Ephraim*, that is, the apostles and evangelists from the Jews. Such people, in fact, are spiritual *warriors*, fighting enemies, repelling adversaries, defeating principalities, powers, and overlords, as well as the spiritual forces of evil, and prevailing effortlessly over the opponents of the divine teachings.[15] They are also called from the mass of the nations through faith in the knowledge of Christ, holy and inspired men, *like the warriors of Ephraim.* They are also imitators as far as possible of the apostles' way of life, following in their virtuous footsteps and locked in combat themselves with the enemies of truth and with passions and sins.

Their heart will rejoice as though from wine, their children (439) *will see and be glad, and their heart will rejoice in the Lord.* Winebibbers' minds are always out of key and heedless, unaccustomed to register grief, but, as it were, relaxed and untroubled by worry. So if they were *like warriors of Ephraim*, it was then that they would have been very satisfied with themselves, and *rejoiced* to be famous and celebrated with the hope of future good things, and would have as imitators of the special way of life the children born to them—spiritually, I mean. Such was the divinely inspired Paul, too, who says in writing to those called by him, "Even if you have countless guides in Christ, you do not have many fathers; in Christ Jesus through the Gospel I became your

14. Rom 3.29.
15. Cf. Eph 6.12.

father."[16] So their *future* children *will see and be glad;* having been born through meditations on Christ, been acquainted with the force of the mystery, and enlightened by the offerings of the Spirit, they will perform acceptable deeds, receive satisfaction in Christ the Savior himself, and make him their gladness, enjoyment, and happiness of soul and heart. This would also be a clear sign of someone's choosing to live in a godly way: people who direct their thoughts to worldly affairs and connive at dishonesty rejoice in it and find their satisfaction there; they take delight in pleasures of the flesh, are in the habit of reveling in the excesses of the present life, and regard the things of God as of almost no importance. Those who by contrast seek him with all their heart, (440) find delight in meditation on him, and those who extend the horizons of the mind will gain satisfaction in him and only in him.

I shall send them a signal and welcome them, for I shall ransom them and they will become as numerous as they were before. I shall sow them among peoples, and those far off will remember me. They will raise their children and bring them back (vv.8–9). Again he mentions the flock of the Jews, and promises to gather them together after their being scattered and assemble them in Judea from the whole earth so as to leave no one abandoned. He likewise indicates the way the gathering would happen. Some people claim that beekeepers are in the habit of giving certain signals, whistling or making some other sounds, and in this way gathering the swarms of bees to visit the hives. Such a practice is mentioned also in the verse of Isaiah, "On that day the Lord will whistle for flies which frequent part of the river of Egypt, and for the bee which is in the land of Assyria." Other people say that also in time of war, if it happens that the fighters are dispersed, either in pursuit or being pursued, some sign is raised aloft by the leaders for them to see, come together, and arrive at the one place. What is found in the prophet Isaiah describes something similar: "It will be like a flag on a mountain, and like a signal on a hill."[17] So (441) the similarity arises from a normal occurrence; he says, *I shall send them a signal and welcome them—*

16. 1 Cor 4.15.
17. Is 7.18; 30.17.

in other words, the cross of the Savior was raised up as a bold, clear sign for us; through it we became acceptable to the God and Father, were in fact redeemed, and as believers we emerged as a vast number beyond counting.

Now, since he went on to say, *I shall sow them among peoples, and those far off* from them will come and *remember me*, again we make that claim, and not at variance with the author's purpose. It is in fact quite logical: as though broadcast among many nations and in every country and city, the divinely inspired disciples and heralds of the divine Gospels caused those who were far removed from God as a result of the sin and error that came between them to *remember* him and bring to mind the Savior and Creator of all, even if formerly paying reverence to creation and consequently forfeiting their relationship with God. The divinely inspired Paul therefore addresses those called through him to the knowledge of Christ in the words, "We who once were far off have now been brought near." So they will *remember* God and come; the blessed prophet Jeremiah will suggest to us something similar in saying as though to Israel, "Remember the Lord, you who are far off, and let Jerusalem come into your heart."[18] If they fully remembered the one who is by nature God, however, they would then also proceed to such a degree of spiritual vigor as to become fathers of children, and by means of words *raise their children* to piety, taking pride in that very fact. To those raised by him, reaching maturity and coming to full stature (442) in Christ, the divinely inspired Paul also writes somewhere, in one case, "My joy and crown," and in another, "Brethren, you are the boast I make in Christ Jesus." Scripture says, remember, "Old people's crown are their children's children; children's boast are their parents."[19]

I shall bring them back from the land of Egypt and welcome them from Assyria; I shall bring them into Gilead and into Lebanon, and none of them will be left behind (v.10). When Nebuchadnezzar took Judea by force, and the divine Temple and Jerusalem itself were set on fire, then the whole of Israel also suffered hardship. Some people in fact were taken off as captives to the Assyrians and Medes;

18. Eph 2.13; Jer 51.50.
19. Eph 4.13; Phil 4.1; 1 Cor 15.31; Prv 17.6.

others escaped their cruelty and managed to flee, in fear and dread of being caught up in a similar fate, choosing to make their way to Egypt and undergo the yoke of servitude under them, not of their own will but imposed by necessity. Since he promised to regather them from all quarters, therefore, he mentions also the places where they had been deported, some made captive, as I said, and some forced by intolerable dread to accept a fate against their will.

Now, since it becomes spiritual people with an ardent love of God to introduce a spiritual interpretation instead, we claim that he is promising to extricate them from the country or the hand of the unseen foes and free them from every fear, (443) captives though they were and, as it were, subject to others, and in a way transformed into liberty. Or, by a different way of interpreting, he says they will be freed from darkness and confusion, Egypt meaning "darkness" and Babylon "confusion." Often the terms Assyrian and Babylonian are applied indiscriminately to the one nation on account of their being under a single rule and the single kingship being exercised over them. So his promise is to introduce those who are ransomed from the hand of arrogant rulers *into Gilead,* a fertile and fruitful part of Judah, and also *into Lebanon,* a high and wooded mountain situated on the boundaries of the land of the Jews and of the Phoenicians. That was the meaning, in my view, of reference to both: our Lord Jesus Christ freed us, as it were, from *Egypt and Assyria* in the sense of the arrogance of the captors, these being evil and unclean demons, and introduced us, as it were, into a wooded and prosperous land, the Church, in which there is a very abundant crop of honorable people, the heads of the saints being innumerable, raised on high through virtue, and flourishing in the manner of cedars. To them would very rightly be applied the saying of David to the God of all, "The cedars of Lebanon which you planted," the divinely inspired Paul also clearly identifying those justified by faith as "God's field."[20]

They will cross by a narrow sea, and strike waves in the sea, (444) *and all the depths of the rivers will dry up. All the arrogance of Assyria will be done away with, and the sceptre of Egypt will be removed. I shall*

20. Ps 104.16; 1 Cor 3.9.

make them strong in the Lord their God, and they shall boast in his name, says the Lord (vv.11–12). By way of similarity to the favors bestowed on the ancients, there is a promise of assistance to those believing in Christ. In other words, just as Israel crossed the Red Sea by controlling its waves (Scripture says, remember, "The waters became as solid as a wall," with God achieving an incredible feat), and just as they crossed the Jordan on foot,[21] likewise (he is saying) those called through Moses to knowledge of Christ and conducted to salvation through initiation by the holy apostles will negotiate the billows of the present life like some fiercely raging *sea,* escape the world's tumult, and be at liberty to serve the one who is by nature God.[22] They will also pass through trials like some surging *rivers,* and thus rejoice loudly on this basis by saying, "If the Lord had not been with us, let Israel say, if the Lord had not been with us, when people rose against us, surely they would have swallowed us alive when their anger raged against us; surely the water would have drowned us. Our soul passed over the torrent; surely our soul passed over the intolerable water."[23]

Now, just as Israel was taken prisoner, he is saying, and was led off to Assyrians and Medes, but escaped their *insolence* or arrogance, being brought back to Judea, and just as it threw off the (445) arrogance of the Egyptians, who were always disposed and given to making war on them, in similar fashion (he is saying) those redeemed by Christ will prevail over the foe, namely, those seen and unseen, who, as it were, force them into slavery against their will, make captives of them, as it were, and shackle them in the bonds of their peculiar malice. But they will prevail over them, escape their insolence and arrogance, with the help of God, in whom they will also *boast.* We glory in Christ, in fact, take him as our strength, trust in him, and place all our hope of life in him. "It was no messenger, no angel, but the Lord himself who saved us," remember, and as the blessed psalmist says, "God is our refuge and strength, help in the tribulations coming upon us in great number."[24]

21. Ex 15.8; Jos 3.14–17.
22. Cyril sees the economy of salvation spanning both Testaments, from Moses to Jesus to the apostle.
23. Ps 125.1–5 LXX.
24. Is 63.9; Ps 46.1.

COMMENTARY ON ZECHARIAH, CHAPTER ELEVEN

Open your doors, Lebanon, and let fire consume your cedars. Let the pine lament because the cedar has fallen, because the mighty were in severe difficulties. Lament, oaks of Bashan, because the dense forest has been felled (vv. 1–2).

HE SHIFTS the drift of his words, then, to another line of thinking. Having delivered in excellent fashion an adequate account of the calling of the nations in Christ through faith, he clearly forecasts the future disbelief in him by the people of Israel, that is, at the time of the Incarnation, and the fact that this was the reason for the burning of the Temple and the city of (446) Jerusalem, the taking of the other cities of Israel, and the extermination of their inhabitants. This was done by the hand of the Romans at the time when Vespasian and Titus were in control. It would probably be unnecessary to recount in detail all that happened to the cities or communities of the Jews on account of their fury against Christ; those interested can read it in the works of Josephus and gain a close knowledge of whatever they wish.[1]

He therefore shifts his attention to those of the line of Israel, comparing Judah to *Lebanon.* On what basis? Lebanon is a mountain with many trees and covered in dense forests, while the country of the Jews is well populated, with a mass of inhabitants beyond number, more famous than others, like very tall *cedars* or *pines,* by which I mean the priests and kings from the tribe of Judah at the time, who excelled for the glories of leadership and were known throughout the land for having a

1. Attentive though Cyril is to the historical situation of the author, and also to future developments in New Testament times predicted in the text (as he sees it), he does not go into details on the latter. Instead, he suggests the reader may wish to find these in the works of the Jewish historian Flavius Josephus. See note 13 below for Cyril's depending on Jerome for reference to Josephus.

high reputation. They acted in impious fashion towards Christ, however, "taking away the key of knowledge, not entering themselves or allowing entrance to those coming in," and finally crucifying him, even despite acknowledging that he was the heir.[2] Consequently, it was right that they should perish along with their homes, cities, and loved ones. By *Lebanon*, therefore, he makes an obscure reference to Judah, likening those in it to the tall trees in being higher than the others and very elevated. The fact that it was destined to be captured easily (447) and as an unwalled city to admit the Roman army flooding in, and thus to be consumed like a forest when set alight, he suggests in the words, *Open your doors, Lebanon, and let fire consume your cedars. Let the pine lament because the cedar has fallen.*

The verse employs a metaphor; by using the term *Lebanon* or likening the country of the Jews to a mountain, he necessarily compares those in it to a *pine* and forest.[3] The fact that it refers to people is not difficult to see; he said at the outset, *because the mighty were in severe difficulties,* and the way the *difficulties* are to be taken he demonstrated by saying, *Let the pine lament because the cedar has fallen.* In other words, when the power of the Romans devastated the cities of Judea, it was a daily event for their prominent citizens to be taken; those who had not yet met this fate lamented those taken, directing the lament also to themselves, being dispirited and fearful that they too would very shortly become victims. This in my view is the import of the clause, *Let the pine lament because the cedar has fallen.* By *oaks of Bashan* he possibly refers in generic fashion to the inhabitants of Jerusalem, Bashan being a region of Judea, fertile and productive, where very tall trees grow. Since the inhabitants of Jerusalem were more famous than the others, by which I mean priests and leaders of the people, he calls them *oaks of Bashan,* which were rightly lamenting, doubtless because *the dense forest has been*

2. Lk 11.52; Mt 21.38.

3. Not finding (in this apocalyptic material) a reference to the time of Zechariah, Cyril perceives an historical reference to the fall of Jerusalem under Titus by way of metaphorical expression, every detail of which he unpacks for his readers. In the course of this interpretation (which is independent of Didymus's more highly allegorical procedure) he is not dogmatic, offering it as "my view," a phrase frequently in his mouth.

felled. They realized, you see, that the populace throughout the country had been consumed like a *forest,* chopped down by the fierce attacks of the invaders as though by axes. By the *dense forest,* which (448) he says was *felled,* you will likewise understand the population of Jerusalem itself; through famine and battle they perished, with the *oaks of Bashan*—that is, the leaders—lamenting them.

A sound of shepherds mourning for the reversal of their greatness, a sound of lions roaring for the reversal of Jordan's insolence (v.3). In this, as I said just now, he makes the explanation very obvious: no longer speaking of pine or oak, he refers unambiguously to the leaders of the Jewish classes, who he says were lamenting and, as it were, uttering cries, bewailing the *reversal of their greatness.* They were miserable and dejected, in fact, pitiable and dishonored, after previously enjoying a very high reputation. But after the shepherds in Christ emerged—namely, the divinely inspired disciples—there was rightly a *reversal of the greatness* of the false shepherds. The Lord of the flock, remember, had blamed them through the holy prophets in these words, "Woe to the shepherds who scatter and destroy the sheep of their pasture," and again, "Because the shepherds were stupid, and did not inquire of the Lord, hence the whole flock had no sense and were scattered." He promised to reveal the genuine shepherds to those believing in him, on the other hand, saying once again, "I shall bring you to Zion, and give you shepherds after my own heart, and they will shepherd you, shepherding with understanding." Who are they, then? (449) The divinely inspired disciples and the leaders of the churches of the time, "explaining the word of truth,"[4] and skilled in bringing the young in their charge to everything calculated to promote spiritual benefit.

It is the false shepherds, then, who *mourn for the reversal of their greatness.* He suggests this also in another way by immediately adding, *a sound of lions roaring for the reversal of Jordan's insolence,* "roaring" applying properly to the sound made by wolves, howling from hunger and thirst, though the divine Scripture uses it also of lions. So those who preside over the ranks of the Jews were found *roaring* like lions, that is, starving and howling,

4. Jer 23.1; 10.21; 3.14–15; 2 Tm 2.15.

presumably for not having the contributions from the people—tithes, first-fruits, thanksgiving offerings. Since they lost their flock, you see, they no longer profited from the offerings from them.

If, on the other hand, you were to think that the scribes and Pharisees in the role of lions were howling against Christ, you would be right to take this view; they bellowed against him, and uttered cries of envy, hatred, and unbridled fury, calling him inebriated and born of lewdness, and saying, "Away with him, away with him, crucify him."[5] But even if they roared, the *reversal* was extreme, affecting *Jordan's insolence.* The meaning of this I shall in turn explain. Jordan, remember, flows past Jericho, and there are a great number of lions in its vicinity, roaring balefully and instilling unbearable fear in the inhabitants. (450) The scribes and the Pharisees were like that in the way they roared at the common people, striking the weaker ones with fear of their authority. But there was a *reversal* of the fear of the lions. He refers to this as *Jordan's insolence, insolence* also being the word used for the snorting that issues from the nostrils of horses and mules and is expelled by fierce breathing, and also used of arrogant behavior. The divinely inspired David, for example, said of those who violently abused Christ, "What was the reason for the nations' insolent snorting and the peoples' vain pondering?"[6] So when he says *Jordan's insolence,* you would understand haughtiness, not at all on the part of the river, but of the lions in its vicinity; from the places he sometimes indicates what is in them.

The Lord almighty says this, Shepherd the sheep of slaughter. Those who acquired them killed them without repenting, and those who sold them said, Blessed be God, we are rich. And their shepherds were unaffected by them (vv.4–5). The passage is directed to the shepherds lamenting and roaring in the fashion of lions, whom he has permitted thus far to pasture *the sheep of slaughter* despite their being very negligent by selling and slaughtering without showing the slightest regret. Those shepherds, in fact, being very unreasonable and interested only in their own pleasure, and

5. Jn 8.41; Mt 11.19; Jn 19.15.

6. Ps 2.1. As Cyril explains (his commentary invoking both topography and linguistics), the word in the Zec text, φρύαγμα, has these related meanings.

very little concerned for the owner of the flock, have no qualms about slaughtering some of the sheep in imitation of the attacks by wild animals, and selling others without showing any regret at all, as I said (451); instead, they rejoice in the impropriety of the profit, and succumb to the base gain acquired in this way. In similar fashion, in my view, the leaders of the Jews would also be found showing no compassion for the flocks in their care, enhancing their wealth and expanding their wallets with their insatiable grasp. The Savior, for instance, said of such people in accusation, "Woe to you, scribes and Pharisees, hypocrites, because you tithe mint, dill, and cumin while neglecting the weightier matters of the Law—justice and mercy and faith."[7] In other words, though so fastidious as to chastise those not observing minutiae in offering tithes prescribed by Law, they gave no importance at all to its more serious, basic, and beneficial requirements. That they were not good shepherds, but interested rather only in their own profit, he makes clear in saying in the verse of Ezekiel, "Ah, you shepherds of Israel, surely shepherds do not feed themselves? Do not shepherds feed the sheep? Lo, you consume the milk, clothe yourselves in the wool, slaughter the fatlings, and feed my sheep."[8] Hence his saying, Feed *the sheep of slaughter;* that is, otherwise they will shortly die by the hand of the Romans, or you will slaughter them yourselves, despite being in the position of shepherds. The time, in fact, has not yet come for them to go to slaughter: after the coming of the Savior the mass of the Jews were consumed by the Romans' swords despite God's patience with them.

Now, the fact that the peoples in their control had become the inheritance of the shepherds he demonstrated in saying, *Those who acquired them killed them without repenting:* just as (452) they made their own the Lord's spiritual vineyard—Israel, I mean, or Judah in person, the newly planted, the beloved—so *they acquired* the flocks, as it were, gaining profit from them, and always treating them as their own inheritance on the basis of greed, and exposing them to theft by anyone interested. Hence

7. Mt 23.23.

8. Ezek 34.2–3, the Pusey ed. not containing the negative in the final clause found in the PG ed. here and in Theodoret's Commentary on Ezekiel.

those who acquired them killed them, and those who sold them said, Blessed be God, we are rich. These people should be understood as judges who put their judgments up for sale as if claiming support from the Law of Moses, despite its saying clearly, "You shall not be partial in judging, because the judgment is God's."[9] They were, in fact, very fond of selling the judgment in each case to interested parties, as is clear again from the words of the holy authors; one of the holy prophets said of Jerusalem, "Its leaders passed judgment by bribery," and the divinely inspired Habakkuk protested, as it were, loudly to God, "How long shall I appeal, Lord, and you will not hearken, or cry to you when wronged and you will not save me? Why have you given me a glimpse of pain and trouble, hardship and impiety? Judgment goes against me, and the judge takes bribes. Hence the Law has lost validity, and judgment does not take effect, because the impious have control of justice, and for this reason verdicts will not be enforced."[10]

So those amassing wealth by illegal profit and perverting justice, and, as it were, *selling* judgments in every case, would be the judges, as I just said. They are also the ones saying, *Blessed be God, we are rich.* And for making these most foolish and outrageous statements (453) they would rightly deserve censure; they pretend they have God to thank for profiting from injustice and growing rich from bloodshed. It would have been better for them to say, however, *Blessed be God* for our paying respect to upright judgment, for emerging as blameless and sincere guardians of the divine prescriptions, delivering upright verdicts in every case. So fine words are deceitful and blameworthy unless what is performed by us is pleasing to God.

Hence I shall no longer spare the inhabitants of the earth, says the Lord. Lo, I shall surrender each person into the hands of his neighbor and into the hands of his king. They will destroy the earth, and I shall not rescue them from their hand. I shall shepherd the sheep of slaughter to the Canaanite (vv.6–7). He threatens the flocks with ruin, removal, and the calamities of war, because, although it was open to them to have recourse to the power of the chief shepherd

9. Dt 1.17.
10. Mi 3.11; Hab 1.2–4.

of all—Christ, I mean—and be subject to him, they stupidly associated themselves instead with those who slaughtered and sold them. The Only-begotten Word of God became man, remember, and clearly said in unmasking both those men's knavery and the sincerity of the divine plan for us, "I am the good shepherd. The good shepherd lays down his life for the sheep, whereas the hired hand, who is not the shepherd and does not own the sheep, sees the wolf coming, leaves the sheep, and takes to flight. (454) The wolf snatches them and scatters them, because he is a hired hand, and does not care for the sheep. I am the good shepherd."[11] Now, the Jews, miserable though they were and needing to voice their criticism of the hired shepherds, did not do so; rather, the good shepherd, who laid down his own life as a ransom for all, they abused in countless ways, stoned, reproached, and in the end opened their mouth wide against him, crying out along with their leaders in demanding from Pilate, "Away with him, away with him, crucify him," and actually bringing down his righteous blood on their own heads in the words, "His blood be upon us and upon our children."[12]

Hence I shall no longer spare the inhabitants of the earth, the text says: they no longer deserved pity from God; instead, *each person* was delivered *into the hands of their neighbor and into the hands of their king* or ruler. In fact, they crucified Emmanuel, and became murderers of the Lord, completely sacrilegious. But God called them to repentance, and did not immediately inflict on them the effects of his wrath. After the lapse of thirty years from the crucifixion of the Savior, however, peace departed from the country of the Jews; there were enemies everywhere, city invading city, people in each one divided among themselves and fighting with one another, the result being that they found themselves in equal trouble from one another as befell them from the enemy. The bold Roman generals were in control of the land of the Jews, burning cities along with inhabitants, (455) and subjecting the country to the yoke of slavery. Those capable of fleeing dwelt in the lands of the nations, which is still the case today.

11. Jn 10.11–14.
12. Jn 19.15; Mt 27.25.

I think this is also the reference in his saying, *I shall shepherd the sheep of slaughter to the Canaanite,* that is, to the country and land of the Canaanites. The Canaanites are the nation among whom the *sheep of slaughter* are shepherded by God to this day, or at least seem to be shepherded; they observe some elements of the Law, and you would find them not totally ignoring the ancient customs. For instance, they circumcise the flesh, observe the sabbath, and in addition to this they judge some other details worthy of care and attention. This, to be sure, was the drift of God's words in Ezekiel, "I shall be a sanctuary for them for a while in the countries where they go."[13] The civil wars throughout Judea and Jerusalem, for example, and in every city, the narrator of the Jews' disasters has narrated—Josephus by name, a man of eloquence and wisdom.

I shall take for myself two staffs; one I called Beauty, and the other I called Cord; I shall shepherd the sheep. The word *staff* is understood in many ways for our benefit by the inspired Scriptures: sometimes it implies (456) a kingdom, as when there is reference to Christ, "The staff of your kingdom a staff of equity," sometimes strength, as in the saying, "The Lord sends out from Zion a staff of power, and you will rule in the midst of your foes."[14] It is also taken as instruction and pastoral practice; there is the expression again in the verse of the prophet to the Son, "Shepherd your people with the staff of your tribe, the sheep of your inheritance." In the present text, however, the *staffs* indicate to us forms of pastoral practice and a twofold form of instruction giving the impression of being blameless. The chief shepherd of all, who "lays down his life for the sheep"[15]—namely, Christ—receives the *staffs* so that with them he may shepherd his own sheep.

In former times—that is, before the time of the Incarnation—the Word from God the Father, being God and Lawgiver, pas-

13. Ezek 11.16. The further recommendation of Josephus carries no indication that Cyril has read him. Kerrigan, *St Cyril,* 345, holds that "finding references to Rome in oracles of Old Testament prophecy bears witness to a vogue that was rather widespread in antiquity." His suspicion that Cyril may be finding such references in Jerome is entirely plausible.

14. Pss 45.6; 110.2.

15. Mi 7.14; Jn 10.11.

tured Israel, using a single staff, as it were, instruction according to the Law. He said to them somewhere, remember, in the statement of the prophet, "I shepherded you in the wilderness."[16] But when he became like us, he received *two staffs;* he pastured as his own worshipers those justified through faith and sanctified by the Spirit through axioms of the Law and the Gospels, not urging them to sacrifice oxen nor teaching them to devote themselves to offerings according to the Law. Instead, he bade them exercise the power of worship in Spirit as a bloodless manner of sacrifice; the shadow gives way to the reality, and (457) what was outlined in types has been changed to the refinement of life in Christ and the Gospel.

Now, the staffs have names: *one Beauty,* a new covenant, fine and admirable, of which the Son himself said, "Charming in beauty beyond the sons of men," the other *Cord*—that is, a division—for us to understand it as the Law, the *cord* that was normally used for educating now being separated from the Lord; Scripture says, remember, "When the Most High divided up the nations so as to scatter Adam's children, he fixed the boundaries of the peoples according to the number of God's angels; the Lord's own division was his people Jacob, Israel the cord of his inheritance."[17] By these two *cords,* then, the great chief shepherd promises to pasture *his own sheep,* and his word is sure: he gathered the people of Israel and also those of the nations into one fold,[18] and for their nourishment he provides instruction both from the Law and from the Gospels, supplying them with a share of spiritual fodder, as it were, and richly nourishing the souls of the saints.

I shall remove three shepherds in one month. My soul will be depressed by them, their souls roared at me. And I said, I shall not shepherd you. Let the dying die, the faulty fail, and what are left eat the flesh each of his neighbor (vv.8–9). At the appearance of the true and good shepherd, it was actually quite likely—or, rather, inevitable—that there should now be hired laborers and false shepherds in their midst (458), that is, the Jews' guides in the Law, some of

16. Hos 13.5.

17. Ps 45.2; Dt 32.8–9. In the Zechariah text the LXX sees "cord" in the Heb. "union."

18. Jn 10.16.

whom "slaughtered the sheep without repenting," while others "sold them and said, Blessed be God, we are rich."[19] Next, what on earth he is referring to in the *three shepherds,* do you think, and in what way they are *removed in one month,* as he says—come now, let us explain, giving credence to the statement of the divine Scriptures. In my view, then, by the *three shepherds* he refers to those acting as priests according to the Law and those appointed as judges of the people; in addition to these there are the commentators on the Scriptures or the Law, they being the ones who pastured Israel. Some of them enjoyed the glory of priesthood, being from the single tribe of Levi, of whom Moses said, "The lips of a priest will guard knowledge, and people will look for the Law from his mouth."[20] Others were assigned to the role of judging, also being chosen but emerging from every tribe. In the same way, in my view, were the commentators on the Scriptures, or, as I said just now, the Law, who were always in attendance on those assigned to judge and provided the texts of the Law as evidence in each case.

The fact that, as I said, the attendants on the divine altars were only from the tribe of Levi requires no proof, whereas confirmation that the judges came from every tribe by selection comes from the words of blessed Moses in Deuteronomy to the children of Israel, "You will appoint judges and scriptural commentators for yourself tribe by tribe in all the cities the Lord your God gives you, and they will render just decisions for the people. They will not distort justice, they will not show partiality (459) or accept bribes, for bribes blind the eyes of the wise and subvert the cause of those who are in the right."[21] Moses reached the point of making such a statement and similar ones and of ordering its fulfillment, partly in obedience to God's ineffable wishes, and partly out of deference to the advice of Jethro, his father-in-law. Scripture says, remember, "The next day Moses sat as judge for the people, and the whole people stood around Moses from morning until evening. Lo, when Jethro saw all he was doing for the people, he said, What is this that you are doing for the people? Why are you the only one sitting while all the people stand around you

19. Zec 11.5.
20. Mal 2.7.
21. Dt 16.18–19.

from morning until evening?" Then when Moses said that it was for the sake of judging fairly and lawfully that he gave himself to the labor of this role, Jethro once more said, "Now listen to me, then; I shall advise you, and God will be with you. Let your role be to represent the people before God, offer their cases to God, convey to them God's commands and his Law, and indicate to them the ways they are to follow and the deeds they are to do. You should also look for able men from the whole people, reverent and just men who abhor arrogance, and appoint them for the people." What does the sacred text say next? "Moses listened to his father-in-law and did all that he said to him. Moses selected able men from the whole of Israel and appointed them as heads over them, officers over thousands, officers over hundreds, officers over fifties, and officers over tens; they judged the people at all times. Difficult cases (460) they brought back to Moses, but easy cases they judged themselves."[22]

The *three shepherds*, therefore, were the priests, judges, and experts in the text of the Law—that is, legal experts. We shall find our Lord Jesus Christ, however, making a point of criticizing Pharisees, scribes, and lawyers in these words, "Woe to you, scribes and Pharisees." And when one of the lawyers replied to him when he said this, "Teacher, in saying this you insult us as well," he replied, "Woe also to you lawyers, because you load people with burdens hard to bear, and you yourselves do not lift a finger to ease them."[23] While I am aware that those reigning in Jerusalem at one time from the tribe of Judah filled the role of shepherds to the people under them, yet at the time of Christ the race of kings had disappeared or had been expelled from control; Herod from Ashkelon, son of Antipater, and Pontius Pilate were in charge of Judea at the time. We consequently kept silence about those from the tribe of Judah; the fact that they had disappeared at the time of Christ's birth is confirmed by the scriptural statement, "A prince will not disappear from Judah or a ruler from his thighs until he comes to whom it belongs, and he will be the expectation of the nations."[24] Since

22. Ex 18.13–26. The whole Jethro incident is missing from the PG ed.
23. Lk 11.44–46.
24. Gn 49.10 LXX. In his attempt to identify the three groups referred to in the Zechariah text, and exclude kings, Cyril (whose historical data can be un-

the expectation of the nations had arrived and was now born—Christ, that is—consequently a ruler disappeared from Judah and a ruler from his thighs.

The *three shepherds*, then, as I said—priests, judges, and teachers of the Law—who held their office (461) or functions and positions up to the time of the Incarnation, were the ones who were *removed in one month*, and rightly so: since they killed the Author of life, consequently they too were cut down *in one month* when Emmanuel endured execution for your sakes. Though in fact they continued to administer Israel even after the crucifixion of the Savior, since God who controls everything was still patient and showing pity on them, and summoning them to repentance, we say they were *removed* when the sentence delivered by God came into effect, at the time when, as I said, they handed over for crucifixion the Savior and Redeemer of all—hence *they were removed in one month.*

So much for the *shepherds* in the passage; the judgment *I shall not shepherd you* affects also the creatures, their *eating* and biting one another at will, smashing and consuming without any mercy. You see, since they were expelled from the divine fold, and did not consider the chief shepherd of all to be deserving of pity, they consumed one another and were rendered ready prey for the snatching. In reference to the *three shepherds* he said, and rightly so, that once they were *removed in one month, my soul will be depressed by them;* that is, I shall impose a heavy penalty on them, because *their souls roared at me;* differing in no way from wild animals, they repeatedly assaulted Christ, finally presenting him to Pilate with the words, "Away with him, away with him, (462), crucify him." He recalls this, saying also in the verse of Jeremiah, "I have forsaken my house, I have abandoned my heritage, I have given my beloved soul into the hands of its foes. My heritage has become like a lion in the forest; she has lifted up her voice against me—therefore, I hate her."[25]

---

certain) cites Herod the Great (only half a Jew, son of Antipater II and appointed king by Rome, alive at Jesus' birth but dead in 4 BCE). Could he have in mind rather the contemporary of Pilate (appointed in 27 CE) and Herod's son and successor, Herod Antipas, a tetrarch, not a king, who outlived Jesus? It seems the former was on his mind when he made a similar point in comment on Hos 1.4.

25. Jn 19.15; Jer 12.7–8.

I shall take my beautiful staff and cast it aside to cancel my covenant that I made with all the peoples. It will be canceled on that day, and the Canaanites will know the sheep that are protected, because it is the word of the Lord (vv.10–11). By *beautiful staff* he refers to the instruction given through the guidance of the Gospel, which is especially charming—namely, for its spiritual quality. By the *casting aside and canceling*, on the other hand, he would probably be indicating not that he dismisses and annuls it by abolition or abrogates it as useless: far from it. I would rather claim that there is need of understanding by us. People normally in charge of flocks, remember, on perceiving that some of the sheep of the flock have run off and are far removed from the others, use their staff to advantage on them at that time, and immediately round them up and force them to join the others. Accordingly, the prophetic passage appropriately applied the practice of shepherds; it says the *beautiful staff would be cast aside*, (463), that is to say, launched at those far off—namely, the nations, these being at a distance but becoming close through faith. It says *the staff would be cast aside* in such a way as to be *canceled* or distributed throughout the whole earth,[26] and to give the impression of the preaching about Christ, or the Gospel message, being disseminated everywhere. *It will be canceled on that day*, the text says—that is, at the time when Christ tramples on the power of death, comes back to life, and says to the holy apostles, "Go, make disciples of all nations, baptizing them in the name of the Father and of the Son and of the Holy Spirit." It was then, you see, that the word of the Savior of us all traversed the whole world under heaven, and it is correct to say of the holy apostles that "their flame went out to all the earth, and their words to the ends of the world."[27]

Now, the benefit of the *casting aside* to the nations and *canceling* or distributing throughout the earth in their own countries the *beautiful staff*, or the *covenant*, which he made no longer with Israel alone but rather with *all the nations*, we would have no trouble establishing in understanding the prophetic passage.

26. Cyril seems to see the phrase "(the peoples) of the earth" in his text, though the Pusey ed. does not include it.

27. Mt 28.19; Ps 19.4.

He says, in fact, *the Canaanites will know the sheep that are protected, because it is the word of the Lord,* by *the Canaanites* meaning "the nations." They would be understood as *the sheep that are protected:* they have been watched for by Christ, he being the "expectation of the nations."[28] When the *covenant with all the peoples* was scattered in their own countries (464), they believed that he is *the Word of the Lord;* we who are called from the nations through faith accept that as God, born of God by nature and being the Only-begotten Word of God, he it is who addressed to us in himself the divine and evangelical laws. Consequently we have adored him and serve him, abandoning that ancient and inglorious error and forsaking polytheistic views. This, to be sure, was the theme of praise raised to him in the statement of David, "All the nations you made will come and adore before you, Lord," for "in the name of Jesus Christ every knee will bend of those in heaven, on earth, and under the earth, and every tongue confess that Jesus Christ is Lord to the glory of God the Father."[29]

I shall say to them, If it is good in your sight, set my wages, and give them or decline. They set my wages at thirty pieces of silver. The Lord said to me, Throw them into the smelter and see if it proves true in the way I was tested for them. I took the thirty pieces of silver, threw them into the house of the Lord, into the smelter (vv.12–13). In the Gospel oracles, or in the *beautiful staff*—that is, the excellent instruction—we learned of the Incarnation of the Only-begotten. We heard and have believed, in fact, that as God, as I said, the Word of God the Father "became flesh and dwelt (465) among us," came in the form of a slave, though being in the form and in equality with the one who begot him, and became "obedient unto death, death on a cross," and, "though rich, he became poor for our sakes so that through his poverty we might become rich";[30] he rescued us from the bonds of death, freed us from sin, and made us children of God. What good thing has not been given? In addition to this we know that we "were bought at a price," "not with corruptible things, silver and gold, but with the precious blood of Christ as of an innocent and spotless lamb." And so we now owe our life to him; if "one person died

28. Gn 49.10 LXX.
29. Ps 86.9; Phil 2.10–11.
30. Jn 1.14; Phil 2.6–8; 2 Cor 8.9.

for all, then all have died in him," and we ought to live no longer for ourselves, according to right and proper thinking, but rather "for the one who died and rose for us."[31]

Consequently he says, *If it is good in your sight,* that is, the mystery of the Incarnation: if you were saved through it and behaved properly, and know me as Savior and Redeemer, who endured death for the life of everyone, *set my wages*—that is, determine them—*and give them or decline.* Only those from the nations were grateful: they *set my wages,* by no means adequate but to some degree appropriate to what we received from him. In other words, just as he died for us, so we also laid down our lives in sincerity and love for him. It would be appropriate for the holy martyrs to say, "Who will separate us from the love of Christ: tribulation, oppression, persecution, famine, nakedness, danger, or the sword?"[32] Nothing, in fact, overcame the saints' courage. So the likeness to us of what was achieved by Christ (466) is suggested by the saying that *thirty pieces of silver* were given to him as his *wages;* the traitor Judas, remember, truly loathsome hater of God as he was, received thirty denarii for betraying Christ to the murderers and selling the source of our salvation to the avengers.[33]

Thirty pieces of silver were brought by the nations as his wages, and by God's orders they were *thrown into the smelter,* thoroughly *tested,* as also Christ himself was tested.[34] Our faith will not go without trial, you see, by God, who knows everything, as our life also will be put to the proof, blessed Paul saying, "Fire itself will test what sort of work each one has done." It is also written about Christ that "the Lord whom you see will come into his temple, the messenger of the covenant whom you desire. Lo, he is coming, says the Lord almighty: who will endure the day of his coming, or who can stand in his sight? Because he enters like a refiner's fire and like a fuller's soap, and he will sit refining and purifying them like silver and like gold." The divinely inspired David also sings somewhere in the person of every be-

31. 1 Cor 6.20; 1 Pt 1.18–19; 2 Cor 5.15.
32. Rom 8.35.
33. Mt 26.15.
34. None of our Greek commentators detects the Heb. "treasury" underlying the LXX's version "smelter."

liever in Christ wishing to live an evangelical life, "Prove me, Lord, and try me, test my heart and my mind."[35] The prophet refers, however, to *the smelter in the house of the Lord;* the Church of Christ *tests* each one's behavior and the sincerity of their love for Christ, and, enjoying a discernment of spirits, it knows precisely who, on the one hand, speaks with the Holy Spirit in naming Jesus Lord, and who, on the other hand, by Beelzebul calls him cursed, and as well who (467) are "the true worshipers" and, moreover, who come to us as wolves in sheep's clothing.[36]

I cast aside the second staff, Cord, to cancel the covenant between Judah and Israel (v.14). He said that Christ would take two staffs, and thus pasture with them his sheep, namely, the mass of holy ones called in faith. We said that the "beautiful staff" was Gospel teaching or proclamation, while the other—namely, "cord"—was the commandments of Moses, coming from God, who, as it were, goes forth to feed with the cord; it was given for assistance according to the statement of the prophet, "I gave the Law for assistance."[37] So in our text he makes clear that it is not only by the Gospel teachings that the mass of the nations is given guidance, but also by the commandments given of old through Moses, the shadow that is the Law obviously being transformed into reality. In other words, just as in reference to the "beautiful staff" he spoke of "casting aside" and "canceling," since the Gospel teaching was scattered, as it were, in the lands of the Canaanites—bruited abroad obviously by the holy apostles—so too the other staff, or instruction—namely, "cord"—or the Law, was set by God as a *covenant between Judah and Israel,* that is, the whole (468) race of Israel, by *Judah* referring to the two tribes in Jerusalem (Judah itself and Benjamin) and by *Israel* to the other ten, those settled in Samaria with Jeroboam.

The Law was also given to those in Canaan, therefore; as I said, we are given guidance by oracles from both the Law and the Gospels—hence Christ's also saying, "Do not think that I have come to abolish the Law or the Prophets: I have come not to abolish but to fulfill. For I truly tell you, until heaven and earth pass away, not one letter, not one stroke of a letter, will

35. 1 Cor 3.13; Mal 3.1–3; Ps 26.2. 36. 1 Cor 12.10, 3; Jn 4.23; Mt 7.15.
37. Is 8.20 LXX.

pass from the Law until all is accomplished." He fulfills the Law, you see, by teaching what surpasses the Law and not by putting beyond the Law the person under guidance, as when, for example, he says, "You have heard that it was said to those of old, You shall not murder, and whoever murders will be liable to judgment. But I say to you that whoever is angry with their brother will be liable to judgment"; and again, "You have heard that it was said, You shall not commit adultery. But I say to you that everyone who looks at a woman with lust has already committed adultery with her in his heart."[38] The commandment "You shall not murder" is fulfilled, you see, by leaving no room either for anger, which is the root and origin of murder; and to allow no entrance at all to lust, or at least to keep pleasures in check, is the way to put a complete stop to adultery, just as of course we say that, with the roots removed, the shoots that spring from them wither, or rather would not even grow at all. (469)

The Lord said to me, Furthermore, take for yourself shepherd's gear of an unskilled shepherd because, lo, I am raising up a shepherd for the land: what has failed he will not take note of, what is scattered he will not go after, what is hurt he will not heal, what is sound he will not guide. The flesh of the chosen he will eat, and their knuckles he will twist (vv.15–16). Some people recognize that the Word of the Lord is referred to in the good shepherd, wise and skillful—namely, Christ—who cast aside the two staffs and scattered them in the lands of the Canaanites, according to explanations previously given. They believe, in fact, as I said, that, though begotten in an ineffable fashion of the God and Father, and being both from him and in him, the Word became like us and was styled chief shepherd of all. To them he proposed instruction and illumination by way of guidance and precise knowledge of himself from both Gospels and Law; (470) these, we said, are the two staffs by which Christ shepherds us "in good pasture and a rich place," as it is written.[39] With no understanding of the mystery, however, Jews were ignorant of the beautiful staff—that is, the Gospel preaching—and furthermore they scorned the other staff called "cord"—that is, the Law of Moses—not accept-

38. Mt 5.17–18, 21–22, 27–28.
39. Ezek 34.14.

ing the faith and not recognizing the one foretold in Law and Prophets. The Savior himself clearly said to them, "Do not think that it is I who will accuse you to the Father: it is Moses himself who is your accuser, in whom you have set your hope. If you believed Moses, you would believe me, for he wrote about me. But if you do not believe what he wrote, how will you believe what I say?"[40] There is no questioning the fact, then, that they believe neither what Moses wrote nor indeed what the Savior said.

Now, since they did not accept the knowledge of the truth, consequently as the most wise Paul says, "God will send them a powerful delusion, leading them to believe what is false." By "powerful delusion" he means the Antichrist, to whom Jews will be assigned for condemnation. The Savior will confirm this in his words to them when they chose to disbelieve, "I have come in my Father's name, and you do not accept me; if another comes in his own name, you will accept him."[41] So Jews were destined to accept without hesitation the son of iniquity when he appeared in due course, "who opposes and exalts himself above every so-called god or object of worship, so that he takes his seat in the temple of God, declaring himself to be God,"[42] the one who does not know how to shepherd properly and skillfully, whom God bids the prophet prefigure (471) in the words, *Furthermore take for yourself shepherd's gear of an unskilled shepherd.* The more reasonable shepherds, you see, skilled in the business at hand, have slender staffs in case at the time for striking they should bruise what is beaten. If, on the other hand, anyone were without knowledge of the trade and out of touch with the skills of a shepherd, they would bruise them with crude staves—the meaning, in my view, of *shepherd's gear of an unskilled shepherd.*

Now, since in due course the son of iniquity, clad in royal trappings, was destined to appear in the role of a shepherd for those on earth, and accord no mercy at all to the peoples subject to him, or even those not subject, consequently the text says, *Lo, I am raising up a shepherd for the land: what has failed he will not take note of,* as if he were to say, Lapsing into little faith

40. Jn 5.45–47.
41. 2 Thes 2.11; Jn 5.43.
42. 2 Thes 2.4.

would not be cured by spiritual guidance. *What is scattered he will not go after:* what veered from the straight and narrow and was in the habit of straying from the flock *he will not go after,* that is, he will not bring to a better and correct state. *What is hurt he will not heal:* anyone hurt, overcome by evil pleasures, unable to withstand the pressure of fleshly desire, or a prey to the deceits of the ungodly heretics, with the mind unable to believe as it ought—something the good shepherd *heals,* but not the *unskilled* one. *What is sound he will not guide,* but *the flesh of the chosen he will eat, and their knuckles he will twist:* the son of iniquity will wage war on the saints, and vent on them his wrath without restraint (472), chewing them up, as it were, and eating them like a wild beast. *Their knuckles he will twist* in case anyone be able to walk upright; he will force them to adore him, confusing them with marvels. His presence occurs, in fact, "by the working of Satan," and by Beelzebul he will work "portents with the result that even the elect will be deceived, if this were possible," and as the Savior says, "No flesh would be saved," with his arrogance raging against everyone, were it not that "those days will be shortened." In fact, the Lord "will destroy him with his breath, and annihilate him with the manifestation of his coming."[43]

O those who shepherd futile things and desert the sheep: a sword is on his arm and his right eye. His arm will completely wither, and his right eye will be completely blinded (v.17). With the treatment of the unskilled shepherd complete, he now, as it were, turns a gloomy eye on the shepherds that are not good, employing language that is to a degree generic, forecasting what will befall those of this mentality. Notice, in fact, how from his innate mildness he is somehow perhaps distressed at those paying the penalty for their indifference. He faults them, on the one hand, for being shepherds of *futile things*—that is, preoccupied with what is passing—and, on the other hand, so indifferent as to rejoice in the wretched fate of the sheep: some sold them and said, (473) "Blessed be God, we are rich," others slaughtered them without feeling anything for them; there was no attention at all

43. 2 Thes 2.9; Mt 24.24, 22; 2 Thes 2.8.

on their part to shepherding them properly. Now, this was what the Jews' teachers were like, shutting the kingdom of heaven, as Christ says, not going in themselves nor letting the others go in, instead traversing "sea and dry land to make a single convert, turning him into twice as much a child of hell as yourselves, if this were possible."[44]

So what in fact will befall such wicked shepherds? *A sword is on his arm and his right eye,* the text says. The word *arm* is used to convey strength and as a type of spiritual energy. When the animals were slaughtered in the holy tent, for example, the arm was the part chosen for the divine altar and as a sacred offering to God,[45] the Law suggesting obscurely, in my view, that one's bodily and spiritual strength should be devoted to God. The fact that the arm indicates force one of the saints confirms where the God of all declares, "By the might of your arm they became still as a stone."[46] The *eye* is taken as a type of the mind; so the one who does not shepherd properly will suffer mutilation of arm and eye; that is, he will be bereft even of spiritual strength; he will be unable to achieve any good deed, God giving him no strength, and he will suffer darkness of mind because he will be in effect without a share in divine light, and thought to be so. In other words, he will be unable to claim confidently, "It is you who light my lamp, O Lord; you light up my darkness, O my God."[47]

It is his right *arm* that is cut with the *sword,* (474) and his *right eye* that is *blinded*—in other words, there was nothing *right* with the Jewish populace, no good deed, no strength in them, nothing of the divine light entered their mind and heart. As Paul said, "To this very day when Moses is read, a veil lies over their heart." David also sings somewhere about them, "Their eyes were darkened so that they could not see."[48] With them, therefore, everything is a disability, be it behavior, thought, anything else they are credited with having. I mean, the loss of what is on the left would possibly be to the benefit of those who sustained

44. Mt 23.14, 15.
45. Dt 18.3.
46. Ex 15.16, in the Song of Moses.
47. Ps 18.28.
48. 2 Cor 3.14; Ps 69.23. Cyril alters the Zechariah text somewhat to make a point (a tendency more frequently found in Didymus), and indulges in word-play.

it; forfeiting a disability would rid them of all blame and guilt. Losing what is on the *right*, by contrast, would do no little harm; it leads completely to dishonorable and loathsome behavior. While it would be quite appropriate for Jews to suffer deprivation of what is on the *right*, for us who are in Christ it would be appropriate to suffer loss of a disability and to take pride in what is on the *right*.

COMMENTARY ON ZECHARIAH, CHAPTER TWELVE

An oracle of the word of the Lord on Israel. Thus says the Lord, who stretches out heaven, lays the foundation of earth, and forms a spirit of a human being in it (v.1).

HE HAD GIVEN quite adequate comment on the good shepherd—namely, Christ—and also on the unskilled one who was cruel and fed off the sheep, whom we claim to be the Antichrist. (475) So now he makes useful mention also of the persecutions that would in time come upon Israel, not at all bodily but rather spiritual, and directed at the truly holy Jerusalem, "which is the Church of the living God." You see, just as we use the term "Jew" in a spiritual sense as the person who has circumcision of the heart, which comes through the spirit, and not at all of the flesh through the letter, so too you would say the term "Israel" is to be understood, not at all of the one of the line of Israel, but rather the one with the spirit that sees God.[1] Or, rather, of this kind are all those called through faith in Christ to holiness, acknowledging through him and in him the God and Father, this being the one, true, and special way of seeing God.

So *the word on Israel* is therefore taken in the sense just explained by us. Now, the fact that it is the all-powerful Creator of all who is making a prediction to us in this verse he makes clear by saying, *who stretches out heaven, lays the foundation of earth, and forms a spirit of a human being in it.* The one who receives *an oracle of the word on Israel,* he says, note, is God, who is capable of everything, "stretching out heaven like a hide," in the words of the psalmist, and making the earth so very firm as to be always and ever stable, though established upon the sea, this being the

1. 1 Tm 3.15; Rom 2.29.

statement of the inspired Scripture.[2] He it is who *forms a spirit of a human being in it.* Would not the Creator and artificer of such wonderful things achieve his will with complete ease and without effort? *A spirit of a human being is formed in it,* not called to the beginning of its being, even if this also occurred through him, (476) but, as it were, transformed, from weakness to strength, from cowardice to endurance, and, in a word, spiritually reshaped from what is worse to what is better. The divinely inspired David also sings somewhere, "Create a clean heart in me, O God, and restore to my innards a right spirit."[3] No one in their right minds would claim to want to receive a heart or spirit as though not having one to begin with; they would be inclined rather to ask for a clean heart or right spirit to be created in them, which is a case of transformation. Now, it is customary with the holy prophets, when on the point of delivering a prophecy of things not easily grasped, to try to present the God of all as all-powerful and almighty so that in every respect the pronouncement may enjoy reliability for belief in their case, even if they are speaking of something surpassing hope and defying understanding and belief as far as we can grasp it.

Lo, I am making Jerusalem like a shaken threshold for all the peoples round about, and in Judah there will be a siege against Jerusalem. On that day I shall make Jerusalem a stone trodden on by all the nations; everyone who treads on it will mockingly mock it, and all the nations of the earth will gather against it (vv.1–3). In what was already announced, the war to be waged against Judea by the Roman army was clearly mentioned. He said, for instance, "A sound of shepherds mourning for the reversal (477) of their greatness," and again later, "Hence I shall no longer spare the inhabitants of the earth, says the Lord. Lo, I shall surrender each person into the hands of their neighbor and into the hands of their king. They will destroy the earth, and I shall not rescue them from their hand."[4] In the present text, on the other hand, he clearly foretells the persecutions conducted against the Church; they waged war against the believers in Christ. Before all the others, in fact, the leaders of the assembly of the Jews bade the

2. Pss 104.2; 24.2.

3. Ps 51.10.

4. Zec 11.3, 6.

holy apostles not to speak in the name of Christ, even scourging them in their councils, causing them to be stoned, and doing and saying goodness-knows-what unholy things.[5] When the word about Christ pervaded the countries of the nations, however, and their inhabitants became attentive to the Gospel preaching, further persecutions broke out from those in power at different times and places, who were anxious to lay claim to loathsome and abominable idolatry and became ministers of the diabolical sacrilege; they put to death the saints by involving them in contests resulting in martyrdom.

The Church gave the impression to some extent of being vulnerable, with no one to lend help, and it resembled *shaken thresholds* that were falling, or *a stone trodden on.* Although the Savior of all was easily able to subdue every conflict, or rather to remove it completely from his adherents and render them proof against every trial and superior to the power of the foe, in his wise design he allowed them to be distinguished (478) for their sufferings so as to become like him and thus be glorified and reign with him. After all, if "we suffer with him, we shall also reign with him," as Scripture says, and if "we are sharers in his sufferings," we shall also be in his glory.[6] The text says, then, *Lo, I am making Jerusalem like a shaken threshold.* If it happened, there would be a *siege* mounted around it, that is, the blockade by all, and when it seemed to be like *a stone trodden on*, then *everyone will mockingly mock it.*

Now, this occurred, as I said just now, in the persecutions at various times; they went after the saints, tormenting them in various ways, and the wretches perhaps in some cases mocked the dying; they probably did not realize the fame that came from suffering, and the fact that hardship would indisputably be a source of undying satisfaction. Consider how he does not say that the Church's being trampled on was an effect of the nations' might, but of his will allowing his adorers to be perfected

5. Acts 4.18; 5.12. While Didymus has also looked to the Roman invasion of Judea and the destruction of the Temple for light on this apocalyptic text, even recommending reference to Josephus (Jerome having cited the *Antiquities of the Jews*), Cyril as usual has a tightly ecclesiological focus, moving to the sufferings of apostles and martyrs.

6. 2 Tm 2.12; 2 Cor 1.7.

through suffering,[7] as I said; the text says, note, *Lo, I am making Jerusalem like a shaken threshold for all the peoples round about.* Relevant to this, in my view, is what is said very clearly to Pilate in the statement of the Savior, "You would have no authority over me if it were not given to you from on high."[8] Likewise, the spiritual Jerusalem, the Church, could rightly say to the world persecuting it, "You would have no authority over me if it were not given to you from on high."

On that day, says the Lord almighty, I shall strike every horse with panic and its rider with shock, (479) *whereas on the house of Judah I shall open my eyes and strike all the horses of the peoples with blindness* (v.4). The fact that he suppresses every war and renders ineffectual the assaults of the persecutors he gives us to understand by saying, *I shall strike every horse and rider with panic and with shock and indeed with blindness.* Now, in my view, to suffer *panic* is the same as to undergo *shock, panic* being understood as being out of one's mind, and rightly so. When it happened and the murderers were affected, it was quite possible for the saints to say about the people fighting against them, "Our enemy are beside themselves," and even, "Some in chariots, some in horses, but our boast is in the name of the Lord God. They collapsed and fell, but we rose up and stood straight."[9] *Shock,* on the other hand, would have been the different effect on the one who in an unholy manner abused the longsuffering of the saints, only to undergo *panic* or amazement on seeing them prevail amidst disasters and still take the crown, even though falling or appearing to be worsted, then most of all in complete control. It is true that they are seen to be extraordinary, especially in their sufferings, and to enjoy grace from on high commensurate with the intensity of their hardship. Further, how would the blessed martyrs fail to astonish their assailants since they overcome Satan himself and bring retribution on the wicked and unclean spirits, sometimes even instilling in their exterminators deep wonderment at the fame accruing to them? Hence his promise to *strike horse* and horseman together, by which we are meant to

7. Cf. Heb 2.10.
8. Jn 19.11. The next sentence does not occur in the PG ed.
9. Dt 32.31; Ps 20.7.

understand the columns of the enemy hostile to the simplicity of the saints. (480)

On the house of Judah he promised to *open his eyes.* By *Judah* here he refers to Christ as the one who sprang from the root of Jesse and from the tribe of Judah, and by his *house* the Church, or the holy mass of those justified by faith. The *opening of his eyes* I think means that he will survey the scene with widespread and total vision, which would be a clear sign of his benevolence, compassion, and love for us, Scripture saying, "The eyes of the Lord are upon the righteous."[10] Those he surveys he renders completely blessed, since it is possible to claim without any falsehood that, whereas he punishes the insolent and vengeful by turning away, he gladdens the pious and virtuous with his oversight. The divinely inspired David, for example, to make clear the loss involved in God's turning away and the gain from his oversight, said in one place, "Do not turn your face away from me, and do not turn in anger from your servant," and likewise in another, "Gaze on me and have mercy on me."[11] Upon his turning away, in fact, follows his anger and the effects of it, whereas of his gaze mercy is the necessary gift.

All the commanders of Judah shall say in their hearts, We shall find for ourselves the inhabitants of Jerusalem, in the Lord almighty their God (v.5). We claim that in the *commanders of Judah* there is reference to the holy apostles, appointed by Christ in the role of generals, as it were, (481) and assigned to leadership of *Judah,* that is, of those called to confession and praise (Judah meaning "praise"). All of them would be those from the nations, whom the divinely inspired psalmist entrusts with the duty of glorifying Emmanuel when he says in spirit, "Bless your God, nations, and make the sound of his praise be heard."[12] So in this verse *Judah* means those called through faith to both praise and confession; the *commanders* are those set over them, both captains and leaders, namely, the divinely inspired disciples. So it is possible to see them calling out and saying to the worshipers of the Savior, as though to some soldiers, "Stand therefore and fasten the belt of truth around your waist, put on the breastplate of righ-

10. Ps 34.15.
11. Pss 27.9; 25.16.
12. Ps 66.8.

teousness, have your feet shod with readiness to proclaim the Gospel of peace, in every situation take up the shield of faith with which you will be able to quench all the flaming arrows of the evil one. Take the helmet of salvation and the sword of the Spirit, which is the word of God."[13]

The divinely inspired Paul also says we should be recognized as conspicuous for living a commendable life "with the weapons of righteousness for the right hand and for the left," and in addition to them he pointed out the columns of the adversaries, as it were, saying, "Finally, be strong in the Lord and in the strength of his power; our struggle is not with flesh and blood, but with the rulers, with the authorities, with the cosmic powers of this present darkness, against the spiritual forces of evil in the heavenly places."[14]

The *commanders*, then, are the divinely inspired disciples, and rightly so, (482) who will also *say in their hearts, We shall find for ourselves the inhabitants of Jerusalem, in the Lord almighty their God.* The divinely inspired disciples, you see, longed for the truly holy Jerusalem—that is, the Church—to be seen thronged with worshipers and, like some famous and celebrated city, glorying in the mass of its inhabitants. So they proclaimed the faith and spread the good news of Jesus, confirming their words with signs and wonders. They did not convince Israel, however: it remained obdurate, rigid, and as untamed as a horse. Consequently, they now sought for themselves *inhabitants* of the holy city *in the Lord almighty their God*, that is, in Christ, and actually turned to the nations, proclaiming to the Jewish population, "It was necessary that the word of God should be spoken first to you; but since you reject it and judge yourselves to be unworthy of eternal life, lo, we are now turning to the nations, for this is what God commanded us."[15] From them they sought members of the Church, which the divinely inspired David also mentions, "Glorious things are spoken of you, O city of God." By seeking they were enriched; they assembled a membership that was su-

13. Eph 6.14–17. The PG ed. omits the final sentence as well as all of the following paragraph.
14. 2 Cor 6.7; Eph 6.10, 12.
15. Acts 13.46–47.

perior in number, and actually said to the holy city, "Enlarge the site of your tent and your halls. Fix your tent, do not be sparing, lengthen your cords, strengthen your pegs, expand further to right and to left." It rejoices in the vast number of its *inhabitants,* as if marveling (483) at the multitude of its own children and saying, "I was childless and widowed: who has given me these children, how did I come by them?"[16]

On that day I shall make the commanders of Judah like a firebrand in wood and like a burning lamp in stubble, and they will devour all the peoples round about on the right and on the left (v.6). By *the commanders of Judah,* as I have already said, he refers to the holy apostles, or simply all the leaders of the holy churches. He said he would develop the word or spiritual guidance of the nations' heart in them to such an extent that it would seem that *a firebrand* had fallen on *wood* or *a lamp in stubble* that easily catches alight; *they will devour all the peoples round about on the right and on the left*—that is, wherever they wish to go, they would be absolutely capable of doing so, summoning them to be sensitive and, as though by a divine and spiritual fire, warming the frozen. The God of all said something like this as well to the blessed prophet Jeremiah, "Lo, I am now making my words in your mouth a fire, and this people wood, and it will consume them"; that is, he will summon to be sensitive those frozen in sin, and in turn will perfect in spirit those already warm. The heart of those in error, you see, is frozen and their mind dead through worshiping "creation instead of the Creator" God, giving reverence to wood and stone.[17]

Since in their fervor they accepted the divine message, as (484) I said, they will be made perfect in spirit, warmly disposed to righteousness; according to the divinely inspired John we are baptized "in the Holy Spirit and fire"[18] of a spiritual kind that normally consumes, like a kind of litter, the sin seething in our souls and purges the stains of fleshly desires. There is a saying in Isaiah, remember, "You have hot coals; sit before them; they will be of help to you"; and he said in reference to himself, "One of the seraphim was sent to me, holding in his hand a

16. Ps 87.3; Is 54.2–3; 49.21.
17. Jer 5.14; Rom 1.25.
18. Mt 3.11 (not John).

burning coal, which he had taken from the altar with the tongs. Touching my mouth he said, See, it has touched your lips, it will remove your iniquities and purify your sins,"[19] probably meaning that the divine and most sacred coal purging sin is Christ.

The divinely inspired disciples, therefore, were *like a firebrand in wood and like a burning lamp in stubble, and they will devour all the peoples round about*—not consuming to the point of destruction, but rather setting alight the defiled and loathsome teachings of the so-called knowledge within them, and purging the stain of the ancient error. They do not allow the mind of those who once believed to be frozen any longer with mindless absurdities, the result being that in their newly found exultation they say to Christ the Savior of all, "Your saying has been put to the proof, and your servant loved it." The fact of the warmth and extreme sharpness of the word of God would be clear from his statement to Jeremiah, "Are not my words like a fiery flame, says the Lord, and like a hammer that cuts rock?"[20] (485) The word of God, in fact, very appropriately is able both to rekindle the mind frozen in sin and easily, as it were, to unfold what is embedded and compressed. Scripture says, remember, "It is living and active, sharper than any two-edged sword, piercing until it divides soul from spirit, joints from marrow, and able to judge the thoughts and intentions of the heart." It is also said somewhere in a statement of the prophets to the harsh and unrelenting Jew, "Circumcise yourselves to God, remove the foreskin of your hard hearts, men of Judah and inhabitants of Jerusalem." "Rend your hearts, not your garments."[21]

Jerusalem will dwell by itself. The Lord will save the tents of Judah as in the beginning lest the boasting of the house of David be exaggerated and the elation of the inhabitants of Jerusalem over Judah (v.7). He means that the Church will not always be subject to alarm, nor does it undergo unending persecutions; instead, it will at times enjoy peace and *dwell by itself*, that is, alone, with no one troubling it, not inflicting tribulation on it, not causing fear, not heaping up the troubles stemming from trials. *The Lord will save the tents of Judah as in the beginning;* it says, note, the Lord of all—

19. Is 47.14–15; 6.6–7.
20. Ps 119.140; Jer 23.29.
21. Heb 4.12; Jer 4.4; Jl 2.13.

that is, Christ—will so protect his own churches, or (486) *tents*, as to accord them attention equal to that given of old to the people of Israel rescued from Egypt. Israel, remember, the God of all brought out of a house of slavery and an "iron furnace," Scripture says, and from unbearable arrogance "with mighty hand and outstretched arm" when he drowned the pursuers in the Red Sea.[22] He covered them in an ocean; they sank like lead in surging water while those who were rescued crossed over. A pillar of fire led them by night, showing them the way, and a cloud hung over them by day.[23] Further, they ate bread from heaven, escaped the bites of the serpents in the wilderness, prevailed over foes, crossed the Jordan, were circumcised with stone knives, entered the land of promise.

These things Christ will bestow on those seeking his *tents*, that is, the Church; this is the way he will save them, by freeing them from slavery—the devil's, I mean—and rescuing them from demonic arrogance, and by making them cross over, as it were, the sea of the world's distractions and idle tumult, raising up himself as a shining pillar and foundation, bathing them in light, and like a cloud bedewing them with spiritual moisture. He has become for them bread of life, rendered the bites of the spiritual serpents ineffectual and harmless, led them across the Jordan, made them pure by the circumcision of the Spirit, and brought them into the kingdom of heaven. These things he will bestow on his own (487) worshipers, and save them by such means *lest the boasting of the house of David be exaggerated*, that is to say, the leaders of the Jews, and lest there be *elation* or occasion for *elation by the inhabitants of* the material and earthly *Jerusalem over Judah*. They took great pride in themselves, you see, and showed great scorn for those who believed in Christ and for Emmanuel personally, flaunting hither and yon the gifts from Moses to their forebears, and using as a pretext the leniency accorded their ancestors. At one time, for instance, they demanded, "What sign are you going to do, then, so that we may see it and believe you? Our ancestors ate the manna in the wilderness, as it is written, He gave them bread from heaven to

22. Dt 4.20; 5.15.
23. Ex 15.4–5, 10; 13.21.

eat." At another time likewise, "We know that God has spoken to Moses, but as for this man we do not know where he comes from."[24] The God of all, therefore, will work marvels in our case also, even if not openly, and of course as he did at that time, even if in a spiritual fashion; and he will save those in his own *tents* in such a way that the Jews or the leaders in their midst will not *boast* against us (the meaning, in my view, of *the boasting of the house of David*).

On that day the Lord will be a shield over the inhabitants of Jerusalem; the infirm will be like the house of David among them on that day, and the house of David like the house of God, like an angel of the Lord before them (v.8). The God and Father crowned us "with favor as with a shield"[25] (488) in giving us his own Son as protector and champion, through whom also we were saved, emerging without difficulty from every trial and from the hostility of the foe, and equipped to prevail over the knavery of the pursuers. Now, in what went before, something similar was suggested, but you would find the language shrouded in deep obscurity. The God of all promised, note, *to be a shield over the inhabitants of Jerusalem* and not rather over those living on its outskirts. Here *Jerusalem* can arguably be taken as Christ's Church; the person who dwells on its outskirts is not safe, subject to instability, as it were, and very prone to incorrect behavior, or in other respects indifferent to a love of learning. On the other hand, the person who lives within is steady and firm in love of Christ, and ever inclined to the benefits coming from the divine teachings, and thus capable of repeating the sentiment of David, "How sweet are your words to my taste, sweeter than honey and a honeycomb to my mouth."[26]

Accordingly, it says, *The Lord will be a shield over the inhabitants of Jerusalem; the infirm will be like the house of David among them on that day*. Here the *house of David*, we claim, refers to those of most importance among the Jews; coming from the tribe of Judah, to which belonged Jesse and David, they ruled at various times in Jerusalem. The *infirm* person whom it mentions among the inhabitants of the holy city—the spiritual Jerusalem, which

24. Jn 6.30–31; 9.29.
25. Ps 5.13.
26. Ps 119.103.

is the Church—is perhaps the one who is still a catechumen, not yet baptized, and is ill, as it were, by being weighed down with the weight of sin, and not rid of former ailments, or passions.[27] Those who are in that condition, however, because they are only believers and have departed from the darkness of the Law and completely opted to observe (489) the way of living by the spirit and the challenges of life in Christ, *will be like the house of David*, that is, in no respect inferior in understanding what is wise and honorable, at least among the Jews.

Paul in his great wisdom also suggested something similar in addressing the Jewish populace in these terms, "When the nations, who do not possess the Law, do instinctively what the Law requires, these, though not having the Law, are a law to themselves in so far as they show that what the Law requires is written on their hearts." And again, "While circumcision is of value if you put the Law into practice, your circumcision has become uncircumcision if you are a transgressor of the Law. So if those who are uncircumcised keep the requirements of the Law, will not their uncircumcision be regarded as circumcision? Will not those who are physically uncircumcised but keep the Law condemn you who have the written code and circumcision but break the Law? For a person is not a Jew who is one outwardly, nor is true circumcision something external and physical. Rather, a person is a Jew who is one inwardly, and real circumcision is a matter of the heart—it is spiritual and not literal. Such a person receives praise not from others but from God." Accordingly, the person who declines circumcision in the flesh as obsolete, and instead prefers that of the spirit and presents himself as a Jew inwardly, "whose praise is not from others but from God,"[28]—how is he not better than and in any respect inferior to those who are experts in the Law and enjoy most honor among the Jews, even if perhaps having some trace of *infirmity* in not yet being baptized?

If, on the other hand, someone from the house of David—

27. The analogy is Cyril's own; Didymus had thought of infirmity in terms of heresy, listing a rogues' gallery of heresiarchs.

28. Rom 2.14–15, 25–29 (the clause containing the repeated phrase from Paul missing from the PG Greek text but not from the Latin version).

that is, from the prominent and most honorable among them—adopts (490) the faith, understands well the mystery of Christ, and becomes a worshiper of his, they will be *like the house of God* and *like an angel of the Lord before them.* This is the kind of thing the Savior himself is also found saying, "Hence every scribe who has been schooled in the kingdom of heaven is like the master of a household who brings out of his storehouse what is new and what is old."[29] In other words, the one who already has the knowledge of the Law stored within himself, and who supplements it with the knowledge of the Gospel, will be rich in understanding, proposing to the scholars both new insights and old, as though from his deposits. Such a person was the divinely inspired Paul, who at times endeavors to confirm the teaching about Christ with proofs from the Law, at other times in some fashion urges his listeners with guidance beyond the Law in the direction of the need to choose by boasting of his faith in him. At one time, in fact, he said, "Tell me, you who desire to be subject to the Law, will you not listen to the Law? It is written that Abraham had two sons, one by a slave woman and the other by a free woman. The child of the slave was born according to the flesh, whereas the child of the free woman was born through the promise. This is an allegory: these women are two covenants; one is Hagar from Mount Sinai, bearing children for slavery. Sinai is a mountain in Arabia, and corresponds to the present Jerusalem, for she is in slavery with her children. But the other woman corresponds to the Jerusalem above; she is free, and is our mother."[30] At another time in regard to the Son, "He is the reflection of God's glory and the exact imprint of his being, and he sustains all things by his powerful word. (491) When he had made purification for sins, he took his seat at the right hand of the majesty on high." Do you understand, then, how he benefits the souls of those under guidance by both old and new teachings?[31] The text says, therefore, *The house of David like the house of God, like an angel of the Lord before them.*

On that day I shall seek to do away with all the nations advancing on Jerusalem. I shall pour out on the house of David and the inhabit-

29. Mt 13.52.
30. Gal 4.21–26.
31. Heb 1.3.

ants of Jerusalem a spirit of grace and compassion, and they will look upon me (vv.9–10). My intention will be, he says, *to do away with all the nations* fighting against the holy city, that is, the Church, and to invest with *grace and compassion* the house of Judah and *the inhabitants of Jerusalem,* that is, the members of the Church arrayed among those obliged to give praise, who would likewise be those worshiping Christ, opting to follow the Gospel oracles and live an upright and blameless life. Proof, in fact, that the enemies of the truth will be completely reduced to impotence the Savior himself clearly provides by saying, "You are Peter, and upon this rock I shall build my Church, and the gates of hell will not prevail against it."[32] He refers by "gates of hell" to those bent on persecuting it, destructive and ruinous as they are, who invariably bring to their lair in hell their (492) adherents. Those warring against her, therefore, will be astonished or, rather, even devastated, and will disappear in ruin. "Many are the afflictions of the righteous," remember, "but the Lord will rescue them from them all"; and it is true that "all who wish to live a pious life in Christ will be persecuted."[33] Yet Christ will render pointless and futile the schemers' wiles and actual plans, since he has given us the authority "to walk on snakes and scorpions and on all the power of the foe," and encourages us in the words, "You will have tribulation in the world, but have confidence: I have overcome the world."[34]

The Church's adversaries at various times are done away with, and on those within her—that is, the believers—a rich infusion is given of *a spirit of grace and compassion.* The God and Father, you see, awards us good things from on high and fills us with spiritual graces so that we may direct the eye of our mind to him and place every trust in him. This, in my view, is the sense of *they will look upon me.* While with these dispositions we are glad at heart, we say at that time in praise of God, "Bless the Lord, O my soul, who forgives all your iniquities, heals all your diseases, redeems your life from corruption, crowns you with mercy and compassion, and satisfies your desires with good things."[35]

Because they have abused him, (493) *and will show grief for them*

32. Mt 16.18.
33. Ps 34.19; 2 Tm 3.12.
34. Lk 10.19; Jn 16.33.
35. Ps 103.5–6.

as for a loved one, and feel pangs as for a firstborn. The Hebrew text puts the words *And they will look upon me* as the beginning of this verse, but it does not appear in the tradition and version of the Seventy. The Hebrew in fact says, "They will gaze," for *They will look upon,* and for *they abused,* "they pierced." But we claim that there is no departure from the true sense, either in the Hebrew or in the Seventy: the Jews *abused* Christ, and in addition they "pierced" him, Pilate's soldiers transfixing his side, as Scripture reports. We shall therefore be correct in applying the verse in this case to the person of Christ.[36]

But we claim that sense occurs in the verse, *They will gaze on him whom they have pierced* (or *abused*) *and will show grief for them as for a loved one, and feel pangs as for a firstborn.* You see, to the cross they nailed the divine temple, and the crucifiers stood around, some saying with unholy mockery, "You who destroy the Temple and in three days rebuild it, save yourself," and others likewise, "He saved others, himself he cannot save." But when he laid down his life for us and preached to the spirits in Hades, he came to life again, and with the occurrence of an earthquake near the tomb those in attendance said in amazement, "Truly (494) this man was the Son of God," many having a sincere change of heart.[37] When the Roman war broke upon them, however, and their country was devastated, cities burned, houses wrecked, Jerusalem itself besieged, and famine consuming the residents, some of them were brought to a realization of the crimes against Christ and finally became aware of the reason for their misfortunes and the fact that their outrageous behavior to him was the basis for their suffering. Since *they abused him,* therefore, *they will show grief for them as for a loved one, and feel pangs as for a firstborn;* in other words, there is always a copious shedding of tears by parents for a firstborn and beloved son lying dead, weeping and wailing un-

36. Cyril's attention to the textual discrepancy between Heb., the LXX and the reading in Jn 19.37 was drawn by Jerome's comments and perhaps by Didymus, who also divides the verse differently to include all of v.10 together. There is a suggestion in both commentators that some hostile exegetes question the departure from the Heb., and Cyril is insistent that the sense is preserved in both. He also goes on to make a case for the rest of the verse being applicable to Christ as well.

37. Mt 27.40, 42, 54.

able to be contained, lengthy and apparently unceasing pangs being felt, wasting the soul with bitter and unbearable onslaughts. Now, the fact that Jews were destined to experience such troubles Christ foretold to the women weeping over him when he chided them in the words, "Daughters of Jerusalem, weep not for me, but weep for yourselves and for your children."[38]

On that day the mourning in Jerusalem will be magnified like the mourning for a pomegranate cut down in the open field. The land will mourn tribe by tribe, each tribe by itself and their women by themselves: the tribe of the house of David and their women by themselves; the tribe of the house of Nathan by itself and their women by themselves; the tribe of the house of Levi by (495) *itself and their women by themselves; the tribe of the house of Symeon and their women by themselves; all the remaining tribes, tribe by tribe, and their women by themselves* (vv.11–14). With Judea ravaged at times by the Roman army, and Jerusalem itself besieged, he says there will be such *mourning* among its residents as would be expressed by a farmer when a *pomegranate is cut down,* this plant being luxuriant and producing thick, long, and upright shoots. If it were also bedecked with the actual fruit, then in particular it would give rise to deep admiration; the pomegranate is marvelous fruit, naturally attractive, suspended from the saplings, with a kind of skin colored red by the seeds inside. But the plant is harmful, as I said, even deadly, and is cut down along with the fruit.[39]

You could see something like this happening with the Jews: those of eminence among them, as far as importance based on the Law was concerned, were likened to the pomegranate fruit. Those from the tribe of Judah, remember, occupied the royal throne and were given a precedence of honor by them, while those from the tribe of Levi were very properly invested with the trappings of priesthood and were conspicuous and celebrated;

38. Lk 23.28.

39. Like Didymus and the Antiochenes, Cyril is challenged by the mention of the pomegranate arising from the LXX's difficulty with the Heb. phrase "like the mourning for Hadad-rimmon in the plain of Megiddo." He does not utilize Jerome's information on this. On the other hand, he resists Didymus's immediate recourse to sustained allegory, preferring (as Theodoret does) to call upon his botanical knowledge and to rationalize, unwilling to accept that the Heb. text might mean something quite different.

and what am I to say of judges, legal experts, and those notable for other positions? Since they vented their spleen on Christ, however, they were handed over to the enemy when Vespasian and Titus ravaged the country, Jerusalem was besieged, (496) everyone in it was consumed by famine, and everything was filled with lamenting and *mourning*. Josephus will confirm this; in composing his books on the capture, he spoke somewhere to this effect about Jerusalem: "There was grief everywhere throughout the city, piercing shrieks and widespread mourning."[40] He had spoken of it as "Lebanon" and a "forest" in these words, "Open your doors, Lebanon, and let fire consume your cedars. Let the pine lament because the cedar has fallen, because the mighty were in severe difficulties. Lament, oaks of Bashan, because the dense forest has been felled."[41] In a similar vein he also speaks of *a pomegranate cut down*. The divinely inspired John also confirms the account when addressing the Jewish masses, "Already the axe is set at the root of the trees; so every tree not bearing good fruit will be chopped down, thrown into the fire, and will burn."[42] So the *mourning in it*, he says, will be as deep as the *mourning for a pomegranate*, obviously when its fruit has appeared and it is unexpectedly cut down.

The land will mourn tribe by tribe, each tribe by itself and their women by themselves. Our claim is not that the prophet meant to suggest that the males in each tribe were placed separately from the females in expressing their mourning; that would clearly be pointless and unlikely. He conveys instead that each tribe with the women in it will have grounds for lament; consequently, he says *the tribe of the house of David by itself and their women by themselves.* Come now, let us explain to the extent possible (497) each tribe's distress. Those of the tribe of David, or Judah, having lost the kingship, will wail unrestrainedly for being deprived of such notable fame; those of the tribe of Levi, with the loss of priestly status, will express grief along with their women. Those will likewise mourn who are of the tribe of Nathan, who was a prophet, though not completely truthful; he was no longer to make false prophecies and speak from his own

40. *Jewish War* 2.1.
41. Zec 11.1–2.
42. Lk 3.9; Jn 15.6.

heart, sell his own words to the gullible as though they were from God, and make a profit from it. Now, tradition has it that the Jews took the men appointed judges at various times from the tribe of Symeon for the reason of its having men of great wisdom and learning and far preferable to the others in opting for a life in keeping with the Law—hence the clause *the tribe of the house of Symeon will mourn by itself.*[43] They too would have something of their own to lament: they had not judged properly nor shown zeal to implement God's will in fidelity to the divine laws; instead, they were grasping and venal, as the prophet says, "Its judges were like wolves of Arabia."[44] The other tribes as well, however, had reason to grieve along with them for being dislodged from the most pleasant rituals and sites, with death instead hanging over their heads and famine itself consuming them like the enemies' sword.

43. Where Didymus and Theodoret read in their text of v.11 the form Shimei, Cyril's text has Symeon, which the LXX employs elsewhere both for Joseph's son Simeon and for Levi's grandson Shimei.

44. Zep 3.3, the LXX seeing "Arabia" in Heb. "evening" (as Jerome mentioned).

COMMENTARY ON ZECHARIAH, CHAPTER THIRTEEN

On that day every place will be open to the house of David and the inhabitants of Jerusalem for transformation and aspersion (v.1).

He moves on to describe what will in turn happen after this to "those (498) who loved the manifestation" of Christ:[1] some in the arrogance of their unbelief will find themselves besieged, he is saying, and will lament the troubles befalling them. In the spiritual and truly holy Jerusalem, on the other hand, and *in the house of David*—that is, the Church of Christ, who sprang from the line of David according to the flesh—*every place will be open*, that is, there will be much space and a relaxed way of living that is very desirable and free from hardship.

Now, it should be realized that once again the Hebrew represents the text differently: in place of *every place will be open*, it said, "every spring will gush forth." It is very likely that the thrust of the version of the Seventy is directed to the same effect despite a difference in the form of words, thus indicating such a sense.[2] Unbelieving and obdurate Jerusalem, you see, being wicked and rebellious, "killing the prophets and stoning those sent to it,"[3] will pay the penalty commensurate with its crimes; namely, it will be cut down like a pomegranate. To the *inhabitants* of the spiritual Jerusalem, or house of Judah—namely, Christ—*every place will be open*, or a fountain in every place, gushing up with the water of purification—in other words, that of holy baptism—so as to be useful to the believers and *for transformation and aspersion*. What is

1. 2 Tm 4.8.

2. Cyril, perhaps through Jerome, detects the discrepancy between "place" in the LXX and Heb. "fountain" (noted by Symmachus and thus by Theodoret), and tries to reconcile the *skopos* of both, unaware of a misreading of similar forms.

3. Mt 23.37.

the *transformation?* On the one hand, of Jews, from living by the Law to a way of life in Christ, from shadow to reality, from type and letter to spiritual worship. On the other hand, there will be a *transformation* for pagans, when they come from unbelief to believing in Christ, from initial ignorance to unalloyed knowledge of the one who is truly God, from (499) darkness to light. The *transformation* is common to both, befitting everyone who is now called through faith, to both Jew and pagan, from thinking of things of the flesh to living in a holy and pure way and walking in the Spirit, as blessed Paul says,[4] from preferring things in the world to loving what excels worldly things. How could you doubt that we who receive the divine and sacred baptism enjoy *aspersion* with the blood of Christ for purification of sin? So the way to *transformation and aspersion* for those in the house of Judah is saving baptism, or *every place open*, or every fountain expanded and gushing with the water of purification.

On that day, says the Lord, I shall eliminate the names of the idols from the land, and there will be no further remembrance of them; I shall remove the false prophets and the unclean spirit from the land (v.2). Everything has been changed for the better in Christ, and what is in him is "a new creation,"[5] with the removal of the blame of the former decay. Now, the meaning in this verse you could easily discern, if you wanted, from the actual events: before the time of the coming, when the Only-begotten was not yet like us, nor had he shed his divine light on all things, there were gloom and darkness in the hearts of the nations. They used to worship idols, in fact, and were so caught up in their misguided ideas as to give reverence to sticks and stones, and assign to the impure demons the honors due to God. (500) While these crimes were due to the folly of people suffering deception, in the case of Israel by contrast, who was chosen and, in the words of Scripture, was "the Lord's portion and cord of his inheritance,"[6] there was such forgetfulness of manners and customs that they accorded little priority to the Law, despite its being given as an aid to them and containing no slight guidance in upright living. Instead, they opted to betake themselves ill-advisedly to the errors of

4. Gal 5.16.
5. 2 Cor 5.17.
6. Dt 32.9.

the nations and to subside into the superstitions of their neighbors: some worshiped idols by becoming devotees of loathsome shrines and acting as augurs and soothsayers; others had the phrase "Long live the Lord" on their tongue and feigned piety, being wolves in sheep's clothing, arrogating to themselves the role of prophecy in their wretchedness and claiming in unholy fashion a reputation for that, giving vent to their own ideas and claiming God's authority for the thoughts of their own heart.

In reference to those given to such crimes the prophet Jeremiah also said to God, who has authority over all things, "Lord, behold their prophets prophesying and saying, You shall not see the sword, nor will there be famine among you, because I shall grant truth and peace on earth and in this place." In reply God said, "The prophets are making false prophecies in my name; I did not send them, I did not instruct them, nor did I speak to them, because false are their visions, oracles, divinations, and velleities of their own heart—it is they (501) who are prophesying to you"; and again, "I did not send the prophets, yet they ran; I did not speak to them, yet they prophesied." They were false prophets, as I said, and under the influence of base oracles they conveyed to the listeners what came "from their own hearts," in Scripture's terms, "and not from the mouth of the Lord."[7] Then, though the Jews should have taken exception to this, on the contrary they paid homage and showed zeal in bestowing on them supreme honors.

When the Only-begotten Word of God finally appeared among us, however, the trivial and childish trinkets of idolatry totally disappeared and were completely destroyed. With them were removed also the absurd and impious activity of the false prophets, who were filled with a wicked and false spirit, and could very plausibly be shown to be suffering from an error similar to that of the idol worshipers, since in both there was the one guiding spirit—namely, Satan. Hence the text says, *I shall eliminate the names of the idols from the land, and there will be no further remembrance of them on that day*, that is, at the time when the divine and heavenly light shines, and the spiritual morning star dawns on the hearts

7. Jer 14.13–14; 23.11, 16.

of those deceived, as Scripture says,[8] and day breaks, driving off the night of former times and what was done in it. The result will be that with the removal of the ancient uncleanness the true and holy worshipers may then appear decked out in the trappings of the holy way of life and lending prestige to life in Christ.

If individuals still prophesy, their fathers and mothers who bore them will say to them, You shall not live, because you spoke falsehood in the name of the Lord; and their fathers and mothers who bore them will bind them hand and foot when they prophesy (v.3). So great will be the reverence of people of that time for the divinity, he is saying, and the interest they take in the summit of simplicity and praiseworthy living, that even parents will be provoked by their children if they should choose to emulate the false prophets by pretending to prophesy and giving utterance to what comes from their own heart as if God were speaking. They will in fact *bind them hand and foot,* that is, imprison them as insane and demented, taking no delay in sentencing them to death if they persist shamelessly in an ailment of this kind; *speaking falsehood in the name of the Lord* will be sufficient reason for them to sentence their child to any penalty.

Now, consider how true the verse is, and the encouragement to faith the prophecy gives. I mean, who of our number would tolerate anyone's prophesying today? Or who would fail at once to consider such a person deranged, and to give a person with this attitude a wide berth? What sort of *father* would allow his child to go uncorrected if he was in the grip of such awful failings? In my view, therefore, it would be very clear evidence for being firmly convinced that the nature of our situation has changed considerably for the better, thanks to God's bringing it to conform to his will and improve on the past. For example, what was previously held in honor and esteem by many people is now (503) scorned and loathed, unacceptable to good people and liable to punishment.

On that day all prophets will be ashamed of their own visions when they prophesy, and will put on a hair shirt as a penalty for lying. They will say, I am no prophet, because a human being brought me up from my

8. Cf. 2 Pt 1.19.

youth. I shall say to him, What are these wounds between your hands? He will reply, I received the wounds in the house of my beloved (vv.4–6). There is no difficulty in seeing even from the drift of the passage that what was formerly an object of admiration is regarded by us as deserving penalty and punishment. False prophets and impostors prophesied in Israel, as I remarked, and were in the habit of deceiving "for a handful of barley and a piece of bread," as Scripture says.[9] No one then corrected them when guilty of this or chose to forbid their involvement in impiety; instead, the wretches preferred rather to crown them with commendation and high honors. Consequently, they got worse, as though the ailment they suffered fed on the exhilaration of their admirers. At the present time, on the contrary, he says, they *will be ashamed,* obviously because false prophecy is not acceptable but rather punished, and an account of their folly will be required of those guilty of such crimes.

The result will be that they will be accused, withdrawn from the evil, and *will put on a hair shirt as a penalty for lying;* that is, (504) they will grieve for their evil behavior, lament their sin, and repent of getting so caught up in ignorant ideas as to prophesy falsely against God. In confusion they will admit their sin and beg pardon, saying clearly, *I am no prophet, because a human being brought me up from my youth;* that is, I am a child of a human being. Nature is very weak, extremely prone to illicit behavior and liable to sin; such would be the sentiments of the repentant. But if I were inclined to ask him (the text goes on) what the meaning is of the stripes or *wounds* visible in his hands, he would reply, *I received them in the house of my beloved*—namely, his mother and father who bound him hand and foot, and exacted punishment for the prophesying. In all our cases, you see, *house of my beloved* is the house of our parents.

Note the difference, therefore, between practices in former times and today. I mean, the false prophets among people then were admired, enjoyed a good name and reputation, and did so without second thoughts. At the present time, by contrast, if anyone chose to follow those people's insanity, they would be chided, put to shame, punished by the sentence of their own parents;

9. Ezek 13.19.

they would repent as sinners and weep and wail, and beg pardon by pleading the weakness of human nature and its tendency to sin. *The unclean spirit has been removed from the land,*[10] you see, by the power and authority of our Savior Jesus Christ. (505)

Sword, rise up against my shepherd and against his fellow citizen, says the Lord almighty. I shall strike the shepherd, and the sheep will be scattered, and I shall raise my hand against the shepherds (v.7). The God and Father gave his own Son for our sake, as part of the divine plan sending him, though he is God and by nature born of him in ineffable fashion, to come in the form of a slave, adopt our humanity, be nailed to a cross so as to save the world and dislodge Satan from his arrogant treatment of all, demolish the loathsome idolatry, eliminate divination, false prophecy, and the fanciful inventions of the heart, and also remove *the unclean spirit from the earth.* In addition to this, the purpose was for him to gain possession of the earth under heaven, and bring those who were deceived to enjoy the knowledge of God by persuading them to choose the pious and seemly way of life and be seen to hold in honor every form of virtue.

This was the reason, then, that he willingly underwent death on a cross, despite its extreme shamefulness, "disregarding the shame,"[11] in accordance with the will of the God and Father. The Son himself conveys to us something of the sort in saying, "I have come down from heaven, not to do my own will but the will of him who sent me. And this is the will of him who sent me: that I should lose nothing of all that he has given to me, but raise it up on the last day." As the divinely inspired Paul writes, "Christ died and lived again for this purpose: so that he might be Lord both of the dead and of the living."[12] So he willingly laid down (506) his life for us, the God and Father surrendering him, as it were, as man to his will and allowing him, as it were, to purchase life for all with his precious blood, as I said. When Pilate had the idea that he was in a position of authority over him, therefore, the Savior corrected him by saying, "You would have no authority over me unless it were given to you from above."[13]

Accordingly, when the statement of the prophet had described

10. Zec 13.2.
11. Phil 2.8; Heb 12.2.
12. Jn 6.38–39; Rom 14.9.
13. Jn 19.11.

in advance how there would occur a wonderful change for the better in human affairs when he suffered death in the flesh, he is anxious, as it were, to give an indication of when this would happen, and orders the mystery of the Passion to be put into effect by addressing the *sword* itself in the words, *Rise up against my shepherd and against his fellow citizen, says the Lord almighty.* We claim that in this there is reference by *sword* to trial under the image of a sword, or even the actual Passion inflicted on Emmanuel from the Jews' folly. This is likewise the way we should probably understand what the righteous man Simeon said when the holy Virgin brought Jesus when he was eight days old, "And a sword will pierce your own soul"; she was, as it were, slain with a sword to see the crucifixion of the one born of her—according to the flesh, I mean.[14] So he says, *Sword, rise up against my shepherd;* that is, let the saving Passion now take effect, and the time come for the display of good things. Christ, you see, is placed over us as chief shepherd, and we believers are all under him, though not out of the hand of the God and Father; he rules us in the Son, through whom and in whom we are saved and enjoy access. (507) The Savior said, for example, "My sheep hear my voice; I know them and they follow me, and to them I shall give eternal life. They will not be lost forever, and no one will snatch them from my hand. My Father, who has given them to me, is greater than all else, and no one can snatch them out of the Father's hand. The Father and I are one."[15] So the Son belongs to the God and Father as shepherd, and the creatures he pastures belong not to someone else but to himself and the Father. The hirelings who slaughtered the sheep are not to be thought of as his; dismissing all pity, "those who sold them said, Blessed be God, we are rich."[16] *Citizens,* or friends and familiars of the good shepherd, are those placed under him, and before all others the divinely inspired disciples, who, when *the shepherd was struck,* were scattered and took to flight; when the retinue of the Jews came and with them the traitor together with the cohort arrested Jesus, "they all left him and fled," in the phrasing of the Gospel.[17]

Now, the fact that in surrendering his own Son to death for

14. Lk 2.35.
15. Eph 2.18; Jn 10.27–30.
16. Zec 11.5.
17. Mt 26.56.

us the God and Father is said to *strike* him, or at least to let him suffer in every possible way, the Son himself confirms in the verse of the psalmist about those guilty of unholy crimes against him—namely, the Jews—"They persecuted the one you struck, and added to the distress of my wounds; add iniquity to their iniquity."[18] He voluntarily underwent the Passion, therefore, as I said, (508) so that the achievement of his sufferings might be resplendent. But the fact that for the crucifiers the crime would be the source of ruin, and that those responsible for such a scheme and such exploits—namely, the leaders of the people—would be subjected to the evils arising from divine wrath, he makes clear in saying, *And I shall raise my hand against the shepherds.* It was they, remember, in the words of the prophet, who "destroyed my vineyard, turned his desirable portion into a trackless waste; it became a desolate ruin."[19] God will *raise his hand,* as though striking with a sword and exacting vengeance for sacrilege, not only because they have vented their spleen on Christ but because, in addition to this and their other crimes, it was the beginning and introduction to unrestrained madness. As the blessed evangelist Matthew says, remember, when Pilate presented to the Jews both Christ and Barabbas, crying out, "Which of the two do you want me to release to you?" "the chief priests and the elders persuaded the crowds to ask for Barabbas, and to have Jesus killed"; and they further persuaded them to cry out, "Crucify, crucify."[20] The statement in the prophet is therefore true that says, "Because the shepherds were deranged, and did not inquire of the Lord, hence all their flock failed to understand, and were scattered."[21] In other words, just as the vigilance of the good shepherds benefits the flock, so indifference ruins it, and what is subject to the shepherds' control completely follows their footsteps.

On that day, says the Lord, two parts (509) *will perish and fail, while a third will be left in it. I shall pass the third through the fire, and fire them as silver is fired, and test them as gold is tested. He will call upon my name, and I shall hearken to him and say, This is my people. They will say, The Lord is my God* (vv.8–9). With the divine hand raised against those sacrilegious people who falsely prophesied

18. Ps 69.26–27.
19. Jer 12.10–11.
20. Mt 27.20–21; Jn 19.6.
21. Jer 10.21.

and destroyed the Lord's vineyard, he says there will be no escape from punishment and justice either for those who ill-advisedly connived at their unholy exploits—namely, the Jewish populace and the vast number of their subjects and followers. They were consumed by war, in fact, and the cities and towns were destroyed along with their inhabitants, burned to the ground; but a bare remnant survived, referred to as *a third* of the whole group, Israel not being completely wiped out, since God took pity on account of the ancestors. Blessed Isaiah also said as much, "If the Lord of hosts had not left us a seed, we would have become like Sodom and resembled Gomorrah."[22] The *third,* or remnant—namely, those from the line of Israel who believed—he says he will *pass through the fire, and fire them like silver and gold,* the life of the saints not being without hardship, since it is true that "all who wish to live religiously in Christ will be persecuted."[23] The divinely inspired disciples and all their fellow workers at that time were tested most of all, (510) and they suffered hardship with them in administering to the nations the Gospel of Christ. They were called, in fact, to experience many tribulations and persecutions, and, as it were, *fired, tested* by trials, so as to be able to say with confidence, "You tested us, O God, firing us as silver is fired."[24]

What, then, is the benefit of this? And what will be the reward for those who suffer such hardship and are *tested?* They became God's own, his familiars and beloved; they were reckoned "a holy nation, a royal priesthood, a people for his possession, in order that they might proclaim the mighty acts of him who called them out of darkness into his marvelous light"; once no people, they have become a people. And whereas once they heard, "When you stretch out your hands to me, I shall turn my eyes away from you, and if you multiply your prayers, I shall not hearken to you,"[25] now instead he says that *he will call upon my name, and I shall hearken to him and say, This is my people.* They have therefore become the special inheritance of the God and Father, and are given to the Son, who rules everything together with the one who begot him; for them the Creator and Lord of all is kind and merciful. Amen.

22. Is 1.9.
23. 2 Tm 3.12.
24. Ps 66.10.
25. 1 Pt 2.9; Is 1.15.

COMMENTARY ON ZECHARIAH, CHAPTER FOURTEEN

Lo, days of the Lord are coming, when your plunder will be divided in your midst. I shall assemble all the nations against Jerusalem to battle, the city will be taken, the houses ransacked, and the women defiled; half of the city will go off in captivity (vv. 1–2).

IN MENTIONING the august and saving Passion on the cross, he said above, "Sword, rise up against my shepherd and against his fellow citizen, says the Lord almighty. I shall strike the shepherd, and the sheep will be scattered."[1] Now, the fact that the mass of the Jews would be subjected to extreme punishment—and rightly so, since their extreme audacity led to the Lord's death—he conveyed, and proceeded to say, *and I shall raise my hand against the shepherds. On that day, says the Lord, two parts will perish and fail, while I shall pass the third through* (512) *the fire, and fire them as silver is fired, and test them as gold is tested.* The way to understand this I shall with some plausibility explain to the extent possible. The thrust of our present text is also directed against Jerusalem's unbridled sacrilege, and indicates to us the manner of its capture. *Lo, days of the Lord* will come, it says, which he will inflict with righteous verdict and holy judgment. There is truth also in what he says through another prophet, "Surely there will be no evil in the city for which the Lord is not responsible"—in other words, nothing that (we claim) he did not allow would happen capable of bringing evil on the whole city, and he would exact an account of their sins from those guilty of unfettered assaults of criminality without his willing it.[2] So he speaks of the *days* on account of their being inflicted in accord with his wrath; after all, their frenzy was no

1. Zec 13.7–9.
2. Am 3.6.

longer tolerable when they killed the prophets and in addition to them the Son.

Now, what is due to come in those *days* he clarifies in saying, *Your plunder will be divided in your midst*, that is, *all the nations* that are congregated and *ransacking the houses* and abusing the *women* along with infants. At that time, in fact, he says, *half of the city will go off in captivity*. They say, remember, that Romans took the city, and, paying no heed to the fighters' best efforts, they burned the Temple itself and the city's houses, but spared the inhabitants of the upper city and sanctuary who embraced them. Now, observe how he says that, though the victors reached such a point of boldness as to *ransack the houses*, (513) they did not immediately depart with their booty and spend the time on the *division* on arriving in their own tents. Instead, they did so in the captured city, which they would not have done if any fighter at all had arrived to assist those who were distressed and robbed. He does say, however, that they *defiled the women*, involuntarily abused by other men and deprived of due respect, often in view of their lawful partners. Such are the sufferings in war and the disasters that befall people once they are captured and completely deprived of help.

But the remainder of my people will not perish from the city. I think this means nothing else than what I said just now, that some compassion was shown the inhabitants of the upper city, and part of Jerusalem was saved. The Roman generals, you see, would put a stop to the fury of the soldiers if they chanced to see some people tearfully submitting and falling down without fighting. So he is saying either that the *remainder of his people* were in the saved part of the city, or perhaps were those who believed in Christ the Savior of all, of whom he also says they would *not perish from the city*. After all, they will always be members of the Church, even if losing the earthly Jerusalem now in ruins; in its place they will have the city on high, of which the divinely inspired Paul also writes, "The Jerusalem on high is free, being our mother." (514) There is also some similarity to what blessed David suggested in these words, "The inhabitant of Jerusalem will not be shaken forever." After all, if the Church is immovable, and "the gates of Hades will not prevail against it," in the Savior's words,[3] having him for foundation, it is inevitable that its inhabitants will emerge resistant to destruction, reckoned as God's people and ranked with his familiars.

The Lord will issue forth and go into battle among those nations, like a day of battle formation on a day of war. On that day his feet will stand on the Mount of Olives facing Jerusalem on the east. The Mount of Olives will be split in two, half of it to the east and half of it to the sea, an immense abyss. Half of the mountain will face the north, and half of it the south. A valley of my mountains will be filled in, and a valley of the mountains will be joined together as far as Azal in the way it was filled in at the time of the earthquake in the days of Uzziah king of Judah (vv.3–5). The passage adopts the metaphor of a noble general exhorting his fellow soldiers to battle and directing the fighting against the columns of the enemy. It is applied to God as though present and positioned in the ranks with the nations devastating Judea and ransacking Jerusalem itself. (515) We recall, on the other hand, that he says something similar in the Gospel parables as well: the king holds a wedding for his son, and sends his servants to summon those invited; but some outrageously abuse and kill those summoning them to the feast, and finally lay hands on the son. What does the text of the parable say next? "The king was enraged, he sent his army and slew those murderers and burned their city." It will be likewise, then, for those nobly resisting *on the day of battle* and wasting the foe. It is a demonstration of the extreme wrath and response from on high as God exacts due vengeance of those offending against him; after all, they killed the Author of life,[4] as I said.

Since, however, it would be fitting for nature alone, the queen of all, to be capable of achieving what surpasses description and admiration, consequently he says that *on that day his feet*—namely, Christ's—*will stand on the Mount of Olives.* It will sustain four ruptures, two to the east and to the west, or *the sea* (the inspired Scripture normally giving that name to the west), and two in other directions, one to the Bear, or *north,* the other to the region of the *south.* He also said the actual pinnacles were split, the result being the filling-in of the *valleys,* struck by an unexpected

3. Gal 4.26; Ps 125.1; Mt 16.18.
4. Mt 22.7; Acts 3.15.

earthquake *as far as Azal*, a town situated at the far point of the mountain, they say. He even likens this serious earthquake to the one that happened in the time of Uzziah, or Azariah. When he occupied the throne in Jerusalem, remember, being from the tribe of Judah, he presumed in lawless fashion (516) to arrogate to himself the priestly office, and was at once struck with leprosy,[5] God in this way demonstrating at that time his wrath at that offense; the region of Judea was fearfully shaken and Jerusalem itself, and they say Mount Zion suffered such a quake as to be cleft in two and its crests plunged into the adjacent valleys. Now, by this description the prophet probably suggests to us the earthquake which the ministers of the Gospel teachings say happened at the time of the precious crucifixion. While the prophet in the passage details at some length what happened, Matthew in his wisdom abbreviates the account in these words, "Jesus cried again in a loud voice and breathed his last. And, lo, the curtain of the Temple was torn in two, from top to bottom, the earth shook, the earth split, the tombs opened, and many bodies of saints who had fallen asleep were raised."[6]

Since it was necessary to present this account of what happened in a plausible way, he probably suggested by the splitting of the *rocks* and the blocking of the *valleys* the Jews' blindness and the recourse to better things by those who had worshiped idols. Those who bow down to the creature instead of the Creator, you see, have a heart like stone, tough and inflexible, like rocks that bear no fruit. What did God say of them in Ezekiel? "I shall pluck out their heart of stone from their flesh, and give them a heart of flesh for them to know me, that I am the Lord." Hence the rending of the hearts of those in error when God strikes them, so that they may receive the saving message of salvation. (517) He suggests as much in Jeremiah, "Are not my words like a flaming fire, says the Lord, and like a hammer breaking rock?" "The word of God is living and active, very sharp and piercing until it divides soul from spirit."[7] The rend-

5. Cf. 2 Chr 26.16–21, which makes no mention of an earthquake (even if archaeologists point to evidence of it in ancient Hazor at that time). Jerome commented that the name arises from a misreading by the LXX.

6. Mt 27.5–52.

7. Ezek 11.19; Jer 23.29; Heb 4.12.

ing of the *rocks*, therefore, as I said, could be a very clear sign of the hasty recourse to better things by those in error. The blocking of the *valleys*, as I said, suggests the blindness of the Jews, the divinely inspired Isaiah saying something similar, "On that day the Lord will block the flow from the river to the Rhinocoloura"—that is, people's understanding throughout all Judea will be blocked—"lest they look and not see, and listen but not hear or understand." "For a veil lies over their heart," as Scripture says, when reading the Old Testament.[8]

The shaking of the earth, in my view, could suggest the transformation from one thing to another; the divinely inspired David cried aloud, for instance, "He sits enthroned on the cherubim; let the earth be moved."[9] We do not claim that he bids the earth under heaven quake in bodily and material fashion, which is a common event that brings us no benefit; rather, the spirit-filled author begs that the earth be transformed from worshiping idols to future knowledge of the one who is God by nature and in truth, from fleshly thinking to wanting to live spiritually, and in short from earthly to heavenly things. Now, if he were also to say that the tombs of those asleep opened, (518) we claim also that he had to be seen overcoming death, since Christ died in the flesh for us by the divine plan "so as to be Lord of both dead and living."[10]

The Lord my God will come, and all his holy ones with him. On that day there will be no light; there will be cold and ice for one day. That day is known to the Lord. Not day and not night, and at evening there will be light (vv.5–7). Having made cursory mention of the Jews' sacrilegious treatment of Christ, the Savior of us all, and the capture of Judea and Jerusalem itself, he now moves on to the very end of the present age and helpfully narrates the coming of Emmanuel from heaven. He will come down, in fact, with the holy angels in the glory of the God and Father so as "to judge the world in righteousness"; as the divinely inspired Paul writes, "We must all appear before the judgment seat of Christ so that each may receive recompense for what has been done in the

8. Is 27.2 LXX; 6.9–10; 2 Cor 3.14–15.

9. Ps 99.1.

10. Rom 14.9. Zechariah is "spirit-filled," *pneumatophoros*, at least in the Pusey text.

body, whether good or evil."[11] So he will come, he says, *he will come, and all his holy ones with him,* namely, the pure multitude of his angels, acting completely as bodyguards and providing ministerial assistance. Emmanuel, after all, is the *Lord* of all, and praised by all as God and fellow ruler with the one who begot him.

If, on the other hand, you were to say that the *holy ones* are those in attendance on him who "are caught up in the clouds to meet him in the air" after the return to life of the dead, as in the view also of the most wise Paul, (519) you would not be wide of the mark. After all, the divinely inspired Isaiah said as much of them, "There deer assembled and saw one another's faces; they arrived in numbers, and not one of them perished; they did not chase one another, because the Lord instructed them, and his Spirit brought them together."[12] The divinely inspired David also sings to us somewhere in forecasting the visit from heaven of Christ the Savior of us all, "The Lord will not repel his people, or forsake his inheritance, until righteousness returns to judgment, and all of the upright in heart possess it."[13] By "righteousness, note, he refers to Christ, saying he returns to judgment; after treading on death he was taken up and ascended to the God and Father in heaven, but will return in due course to judgment, and with him all the "upright in heart," that is, the *holy ones,* as I just said.

Now, the fact that at the end-time there will be a different condition for visible creation, which will change for the better through Christ, the prophet confirms in these words, *On that day there will be no light; there will be cold and ice for one day. That day is known to the Lord.* In other words, at present day and night are distinct, and by the will of the Creator they are given different times, the light rising in the day and then night succeeding to it. But when the Judge comes, changing everything according to his will, creation will take on a different aspect, as I said; *there will be no light, and there will be cold and ice for one day.* By *light* he means day, and by *ice* (520) *and cold* night, since the day and night period is classed as *one day.* It is as if he were to say,

11. Ps 96.13; 2 Cor 5.10.
12. 1 Thes 4.17; Is 34.15–16.
13. Ps 94.14–15.

At that time when he comes from heaven to change everything and transform it for the better as Creator, *there will be no light* and no night *for one day*. The blessed prophet Isaiah also said something like that, "The sun will no longer be light for you by day, nor will the rising of the moon shed light on the night for you; instead, the Lord will be eternal light for you, and God your glory." The fact that the very elements will in time be irrelevant Christ himself will confirm in the words, "Immediately after the tribulation of those days, the sun will be darkened, and the moon will not give its light";[14] Christ will suffice for light eternal for us; he will be a long and uninterrupted day.

That day, he says, *is known to the Lord;* only the God and Father knows the end-time. The Son himself also establishes this for us in saying, "Concerning that day or hour, no one knows, neither angels in heaven nor the Son, only the Father"[15]—that is to say, as man like us he would not know what is in the Father, but as by nature God and coming from him, he would definitely know also the last day, even if he admits to not knowing it as man. Now, to interpret for us and render clearer what I said, he proceeds to say, *Not day and not night, and at evening there will be light;* in other words, at night time there will again be light (521) that comes through Christ and lights up the earth under heaven, darkness being completely dissipated and no longer affecting the eyes of the holy ones. The Savior's disciple also has reason in his favor in thinking that creation itself will be adjusted for the better, and in saying that the day of the Lord will come like a thief, when the heavens will pass away with a loud noise, the elements will be dissolved with fire, and the earth and everything done on it will be disclosed, and in saying that we are expecting a new heaven and a new earth in accord with his promises.[16] We have no choice but to move to that idea: if our situation will enjoy complete newness of life, we shall have need also of a new creation; as the divinely inspired Paul also writes, "Creation itself will also be set free from the bondage to decay to obtain the freedom of the glory of the children of God."[17]

14. Is 60.19; Mt 24.29.

15. Mk 13.32, a text which the Arians cited to support their subordinationist position, and so required clarification.

16. 2 Pt 3.10, 13.

17. Rom 8.21.

On that day living water will come out from Jerusalem, half of it to the first sea and half of it to the last sea. It will be like this in summer and spring. The Lord will be king over all the earth (vv.8–9). He continues in obscure fashion to narrate that the outpouring of the Holy Spirit will be accorded the saints in a most generous and abundant measure, especially at that time when they would be conveyed to a holy and unending life—I mean, (522) in the age to come. You see, whereas at the present time we are enriched through faith in Christ with the first-fruits of the Holy Spirit by way of a pledge, after our return from death to life and the complete removal of sin it will not be by way of a pledge or measure that the divine Spirit will be in us. Instead, in a rich and abundant fashion, as I said, and in a perfect degree we shall by then luxuriate in his gifts through Christ. Hence his calling the Spirit *living water*, which he says *will come out of the Jerusalem* on high; since the inspired Scripture says the God of all dwells in heaven, consequently the text says the life-giving Spirit will also *come out* from heaven.

Now, the fact that the divine writings have the habit of comparing the divine Spirit to waters is confirmed in person by the one who bestows it—namely, the Son—when he says, "Whoever believes in me, as Scripture said, rivers of living water shall flow from his belly." The divinely inspired evangelist interpreted and clarified this, "Now, he said this about the Spirit, which believers in him were to receive."[18] In other words, since the Spirit is life-giving, consequently he compared him to water that gives life to bodies, and rightly so. And the fact that it falls to those judged worthy of a holy life to have a rich share in the Holy Spirit and be filled with the life-giving waters, as it were, he suggests by saying that of the water that is expected in due course to *come out of Jerusalem, half of it will come to the first sea and half of it to the last sea.* (523) What does that mean? The divine Scripture frequently compares the many nations and the vast number beyond counting of human beings to seas and waters; it speaks this way in one of the holy prophets, "Everything was full of the knowledge of the Lord, as floods of water will cover seas." The divinely inspired Daniel also said somewhere in forecasting what would

18. Jn 7.38–39.

happen at the end-time to people throughout the world, "I, Daniel, had a vision, and, lo, the four winds of heaven buffeted the great sea, and four great beasts came up out of the sea, different from one another." Blessed David made this clearer in his song, "This sea is deep and wide, creeping things are there beyond number, living things small and great; ships pass that way, there is a monster you formed to play in it."[19] I mean, what do we say is the monster in the material sea that is formed for playing by God who controls everything? It is therefore customary with the divine writings to compare the whole world to seas, and sometimes the vast mass of humanity as well.

Accordingly, the fact that the grace of the Spirit is distributed by God in equal measure to believers both from Israel and from the nations he suggests in saying of the life-giving water that *half of it will come out to the first sea and* the other *half of it to the last sea.* By *the first sea* he refers to Israel, and by *the last* to the vast number of those who came to faith after them, namely, the nations. We are by no means claiming that the Holy Spirit is divided and will be incomplete in each, despite reference to *half:* (524) far from it. Our view rather is that the prophet meant to indicate that the distribution of grace to one group and the other will be made equally, *half and half* suggesting equality of esteem and quantity. That the grace is unending and the participation is at every moment it is not difficult to see from his proceeding to say, *It will be like this in summer and spring.*

We should note, however, that instead of *in spring* the Hebrew text says "in winter." *It will be,* therefore, he is saying, at these times, as also the flow of the spiritual waters, both in winter and *in summer*—that is, at every time.[20] Now, it is not a problem that mention is made in the text of the Seventy of *spring* instead of winter, that season being between winter and summer, so that if you were to assign the event to the season of winter, you would not be at variance with what is likely or correct. If, on the other hand, you wanted to understand in another way the reference to the spiritual water, *half of it will come to the first sea and half of it to the last sea. It will be like this in summer and spring,*

19. Is 11.9; Dn 7.2–3; Ps 104.25–26.
20. Jerome had noted the discrepancy in Heb. and Greek texts.

you would give the text the following interpretation. By *first sea* he refers to what lies to the east, namely, beyond the limits of the whole earth, and by the *last sea* to the very extremities of the west, since by east he defines the world's face and beginning, as it were. In my view, he refers by *summer* to the hot southerly parts of the world, and likewise by *spring* to the cold northerly parts. The divinely inspired David likewise, remember, (525) in wanting to indicate the four regions of the earth under heaven, cries out to God, "You made summer and winter," and again, "The north and the sea you created."[21] So the living water, he is saying, *will come out* in equal measure *to the first sea and* likewise *to the last,* that is, to the east and the west, *in summer and spring,* that is to say once more, to south and north. In other words, the land under heaven will be filled with graces through Christ, and will abide altogether in those receiving the gifts. Then it is, in fact, that *the Lord will be king over all the earth:* we shall be under him alone; he it is who will rule when all the cosmic powers of this age are completely destroyed, every evil principality is led away in triumph, and the arrogance of Satan himself is expelled and the wicked powers with him.[22]

On that day the Lord will be one, and his name one, encompassing all earth and desert from Geba as far as Rimmon south of Jerusalem; Ramah will remain in its place from the gate of Benjamin as far as the first gate, to the corner gate and to the tower of Hananel, to the king's winepresses. They will occupy it. There will be no further curse, and Jerusalem will abide confidently (vv.9–11). The discourse of the holy authors is generally obscure—(526) something that in my view is part of God's wise management to prevent holy things from being set before dogs, and the really precious pearl from being cast under the feet of swine and abused.[23] To the saints, by contrast, Christ reveals knowledge through the Spirit and makes clear the powers of the age to come. In sensible realities, hidden and spiritual things are generally outlined, and the substance of what is more obscure becomes evident. He said, therefore, that *on that day,* or at that time, our condition will be transformed into newness of life, creation itself will be reformed

21. Pss 74.17; 89.12.
22. Eph 6.12.
23. Mt 7.6.

as better than before, and *the Lord will be one, and his name one, encompassing all earth.* In fact, the Lord always has been, is, and *will be one,* being by nature and in truth the God of all, bringing into being what at one time had no being. But since the author of sin—namely, Satan—had led astray the earth under heaven, we wretches were inveigled into his false and loathsome service and passed our life in the world without sight or hearing, calling our deceivers lords and stupidly giving the title of divinity to the unclean demons.

We have been called to knowledge of the truth even in this world through Christ, and with the passing of the present age, then and only then will all madness be removed from us, the foes will be put under the feet of Christ, and then *the Lord will be one over the whole earth,* with no one in it wresting the glory of lordship. In another sense Christ *will be one Lord,* when every earthly kingdom is ineffectual, (527) and the earth under heaven dedicates to him alone the rule of all things. Daniel in his great wisdom also said as much; in describing the form of his visions he said, "As you saw a stone cut from the mountain without human hands, and it crushed the clay, the iron, the bronze, the silver, the gold. The great God has informed the king what must happen after this. The dream is certain and its interpretation trustworthy."[24] Therefore, he *will be one* and only, and will fill with his glory the holy city—that is, the spiritual Jerusalem—whose length and breadth he brings out also in the earthly Jerusalem as in a type when he says that it will extend *from Geba as far as Rimmon.* Geba is a town or allotment of the tribe of Benjamin; they say it is situated in the northern parts of Jerusalem. Rimmon is a rock in the southern desert. While the length of Jerusalem is defined, therefore, *from Geba as far as Rimmon,* likewise the breadth when he says, *from the gate of Benjamin as far as the first gate, to the corner gate and to the tower of Hananel, to the king's winepresses.* Some gates in Jerusalem were given these names, *the first gate* and *corner gate,* and in-between was what was called *tower of Hananel,* immediately after which were *the king's winepresses.*

24. Dn 2.45.

Now, these places in Jerusalem indicate its length as in a type: just as the God of all bade the blessed prophet Ezekiel measure the Temple with a reed, surveying it in this direction and that, his purpose being to suggest (528) that there are many mansions in the Father's house, and countless numbers of dwellings for the saints, so too here he seems to me to describe to us by mention of these places the length and breadth of the spiritual Jerusalem—that is, the Church of Christ, which the divinely inspired Isaiah also addresses in the words, "Enlarge the site of your tent and your halls, fix it firm, do not hold back, lengthen your cords, strengthen your stakes, spread out further to the right and to the left."[25] Once the holy city is expanded, then, and broadened to a width befitting it, the saints *will occupy it, and there will be no further curse;* that is, it will in no way be alienated from God, for he will grant it his unwavering love. They would no longer relapse and offend God, since, as I said, sin was eliminated completely along with the tempter Satan. "No lion will be there," remember, "nor shall any wild beast come upon it or be discovered there."[26] Accordingly, *they will occupy it confidently.*

Since the clause *Ramah will remain in its place* occurs in the middle, we have this to say in turn by way of interpreting the sense of the passage to the extent possible. *Ramah* is a town or village, and an allotment to those of the tribe of Asher; a different Ramah from this belongs to those of the tribe of Naphtali. The holy prophet mentions one of these, or another Ramah, in saying, "A voice was heard in Ramah, lamentation and weeping and groaning: Rachel was crying over her children, and she refused to be comforted, because they are no more."[27] We say such a thing happened (529) at Bethlehem when Herod ordered the babies in it to be killed. So he calls Jerusalem *Ramah,* probably on account of what happened in it, the lamenting at its capture. At any rate, the prophet Jeremiah introduced it as though it were weeping and wailing over its own lost children, saying, "She wept bitterly at night, her tears on her cheeks." And what was her lament? "My maidens and my young men were car-

25. Ezek 40; Jn 14.2; Is 54.2–3.
26. Is 35.9.
27. Jer 31.15; Mt 2.18.

ried off in captivity; you killed them by sword and by famine; on a day of your wrath you butchered them; you showed no pity."[28]

If, on the other hand, you preferred that the name *Ramah* here be applied to the spiritual Jerusalem—namely, the Church—our comment is that that is perfectly reasonable. There are, in fact, many in the churches weeping and "having godly grief, which produces a repentance that leads to salvation and brings no regret." Christ himself welcomes such people with the words, "Blessed are those who mourn now, for they will be comforted," and again, "Blessed are you who weep now, for you shall laugh."[29] So even if the Church were named as the Ramah referred to in the prophet's statement, the claim would be quite plausible. *It will remain in its place,* the text says—that is, it will not be moved; the Church of Christ is firmly based, as I said, and unshakeable.

This will be the downfall with which the Lord will strike all the peoples who attack Jerusalem. Their flesh will wither while they are still on their feet, (530) *their eyes will run in their sockets, and their tongues will rot in their mouths* (v.12). "You will have tribulation in the world," Christ predicted to those who believed in him; but he made them more confident by proceeding in a kindly manner, "Yet have confidence: I have overcome the world." "For I have given you the power to walk on snakes and scorpions and on all the power of the foe."[30] The snakes and the scorpions are clearly no other than the loathsome and deadly ranks of the destructive demons who pursue the saints and minister to the unmitigated frenzy of the spirits in the world, who roam in all directions scheming against the saints in multifarious ways despite having been conquered triumphantly by Christ, who nailed to his own cross the record against us so as to rid us of their arrogance.[31]

Since, therefore, he had said that Jerusalem—that is, the Church of the living God[32]—would dwell in confidence, and had every right to look forward to achieving this with the removal of the foe and of those bent on persecuting it, he consequently delivers us this account as well, *This will be the downfall with which*

28. Lam 1.2; 2.21.
29. 2 Cor 7.10; Mt 5.4; Lk 6.21.
30. Jn 16.33; Lk 10.19.
31. Col 2.14–15.
32. 1 Tm 3.15.

the Lord will strike all the peoples who attack Jerusalem. Their flesh will wither while they are still on their feet, their eyes will run in their sockets, and their tongues will rot in their mouths. In other words, on the one hand this death, which affects all in common and is in accord with nature, wastes the *flesh* of everyone, gouges their eyes, and rots their tongues. (531) On the other hand, there would be justice in the terrible fate and approaching calamity, in which *their flesh will wither while they are* alive and *still on their feet, their eyes will run, and* even *their tongues* will be punished. He says that such a fate will very properly befall those who hate God and pursue an accursed life; they will pay the penalty not only for their sins against the saints, but also for their fleshly delights in this world, which were the cause of their not embracing the faith and choosing to live a pious life and to love the glory of life in Christ. They had, in fact, acquiesced unrestrainedly in improper pleasures, and kept their eyes fixed on every pleasurable sight as though greedily imbibing it; they sharpened their tongue against Christ and delivered sacrilegious outbursts against the sacred teachings of the Church.

Rightfully, therefore, they paid the penalty in their *flesh, eyes, and tongues:* just as the woman who drank the water of accusation and broke her oath was punished in the thigh where the crime of adultery took place, the text saying, "Her thigh will be damaged and fall,"[33] in similar fashion (in my view) there is for those persecuting the holy city the punishment affecting *flesh, eyes, and tongues*—namely, fleshly delights, indulgence, and as well sinful use of the eyes and words from an undisciplined tongue. (532)

On that day deep astonishment from the Lord will fall on them. Each will seize the hand of their neighbor, and their hand will be interlocked with the hand of their neighbor. Judah will deploy its forces in Jerusalem and assemble the might of all the peoples round about, gold and silver and garments in great abundance (vv.13–14). Again in this passage by *astonishment* he means "fear" or "amazement." At that time, then, he is saying, when the Church's enemies gaze at one another, and thus are subjected to dire penalties, they

33. Nm 5.17.

will be amazed at the horrors and will thus desist from daring to persecute the holy city any longer; they will take to flight, *seizing* one another's *hands,* as it were, looking vainly for help from one another, and will become pitiable, dejected, and trodden under foot by the saints.

Judah, he is saying—that is, those justified by faith in Christ and representing a Jew in a spiritual sense, boasting also of circumcision in the Holy Spirit—*will deploy its forces in Jerusalem;* that is, they will engage the foe, prevail over their adversaries, trample them like scorpions, walk on them like asp and basilisk, and scorn them completely like lion and dragon.[34] Attracting fame and admiration, they will amass from such doughty deeds wealth like *gold and silver and garments.* You see, how could anyone be in doubt that the sense of the prophecy does not lie in material realities? The wealth of the saints, after all, far from being corruptible and earthly, is spiritual, heavenly, and unending, and (533) is gathered for their own souls by the teachers and those distinguished in other ways in the churches. They laid hold of it, in fact, as though it were *the might of all the peoples,* by bringing forward through faith in Christ the elite of the nations, which is the way Christ himself spoke of plundering the strong man's possessions.[35]

If, on the other hand, you were to speak of the Jew *assembling the might of all the peoples round about, gold and silver and garments* so that we might understand that by collecting the wisdom in the world they would be conspicuous for it by upholding the doctrines of religion, the interpretation would be plausible. The wise women of Israel, remember, plundered the Egyptians, making use of "gold and silver vessels and clothing from neighbor and fellow tenant."[36] The splendor of the good things of the spirit, therefore, is suggested by what is physical and material; the divinely inspired Paul, for example, addresses the believers saved by him, "This is as certain, brethren, as the boast I make of you in Christ Jesus," and he calls them his "crown and joy."[37]

And this will be the downfall of the horses, the mules, the camels, the asses, and all the cattle in those camps through this downfall (v.15).

34. Rom 2.29; Ps 91.13.
35. Mt 12.29.
36. Ex 3.22.
37. 1 Cor 15.31; Phil 4.1.

He had already specified the forms of punishment suffered in every possible way at times by those who persecuted and abused the holy city in their campaigns, loathsome and (534) contumacious as they were, making iniquitous statements against God, and "lifting their horn on high," in the psalmist's words.[38] Now he usefully proceeds, *This will be the downfall of the horses, the mules, the camels, the asses, and all the cattle.* By mention of the beasts of burden he suggests their riders; nations from far and near harassed the Jews and even Jerusalem, some riding *horses*—Babylonians, Syrians, and even the nations of Egypt—some mounted on *camels, asses, and mules,* such as the Moabites and nomads of the desert, whom the prophet Isaiah also mentions, "In tribulation and distress, lion and cub of a lion, from there also asps and offspring of winged asps, which carried their riches on asses and camels"; and elsewhere he says he saw "a rider on an ass and a rider on a camel."[39] So by reference to the nations as a type, those always making war on the earthly Jerusalem, he is writing of the enemies of truth, for us to understand from them our visible and invisible foes with whom we are fighting.

If, on the other hand, you wanted to apply the characteristics of *cattle* to the behavior of the Church's enemies, there would be nothing wrong in saying so and taking it that way. Some are headstrong and audacious, perhaps like *horses,* and you could properly assert of them a love of pleasure and a frenzy for women; others, like *mules,* are wild and untamed, and it is customary even for the Greek poets to call them very wild; and some resemble the behavior of *camels,* those who are unbalanced and arrogant, with a mind conceited owing to derangement; while others are no different (535) from *asses* in suffering the worst irrationality of all, the ass being sluggish and slow to respond, proverbial for extreme irrationality. Now, we should note that those hostile to the Church are not compared with tame and clean animals, like sheep and ox; rather, they are likened to the loathsome and untamed ones, which are condemned by the clauses of the Law as profane and unclean.

As many as are left of all the nations advancing on Jerusalem will

38. Ps 75.6.
39. Is 30.6; 21.7.

come up year by year to worship the King, the Lord almighty, and to celebrate the festival of Tabernacles. All who do not ascend to Jerusalem from all the tribes of the earth to worship the King, the Lord almighty, will be added to the others (vv.16–17).[40] After saying that those making war on the churches and directing a lofty and arrogant attitude against holy Jerusalem would be caught up in penalties befitting them, he forecasts adoration by those left in their wake—namely, adoration in Christ through faith. It is he, after all, who is the "expectation of the nations," as the patriarch put it; he is also set to be "light of nations, a covenant for the race, to open eyes of the blind, and bring out from their bondage those who are bound, and from prison those seated in darkness."[41] Accordingly, he makes clear that, on leaving the gloom of idolatry and having broken the bonds of the devil's knavery, those (536) from the nations will come to the light of truth and hasten to the yoke of the Savior. He means that the survivors from those who were punished, or those fighting against the churches, who are innumerable, *will come up year by year to worship the King, the Lord almighty, and to celebrate the festival of Tabernacles.* The Law of Moses, remember, ordered the feast of Tabernacles to be celebrated on the fifteenth day of the seventh month when the harvest had been brought in to the storehouses from the fields; consequently, he calls the feast "finale" since work in the fields was now complete. They were bidden take "fronds of palm trees, fruit of a handsome tree, dense foliage of a tree, willow branches," drink water from a brook, and rejoice in it.

While the Law cited as the basis of the feast Israel's dwelling in tents when rescued from the oppression of the Egyptians,[42] the event was in fact a type of the mystery of Christ. We too, in fact, were rescued from oppression by the devil, called to free-

40. In the Heb. and the Antioch text the final clause reads, "no rain will fall upon them," a significant reference to the expectation of good rains only for those who observe the feast, still associated with the celebration (Brown tells us, *The Gospel according to John I–XII*, 327).

41. Gn 49.10 LXX; Is 42.6–7.

42. Lv 23.34–43 LXX. Cyril shows how an originally agricultural festival took on historical significance, as with other Jewish festivals (an accent he does not find in Didymus), and was then later reinterpreted in the Christian calendar and theology. Cyril also picks up the accent in Zechariah on the Gentiles joining in the celebration (likewise not found in Didymus).

dom through Christ, as I said, and became subject to him, the King and God of all, spurning the knavery of those formerly in power. We celebrate the real feast of Tabernacles, that is, the day of Christ's resurrection, when the bodies of all, despite being dissolved in corruption and in thrall to death, become solidified in him, as it were. After all, he is the resurrection; he is the life, the spoils of the dead, so to say, and "first-fruits of those fallen asleep,"[43] filling us with spiritual harvest and, as it were, causing the produce collected from the fields (537) to be stowed in the storerooms on high. He it is who will reward us with life and enjoyment in paradise—obviously of a spiritual nature—now that we have conquered sin, exude spiritual fragrance, and bear the handsome and commendable fruit of the evangelical way of life by living in a pure and holy manner. A further sign of this would be having the palm fronds and fruit of a handsome tree combined with the other foliage. He is the brook of delights from which the God and Father has given us to drink; he is the fount of life and the river of peace,[44] who directs to us those called from the nations.

To these matters, however, there has been partial reference by us in other places. Those *coming up to worship the King, the Lord almighty, and to celebrate the festival of Tabernacles,* therefore, are those who are justified through faith in Christ. Those not coming up, by contrast, he threatens with ruin and punishment equal to that sustained by the persecutors and abusers; those opting not to love will suffer the same fate as the enemy. In my view, this is the meaning of what Christ himself said, "He who is not with me is against me, and he who does not gather with me scatters."[45]

If the tribe of Egypt does not go up or travel there, on them will occur the downfall with which the Lord will strike all the nations that do not go up to celebrate the feast of Tabernacles. It will be the sin of Egypt and the sin of all the nations that did not go up to celebrate the feast of Tabernacles (vv.18–19). By reference to one nation—the Egyptians, I mean—he indicates those reaching the height of error and opting for the extreme absurdity of idolatry, on whom will fall

43. Jn 11.25; 1 Cor 15.20.
44. Ps 36.9; Is 66.12.
45. Lk 11.23.

a dire and ineluctable penalty, and for whom their option not to respect the desirable grace of salvation in Christ will be productive of ruin. It is, in fact, as if they were convicted of being killers of their own souls, especially as it is true that they had the chance to lay hold of eternal life and the indulgence from on high available to those willing to opt for it, and to be relieved of the burden of sin. Instead, they gave free rein to their own errors, maintained undiminished the blight of being deceived and the defilement of sin, and persisted in error. This was in spite of the illumination of all things by the divine light, which summoned to clear vision those in gloom and darkness. It could be said of every such person, "A stillborn child is better off than he; for it came in vanity and departs in darkness, and its name will be covered in darkness." "Better for them if they had not been born," in the Savior's words.[46]

Now, the fact that the verse not only is directed at the Egyptians but also will affect *all the nations*, who will all and in every way be punished for spurning salvation in Christ and not respecting the celebration of it, he confirms by saying, *It will be the sin of Egypt and the sin of all the nations that did not go up to celebrate the feast of Tabernacles.* That is to say, before the coming of Christ there was perhaps still some excuse on the part of the nations, who could claim not to be called by anyone, since no one announced it to them. Accordingly, the Savior also in the Gospel parables, to make the same point to us, said that the workers (539) called at the eleventh hour said, "No one hired us." But now that Christ has shone his light, bound the strong man,[47] rescued from their perversity those subject to it, justified by faith those who came to him, and has given himself for the life of all, they will no longer find any adequate excuse for not taking advantage of the august grace. Christ would therefore be right in saying of the nations, "If I had not come and spoken to them, they would have no sin; but as it is, they have no excuse for their sin."[48]

On that day, what is on the bridle of the horse will be holy to the Lord almighty (v.20). When every war has been terminated, fighting

46. Eccl 6.3–4; Mt 26.24.
47. Mt 20.7; 12.29.
48. Jn 15.22.

suppressed, and enemies put down, and when the peace crowning the holy city—that is, the Church—is now unimpaired, there will be no call for the instruments of war, he says, for ornamented bridles. What need would the rider skilled in the art of war have of such a thing, after all, if there were no one to oppose him? So the useful accoutrements of war, he is saying, will be sacred and dedicated to God; since it is he who is the arbiter of peace, the weapons of war will rightly be dedicated to him as pointless and ineffectual. The blessed prophet Isaiah, remember, said of some people, "They will beat their swords into ploughshares, and their spears into scythes; nation will not lift up sword against nation, neither will they learn to go to war any more,"[49] (540) now that the time of peace convinces them to allow warfare to yield to the needs of farming, and to follow other pursuits by setting aside concern for military affairs. Likewise, the divinely inspired Zechariah, as though the peace given by God is now unimpaired, says that warriors' useful accoutrements will be used instead as an offering to God; fighting will come to a complete end, no thought given to horse or ornamented bridle—instead, attention will be directed to the need to opt for the pursuits pertaining to virtue and piety.

Some commentators, on the other hand, take the view that the intent of the prophecy has been fulfilled in a different way, claiming that the Cross was discovered at a certain time with the nails still embedded; the pious Constantine took one of them and made it into a bridle for his own horse in the belief he was blessed by God for so doing. Now, it would not be implausible for someone to make this claim, if it really happened, nor would the interpretation be irrational for it to be brought to notice by God and for respect to be paid to the pious emperor in the inspired prophecy. The Scriptures, in fact, record many such prophecies by the holy prophets, including of course the one having to do with Josiah and some others. Sometimes the tranquility and piety of the times are conveyed by those who ruled at the time. It is therefore not unlikely that in this case as well the prophet Zechariah refers to a commendable event, a truly godly and pious reign, and an age dedicated to love in Christ. After

49. Is 2.4.

all, as to the appropriateness of using the nail taken from the precious Cross for the kings' horses, (541) what other impression could we form than the deepest and truly most admirable piety of the rulers?

And the pots will be in the house of the Lord like bowls before the altar. There were *pots* in the holy tabernacle and in the Temple built later, in which the meat of the sacrifices was cooked; the priests consumed it in a holy place, the Law providing for such a ritual lest sanctified things be taken somewhere outside the precincts.[50] With the cessation of those ancient rites, however, the mysteries moved to another form of worship for us; we were taught by our faith to honor the God of all, no longer with slaughtering of sheep and with offering of incense, but rather with bloodless sacrifices, and to perform sacred rites of a spiritual nature in churches to Christ the Savior of all, using, instead of *pots,* other sacred vessels, which the prophet here calls *bowls,* vessels very useful for drinking. The wise listener will completely grasp the force of what is suggested, even if what is said by us is vaguer than it should be on account of the need to make the narration of hidden things succinct.[51] While once there were *pots,* therefore, now there are *bowls before the altar.*

Every pot in Jerusalem and in Judah will be holy (542) *to the Lord almighty. All those sacrificing will come and take some of them and cook in them* (v.21). He speaks of *pots,* still employing the ancient terms for the sacramental vessels; they are *holy,* venerable, and precious, both to those *in Jerusalem,* or the Church—namely, to the divine ministers—and in *Judah* itself, that is to say once more, those given a share in circumcision in spirit. Once more, these would be the believers; the vessels of the holy altar, of course, are not to be taken for common use by anyone at all—instead, as I said, they are *holy* and kept for the glory of God and in normal use only for the ministers of the holy table. It is through them and in them that the sacrifices of the offerers are performed; instead of each person having his own vessel, every-

50. Lv 6.16, 26; Nm 18.9–10. OT sacraments, *mysteria,* moved to another level in the NT dispensation.

51. Both Didymus and Cyril look for convincing significance in the distinction between pots and bowls (Cyril assigning one to the OT and the other to the NT, Didymus typically resorting to allegory).

one uses only the sacred ones. (*Every pot will be holy to the Lord almighty,* the text says.)

While the prophet is talking about sacrifices according to the Law, therefore, and referring to *pots* and *cooking* and the people *sacrificing,* we for our part shall properly apply it to the times in Christ and to the worship performed by us in the Spirit. Now, our claim is that in the scheme of things the discourse of the holy prophets is obscure, and simply not accessible to everyone, lest the holy things of theirs be thrown to dogs, and lest the message that is fit for the saints alone be revealed even to profane and impious people.[52]

And there will be no Canaanite in the house of the Lord almighty on that day. You could detect that the resolve of the ancients was feeble, fragile, and (543) very easily wearied. After all, the people of Israel had been rescued from Egypt by Moses, had shaken off the insupportable yoke of slavery with the performance of innumerable and admirable signs, managed to make their escape, crossed even the sea, eaten bread from heaven, and drunk water unexpectedly made available from a rock in the wilderness. So why were they a wretched lot? Despite Moses they had made a calf, and as the prophet says, they had "adopted the tent of Moloch and the star of their god Raiphan, the images they had made for themselves to worship." Yet they perished, their limbs collapsing in the wilderness, as Scripture says.[53] When those after them crossed the Jordan under Joshua's leadership, however, and when, with the lapse of more time, they were subject to the judges, they worshiped the idols. And in the time of the holy prophets, they sacrificed to golden heifers that the accursed Jeroboam had made for them; in addition to this, they erected shrines and altars, and bowed down no less to Baal, Chamos, Astarte, and Baal of Peor. Surpassing even these evils was the fact that we have to admit that it was not only the mob and rabble engaged in these doings; instead, we shall find a great number of the priests themselves following this path.

Accordingly, God said through the prophet, "The priests did not say, Where is the Lord? Those who handle the Law did not

52. Mt 7.6.
53. Am 5.26; Heb 3.17.

know me; the shepherds offended against me; the prophets prophesied by Baal, and sold themselves to worthless things." The prophet Ezekiel also saw "twenty-five men of the (544) elders of Israel, with their backs to the Temple of the Lord and their faces in the opposite direction, prostrating themselves to the sun towards the east."[54] While it is not difficult to accumulate many other examples in addition to these, in my view they suffice as proof of their obduracy.

The mind of the ancients was unstable, therefore, and easily swayed. Accordingly, God said of them, "They were footloose and fancy-free, and God was not pleased with them," easily betaking themselves to the absurdities of idolatry and, though born of the line of Israel, showing enthusiasm in imitating the foreign *Canaanites*.[55] Since the Only-begotten Word of God has become like us, however, and justified by faith those who made their approach by grace given by him, and sealed them with the Holy Spirit, our resolve has become stable, secure, and unshakeable, fixed, firm in piety. No one, in fact, will convince the sanctified to acknowledge any other than the one who is by nature and in truth God, whom they recognize as God in Christ. He made the Father clear to us in himself by saying, "The one who has seen me has seen the Father."[56] So *on that day*—that is, at that time—*there will be no Canaanite*, that is, no foreigner and idolater, *in the house of the Lord almighty*. Our reliance, as I said, is on faith, and we are surrounded with the guarantees of security in Christ, to whom with the God and Father with the Spirit be the glory for the ages. Amen. (545)

54. Jer 2.8; Ezek 8.16.

55. Jer 14.10.

56. Jn 14.9.

COMMENTARY ON THE *PROPHET MALACHI*

PREFACE TO THE COMMENTARY ON MALACHI

IT IS NECESSARY ALSO to give a short introduction to the prophecy of Malachi in view of the readers' readiness to learn, and for the purpose of grasping all its contents. At the conclusion of the period of the captivity, Israel returned from Babylon to Judea and once again occupied the holy city, having cast off the yoke of slavery. The divine Temple was also rebuilt, governance of the work being by Zerubbabel son of Shealtiel of the tribe of Judah and Joshua son of Jehozadak the high priest. At the time of the captivity Haggai and Zechariah were prophesying to those released from captivity, and Ezra and Nehemiah were associated in ministering to them. A contemporary of the aforementioned holy prophets, or coming a little later, was the divinely inspired (546) Malachi, who is also called "Messenger," a translation of Malachi.[1]

There are no grounds, however, for accepting the statements by some commentators who have given voice to an idle claim about him in their belief that he really was an angel but by God's will took bodily form and acted as a prophet to the people of Israel. Admittedly, he was called "Messenger," as I said, especially as his name has this meaning; as well, he could not unreasonably be called "Messenger" in announcing the words from God on high to the people of Israel. The prophet Malachi himself, for instance, says in what follows in reference to every priest, "A priest's lips will protect knowledge, and from his mouth they will look for law, because he is a messenger of the Lord almighty." The prophet Isaiah says in reference to Em-

1. Cyril characteristically situates the prophets in their historical situation; Malachi is no exception. The personal pronominal suffix to the prophet's name in Heb., "*My* messenger," escapes him (despite Jerome). The twofold meaning of *angelos*, "angel, messenger," gives rise to the "idle" opinions about an angelic origin for the prophet, dismissed by Cyril (already in commentary on Hg 1.13).

manuel, "They would prefer to be burned alive because a child has been born and a son given to us, and he will be called Messenger of Great Counsel."[2] Do you note that the announcement to others of the will of the heavenly nature[3] caused some people also to be called messengers without their being angels by nature? While some human beings—namely, priests—interpret the divine law to us, it is the Son who by contrast is by nature God and from God. The prophet Malachi was in fact a human being like us, then.

The overall thrust of his prophecy is, as it were, in two directions.[4] The Temple, remember, had been rebuilt, and the occasion required the leaders of the people—namely, those of the line of Levi—to render priestly service, and encouraged the people of Israel themselves, if they were willing, to perform prayers according to the Law. While they kept the commandments given through Moses, it was not done (547) blamelessly or properly: whereas the people brought the usual offerings to sacrifice, they showed little interest, being instead lazy and negligent, offering at the altar inferior animals from the flocks, maimed and of less value. The priests accepted them without looking for flaws, as the Law required, whether an animal was lame, had an ear cut off, was missing a nose or a tail, had scabies or rash or only one testicle—defects the Law rejected,[5] amounting to nothing less than an insult. The priests' negligence was of a different kind, affecting the people for whom they were responsible by not introducing them properly to the requirements of the Law or providing adequate guidance in God's will, and instead allowing them to be involved in improper diversions and to stray from the straight and narrow.

While this was one basis for correction, the other in addition to this applied to the people of Israel on the following grounds. Some men claimed to have a strong love for their wives, but

2. Mal 2.7; Is 9.5–6 LXX.

3. A phrase like "the will of the heavenly nature" in reference to God is reminiscent of Cyril's famous *mia physis* in reference to Jesus, which is open to misinterpretation.

4. Having set the historical scenario in which Malachi exercises his ministry, Cyril now, as usual, turns to the *skopos* of the work.

5. Lv 22.21–25.

then served them with a bill of divorce when in some cases they were guilty of no fault, and had relations with other women in the belief that they in no way offended God even if they chose to do it. Still others associated with the daughters of foreigners, even though the Law explicitly forbade it: "Do not give your daughter to his son, nor take his daughter for your son, for it would turn away your son from me, and he will go and serve other gods."[6] There was a long treatment of this also in the books of Esdras;[7] hence some people presume it is Malachi, but this is not the case. While there is an element of correction in them, at least at the end of the prophecy he discourses on the revelation of our Savior under the aspect of a (548) pure and bloodless sacrifice being offered to God in the future, the abolition of charges against everyone through the removal of sin, and the transformation of those on earth to newness of life. What is in Christ, in fact, is a new creation, now that what is old has passed away, as Scripture says.[8]

6. Dt 7.3–4.

7. 1 Esdras 9.7–9.

8. 2 Cor 5.17.

COMMENTARY ON MALACHI, CHAPTER ONE

An oracle of the word of the Lord to Israel by means of his messenger (v.1).

BY SPEAKING OF *an oracle of the word* he implies reception of the prophecy from God. The blessed prophets, you see, received through the Holy Spirit knowledge of future events; to some people they directed advice and correction, not singling out on their own initiative whatever they chose nor giving false information to individuals, but interpreting what came from God and sincerely and irreproachably conveying to others the words from on high.[1] So he is saying that the prophecy he received came from *the Lord,* thus suggesting that the prophetic word did not convey what kind of harsh and calamitous event was due to befall the people of *Israel* nor what commendation of their upright life—rather, it was correction directed at priests and people. That is the way you will understand the phrase *by means of his messenger: the oracle to Israel* came to the one called *messenger,* who was conducting or discharging the ministry of prophecy, Malachi being called *messenger* for reasons I have already explained.

Take it to heart. I have loved you, says the Lord (v.2). He bids them give no idle reception to what will be said; (549) rather, they should do so enthusiastically and with deep attention and understanding. It is necessary, you see, for those due to hear the divine words to be so inclined, as the benefit coming from them is considerable and very abundant when communicated to their minds. The divinely inspired David, remember, also sings some-

1. While Didymus and even Theodore made much of this word "oracle," *lēmma,* as suggesting ecstatic possession of a prophet, Cyril, in meeting it at the beginning of Habakkuk, Nahum, and Deutero-Zechariah, and warned by Jerome of its Montanist interpretation, had restricted himself to saying that it implies only a prophet's direct influence by God as distinct from personal invention.

where, "I hid your sayings in my heart in case I should sin against you"; it is possible, in other words, it is possible for the person hearing to give the impression of not hearing if the words do not affect the mind but, as it were, merely fly off the tongue of the speaker and then strike the bodily ear and are considered idle and virtually unintelligible. One of the holy prophets refers to such words in this way, "Lo, a foolish and senseless people, who have eyes and do not see, ears and do not hear."[2] Consequently, the prophet therefore urges them in these words, *Take it to heart,* that is, lay up the divine words interiorly even in your heart, understanding the force of the oracles from on high and giving them full acceptance because *I have loved you* and accorded you complete benignity, compassion, and regard befitting those who are loved. Now, it is a further and well deserved example of his reproaching them for repaying him with evil for good when, after being accorded love, they ought to have responded to all the pleasing gifts by rejoicing with simplicity, zeal, and enthusiasm. After all, if it is wrong not to want to make recompense to people like ourselves, what grounds would there be in the case of God, who has richly provided us with everything for our satisfaction, for anyone (550) not to want to repay him for his gifts, especially when it befits really sensible people to say, "How shall we repay the Lord for all his bounty to us?"[3]

You said, How have you loved us? Was not Esau the brother of Jacob, says the Lord, and did I not love Jacob but hate Esau? I made his territory a wasteland, and his inheritance a house of desolation (vv.2–3). At times the Jews were punished by the onset of the divine wrath for the manifold acts of impiety: they went off into captivity, their land ravaged, houses ruined, and Jerusalem burned along with the divine Temple. The occasion of this suffering of theirs was their opting to abandon their obligations towards God and to entertain little regard for the Law. So when God said he loved them even dearly, it was natural for them to recall the hardships of the captivity and actually say, *How have you loved us?* In his wise providence the God of all bypasses what had happened in the meantime and dismisses their version; instead, he recalls

2. Ps 119.11; Jer 5.21.
3. Ps 116.12.

the demonstration of his love for the head of the race, namely, *Jacob whom he loved*, he insists, and he treated *Esau* as loathsome, even though by the laws of nature (551) he was bound to him in brotherhood. The divinely inspired Paul writes, remember, "Even before they had been born or had done anything good or bad,"[4] he made Jacob his chosen one, and from him the Jewish race sprang, whereas he rejected Esau.

We make no mention of partiality: God is not unjust, nor does he give to anyone on earth a judgment that is unfair or harsh; instead, as God he foreknew the future behavior of both, and accorded love to the one who was better and godlier. Blessed Jeremiah, for example, Scripture tells us, he knew before he was formed in the womb, and sanctified him before he left the womb; he was aware, you see, he was aware he would be a prophet, and would be suited to the mission of forecasting the future. Likewise, Paul says that we were sanctified after being justified by faith: "Those whom he foreknew the God and Father also predestined to be conformed to the image of his Son," and is said to have called and sanctified them.[5] It was therefore in his foreknowledge that he accorded Jacob love, and was right to hate Esau.

O Israel, he says, I have loved you; I would in no way be guilty of invention if I were to say so to you. Instead, you would know that the claim is right and true by tracing the course of the love to the head of the race. While both men sprang from Isaac, remember, Jacob was well-behaved and showed love for God, whereas the other was obdurate, intractable, and given to profane interests. Consequently, I was inclined towards Jacob, and devastated the inheritance allotted to Esau, leaving it a desert. In my compassion I supported Jacob—you, that is, (552) or the land you occupy. Now, it should be realized that Esau means "oak"; Esau was obdurate and inflexible, and hardly differed from the wood of an oak, even selling his birthright for a single meal. He was also called Edom, which means "earthy"; consequently, sacred Scripture says Idumea was the name given to the land of his descendants, which the Jews at one time took over and made completely trackless and uninhabited. What is sug-

4. Rom 9.11.
5. Jer 1.5; Rom 8.29–30.

gested for the people of Israel from the prophecy? In my view it is as follows: it says he loved Jacob, and for no other reason than that he was "unaffected, a home lover," whereas he hated Esau, because he was earthy and "godless," in Paul's words.[6] The Jews therefore should have known that they would not have suffered the devastation and the flight from their own country to a foreign land if they had imitated Jacob. Since, however, they proved imitators of the behavior of Esau, and opted to follow in the footsteps of his knavery, they were then surrendered to the foe.

If, on the other hand, you wanted also to derive a spiritual interpretation from the text, you would show wisdom in reasoning that Jacob means "supplanter," and would be a type of everyone supplanting sin.[7] Esau, on the other hand, is "oak," and Edom "earthy"; he would be a type of everyone who thinks only of what is on earth. So God loves the supplanter Jacob, and hates the inflexible and obdurate Esau, or Edom—that is, the one inclined to earthy things, foolishly preferring passing and corrupt things to spiritual goods; our God, in his love for virtue, undermines the inheritance of those accustomed to living this way. What is on earth, you see, is assuredly not permanent, nor does it have an unshakeable basis, and its utter collapse is made clear by the complete devastation of the inheritance of the Idumeans. The person attached to God, by contrast, will have sound and reliable hope, and will proclaim to God the giver of good things, "In your hands my inheritance."[8]

Hence if he says, Idumea was overthrown, let us return and rebuild its ruins, the Lord almighty says this, They will rebuild and I shall overthrow, and they will be called territory of iniquity and a people against whom the Lord is arrayed forever (v.4). Though the sequence of thought in the passage is very difficult, the sense of the text is not hard to perceive: I assigned the inheritance of Esau, he is saying, to destruction and devastation as a result of your plundering, people of Jacob. Perhaps the Idumean would reply, Even if the country we inhabited has been completely overthrown and reduced to utter misfortune, we shall still *return* and rebuild

6. Gn 25.27; Heb 12.16.
7. This etymology results from the word play in the Heb. text of Gn 25.27.
8. Ps 31.15 LXX.

the *ruined* cities and towns, and the survivors will occupy them. What, then, is his reply to this? *The Lord almighty says this, They will rebuild and I shall overthrow.* Now, Idumea is called *territory of iniquity* for being *overthrown* for extremely grave sin, *and a people against whom the Lord is arrayed forever.*

The meaning of the text, therefore, is in my view something no different from this. On the other hand, the further interpretation could be made that the inheritance of those with a fleshly and earthy mentality ("Idumean" meaning "earthy," as I said) will completely and utterly (554) collapse when God *overthrows* it, the things of this world having no firm basis nor allowing any lasting participation. A temporary longing deserts those who possess it, and can be compared to a shadow, or something snuffed out by death, or the onset of an unexpected disaster. If, on the other hand, any of the spiritual Idumeans were to choose to *rebuild* their inheritance by amassing wealth from unjust dealings, or by luxuriating in idle fancies and wanting to be carried away with self-importance in this life, they would find the God of all in person resistant and hostile. As the divinely inspired disciple wrote, remember, "If you want to be a friend of this world, you become an enemy of God";[9] in other words, he will not cease to be opposed to those who choose an earthy mentality, nor will he desist from warring against them. He always shows hatred for the vengeful, and keeps at arm's length those who love sin.

Your eyes will see, and you will say, The Lord has been magnified beyond the territory of Israel (v.5). When you consider the nature of things, he is saying, and clearly grasp with mind unshuttered, as it were, what I said above, then definitely *you will say* with proper deference, *The Lord has been* glorified and *magnified in the territory of Israel.* Those springing from Jacob, of course—namely, Jews—offended through grave impiety, and became refugees, captives, and a prey to the foe. When God took pity on them in their miserable condition, however, after adequate punishment they returned to their original state, (555) and things took a turn for the better for them. The country enjoyed prosperity; in fact, they occupied the cities, rebuilt the Temple, restored the walls of Jerusalem, and once again enjoyed what they hoped and

9. Jas 4.4.

prayed for. On the other hand, the country of the Idumeans was devastated and continued to suffer misfortune, there being no improvement in their security. God was therefore glorified in *the territory of Israel.*

Now, it should be understood that, even in the most profound interpretation, if some people with knowledge of God were guilty of offending, even if they suffered correction for sin, they still would not perish altogether. Instead, after adequate correction God shows pity, and restores their good spirits. By contrast, with those who are attached to an earthy mentality and have eyes only for things of the flesh, he is constantly at odds and extends the period of his wrath against them. *They will be called a territory of iniquity,* remember, the text says, *and a people against whom the Lord is arrayed forever.*

A son honors his father, and a slave will be in fear of his master. If I am a father, where is my glory? And if I am Lord, where is the one to fear me? asks the Lord almighty (v.6). He everywhere highlights those who surpass due limits and choose to scorn what they should not. It would surely befit dutiful children, for instance, to take pains to promote their parent's good name so as to gain the reputation of being children of a distinguished father. If one were a loyal servant, on the other hand, one would wish that the master be quite famous and celebrated, and not unknown and inconspicuous. This is the way, in fact, for the person to participate in the enjoyment of such matters, boast of it, and consider it the basis of the highest satisfaction. You ought to glorify me as a father, the text is saying, and respect me as a master, and thus you will not be guilty of falling short in what is proper in both cases by failing to apply *glory* to me as father and fear of me as master. *Where is my glory? Where is fear of me?*[10] If you cannot bring yourself to do anything in regard to my glory, nor to dread punishment, would you respond to the master's laws? He said as much also in the statement of Isaiah, "Hear, O heaven, and listen, O earth, for the Lord has said, I gave birth to children and reared them, but they spurned me."[11]

10. The latter clause occurs in two forms in Cyril's text. Contrast this version with the text of v.6 in the scriptural lemma immediately above.

11. Is 1.2.

We ought therefore to seek God's glory, and also strive to do good in the knowledge of the text, "As I live, says the Lord, those who glorify me I shall glorify, and anyone who despises me shall be despised."[12] Now, the God of all will be glorified by us as *father* if our efforts are not directed to what is pleasing and attractive to us, but rather if we dedicate our thinking to him and in every case follow his wishes. And we *shall fear* him as *Lord* if we check our inclination to depravity by the fear of offending him, and ponder the charge made at the divine tribunal. "For all of us must appear at the tribunal of Christ so that each may receive recompense for what has been done in the body, whether good or evil."[13]

You priests who disparage my name and ask, How have we disparaged your name? By bringing to my altar (557) *spoiled bread, and saying, How have we spoiled it? By saying, The Lord's table is worthless, and the food placed on it worthless* (v.7). The Jews' indifference is severely blamed on those to whom the Law proclaims, "Make the children of Israel pious."[14] The subject populace, remember, will follow in every respect the example of the leaders, and will offend in no small way when they see them failing in reverence for God. It is, in fact, by the apathy of those in charge that indifference to piety develops, worsens, and is compounded. The truth of this account is confirmed by the God of all when he says, "Because the shepherds have lost their senses, and do not inquire of the Lord; hence the whole flock had no understanding and was scattered."[15] The ministers of the divine sacraments are therefore generally found to be an encouragement to upright living in other people if they opt to live a moral life and to accord reverence to God in the manner expected, but an encouragement to vile and profane pursuits if they are found before the others to be affected by such vices. Consequently, the divinely inspired Paul also proclaims to those engaged in teaching that they should be an example to their flock.[16]

You it is, then, he is saying, though bearing the trappings of priesthood, are the ones *who disparage my name.* If you want to identify the kind of disparagement, listen to him exclaiming,

12. 1 Sm 2.30.
13. 2 Cor 5.10.
14. Lv 15.31 LXX.
15. Jer 10.21.
16. Cf. 1 Pt 5.3; the PG text speaks of Peter as the writer.

By your offering *at the altar spoiled bread.* And if you were to ask further, In what way were they *spoiled,* I shall reply to you, As you perhaps are aware, (558) or rather cry aloud in your very actions, *The Lord's table is worthless, and the food placed on it worthless.* Now, since each of these statements should be explicated and receive clear comment, come now, let us explain what is the meaning of *spoiled bread.* By *spoiled,* then, he means "defiled" and "unclean." Now, we should understand that according to the wishes of the lawgiver, bread was also brought for performing sacrifices, both unleavened and clean, and he ordered the sacrifice of praise to be performed with leavened bread. The eucharistic interpretation of this we gave sufficiently in other works;[17] here too we shall explain it in cursory fashion lest I seem to be wanting in matters of such importance. The unleavened bread, then, would be a symbol of life that is unleavened and clean; the divinely inspired Paul, remember, writes in these words to those justified by faith, "And so let us celebrate the festival, not with the old leaven, the leaven of malice and evil, but with the unleavened bread of sincerity and truth"; and again, "Clean out the old leaven so that you may be a new batch, as you really are unleavened." Christ urges the holy apostles in these words, "Beware of the leaven of the Pharisees and Sadducees."[18] So the bread is a symbol of unleavened bread that is clean and sanctified. Those who brought unleavened bread and took unleavened things according to the Law, therefore, offered it in place of themselves as type and shadow.

Since, however, those who are still catechumens and not yet purged of sin through holy baptism we do not send out of church when we praise God, but rather make them partners when we perform the sacrifice of praise,[19] (559) consequently the Law also says they must do so "with leavened bread." He refers figuratively by "leavened bread" to the one not yet cleansed, as I said, by holy baptism, and, as it were, having some leaven in them left over from their former depravity.

17. Cf. Lv 7.12. In Book 16 of the *De adoratione* Cyril had made comparisons between OT and NT worship; by "sacrifice of praise" he refers to the Eucharist.

18. 1 Cor 5.7–8; Mt 16.6.

19. An example of Cyril's references to the discipline of sacramental initiation in his church.

You priests, he says, then, *who disparage my name* on account of offering at *my altar spoiled bread.* Accordingly, those invested with the divine priesthood must take great care to avoid doing any such thing in church, and also must realize that while precise observance gives joy to God, indifference and neglect of such venerable things severely grieves him. It would, in fact, be nothing but distressing to see the failure by the apathetic to provide unleavened bread, since they heard it said, *You priests who disparage my name,* the disparagement being, as it were, the priests' indifference to God and the sin against the glory fitting and due to him.

Hence, if you offer a blind animal for sacrifice, is it not wrong? And if you offer a lame or sickly one, is it not wrong? Offer it to your leader and see if he accepts you, if he welcomes your approach, says the Lord almighty (v.8). Although the Law required inspection of the offerings, rejection of maimed animals, and sacrifice of flawless ones,[20] they kept bringing them to the altar at that time indiscriminately and at random, little account being taken of the glory due to God. By contrast, extreme interest was shown (560) in amassing the greatest possible number of victims and in having an abundance of rams at home and even in the holy tabernacle itself. As a result, you guardians of the Law, *if you offer a blind animal for sacrifice, is it not a wrong* sacrifice? And if *a lame or sickly one,* will it escape blame for its faulty condition? Do you not think such flawed animals *wrong* and unsuited *to sacrifice?* If you think otherwise within yourself, however, offer them as a present and by way of a gift to one of the leaders.[21] He would not accept it, the text says, and would not consider the action tolerable even out of regard for the person of the offerer; instead, he would be extremely angered by the insult.

It is therefore very wrong to presume to offer God something that one of us would not be ready to accept. It is a grave fault on our part, after all, if we were on the point of offering something to God, and we wretches looked for something worthless and second-rate, forgetting that he did not find Cain's sacrifice ac-

20. Lv 22.21–25.

21. The loan word for "governor" in the Heb. text here implies an official appointed by the king of Persia, and thus confirms a post-exilic date for Malachi. Cyril would be unaware of this clue, of course.

ceptable:[22] though he was right to make an offering, his choice was not right, because he kept for himself the first and best things and chose to honor God with second-rate ones. It was not to his offerings that God gave attention, however; it is indifference on the part of the offerers that he reckons as a failing in honor.

The Law, in fact, rated as unacceptable for sacrifice blind animals, as well as lame and sickly ones; a blind animal referred figuratively to the people who do not have the divine eye in their heart, the lame to those unaccustomed to correct procedure in good works, and the sickly to those who discharge service to God not very consistently, but loosely and negligently. He said somewhere also in a verse of a prophet, "Woe to those who perform the work of the Lord carelessly."[23] We therefore need to keep our mind enlightened, (561) operating properly and at full strength; then we shall be acceptable to the Lord and devoted to the loving God.

Now appease the person of your God, and implore him, says the Lord almighty; this was done by your hands. See if I welcome your approach, says the Lord almighty (v.9). He calls the impious to repentance, and very rightly says that the wrath falling on the offenders must be forestalled by a turn for the better. God is good, remember, raising up the dejected, healing the bruised, and bringing back the wayward.[24] Now, by saying *Appease the person of your God,* he would highlight the fact, and rightly so, that God will turn away from those not declining to offend him, and that he averts his eyes, as it were, from those not seeking his glory, according them no pity, love, or supervision. "The eyes of the Lord are on the righteous," Scripture says, remember; and he said also to some of the sinful in the verse from Isaiah, "When you stretch out your hands to me, I shall avert my eyes from you; and if you multiply your appeals, I shall not hearken to you, for your hands are stained with blood."[25]

It is therefore necessary for sinners to appease him in the hope that they may somehow bring the face of God to shine once more on them, and divert the harm stemming from his

22. Gn 4.7.
23. Jer 48.10.
24. Pss 145.14; 147.3; Ezek 34.16.
25. Ps 34.16; Is 1.15.

ignoring them. He specifies the sins of the ministers, note, and brooks no denial, guilty of no falsehood in saying, *This was done by your hands.* (562) In other words, it is as if he were saying, Though not keeping silent about other sinners,[26] you were responsible for impious actions against me as though personally involved, and they were the results of your indifference, since none of you intervened. If, on the other hand, some people are perhaps reluctant to bring charges against you on these matters, I shall not be like you and one of them, nor would I respect the *person* of the impious. The verse from David resembles this, "You undertook iniquity in the belief I was like you; I shall accuse you, and to your face I shall present your sins."[27] The judge does not discriminate between persons, you see; being God, he is honest and incorruptible.

Hence the doors will be closed on you, and you will not light a fire on my altar in vain (v.10). He very appropriately forecasts the beauty of life in Christ by way of a prophecy: the shadow in the Law and that ancient priesthood would soon come to an end, and the ministers of truth, who would also be servants of the worship in spirit and ardently seek the glory of God, would in due course be revealed. He says *the doors will be closed* on the former, and no fragrance will be associated with those serving as priests according to the Law: "If he closes the doors against someone, who will open them?"[28] In other words, when the true tabernacle is revealed—namely, the Church—those still performing priestly duties according to the Law will not enter, being shut out as a result of unbelief, will remain outside, and *will not light* holy things. The fact that (563) they have forfeited priesthood, you see, would be clear from God's statement in Hosea, "The people of Israel shall remain for many days without king, without ruler, without sacrifice, without altar, without priesthood, without divination."[29] He would therefore be indicating the lapse, as it were, of worship according to the Law, and the

26. The negative does not appear in the clause in the PG text (understandably).

27. Ps 50.21.

28. Jb 12.14.

29. Hos 3.4. Cyril is not acknowledging the eighth-century situation of the northern kingdom referred to by Hosea in applying this verse to Malachi's community and beyond it to NT worship.

closure of priesthood according to it, in my view, when he says there was need to *close the doors* on them, since the Church does not admit them, so to say. It is, in fact, no longer the time to sacrifice sheep; instead, the God of all is in the future honored with unbloody sacrifices.

Now, since he proceeds to follow this with the statement, *You will not light a fire on my altar in vain,* our claim is that the meaning has moved to moral considerations. He wants to indicate, in fact, that they had been called to priesthood and to putting *fire on the altar* not for the purpose of undermining the glory of the one who called them, but to honor him in appropriate ways and enjoy the privileges of priesthood. They did not attend to such august pursuits, however, nor were they deterred by respect for sacrifice from offending God, and would then be justly punished. It would, in fact, be no small accusation, and well deserved, to set at nothing the share in the gifts of God and divest themselves inadvisedly of the honors from God; Esau, for example, was called earthy and profane because "he surrendered his birthright for a single dish."[30] When he says, then, *You will not light a fire on my altar in vain,* he means to say that while the priesthood is not without its recompense, one would not escape punishment unless one were to discharge it in the right and proper fashion.

It should be noted, on the other hand, that the Hebrew text yields a different (564) sense and even a different context. It says, The Levites and priests who have the lowest ranking in the Temple and are charged by you with closing the doors *will not light a fire on my altar in vain;* that is, you do not perform the service (or priesthood) for nothing, since the people offer you tithes, first-fruits, and thanksgiving offerings.

In return for your neglect of the things of God, then, and for their not being given precedence, *I have no pleasure in you, says the Lord almighty, and shall not accept sacrifice from your hands. Hence, from the rising of the sun to its setting, my name has been glorified among the nations, and in every place incense is offered to my name and a pure offering; because my name is great among the nations, says the Lord almighty* (v.11). He now clearly repudiates the offer-

30. Heb 12.16.

ing of sacrifice according to the Law, and, as it were, abandons his love for Jews, and regards the priesthood as unacceptable and the shadow as inadmissible—animal sacrifice and incense, I mean—this not being his original intention. He makes this clear also in other prophets, as when he says in the statement of Isaiah, "I am fed up with burnt offerings of rams; fat of sheep and blood of bulls and goats I do not want, not even if you come to appear before me. After all, who asked this from your hands? Do not continue trampling on my court. (565) If you bring the best of flour, it is a waste of time; incense is an abomination to me." And in Jeremiah, "Assemble your burnt offerings along with your sacrifices and eat the meat, because I did not speak to your fathers about burnt offerings and sacrifices on the day I brought them up out of the land of Egypt."[31] The Law, you see, was a prefiguring and foretelling of worship in spirit and in truth, and "regulations for the body," as the divinely inspired Paul writes, "until the time comes to set things right." Now, the time for reform would, in my view, be no other than the coming of our Savior. The first covenant, on account of its not being faultless, is said to have disappeared, being obsolete; a place was sought for a new and second one, which would be proof against any blame or fault. This, in fact, is said by the Son himself, who bears the name also of Angel of Great Counsel—hence his saying, "I do not speak of myself: the Father who sent me is the one who gave me instructions as to what to speak and what to say."[32]

Accordingly, he clearly told those exercising priesthood according to the Law that they are unacceptable to him or, rather, *I have no pleasure in them* as they perform sacrifices in shadow and type, and that he would *not accept* what was offered by them. He predicts that his *name* will be *great* and famous among people everywhere throughout the earth under heaven, and that *in every place* and nation pure and bloodless sacrifices will be *offered to* his *name,* now that the ministers no longer diminish his honor or pay him spiritual worship in indifferent fashion. Instead, with enthusiasm, simplicity, and holiness they will be zealous in offering the pleasing odor of the spiritual incense—(566) namely,

31. Is 1.11–13; Jer 7.21.
32. Heb 9.10; Jn 4.23; Heb 8.7, 13; Is 9.6; Jn 12.49.

faith, hope, love, and the ornaments of good works. This is obviously when Christ's heavenly and life-giving sacrifice is instituted, through which death is destroyed, and this corruptible flesh from the earth puts on incorruptibility.[33]

You by contrast profane it in saying, The table of the Lord is spoiled, and the food on it is of no value (v.12). In this he also makes clear to us that those called from the nations will be better and more honest than those from Israel; their sacrifices will be pure, their incense fragrant, and his name will be great from east to west, whereas among you (he says) the altar is not held in the high regard that befits God. *You profane it by saying, The table of the Lord is spoiled, and what is on it is of no value.* While it is likely that the priests did not use those words, they proclaimed it in their actions, as likewise "The fool says in his heart, There is no God."[34] In other words, even if the person seen to be scornful were to say nothing verbally, by his very actions and the depravity of his life he is, as it were, crying aloud, There is no God. After all, those who normally live as if God were not watching, who do everything heedlessly and are guilty of unholy behavior, even in their deeds and actions deny God. In this way, therefore, those who make no effort to preserve for the holy altar the reverence that is fitting and due to him (567) say through their very actions, *The table of the Lord is spoiled.* Indifference in these matters is therefore to be avoided; the person choosing not to do so will definitely hear God say, *I have no pleasure in you, and shall not accept sacrifice from your hands.* How could anyone of sound mind and intention doubt that offending God is a dreadful thing?

You said, This is a burden. I blew it away, says the Lord almighty. You bring stolen goods, lame and handicapped things, and present them as offerings: am I to accept them from your hands? says the Lord almighty (v.13). He soundly upbraids the priests for opting not to scrutinize the offerings of victims, and instead idly and indifferently accepting what was lame, blind, and sickly despite the Law's clear directions that flawed victims should be rejected. If out of adherence to the Law any of the priests discouraged a person offering what was worthless *as an offering,* the offer-

33. 1 Cor 15.53.
34. Ps 14.1.

ers would persist, citing the captivity over and over again, and claiming with great insistence that they were not unsuitable but had suffered injury on the way when they were traveling from Babylon to Judea.[35] They kept bringing *stolen goods, lame and handicapped things.* Sometimes, you see, wild animals attacked and did damage to the flocks, and (568) perhaps stole some, and then the shepherd ran up and rescued the stolen one from their jaws, scaring them off with the barking of dogs or throwing the staff at them—hence, in my view, the reference to *stolen goods.* They kept offering these animals together with the lame ones that were no longer capable of grazing with the others; they also offered *handicapped* ones, that is, those as good as dead, thus insulting rather than honoring the God of all. But *I blew it away, says the Lord almighty,* the text reads: since they kept sacrificing in a sacrilegious way, I would in no way accept anything from them, nor reckon as an odor of sweetness offerings that were so illicit and unclean.

It therefore behoves us, to be sure, to sacrifice with great simplicity and zeal, and honestly offer to God, not what is rejected, dishonorable, and of no account, but what is choice and special. If, on the other hand, you are offering yourself to God (we remember Paul writing in these terms, "Present your bodies as a living sacrifice, holy and acceptable to God, which is your spiritual worship"), examine carefully your situation, and become, as it were, a precise inspector of your own soul. Be careful not to be blind—by not having the light of truth, I mean—nor to be limping in the inability to proceed properly to any kind of good work, nor to be possessing *stolen goods* or anything sickly. We must never sleep, "because our adversary the devil like a lion prowls about, looking for someone to devour."[36] So when we are found awake and alert, the wild beast passes by, whereas if he sees us dozing and negligent, he makes *stolen goods* of us and reduces us to a sickly condition—dead, in fact, (569) and quite incapable of being active in pursuing virtue. Let us keep

35. Malachi's ministry, Cyril implies here, is exercised only a few years after the exiles' return from Babylon, though at the outset he said the Temple had already been rebuilt.

36. Rom 12.1; 1 Pt 5.8.

ourselves far from disquiet, that is, proof against depression and conspicuous for patience; just as a habit of patience contributes to living, so too depression does to dying, since it involves weakness and faint-heartedness. Accordingly, the blessed prophet Isaiah advises us to rid ourselves of such feelings, "Be strong, limp hands and feeble knees; take comfort, you faint-hearted; be strong; do not fear. Lo, our God, lo, the Lord comes with strength, and his arm with lordship."[37]

Cursed be a man of means who had a male in his flock, and his vow involved it, and he sacrifices spoiled things to the Lord. Because I am a great king, says the Lord almighty, and my name is illustrious among the nations (v.14). He now very rightly specifies the oath taken by the person who sacrifices in a sacrilegious manner. If you made a vow, he is saying, and have a faultless male in your own flock, but, rather than offering it to God, you take instead something of no value, that would be nothing less than an insult. After all, we do not serve sticks and stones as do some people seated in darkness and the errors and abominations of idolatry; instead, we serve almighty God, Creator of all things, at whom the heavens tremble, and (570) of whom the earth and all who are in it are afraid. He likewise gives testimony to the great probity of those from the nations, saying that the name of the Godhead is *illustrious,* revered, and praised among them, this in fact and no other being our disposition.

Our Lord Jesus Christ also accepted the centurion, idolater though he was, and even said, "Truly I tell you, in no one in Israel have I found such faith."[38] Cursed is the one, therefore, *who sacrifices spoiled things to God,* though in a position to honor him with better things, especially if he *has in his flock* the one that is flawless and *a male,* as I just said. Now, it should be noted that he asks for *a male* for sacrifice, even though the Law required also a female. We are saying, then, that sacrifices by vow, or voluntary ones, required a victim that was flawless and male; for the offerer it was a type, as though the Law were recommending that those wishing to ascend as an odor of sweetness to God

37. Is 35.3–4; 40.10.
38. Mt 8.10.

should be virile, superior to passions, and free of every fault.[39] Sacrifices offered for sin, on the other hand, clearly required a female from the lambs and goats.[40] Now, this involved a hidden reference to the weakness of the offerers: the female was weak, inferior to the male in strength; and every sin is committed with a weak mind that no longer preserves spiritual strength.

39. Lv 1.
40. Lv 4.28; 5.6.

COMMENTARY ON MALACHI, CHAPTER TWO

And now this command is for you, O priests: if you do not listen, and if you do not set your heart on giving glory to my name, says the Lord almighty, I shall send the curse on you, and I shall curse your blessing and curse it. I shall annul your blessing; (571) *it will not remain with you because you do not take it to heart* (vv. 1–.2).

He lovingly passes over the faults in what had preceded, and accords mercy, restoring, as it were, the sinners to their former probity—the meaning, in my view, of his saying in kindly fashion, *And now this command is for you, O priests:* He then makes the threat, on the other hand, that if they do not choose to do what they should be seen doing, and to interiorize in their mind and *heart* a sense of the divine oracles, and to become better than they were before by seeking out God's glory and not continuing to belittle the altar or performing legal requirements casually and without scrutiny, he would utterly make them cursed and the object of divine wrath. For my part, I think the clause *I shall curse your blessing and annul it* has perhaps this meaning: when God wills the prosperity of some people, the produce of the fields will multiply, there will be abundant and rich crops, cattle will grow to immeasurable numbers, and they personally will be proof against bodily decay. When by contrast he revokes his *blessing,* things will take a complete turn for the worse, fall far short of prosperity, and instead conditions will prevail at which one would rightly be dejected.

While this is the sense at a material and this-worldly level, it is necessary to recognize that if you were not to keep in mind the divine commands, the good things in your mind would altogether come to nothing, and bear no fruit in a godly life. Instead, you would be deprived even by God of blessing from on high, and would fall foul of curses and punishments from him. God's gift[1] is therefore to be sought; and (572) the way we shall achieve it the Savior himself taught us in saying, "Let your light shine in people's sight so that they may see your good works and glorify your Father in heaven."[2] Then it is that we shall also receive abundant blessing and unalloyed satisfaction, enjoy spiritual fertility, be filled with every good, and live a truly commendable and praiseworthy life.

Lo, I dedicate to you the upper arm, and shall scatter offal in your faces, offal of your festivals, and I shall take you to it. Know that I the Lord have sent to you this commandment so that my covenant with the Levites may hold, says the Lord almighty (vv.3–4). Some meaning is once more hidden in the present text, which I think should be clarified for studious readers, this being the way for them to grasp what is signified. The Law given through Moses, then, gave a role almost equivalent to God to the attendant and minister at the divine altars, crowning him with honors from on high; it said, remember, that his allotment was the Lord's share. The divinely inspired Paul also said somewhere, "Consider Israel in the flesh: are not those who approach the altar sharers of the altar?" It was the custom, you see, to dedicate to God from every victim the breast and the arm, the lobe of the liver, the two kidneys, and also the *offal,* or belly.[3] The text of the Law thus suggested metaphorically that we are completely dedicated interiorly (573) as an odor of sweetness to God, and should be sacred and sanctified. They bring the innards, note, with no impurity attached to them. The arm would be understood as a symbol of strength—that is, we should be strong in every good work and resolute in singing that wise verse with the psalmist's lyre, "Bless the Lord, my soul, and all that is within me, bless his holy name."[4]

Comment on the innards and the sacrifices performed according to the Law has briefly been given in our other writings.[5] Omitting this for the present, therefore, we shall give our atten-

1. For "gift," *dosis,* the PG text reads "glory," *doxa* (encouraged by the preceding scriptural citation).

2. Mt 5.16.

3. Dt 18.1; 1 Cor 10.18; Lv 3.4; 10.15.

4. Ps 103.1.

5. For example, in Book 11 of his *De adoratione.*

tion to clarifying the text as far as possible. The Law required, therefore, that the offerings be scrutinized, that no victim be brought to the altar without inspection, and that those assigned to sacrifice separate the limbs from the offerings. While they were negligent in their duty of scrutiny, they observed the commandment about the so-called cast-offs, giving preference not to God's pleasure but to their own wishes, taking control and exerting themselves to establish what was of value to them as they collected the meat from the sacrifices. He levels an accusation at this practice when he says, *I dedicate to you the upper arm,* meaning, I assigned it already, and for a second time my wish is that the custom be observed. But I threw, as it were, or I throw also *the offal in your faces;* since they dishonored the altar, consequently God says, *I shall scatter* as though returning the insult; "the one despising me will be despised," Scripture says, remember.[6] *I shall therefore take you to it,* that is, in this very (574) practice I shall prevail and shall level accusation at the offenders. In fact, because you have observed the law about the cast-offs to your benefit, and do not allow yourself to be remiss in any way about the part given to you while you seem to suit yourself when it comes to the duty of inspection, know therefore that the doors are closed to you—that is, you are excluded and disqualified from priestly service. Because it was I who gave *this commandment* or *covenant,* which I made with *the Levites.*

So what follows from this? The ministers of the divine sacraments should realize that they ought to do what God wants, and that whatever else seems of benefit to them should be subordinated to the Lord's commands. They will thus be sacred ministers, in fact, and not attached to things of this world or in thrall to base gain.

My covenant with him was one of life and peace (v.5). He directs his attention to those serving in a holy and commendable manner, and presents the priesthood as a truly praiseworthy institution, in keeping with the Law and the benefit and security coming from the divine oracles. As Paul in his great wisdom writes, "The Law is holy, and the commandment is holy and good."[7]

6. 1 Sm 2.30.
7. Rom 7.12.

So when he seems to make reference to Levi, the sense of the thought is properly directed not at the one who sprang from Jacob and was numbered among his twelve sons, for he did not act as a priest in the full sense. Instead, let us understand the fullness of priesthood and what priestly service involves, prefigured in the person, as it were, of Levi. It was with him, the text says, *my covenant of life and peace* was made; (575) the Law was communicated in writing to the most sacred Moses through the mediation of angels,[8] and through Moses as mediator it was given to those of the line of Israel, carrying an announcement of *life and peace* to those willing to live an upright life and to take as their norm of life the will of the Lawgiver.

Now, the text also seems to suggest to us in the present a more pressing level of meaning. I mean, the Law was given to the ancients, namely, those of the line of Israel,[9] to point in the direction of Christ and provide an image and type of what is real; the reality is Christ, who is *life and peace,* and the shadows in Moses delineate him for us. Accordingly, he said in addressing Jews, "If you believed Moses, you would believe me, for he wrote about me."[10] The lamb slain on the fourteenth day of the first month referred to him, intended as it was to save those who chose to anoint the doorposts of the houses; he was referred to by the red and flawless heifer, whose ashes mixed with water sanctified the participants "for cleansing of the flesh," as Scripture says; he was referred to by the unleavened bread, the turtledoves, the pigeon chicks—in short, the Law was full of insight into Christ. He is rightly spoken of, then, as a *covenant of life and peace;* by him we are brought to life, through him likewise we have access to the God and Father, and are at peace with him through obedience and faith.[11]

And I gave it to him to have deep fear for me and for him to shrink before my name. (576) There is a useful listing of the conspicuous ornaments of priesthood, highlighted in the Law's ability to point to the sacraments; most of all they instill the *fear* of God

8. Gal 3.19.
9. The PG text reads, "the line of Levi."
10. Jn 5.46.
11. Ex 12.2–15; Lv 1.14; 12.6; Nm 19; Heb 9.13; Eph 2.18.

in the ministers, encouraging them *to shrink before* his *name,* that is, causing them to have dread and respect for the Lord's name, and imparting to them the need to show a reverence for it that is not casual but devoted. Scripture says, remember, "The one who fears the Lord prospers," and again, "The fear of the Lord is our glory and boast."[12] To those serving in a holy and proper manner, therefore, he testified to the certainty of security, saying that they have not simply *fear* but *deep fear,* that is, that they entertain fear of God in all their soul and heart. There is a reinforcement in the expression, note, and a duplication of the sentiments that convey to the listeners a recommendation of the virtue of those being commended.

A law of truth was in his mouth, and iniquity was not found on his lips (v.6). In other words, the Law ordered the avoidance of falsehood, upright and just speech, and a commitment to delivering in every case a right and incorrupt judgment.[13] By *truth* he once again seems to refer to our Lord Jesus Christ, whose *law* is found *on the lips,* he says, of those living a life befitting priesthood. After all, even though the Law was in shadows, as I said, nevertheless it contained the shape of reality, and in the text there was, as it were, the outline of the evangelical oracles. We shall find, in fact, the force of worship in spirit in the types. (577) The fact that what was communicated of old to the ancients through Moses was the *law* of Christ, the Savior himself confirms in saying, "Do not think that I have come to abolish the Law or the Prophets. I have not come to abolish but to fulfill. For I tell you truly, until heaven and earth pass away, not one letter, not one stroke of a letter will pass from the Law until all is accomplished."[14]

Conducting himself in peace, he walked with me, and turned many from iniquity. What should be understood as being at peace with God by ourselves and others, especially if they understand the divine sayings, is nothing else than thinking and doing what he wishes, not offending him in any way, and instead endeavoring to live a life in great fidelity to law and in a creditable and praiseworthy manner. The divine Paul also made such a declaration

12. Prv 13.13; Sir 1.11.
13. Lv 19.11; Ex 23.1, 2, 6, 8.
14. Mt 5.17–18.

to us, "Justified by faith, then, let us have peace with God,"[15] this being the way to honor the one we know to be by nature and in reality the Lord. By paying homage to creation, on the other hand, when profane and sordid sin rules our thoughts, we are at odds with the Lord and, as it were, locked in battle with him, rearing our stiff necks and continuing to entertain disobedient and rebellious thoughts. The Savior's disciple will confirm this in saying, "Do you not know that friendship with the world is enmity with God? Whoever wishes to be a friend of the world becomes an enemy of God."[16] There is no obstacle, however, to our turning back to the God of all in faith when sin is removed, nor would anyone impede our relationship with him; (578) instead, let us, as it were, cling to him in complete sincerity, walk the straight and narrow, and tread the truly right path, directing ourselves and others into it.

Now, the contents of the passage would be particularly applicable to holy ministers of whom it could rightly be said, *Conducting himself in peace, he walked with me, and turned many from iniquity.* In other words, subjects follow in the path of their leaders' uprightness, and if they take the straight and narrow, they save many and easily persuade them to abandon a wanton and execrable life and the ways of *iniquity,* and to choose to love things that are better and praiseworthy and whatever deserves commendation from God and man.

Because a priest's lips will preserve knowledge, and they will look for a norm from his mouth, for he is a messenger of the Lord almighty (v.7). The way he diverted many from iniquity and proceeds by guiding them in peace with God he makes clear by saying that he bore on his lips, or tongue, the knowledge of everything necessary for living. He became "a corrector of the foolish, a teacher of children," and a true and honest expositor to those willing to learn the ruling of the Law. Far from distorting the sense of the divine sayings, and far from teaching "teachings, human precepts," he was like a *messenger* of God,[17] nicely illuminating for the subject populace the oracles that are sometimes obscure. In other words, he does not proclaim his own wishes or give

15. Rom 5.1.

16. Jas 4.4.

17. Rom 2.10; Mt 15.9.

vent to statements of his own opinion, ministering rather to the Lord's pronouncements. I would say that we see in (579) this the truth found in the book of Proverbs, "A desirable treasure will rest in the mouth of the wise, but foolish men devour it."[18] It would be to the credit of those announcing something from God to add nothing in addition to what they announce nor subtract anything. Giving this very little heed, the unholy bands of the Pharisees in their ignorance went to such a degree of nonsense as to teach "teachings, human precepts," and on the basis of their own tradition to disallow the divine commandments; such, in fact, were the charges leveled against them by Christ. So the *norm* of the divine sayings gives security: nothing is to be added to them, nor anything taken from them.[19] The *lips of priests,* therefore, *will preserve knowledge* of the Law, and announce it without adding anything. Consequently, he is also called *a messenger of the Lord almighty* despite being by nature human, because he clearly announces God's will, and has the Law to set his tongue in motion.

For your part, however, you veered away from the path, and caused many to be weak in performance of the Law; you corrupted the covenant of Levi, says the Lord almighty (v.8). In a fashion he ranges against the uprightness of creditable people the faults of the indifferent, and charges with depravity those opposed to reform. In other words, just as light shines in darkness, "and power is made perfect in weakness,"[20] so too the beauty of virtue would be more conspicuous for its absence if it were contrasted with some depravity or sin. (580) Some lived in a manner befitting a priest, therefore, directing themselves and others in peace; they were with God, and turned many away from iniquity, bearing knowledge on their lips and proving to be precise commentators on the divine sayings. Others, by contrast, who came after them and to whom the verse is directed, *veered away from the path,* deviating from the proper course and doing no little harm to themselves and others; *they caused many to be weak in performance of the Law;* that is, they made them weak and slothful in their obligation to live a lawful life. After all, if the leadership

18. Prv 21.20.
19. Dt 4.2.
20. 2 Cor 12.9.

fails in what is required, how could the subjects not be completely and utterly delinquent, and those of lower rank and less gifted with understanding not be dragged down with their betters? In other words, just as a law-abiding and holy priest makes his people imitators of his own good deeds, so too the opposite; if they *corrupt the covenant of Levi,* what likelihood would there be that those depending on them for spiritual guidance would consider the Law worth venerating?

I made you contemptible, cast you out into all the nations for not observing my ways and instead showing partiality before the Law (v.9). He returns to the sins of their fathers, and reminds them of their ancestors' faults. Since they had not been constant in observance of the Law, consequently (he says) they were given over to those who deported them into captivity in a pitiable and abject condition and bereft of all mercy. What disasters, in fact, did they not suffer? Or in what calamities did the wretches not share? But if you wish (581) to learn the cause of the wrath vented on you, he says, listen to the words, *Because you did not observe my ways and instead showed partiality before the Law.* This, I think, was the corruption of the covenant of Levi, not observing the way of life in the Law and making very wrong judgments in all cases, despite God's saying clearly, "Do not show partiality in judgment; judge the small and the great alike."[21] The crimes for which they were handed over to the enemy and became rejected are exactly those for which he makes the threat that unless they choose to live an upright life, he will not refrain from punishing them, and a most appropriate penalty will befall those abusing the Law, as befits those in the habit of doing so.

Did not one God create you? Is there not one father of you all? Why is it that each one of you has abandoned his brother so as to profane the covenant of your fathers? Judah has been abandoned, and an abomination has happened in Israel and in Jerusalem (vv.10–11). In beginning our composition on the prophet we said that after the return from Babylon and the land of Assyria the people of Israel paid little heed to the commandment of the Law and had relations with foreign women. Their behavior reached such a degree of neglect that even those serving as priests were led astray

21. Dt 1.17.

with the others; they treated their partners with little esteem, though they were of the line of Israel, dismissed them from hearth and home, and introduced (582) in their place foreign women, Ammonites, Moabites, and Idumeans. This represented a great abomination for Israel; far from abandoning their ancestral ways, those women still worshiped idols, even paying homage to the heavenly host, and it was inevitable that those having illicit intercourse with women of such corrupt mentality would likewise be contaminated and offend God. There is lengthy treatment of this, for example, in the books of Esdras.[22]

Accordingly, the God of all charged them with dishonoring their wives from the line of Israel, or Judah, and associating in an unholy manner with daughters of foreigners, despite the Law's forbidding the association. In somehow treating such august requirements as of little account, however, they were either seduced into illicit pleasures by the women's charms or perhaps wanted to gain an advantage from their friendship with the foreigners to avoid fighting them when already known to them and having a connection with them by marriage. It amounted, however, to an insult to God by people who had little faith in his ability to save them from their hands or make them proof against the oppression of foreigners. In every way, therefore, the practice disappointed God.

Consequently, he says on seeing their lack of appreciation for his innate affection, *Did not one God create you? Is there not one father of you all? Why is it that each one of you has abandoned his brother?* In other words, there is *one* Creator of all, and all of us belong to one Lord, who wishes that what has been created be bound together in unity and fellow-feeling by the bonds of love. After all, if there were two gods and lords, or even more, it would not be unlikely that the creatures would be under pressure from the wills of the creators and would appropriately experience opposition to one another (583) in response to the wishes of those in charge. Since instead there is *one* God, who is through all and in all and over all,[23] what basis would there be for any dissension? And since in addition to this there is *one*

22. 1 Esdras 9.7–9.
23. Eph 4.6.

father of all Jews according to the flesh—namely, the divinely inspired Abraham—what encouragement is there to give entrance to the disease of mutual hostility? How is it not a consequence of blood relationship to lay up love, as it were, by way of a debt? How is it not, on the other hand, akin to madness to be contaminated with the daughters of foreigners, and to dishonor house and race *so as to profane the covenant of your fathers?*

In fact, they perpetrated what was forbidden by the divine laws in regard to women from outside; they had been told, "You shall not give your daughter to his son, nor take his daughter for your son, for she will turn away your son from me, and he will go off to serve other gods."[24] But they set at naught the oracles, trampled on the Law, and to the extent possible weakened and profaned the covenant, grieving their champion by transgressions of the laws. Astonished, as it were, at their crime, and beholding the women of the nation of Judah being oppressed with most unjust hatred, he goes on to say, *Judah has been abandoned*, especially in the case of the inhabitants of *Jerusalem.* O what awful irony! It is not to Assyrians, Medes, Persians, Elamites, or nearby enemies, but to Israel itself and the inhabitants of Jerusalem that Judah has become loathsome and odious—that is, the race of Judah and the wretched mass of neighboring women.

Now, it should be realized that *Israel* refers to the ten tribes (584) who occupied Samaria before the time of the captivity and whom Shalmaneser had first deported to the Assyrians and Medes, whereas by the inhabitants of *Jerusalem* he means those whom Nebuchadnezzar took at the final captivity after burning Jerusalem and the divine Temple itself and whom he deported to Babylon. So he is accusing them or, rather, delivering no slight condemnation of them, for dismissing their wives from Judah and for illicitly taking those from the foreigners despite, as I said before, their holding tightly to their ancestral ways and still wallowing in the mire of idolatry.

Now, care should be taken also by us, who have been justified by Christ and vouchsafed a share of the Holy Spirit through faith in him, not to mingle with people of distorted thinking,

24. Dt 7.3–4.

who have a profane mentality and a faith that is incomplete. Such people, in fact, are foreigners, speaking a foreign language and uttering distortions of the truth; anyone mingling with them will be completely and utterly defiled, Scripture saying, "Whoever touches pitch gets dirty."[25] Since it is quite possible to bear fruit spiritually in the Church of Christ, then, what reason would there be for wanting to have intercourse, as it were, with other assemblies, to participate in profane gatherings, and to bring on us the wrath of the God of all?

Because Judah profaned the sanctuary of the Lord, which he loved, and went after foreign gods. The Lord will destroy the people who do this until they are humbled in the tents of Jacob and among those offering sacrifice to the Lord almighty (vv.11–12). He says that (585) Judah was hated, not by the foreigners, but by Judah itself for having *profaned* the Law as a result of a decadent fondness for exotic women and choosing to imitate their ways, to relish abandonment of God, and to adopt worship of idols. Some in fact, as I said, were brought to that point by following the women they were illicitly associated with, and obeying their wishes in everything. For instance, at Shittim they had relations with the women of the Midianites, or Moabites, when they were rescued from Egypt, descending in a short time to such depths of folly and sacrilegious thinking as even to join the ranks of Baal. For this reason the wretches perished.[26]

The God of all therefore cursed *the person doing this* out of an unholy fondness for such deviant activities, should there be anyone left among the people not yet exterminated from the *tents of Jacob,* that is, not yet completely annihilated, and the memory of the deed lost; and should there be anyone left in the ranks of priesthood *and* not yet *humbled among those offering sacrifice to the Lord almighty,* that is, not yet annihilated and struck off the list of priests. Some of the priests, you see, along with the others, as I said, had been caught up in the people's crimes and captivated by exotic women, with complete disregard of the divine oracles.

25. Acts 20.30; Sir 13.1.

26. Nm 25.1–5, which describes the incident at Shittim involving Moabite women. Cyril's uncertainty about their identity stems perhaps from the following incident involving a Midianite woman and an Israelite, both of whom Phinehas killed with a spear.

Accordingly, if the one who provokes God and endeavors to set the delights of the world in opposition to pronouncements from him is accursed, let us avoid the curse. Far from giving any importance to them, (586) let us make it our aim rather to add luster to our souls with the ornaments of obedience. This in fact is the way we shall have no experience of the effects of a curse, and the Lord of all will regale us with the good things stemming from his characteristic goodness.

You did what I hated: you covered the Lord's altar with tears, with weeping and groaning from hardship. Is it still worth having regard to your sacrifice, or taking it as acceptable from your hands? (v.13) There were many types of sacrifices in keeping with the Law: some were votive offerings, others by way of thanksgiving, and still others for sin. There were, on the other hand, also tithes, first-fruits, and the drachma tax, which were offered by the Law's requirements on the priests' account. In making votive offerings in sacrifice to God, then, they were in the habit, as I said, of offering lame and blind animals and stolen goods from the time of the captivity, constantly citing their misfortunes, over and over again adducing the devastation and the poverty affecting them from that fact. This was despite almighty God's gladdening them with incomparable kindness after the return from Babylon, and generously according them good things in which they probably luxuriated greatly. They made their offerings, therefore, weeping and wailing, as if to say to the ministers in decrying their offerings, This involves *hardship;* that is, it has not been acquired without effort, but is the result of sweat and tears. Then, he asks, how *is it still worth my having regard to your sacrifice,* or how am I to regard as acceptable what does not come from a good intention?

One should, in fact, offer sacrifice in good spirits, in a spirit of festivity and happiness. This, in my view, is the sentiment properly stated in the verse from Paul (587) to those making their contributions, "Not reluctantly or under compulsion, for God loves a cheerful giver."[27] So if we offer our sacrifice in good spirits, then, God will have regard for it, accept and commend

27. 2 Cor 9.7.

it, and in accepting it he will accord it respect and blessing. My view is that applying a sentiment different from that in the text contributes greatly to it. The God of all, note, rightly regarded as accursed the one who profaned the covenant of the ancestors by having intercourse with foreign women when those from their race were driven out and condemned, often for no fault of theirs. He blamed in addition to them some of the priests for showing partiality when dealing with people in administering the Law: *The Lord will destroy the people who do this until they are humbled in the tents of Jacob and among those offering sacrifice to the Lord almighty.* He then went on to say, *You covered the Lord's altar with tears, with weeping and groaning from hardship.* The word *covered* is to be taken to mean, You caused the divine altar to be awash with weeping and wailing: women are unreasonably driven out, and people who are victims of unjust judgment from the priests themselves surround the altar, lamenting the forms of injustice and incessantly weeping for the *hardships* imposed on them.

He then asks, *Is it worth having regard to your sacrifice, or taking it as acceptable from your hands?* In other words, just as there is truth in the saying in the book of Proverbs, "Offerings from a whore's fee are sacrilegious,"[28] so a priest would not be reckoned pure and blameless if he claimed to have the support of the divine oracles, as it were, and trampled under foot an (588) ordinance of sacrifice as if he were offering sacrifice without offending in any way. It is surely a fearful thing, therefore, to sacrifice to God with unwashed hands, so to say. My view, in fact, is that there is need to perform such august ministry in a state of purity to the extent possible; such a person proves to be immune to any accusation and the effects of divine wrath.

You asked, Why? Because the Lord was a witness between you and the wife of your youth, whom you have abandoned; she is your partner and your wife by covenant, whom he made no differently, and a remnant of his spirit. You claim, What else is God seeking but offspring? (vv.14–15) Despite God's constant deploring such behavior, and urging them to love the women from their own race, expel the foreigners, and

28. Prv 19.13 LXX; cf. Dt 23.18.

avoid marriages condemned by the divine Law itself, they kept saying in their stupidity, *What else is God seeking but offspring?* It was said in the commandment of Moses (he says), "No one will be without children or offspring among the sons of Israel." The God of all also said somewhere to Abraham, "I shall multiply your offspring to be like the stars of heaven in number."[29] God's intention, therefore, he says, is for large numbers and big families so that the gift of large families may lead to a fulfillment that befits the promise to Abraham; whether this is achieved by us from foreigners or from people of our own kind, however, is a matter of indifference to God, for the promise takes effect. Accordingly, he says, *You asked, Why was the Lord a witness between you* (589) *and the wife of your youth whom you have abandoned?* If you prefer to say, *Why was the Lord a witness* and why did he order you not to dismiss your partner, my reply to this is, Consider that *she is your partner and your wife by covenant;* that is, she is of one flesh with you, she is your lawful partner, and God created her in no different fashion. In my view, the phrase *and remnant of your spirit* means, In body and in soul the husband is closely attached to his lawful partner; just as they are one body, so too in some way one soul, love binding them together and the divine Law bringing them together in harmony. Accordingly he refers to the wife as the *remnant* of the husband's *spirit,* and, as it were, part of his soul, as a result of the unity which exists, as I say, in the harmony of love.

Do not, therefore, surpass the bounds of reason in blaming God for perhaps unfairly correcting those who dismiss the *wife of their youth* and *partner by covenant and spirit,* who is united to them in the flesh. For my part, at any rate, I think Paul was moved by this to write to the believers in Christ, "Are you bound to a wife? Do not seek release." The Savior himself also said somewhere, "Whoever divorces his wife, except for unchastity, causes her to commit adultery; and whoever marries one who is divorced commits adultery." And when the Sadducees and querulous people asked the reason why Moses ordered them to give a certificate of dismissal and be rid of a wife, he replied once more, "It was because of your hardness of heart that Moses gave you the command, but from the beginning it was not so. He made them male

29. Ex 23.26; Gn 22.17.

and female; so what God has joined together let no one separate."[30] (590)

Be on the lookout in your spirit, and do not abandon the wife of your youth. But if you hate her and send her away, says the Lord almighty, the God of Israel, impiety will unmask your desires, says the Lord. Be on the watch in your spirit, and do not renege on your agreement (vv.15–16). Though the Law had clearly and openly declared the possibility for those wanting to serve a bill of dismissal on their partners and be freed from their wife without blame, there seems to be some objection to the former ruling in the prophet's statement, which subjects to accountability and brings a charge of lawlessness against the man who presumes to dismiss and divorce his wife. Providentially in this text, therefore, he presents the ancient commandment as inapplicable, and discourages some people from making it the pretext for unholy procedures. Although the Law had allowed the bill to be served, he is saying, you are not on those grounds guiltless in having relations with foreign women. On the contrary, even if you are allowed to separate from your wife, and do so with the sanction of the Law, *Be on the lookout in your spirit not to abandon the wife of your youth.* It would, in fact, be better if the Law did not allow those wanting separation. *But if you hate her and send her away, says the Lord the God of Israel,* that is, if you make a plausible and convincing case for dismissal and write on the bill, Because I hate you, I dismiss you, then *impiety will unmask your desires.* In other words, if (591) impious and loathsome passion gets the better of your desires, and there is a specious pretext for *hating,* and if you prove to be won over by others' charms and want to have relations with foreign women, *be on the watch, do not renege,* or you will be utterly accursed. He had said, remember, *The Lord will destroy the person who does this until humbled in the tents of Jacob and among those offering sacrifice to the Lord almighty.*

While such is the extent of the clear and obvious sense, care should be taken also by those called in faith to holiness not to be seduced by loathsome heresies as though by foreign women at odds with God. Sufficient for their spiritual fruitfulness, in fact, is the pure and faultless guidance of the teachers of the

30. 1 Cor 7.27; Mt 19.4–9; 5.32.

Church for making them, as it were, parents of well-born children by giving birth spiritually from a good heart to the ornaments of love for God, to whom be glory and power, for ages of ages. Amen.[31] (592)

You provoke God in your words, and yet claim, In what way have we provoked him? By saying, Everyone doing evil is good in the sight of the Lord, and he is pleased with them. Where is the God of righteousness? (v.17) I previously said that it was not in only one way but rather in many that the God of all was provoked by those of the line of Levi. In criticizing the indifference of the ministers he said, "You offer stolen goods and lame and maimed animals," to which he added, "In administering the Law you show partiality to some people."[32] While giving improper consideration and treating some of those who had access with undue regard, in fact, they impiously ruled against the weak and were oppressive to some people by not rendering just verdicts according to the Law, delivering instead biased and partial sentences. Perhaps they also seized inheritances to which they had no right, took advantage of bribes, (593) abused the entitlements of priesthood, and exploited those under them. Some of the victims of injustice were astonished, so to say, on seeing them living such a shameless and lawless life; they did not meet with retribution from God or with the effects of his wrath that sometimes befall those in the habit of despising him.

Dismayed at such things, and perhaps no longer able to bring themselves to entertain the idea of God's incomparable tolerance, they, as it were, cried aloud in desperation, *Everyone doing evil is good in his sight, and he is pleased with them*—that is to say, perhaps the evildoer is good in God's eyes, and he finds to his liking those living so shamefully. Otherwise, they said, *Where is the God of righteousness?* It is not proper, in fact, not proper for the dispenser of righteousness to show such longsuffering for oppressive priests, who defile the altar and devote themselves as far as possible to what is unjust, sacrilegious, and beyond the Law.

Now, it should be realized that according to the drift of the text those who utter such naïve sentiments provoke God; they

31. Thus closes Cyril's first volume on Malachi.
32. Mal 1.13; 2.9.

are, as it were, in the habit of chiding God for his longsuffering and for his very kind readiness to wait for the conversion of the wayward and a turn for the better in those caught up in sin. The divinely inspired Paul, for example, chides those reluctant and shrinking back from repentance, "Or do you despise the riches of his kindness, forbearance, and longsuffering, unaware that his kindness is drawing you to repentance? But by your hard (594) and impenitent heart you are storing up wrath for yourself on the day of wrath when God's righteousness is revealed."[33] Those people definitely offend, therefore, who are overcome by their own mean-spirited desperation and direct unbridled words to God, while those who provide them with the occasion for such a failing would be guilty of sin.

It is therefore necessary for the priestly elite or those called to priesthood in the Church to live a holy and upright life. They will thus be, in fact, a model of decorum and every virtue for the people in their charge, who will honor the God of all when they see the exemplary and special attraction of the priests' way of life. This, in my view, is the correct meaning of the Savior's statement, "Let your light shine in people's sight so that they may see your good works and glorify your Father in heaven."[34] You see, just as the people are scandalized when ministers opt for an improper life, so they gain the greatest possible benefit from seeing them involved in good work and choosing to live in a way pleasing to God.

33. Rom 2.4–5.
34. Mt 5.16.

COMMENTARY ON MALACHI, CHAPTER THREE

Lo, I am sending my messenger, and he will have an eye to the way before me, and the Lord will suddenly come into his Temple, whom you seek, and the messenger of the covenant, in whom you delight (v.1).

WITH THEM ASKING, Where is God? (595) the text before us appropriately moves to the mystery of Christ. Emmanuel came from the God and Father, remember, as our "righteousness and sanctification and redemption,"[1] a cleansing of every stain, removal of sin, abolition of shame, a way to better and more fitting things, a door, as it were, and introduction to eternal life. Through him came complete reform, overthrow of oppression, and emergence of righteousness—in fact, with which marvelous things have we not been enriched through him? Accordingly, *Lo, I am sending my messenger, and he will have an eye to the way before me.* In this there is an apparent prediction of the ministry of the holy Baptist; Christ himself said, remember, "This is the one about whom it is written, Lo, I send my messenger before you, who will prepare your way before you." The divinely inspired Isaiah also indicated him to us likewise in the words, "A voice of one crying in the wilderness, Prepare the way of the Lord, make straight the paths of our God."[2]

Once he came, the text is saying, as a forerunner he was under orders briefly to make this announcement, *the Lord will suddenly come into his Temple, whom you seek, and the messenger of the covenant, in whom you delight.* Blessed John also gave confirmation in saying to those coming to the baptism of repentance, "While I baptize you with water, there is coming after me a man, the thongs of whose sandals I am not worthy to stoop and untie; he

1. 1 Cor 1.30.
2. Mt 11.10; Is 40.3.

will baptize you with the Holy Spirit and with fire."[3] You understand, therefore, how Christ immediately afterwards walked in the footsteps, as it were, of the foreteller, making himself known to people throughout Judea, appearing *suddenly* and unexpectedly, so to say. (596) We actually say the divinely inspired Baptist is called an "angel," though not by nature, since he was born of a woman and was a human being like us; rather, it is because he was entrusted with the mission of proclaiming and announcing such things to us. The title, therefore, comes from his role, and does not suggest an angel's being.[4]

He will come into his Temple, the text says, either meaning that the Word became flesh and dwelt, as in a temple, in the pure body from the holy Virgin (or rather in a perfect human being—which, I mean, is believed to be directly and in the divine plan a unity of soul and body), or by *Temple* he refers simply to the sacred city dedicated to him, as it were (Jerusalem, that is), or to the Church as in a type. Now, he made the announcement of his own coming by working wonders in various ways, "preaching the good news of the kingdom and curing every disease and every sickness among the people," as Scripture says.[5] So he says, *The Lord whom you seek will come,* namely, those asking in desperation, "Where is the God of righteousness?" *He will come* to teach what is beyond the Law and what surpasses shadow and types, being a *messenger of the covenant* that was prophesied of old in the word of the God and Father. He said somewhere to the revealer Moses, "I shall raise up for them a prophet like you from among their own people, I shall put my words in his mouth, and he will tell them everything I command him."[6] Now, the fact that Christ was the *angel of the* new *covenant* blessed Isaiah also makes clear in saying of him, "Because they will return with transformation all apparel assembled by deceit and every garment. They would prefer to be burned alive because a child has been born to us and a son given to us; government is on his shoulder, and he will be called (597) Angel of Great Counsel." Hence he also

3. A conflation of Mt 3.11 and Mk 1.7.

4. At the outset of commentary on Malachi (as on Hg 1.13), Cyril noted the twofold sense of *angelos.*

5. Mt 4.23.

6. Mal 2.17; Dt 18.18.

said, "I do not speak on my own, but the Father who sent me has himself given me a commandment about what to say and what to speak." In other words, the Savior's words, far from being human, came to us from the God and Father through his Son by nature; he is the Word of the one who begot him, and confirms it in the statement of David, "My heart gave vent to a good word."[7]

Lo, he is coming, says the Lord almighty. Who will endure the day of his entering, who will stand it when he appears? (vv.1–2) The similar statement of Isaiah closely resembles this: "Be strengthened, weakened hands and loosened knees. Give comfort, you faint of heart, be strengthened, do not fear. Lo, the Lord comes with might, his right arm with lordship."[8] He clearly shows, in fact, that he will really come—or, rather, he presents him as already here—and that the time of his coming in this world will not be long delayed. Now, the fact that the force of the divine plan will not be easily scorned by some people, nor would it be tolerable to unbelievers, he conveys by saying, *Who will endure the day of his entering, who will stand it when he appears?* And by *entering* he refers to the arrival in this world of the Only-begotten in the flesh, and refers to his epiphany, as it were, by *when he appears;* being God by nature, he is invisible, but he became visible by taking the likeness to us. The psalmist also proclaimed this clearly by saying in the spirit, "God (598) will come in obvious fashion, our God, and he will not keep silence"; in the words of the divinely inspired John, "The Word was made flesh, and dwelt among us," being in the "form of a slave." He was in no way troublesome "to those who have longed for his appearance";[9] rather, he was kindly and gentle, and a giver of life eternal. The God and Father also said of him somewhere, "Lo, my beloved Son, with whom I am well pleased, will understand. He will not quarrel or cry aloud, nor will his voice be heard outside. He will not crush the bruised reed nor extinguish the smoking wick; instead, he will deliver judgment in favor of the truth."[10]

7. Is 9.5–6 LXX; Jn 12.49; Ps 45.1.
8. Is 35.3–4; 40.10.
9. Ps 50.3; Jn 1.14; Phil 2.7; 2 Tm 4.8.
10. Is 42.1–3 in a form not generally represented in the LXX, nor in Theodoret's Isaiah Commentary.

The fate of those who spurned the salvation coming through him and did not take advantage of purification through faith was to suffer the worst of all evils: the wretches perished. Accordingly, he also said to the Jewish crowds, "I tell you truly, if you do not believe that I am he, you will die in your sins." John also said somewhere, "The one believing in him is not condemned, whereas the one not believing is already condemned for not believing in the name of the Son of God." The Baptist also proclaimed to the people of Israel, "Even now the axe is lying at the root of the trees; every tree therefore that does not bear good fruit is cut down and thrown into the fire."[11] So the time of his *entering when he will appear* was unbearable and quite intolerable to the unbelievers; they were accused of ruining their own souls and being destined to die in their sins on account of a faulty attitude and a refusal to apply to mind and heart the purification that comes through faith. He therefore asks, *Who will endure the day of his entering, who* will *stand it when he appears?* In other words, Who will be so rigid and (599) inflexible as, at the time and on the day of his entry into the world—that is, in the flesh, by which he would be able to be touched or seen—to *stand it* and remain unimpaired? In fact, they will be completely and utterly punished, and pay a harsh penalty for their folly.

Because he is coming like a fire in a smelter, and like fullers' soap. He will sit refining and purifying, like silver and gold. He will purify the sons of Levi and refine them like gold and silver (vv.2–3). While in this passage the words are expressed on the basis of a comparison of things familiar to us, they would convey an ineffable hint of a mystery to the more thoughtful readers. Experts in these matters, you see, conduct a test on *silver and gold,* removing by *fire* everything in them that is faulty and unsightly. There is also a fire that is divine and heavenly, namely, the grace of the Holy Spirit, by which we would be brought to life in spirit when it penetrates to mind and heart; when Christ imparts it, then and only then it cleanses every stain of sin, and consumes the defilement of previous falls. It renders those who possess it purified and acceptable, transforms them spiritually, as it were, to newness of life, and then leaves utensils shining and sanctified,

11. Jn 8.24; 3.18; Lk 3.9.

ready for respect and for use in the great house—that is, the Church. This divine and spiritual fire the divinely inspired John indicated by saying, "I baptize you with water, but there is a man coming after me (600), the thong of whose sandals I am unworthy to untie; he will baptize you with the Holy Spirit and with fire." We also recall Christ himself saying, "I have come to cast fire on the earth, and how I wish it were already enkindled."[12] Since, then, those of the line of Israel raised an inordinate outcry against the impurity or injustice of the Levites, or rather continued to provoke the God of all on their account, uttering criticism and saying outrageously, "Everyone doing evil is good in the sight of the Lord, and he is pleased with them. Where is the God of righteousness?"[13] he makes the helpful prediction that in due course Christ will shed his light, removing every sin from our midst, making his own priests holy, and testing them in fire like *gold and silver,* that is, rendering them proven and illustrious.

Of such a kind, in fact, are the Church's ministers in general, and it would be very fitting to apply to them the saying of David, "Because you have tested us, O God, purifying us by fire as silver is purified."[14] An adornment for the successors of Aaron, remember, was the garment prescribed by the Law; for those chosen in Christ and appointed to priesthood there will be the splendid robe that is holy and fit for a priest, namely, Christ himself. Accordingly, through the lyre of the psalmist the God and Father said in reference to the Church from the nations, "Its priests I shall clothe with salvation, and its holy ones will shout for joy," Christ himself being salvation that acts as the commendable robe of his own priests, or rather of all the believers as well. "All you who were baptized in Christ," Scripture says, "have put on Christ."[15] (601)

They will be to the Lord offerers of sacrifice in righteousness. The offering of Judah and Jerusalem will be pleasing to the Lord, as in the days of the age, and as in former years (vv.3–4). They will be dedicated to God—the meaning in my view of *They will be to the Lord*

12. 2 Tm 2.20–21; Mt 3.11; Mk 1.7; Lk 12.49.
13. Mal 2.17.
14. Ps 66.10.
15. Lv 16.4, 32; Ps 132.16; Gal 3.27.

offerers. Now, we shall be dedicated to God when we live no longer for ourselves but are wholly devoted to love for him and choose to carry out with all our strength what is pleasing to the divine will. The divinely inspired Paul also said something similar in reference to Christ the Savior of us all, "One person died for all so that those who live might live no longer for themselves but for him who died and was raised for them." And describing for us, as it were, the beauty of his own way of life, and making clear the force of the mystery of Christ, he said again, "I have been crucified with Christ, and it is no longer I who live, but it is Christ who lives in me. And the life I now live in the flesh I live by faith in the Son of God, who loved me and gave himself for me."[16]

He says, then, *They will be offerers to the Lord;* that is, they will be dedicated only to his wishes, "their minds not set on earthly things," having no love for the defilement of iniquity, showing no inclination for oppression of some people, but rather *offerers of sacrifice of righteousness.* There seems to me great wisdom in Paul's saying, "When there is a change in the priesthood, there is necessarily a change in the law as well."[17] In other words, we who are called in Christ are not involved any longer in sacrifices of blood and smoke, nor do we offer to God lambs and goats; rather, we celebrate in the churches the sacrifice that is understood in Christ to be holy and spiritual. (602) By performing it also for sanctification and for participation in eternal life, we offer like some special incense the sweet odor coming from our good works, and by making a sacrifice of *righteousness* we are confident that we shall be acceptable. Scripture says, remember, "Honor the Lord with your righteous efforts, and from your fruits of righteousness offer him the first-fruits."[18] The God of all will in fact be pleased, in my view, with no other sacrifices than these.

Accordingly, in reference to those called in Christ to sacred ministry, he said that they will be better than the first ones, not involved in animal sacrifice like them, or defiling the altar by offering "spoiled bread,"[19] but by offering to God *righteousness*

16. 2 Cor 5.15; Gal 2.20.
17. Heb 7.12.
18. Prv 3.9.
19. Mal 1.7.

and the spiritual fragrance of the Gospel way of life in place of incense. They will perform a liturgy that is so acceptable as to be in no way inferior to the fitting sacrifices *in the days of the age*, that is, the life of the holy spirits in heaven, who spend their *days*, or time, ceaselessly and at length. It will also be equal to the *former* times, that is, to the worship of the saints who lived in *former* times. The acceptability of the ancients, remember, lay in obedience; thus Abraham offered his son to God, "and it was reckoned to him as righteousness, and he was called God's friend," and likewise Noah "built the ark to save his household," as Scripture says.[20] So he says, *The offering of Judah will be pleasing*—that is, the people who have a circumcision in heart and spirit—and *of Jerusalem*, namely, the spiritual one—that is, (603) the Church—which will be like the sacrifice of those who had *the days of the age* and that of the saints who lived in *former times*, who were pleasing by obedience and faith. The divinely inspired Paul also lists these people in the letter to the Hebrews,[21] saying that many were justified by faith.

I shall draw near to you in judgment, and I shall be a speedy witness against the sorcerers, the adulterers, those swearing falsely in my name, those depriving a hireling of his hire, oppressing widows, abusing orphans, those diverting justice from a sojourner, and those not fearing me, says the Lord almighty (v.5). In this passage, too, the thought continues for us in the same vein. The people of Israel, remember, had said in foolish fashion, "Everyone doing evil is good in the sight of the Lord, and he is pleased with them. Where is the God of righteousness?"[22] And though an explanation was previously given of such dreadful babbling, it will be given here again. Some of the sacred ministers, remember, and in fact others who were prominent and notable for positions of eminence, were involved in every form of knavery and evil exploits, and God seemed to be showing excessive tolerance of them in his goodness, kindness, simplicity, and love; consequently some people gave vent to words of unalloyed desperation. The fact, however, that in due course there will be a turn for the better in those appointed to ministry, (604) when Christ transforms

20. Jas 2.23; Heb 11.7.
21. Heb 11.
22. Mal 2.17.

them to newness of life and brings a change to a life of sweet odor and to respectable living, we explained clearly.

Now, proof that he would not at that time accept those guilty of depravity, or judge them worthy of praise and regard, but will rather judge them and require an account of those of criminal life, he gives in the words, *I shall draw near to you in judgment*—that is, I shall prosecute you as a judge—*and I shall be a speedy witness*—that is, independently and without being summoned by anyone. In other words, I shall deliver a condemnation of the evil ones, and bring justice upon them without anyone else exposing their guilt, knowing as God what is concealed and hidden, and through conscience testifying against each of the sinners. The divinely inspired Paul also said somewhere that people throughout the world will in due course appear before the judge: "Their conflicting thoughts will accuse or perhaps excuse them on the day when, according to my gospel, God through Jesus Christ will judge people's secret thoughts."[23]

Now, consider how those guilty both of hidden and of notorious crimes will, he says, be brought *to judgment*. Firstly, note, he mentions *the sorcerers* and *the adulterers*, then *those swearing falsely*. These crimes are concealed and committed furtively; after all, who would be completely open in deceiving people? Or why would an adulterer choose to be seen by anyone? And I think concealment is the intention also of those opting to take a false oath. Blessed David classes such people as stupid, saying, "Get some sense, you fools among the people. When will you dullards come to your senses? He who planted the ear, does he not hear? He who formed the eye, does he not observe?"[24] There is nothing at all, in fact, beyond God's vision: he alone knows evils that are hidden and those notorious. (605) While the former are committed furtively and, as it were, in darkness, he goes on to add to them as well the notorious ones, namely, *depriving a hireling of his hire*, arrogance and *oppression*, which some people would commit against the weak, that is, *widows* and *orphans*. To these he adds also those who corrupt justice in verdicts and those *not fearing* him, these being the people who offend God

23. 2 Cor 5.10; Rom 2.15–16.
24. Ps 94.8–9.

in some other way than those mentioned by us just now. Accordingly he says, *I shall be a* judge and a *speedy* and independent *witness against sorcerers* and *adulterers* and the perpetrators of the other evils. It is likely that at that time such crimes were committed by some people, and in those cases there happened the babbling against God by many people.

It is surely necessary, therefore, to avoid wickedness with all our strength, have recourse to better things, and strive to achieve that which is the means by which a person is filled with all goodness and commendation. This, in fact, is the way not to share in the effects of divine wrath that will be inflicted on those addicted to sin, and to enjoy honor and glory, which God would award to those who love him.

Because I am the Lord your God, and I do not change. You children of Jacob have not abstained from the sins of your ancestors; you departed from my laws and did not observe them (vv.6–7). He discourages them further from unholy thoughts and also words. After all, to think that the God of all changes from intending good and does the opposite, that he no longer loves righteousness but instead welcomes the (606) addicts of depravity—how would that not be foolish, or rather completely absurd and sacrilegious, and typical of extreme impiety? So when you see those called to justice—namely, the sorcerers among you, or soothsayers (these whisperers and chatterers being generally females), and the perpetrators of the other evils—then it is (he says) that you will know from experience that *I am the Lord your God*, who of old and also at present am both good and a lover of virtue. I experience no change or alteration, you see; instead, I am ever and unchangeably what I am. You, on the other hand, he says, despite being of the line of Jacob, a good and God-loving man, who always hated stubbornness and was a servant of God—you have proved to be no imitator of his ways. Instead, you imitated the disobedience and obduracy of your fathers, who for this reason were deported as captives, left their homeland, and were enslaved to the enemy who captured them. As well, *you departed from my laws and did not observe them.* While God is unchangeable, then, and, as it were, rooted in good and set in righteousness, you proved to be inveterate observers of evil, so to say, and devoted imitators of your fathers' infidelity.

Christ is also found saying as much; he rightly deplores the practice of the ignorant scribes and Pharisees, speaking in these terms, "Woe to you scribes and Pharisees, hypocrites: you build the tombs of the prophets, and decorate the graves of the righteous, and say, If we had lived in the days of our ancestors, we would not have participated with them in shedding the blood of the prophets. Thus you testify against yourselves that you are descendants of those who murdered the prophets. Fill up the (607) measure of your ancestors."[25] It behoves us, therefore, if we are truly of a right attitude and settled mind, to imitate in particular the most upright of the ancestors and eschew imitation of those who were not good. Or if someone should choose not to do this, and naïvely and indiscriminately follow the example of their predecessors in time, they would resemble completely the pagans; if you were to blame them for abandoning the knowledge of the truth and forsaking the one who is God by nature, and worshiping stones, they would repeat their claim to be following the custom of their fathers.

Return to me, and I shall return to you, says the Lord almighty. You ask, How shall we return? Does a human being cheat God? Because you cheat me, and ask, How have we cheated you? Because tithes and first-fruits are in your possession. You continue to look at them, and you cheat me. The year has finished, and you brought all the produce into the storehouses, and robbery of it will be in your house (vv.7–10). After very properly discouraging them from their babbling against him, and after shaming them to deter them as far as possible from making their customary defense, he summons the offenders to repentance, promising to bestow on them once more his habitual clemency with great readiness. In other words, just as he inflicts on those intent on a bad life the penalties befitting them, so with those who go back and actually desist from sinning further he is truly (608) glad, in every case stifling despair as the cause of ruin. From this it is possible to see how awful an ailment is introduced into our life by those who adulterate the grace of repentance and misguidedly apply to themselves the name of purity. Would it not be better to admit that believing

25. Mt 23.29–32.

and claiming to be pure brings on them the accusation of extreme impurity? Scripture says, in fact, "Be the first to state your sins if you are to be justified," and the divine David also sings to us somewhere, "Because I acknowledge my sin, and my sin is always before me," or, as it is written, "No one is clear of stain."[26] For people suffering such weakness, therefore, there is surely need of the good effects of repentance and clemency from on high, which thoroughly cleanse the person stained and which justify the impious. This is the reason that in his clemency he calls sinners to repentance.

To those who inquire again in their wish to learn the nature of their sin he replies, *Does a human being cheat God? Because you cheat me.* The word *cheat* means to rob, or to deceive and think to escape the notice of those hoodwinked or those doing something out of the ordinary. Esau was angry with Jacob, for example, and in explanation of his thirst for blood he said, "This is the second time he cheated me: he took away my birthright, and now he received my blessing."[27] Surely man does not get the better of God, he says, therefore, or rob the one who knows everything? So why *do you cheat me?*

Now, I believe that for a precise clarification of our text there is need to mention a few details at this point that are found in the books of Esdras. When the people of Israel left Babylon and returned (609) to Judea, they occupied Jerusalem. The divine Temple was also rebuilt, and ranks of priests then developed, chanters and singers and gatekeepers.[28] Then what happened? Those who had been released grew indifferent to the need to observe the divine oracles; they did not carry out the Law, and instead transgression of the divine commandment was regarded as of no significance; only reluctantly did they bring offerings for sacrifice, and these were blind and stolen animals, lame and handicapped. Then, when they harvested in the fields sheaves of corn and other crops, picked the grapes from the vines, and pressed the fruit of the olive trees, they did not offer tithes and first-fruits according to the Law so that the ranks of priests

26. Is 43.26; Ps 51.3; Jb 14.4.
27. Gn 27.36.
28. Cyril seems to be referring to Neh 7.1.

might keep what they needed, and thus devote themselves to the worship of God without distraction, and occupy themselves with the actual rituals prescribed by Law.

With nothing being offered, therefore, the ministers of the divine altars diminished and the Temple thus remained desolate, no sacrifice being offered and nothing else done that contributed to the glory of God. As a result, everything in the fields now deteriorated; they were affected by hunger, and reached such a degree of necessity and need as to be willing to sell their children to those who had food, until Ezra was brought to a sense of the divine wrath, and upbraided the leaders of Israel about this.[29] Thus they finally began offering tithes and first-fruits, and the priests came forward and began performing the rituals that were customary by Law. So he asks, Why (610) *do you cheat me? The year has finished*, the crops are harvested, and *the tithes and the first-fruits* prescribed by Law are still with you. *And robbery of it will be in his house*, it says, meaning, Whereas you gathered the crops from the fields in your houses, perhaps you also had the idea of saving them for yourselves and keeping them properly stored. In these very houses, however, they will be frittered away, and your action will be no different from *robbery*. You will, in fact, be consumed with hunger, he says, despite amassing what you find with sweat and tears.

We shall therefore understand from this that we shall incur serious blame for not making thanksgiving offerings to God and giving adequate thanks for his glory, for what he has given. If we do so, on the other hand, he will doubtless give us every blessing, and generously bestow good things on us. If, on the other hand, we were to withdraw our hand, and keep what is given for our own satisfaction, he would not be quick to make any recompense; instead, he will scatter, as it were, even what had been gathered. We must, you see, be generous and ready to share,[30] making others participants in what is given by God.

Turn back with this, says the Lord almighty; unless I open to you the gates of heaven and pour out on you my blessing to the point of sufficiency, I shall distribute food among you, and not destroy the crops of the

29. Neh 5.
30. Cf. 1 Tm 6.18. The final lines are abbreviated in the PG ed.

earth, and your vine will not wither in the field, says the Lord almighty. All the nations will count you happy, for you will be a chosen land, says the Lord almighty (vv.10–12). Once again (611) he forgives their faults, rids them of all blame, and promises generously and ungrudgingly to grant their petitions and gladden them with a liberality beyond description. On the other hand, he wants them to learn from actual experience of events that bearing fruit will be completely beneficial for them. If they were to opt to do this, he would promise to grant even an abundant supply of rain, and accord them such generous *blessing* that they would have an ample sufficiency of foodstuffs, and in short an adequate share of the goods of the earth. *I shall distribute food among you,* he says, note, and by *distribute* you should understand "apportion," that is, that each season will have some of the produce *of the earth,* when it will grow and ripen. Now, the fact that *the crops of the earth* will be proof against all damage, and the vine in the fields will produce many grapes and much wine, he clearly promises and will bring it to fulfillment. He says they would then be *happy* and the land, as it were, be called *chosen,* that is, esteemed for its productivity and fertility.

If you were to have feelings of compassion, therefore, you would definitely encounter a God of that kind, heap up stores in heaven, and eat the fruit of your own labors, as Scripture says. You will not be like that harsh and most foolish man of wealth who, the Savior in the Gospel parables said, filled his place with good things and said, "What am I to do? I shall pull down my barns and build bigger ones, and I shall say to my soul, Soul, you have many goods stored up for many years; eat, drink, be merry." As he considered such things in his ignorance, God said, "You fool, this night they require your soul of you. What (612) you have prepared, whose will it be?"[31] As I said, therefore, the one who shares is filled with *blessing;* such a person will have spiritual rain bedewing his heart and giving him considerable joy; he will produce the fruits of piety, *distributed,* as it were, in different ways at different times, being conspicuous at one time for love, at another for kindness and brotherly love. He will be like some fruitful and fertile *land,* famous and celebrated

31. Col 3.12; Ps 128.2; Lk 12.17–20.

and truly thrice-blessed; as Scripture says, "A good name is preferable to great wealth."[32]

You leveled your harsh words at me, says the Lord, yet you said, In what way did we revile you? You said, The one serving God is wasting time; what value is there in our observing his observances and in our going about as suppliants before the Lord almighty? As it is, we count foreigners blessed; all who commit crimes are built up, they forsook God and did well. Those who fear the Lord said this in reproach, each one to their neighbor; the Lord gave heed and hearkened (vv.13–16). When God wants to correct some of his intimates who are drawn into sin, he parades their faults and makes a clear accusation, as it were, smiting them with guilt, so that they may be ashamed of their sins and decide to take a turn for the better, and thus be saved by seeking mercy from him. Accordingly, he reproves the people of Israel also on another account, and composes, as it were, a common rebuke for those coming after them as well, though aware that it is beneficial and saving for them all; everything that happened as a type to those before our time, after all, "has been written for (613) an example to us,"[33] as Paul in his great wisdom said. He therefore reproves them for their extreme babbling and choosing to offend him with critical remarks; *you leveled your harsh words at me,* he says. And what actual form did the criticism take? *You said, The one serving God is wasting time,* and it is pointless wanting to keep *his observances,* that is, the oracles of the Law. In addition to this, it is useless, you claim, making *supplication* to him, that is, offering prayers for what you want.

While the God of all is completely reliable in saying this and accusing the people of Israel, it should be mentioned what basis the babblers had for their sinful talk. Whereas God pastured countless races on earth, of them all God chose the race of Israel, who were known as his portion and cord and inheritance.[34] In his relationship with them he provided them guidance in the Law and assistance through the Prophets. And what did the insane Israel do in response to this? It worshiped the host of heaven, it served idols, it said to statues, You are our god.[35] Rightfully

32. Prv 22.1.
33. 1 Cor 10.11.
34. Dt 32.9.
35. Hos 14.3.

indignant at such awful sacrilege, the God of all corrected them in many ways, calling them to repentance by famines, scorching winds, shortage of crops, and locusts of various kinds. He did not yet wish to strike them with a firm hand, you see, but, as it were, to frighten them with threats and moderate prompting to opt for action to their benefit, and to love the one who is God by nature and in truth.

Since, however, they took no notice of moderate correction, but devoted themselves unrestrainedly to every form of impurity, he sent them off to captivity, and caused them to come under the control of the Babylonians. But when they were called (614) back to Judea through God's compassion, fortified the city, and rebuilt the Temple, they once more turned to indifferent ways, not fulfilling vows, not following the oracles in the Law, not offering tithes and first-fruits; instead, they were slow and reluctant to go to sacrifice, slaughtering animals that were lame, blind, and handicapped, which was wrong conduct, which God corrected no less by famine and infertility. Some of them, on the other hand—who were good people and understood what was to their own good, and should by a turn for the better have paid homage to the God of all, who had been offended—raised a foolish outcry. When in fact they saw neighboring nations, who did not know God and instead worshiped statues, and were guilty of extreme error, living in prosperity and luxury, they foolishly claimed, *The one serving God is wasting time; what value is there in our observing his commands?* We the law-keepers suffer want and trials, yet even live as captives despite always adoring and being suppliants of the Lord almighty, whereas they do nothing like that and yet suffer no trials, no hardship. Therefore, *we count foreigners blessed; all who commit crimes are built up, they forsook God and did well;* those in error rebel in reality against the glory of God in manifold ways, offering sacrifices to graven images and "saying to a tree, You are my god, and to a stone, You begot me."[36]

Those who fear the Lord said this in reproach. The crime again is using language of ill-omen, and a clear example of the worst insanity; they are the words of a demented brain, and speaking

36. Jer 2.27.

against God is a drunken intellect's rejection that is hateful to God. Now, the fact that (615) he listened to such words not idly but intently is confirmed by the statement, *The Lord gave heed and hearkened.* "Because the Spirit of the Lord has filled the whole world, and that which holds all things together has knowledge of what is said."[37] Now, if there were any remark passed against his divine glory, it would be serious and, as it were, intolerable, despite his normally being patient—hence his saying as well, *You leveled your harsh words at me.*

It behoves us, therefore, even if we suffer hardship when God kindly chastises us, not to be completely heedless nor to conclude that the one who so loves virtue spurns good people. We should rather take particular note of the things in which we give offense, mitigate them, and ask for mercy. Even if, on the other hand, some of the people addicted to sin experience this-worldly prosperity by enjoying temporary success, we ought to attribute the reasons for his tolerance of them to his ineffable providence.

He wrote a book of remembrance in his sight to those fearing the Lord and to those reverencing his name. They will be to me, says the Lord almighty, as a special possession on the day which I hold, and I shall give them preference as people give preference to their children who serve them well (vv.16–17). To those of the people of Israel jeering at him and mouthing sacrilegious things against him, he *gave heed and hearkened.* Though he should have imposed a due penalty on the sinners, and required an account of their babbling, he patiently passed over even that, and *wrote a book of remembrance to those fearing him;* in my view, (616) David also referred somewhere to the one writing a book about them, "In your book they will all be written."[38]

Now, we shall find our Lord Jesus Christ himself saying to the holy disciples, "Do not rejoice that the demons submit to you; rejoice rather that your names are written in heaven." The divinely inspired David also very rightly cursed the Jewish crowds who killed Christ by speaking this way, "Let them be blotted out of the book of the living, and not be enrolled among the righteous." So the *book of remembrance* is written *to those fearing him,*

37. Wis 1.7.
38. Ps 139.16.

who he says will be his intimates and familiars at the time of the *possession,* when Christ is seated on his throne of glory, with angels attending him, "and he will put the sheep at his right hand and the goats at his left, and he will say to those on his right, Come, you that are blessed by my Father, inherit the kingdom prepared for you from the foundation of the world."[39] Then it is, in fact, that *he will give them preference;* that is, he will prefer them, having no less affection than our parents, who rejoice in their children when they are sensible and obedient and treat with greatest respect those who gave birth to them.

You will be converted and see the difference between right and wrong, and between serving God and not serving him (v.18). Then it is, he says, then it is that, with the cessation of such unbalanced gossiping and their desisting from unalloyed and ignorant babbling, they will no longer misrepresent the God who loves virtue; dismissing their inebriation, as it were, and, so to say, (617) being *converted* from error, they will clearly consider *the difference between right and wrong, and between serving God and not serving him.* Lawless and rebellious people, who throw off the yoke of service to him, will be consigned to ruin and unending punishment, "where there will be weeping and gnashing of teeth," as Scripture says. Good and godly people, on the other hand, who understand the divine laws and are conspicuous and sanctified devotees of every virtue, will don the crown of incorruptibility. Living in the heavenly mansions, they will pass their time with the holy angels, emerge as sharers in the glory of Christ, and in a life without end will enjoy the blessedness, "which eye has not seen, nor ear heard, nor has it entered the human heart," as Scripture says.[40]

With the sight of the lovers of depravity happily going from day to day in this life, however, some of the holy ones gave thought to this, though not unaware that destruction will be the end of their life. Blessed Jeremiah, for instance, somewhere says this, "You are righteous, O Lord, because I shall lay charges against you; yet I shall put my case to you. Why does the way of the guilty prosper? Why do all who commit crimes thrive?

39. Lk 10.20; Ps 69.28; Mt 25.33–34.
40. Mt 8.12; 1 Cor 2.9.

You planted them, and they took root; they generated and produced fruit. You are near in their mouth, and far from their hearts. You, Lord, know me; you tested my heart in your sight." Then he goes on, "Sanctify them on the day of their slaughter. How long will the land mourn?" Do you see how he fell foul of disgruntled thinking, yet was not ignorant of the end of offenders? "Hence all flesh is grass, and human glory like a flower of a plant," as Scripture says.[41]

41. Jer 12.1–4; Is 40.6.

COMMENTARY ON MALACHI, CHAPTER FOUR

Hence, lo, a day is coming, burning like a pan, and it will set them alight. All the foreigners and all those doing wrong will be straw, and the day that is coming will enkindle them, says the Lord almighty, and no root or branch of them will be left (v.1).

IN OTHER WORDS, it follows that the day of judgment will involve fire, when "the heavens will pass away with a loud noise, the elements will be dissolved with fire, and the earth and everything that is done on it will be incinerated. We wait for a new heaven and a new earth in keeping with his promises,"[1] these being the terms in which one of the holy disciples spoke. He is saying, therefore, that *the day* of the Lord *will come like a pan,* and *will set alight all the foreigners* and in addition to them *those doing wrong,* the one penalty befalling both groups. Note how he cleverly makes mention here of *the foreigners:* since he had blessed them in the words, "As it is, we count foreigners blessed; all who commit crimes are built up, they forsook God and did well," consequently he says they will be set alight for warring against God's glory and choosing to worship creation instead of the Creator.[2]

In a different way we see reference in *foreigners* also to idolaters and those who are in any other way foreign to the sacred and chosen race—the heretics, I mean—of whom it would very rightly be said, "They went out from us, but they did not belong to us, for if they did belong to us, they would have remained with us." (619) Having rejected their divine lineage, and separated themselves from the sacred and chosen race that became his possession[3]—through faith in Christ, that is—such people

1. 2 Pt 3.10, 13, in Cyril's text, which reads "incinerated," not "disclosed."
2. Mal 3.15; Rom 1.25.
3. 1 Jn 2.19; 1 Pt 2.9.

will be fuel for the all-consuming fire. Now, in the same position with God are placed also *those doing wrong*, even if perhaps mingled with the believers and the elect, with those who know the one who is by nature and in truth God. For them, in fact, it does not suffice for washing away of sin, especially as it is true that "faith without works is dead";[4] while faith in Christ justifies, and rids us of the stain of past sins, yet if they are afterwards found to be indifferent and to have succumbed to the passions of the flesh and the world, they have put faith to death, as it were, within them, acquiring nothing deserving of commendation, but rather relapsing into their former depraved life. Of such people the divinely inspired disciple also says, "It would have been better for them, in fact, not to have known the way of righteousness than, after knowing it, to turn back from the holy commandment that was passed on to them. It has happened to them what is said in the true proverb, A dog turns back to its vomit, and, A sow is washed only to wallow in the mud."[5]

Accordingly, *those doing wrong*, who also will be *straw*, are in a situation similar to that of the *foreigners*, and will likewise be incinerated in the way straw is set on fire; the grain is gathered into the barn, as the Savior also says about the holy reapers, but the chaff will be burned with unquenchable fire.[6] *And no root or branch of them will be left;* that is, they will have no hope of growing up again to life, by which I mean the life that is desirable and, as it were, in glory with God, and understood as achieved by holiness and blessedness. If a *root* is not completely pulled up and a branch not removed from the base, there is still hope (620) of future growth. "There is hope for a tree," Scripture says, remember, "even if it is cut down, that it will sprout again, and that its shoots will not cease." If, however, it is pulled up from below and from its very root, and suffers a severe pruning, all hope completely disappears of its being able to grow again to life. On the basis of comparison with plants, therefore, he says that all hope is lost for lovers of sin. The divinely inspired Isaiah

4. Jas 2.20. This is a significant qualification for Cyril, who often asserts simply that justification comes through faith in Christ.

5. 2 Pt 2.21–22; Prv 26.11.

6. Mt 13.30; 3.12.

also makes this promise clearly, "Their worm will not die, nor their fire be quenched, and they will present an awful sight to all flesh."[7]

There will arise for those who fear my name a sun of righteousness, and healing is in his wings. You will go out leaping like calves released from bonds: You will trample down the lawless; hence they will be ashes under your feet on the day of my making, says the Lord almighty (vv.2–3). On appearing in this world the Only-begotten Word of God was resplendent, adopting a likeness with us; "the Word was made flesh," Scripture says, "and dwelt among us."[8] Like a *sun* he sheds the light of his own beams on us in our gloom and darkness, shedding the clear radiance of the true knowledge of God on the hearts of believers, making them pure and wise and ready for every good work. He revealed the Father to us in himself, (621) rendering us most skillful and enlightened with his ineffable guidance, and filling their minds with knowledge of him. By being brought to this degree of brightness, and, as blessed Paul says, "enriched in all speech, all knowledge, and all wisdom," "we now see as in a mirror, dimly, and we know in part." In due course, however, what is perfect will come, and we shall then enjoy complete knowledge when Christ shines on us again from heaven, abolishing the knowledge that is partial and dim, and illuminating those that are perfect, as it were, filling their mind with a divine and indescribable light, and buoying it up with an outpouring of the Holy Spirit. While the divinely inspired Paul said, remember, "Prophecies will come to an end and knowledge will cease,"[9] our claim is that we do not proceed from knowing in part to knowing nothing—far from it.

Otherwise, in what way would the time of future hope not come at a cost for the souls of the saints if it were completely necessary for them to lose what they have, not by gaining what is better, nor by proceeding to an understanding of sublime things, but rather by selling even what has already been acquired, sometimes not without hardship? Prophecies will cease and knowledge will come to an end, namely, when that which excels them takes possession of our souls. In other words, just as if you were

7. Jb 14.7; Is 66.24.
8. Jn 1.14.
9. 1 Cor 1.5; 13.12, 9, 8.

to bring a lamp into a house where there was one light shining that provided a slender beam to the onlookers, it would be inevitable that that light would give way to the bright beams of the stronger one, (622) and just as, when the sun is illuminating the earth under heaven, the brightness of the stars is ineffectual and fades, so when clearer knowledge is introduced to us, the lesser kind is lost. Christ also said somewhere to the holy apostles, "I have said these things to you in figures of speech. The hour is coming when I shall no longer speak to you in figures, but shall tell you plainly of the Father."[10]

On the saints, therefore, who have intense respect for God's *name,* and are devoted to every virtue in this world, Christ shines like *a sun of righteousness,* shedding beams of perfect knowledge, freeing them from every ailment of the soul, and distancing them from past tribulation. This, in fact, is the meaning of *healing is in his wings,* as if in reference to an eagle and its young, like the statement by the all-wise Moses about God and those rescued from Egypt, "As an eagle hovers over its nest, spreading its wings, he took them up."[11] Accordingly, he says there will be *healing in his wings,* that is to say, in this age there is dire rebellion of the flesh, prompting the mind to improper pleasures, while the law of sin rages in our limbs, even if it is overcome by the continence of the saints with Christ's assistance. Yet the mind is in some way inebriated and in a different way tested by the passions; arrogance goes on the attack along with worldly vainglory, anger, avarice, and the other vices. Since we have been enriched with the pledge of the Spirit through Christ, however, we are accustomed to dominating the passions, though not without effort; with the full light of the knowledge of God in the age to come, enriched with the perfection of the gift of the Holy Spirit, and relieved of the corruption and passions of the flesh, we shall serve God in every way, not half-hearted because of sin nor distracted by the passions of a former time, but living a pure and innocent life on a level with the holy angels. In reference to the saints Scripture says, in fact, that they will forget their tribulation and not take it to heart; instead, "everlast-

10. Jn 16.25.
11. Dt 32.11.

ing joy will be on their head, for praise and joy will be on their head, and happiness will take hold of them, when pain takes its leave along with sorrow and grief."[12]

Consequently, the prophet says—or God, the agent and giver of these ideas—that *you will go out leaping like calves released from bonds:* just as suckling calves, when released from bonds, go leaping around the fields, rushing about the rich feed, and lowing, so at times the saints, released, as it were, from the bonds of tribulation and care in this life, and from effort and hardship, will embark on the enjoyment that is proper to the holy ones, *trampling down the lawless* who are no longer still fighting and resisting but now fallen and vanquished, and, as it were, lying under their feet through the complete abolition of warfare on their part. "No lion will be there, nor any wicked beast come up on it," Scripture says; "rather, there will be a pure path, and it will be called a holy way";[13] being rid of war and every stain at that time in particular, it will be life for the saints.

Lo, I am sending you Elijah the Tishbite before the great and glorious Day of the Lord comes. He will turn a father's heart to his son, and people's hearts to their neighbors, lest on coming I strike the earth severely (vv.5–6). It is an index of God's clemency and longsuffering that Elijah the Tishbite will in due course shine forth and foretell to people throughout the world the time when Christ will come. The Son, in fact, will descend as Judge in the glory of the God and Father, with angels attending him, will sit "on the throne of his glory" to judge the world in righteousness, and will render to all according to their works.[14] Since we bear many sins, however, it is of help that the divinely inspired prophet comes in advance, encouraging harmony in those on earth, so that when all are joined in unity through faith, and have renounced their involvement in depravity, they may opt for doing good and thus be saved when the Judge arrives. Blessed John the Baptist anticipated him, therefore, by coming "with the spirit and power of Elijah"; but just as he preached the message, "Prepare the way of the Lord, make straight his paths,"[15] so too the divinely inspired Elijah announced of him, at that time when he was near and had

12. Is 65.16; 35.10.
13. Is 35.9.
14. Ps 96.13; Mt 25.31; 16.27.
15. Lk 1.17; Mt 3.3; Mk 1.3; Is 40.3.

not yet come, that he would judge the world in righteousness.

Today some people disagree: a father is at odds with his son, a son with his father; one believes in Christ, another is in the ranks of the unbelievers;[16] some are distinguished by love of one another, whereas others are divided by hostility and implacable anger and enmity over every matter in the world. The prophet will bring about a restoration, uniting in one (625) faith those long divided and *turning people's hearts to their neighbors, lest on coming I strike the earth severely,* that is, completely and utterly. Do you see, then, the clemency of the Lord of all? He encourages in advance people on earth, adjuring them, as it were, through the voice of Elijah that the Judge will come, his purpose being that those living on earth at that time will reform their life by a turn for the better, and thus will not fall foul of the harsh Judge, who dispatches the guilty to fire and exterior darkness, but rather will hear, "Come, you blessed of my Father, inherit the kingdom prepared for you before the foundation of the world."[17]

Remember the Law of Moses my servant, as I passed on to him at Horeb commandments and ordinances for all Israel (v.4). Once more he recommends that the readers consider the prophet's words, the fact that preaching about Christ is not new or unfamiliar, nor was it announced only in the words of Malachi—rather, it was in fact originally from the outset and, so to say, from early times when Israel was called to knowledge of God at the time when God through Moses uttered the laws on Horeb. The God of all, remember, descended in the form of fire on Mount Sinai; there was a vision of smoke and flames rearing up and instilling great fear in those watching; there were darkness, gloom, and a tempest, and "a trumpet made a loud noise." (626) At this the people of Israel were terrified, and they came to speak to their mediator and guide—Moses, that is: "Speak to us yourself; let it not be God who speaks, lest we die." God replied, "They are right in what they have said. I shall raise up a prophet like you from among their brethren; I shall put my words in his mouth, and he will tell them all I command him."[18] Do you see how from

16. For "unbelievers" the PG text reads "apostles."

17. Mt 25.30, 34.

18. Ex 19.16; 20.19; Dt 18.17–18.

that great distance the sacred text foretells Christ? If, however, you were prepared to examine the very shadows of the Law, you would find Christ referred to as well as the mystery concerning him; he said to the Jews, remember, "If you believed Moses, you would believe me, for it was of me he wrote."[19] Christ, you see, is the fullness of Law and Prophets; through him and with him be glory to the God and Father with the Holy Spirit, now and forever, for ages of ages. Amen.

19. Jn 5.46.

INDICES

INDEX OF PROPER NAMES

For names of biblical books, please see the Index of Holy Scripture.

INDEX OF HOLY SCRIPTURE

Old Testament

New Testament